AF674141

A MASTER AND A SEEKER

श्री सद्गुरुदेव मंगतराम जी महाराज

A MASTER AND A SEEKER

Life of Śrī Maṅgatrāmjī Mahārāj

Som Raj Gupta

MOTILAL BANARSIDASS PUBLISHERS
PRIVATE LIMITED • DELHI

First Edition : Delhi, 2017

ISBN : 978-81-208-4159-8

<u>*Also available at*</u>

MOTILAL BANARSIDASS
41 U.A. Bungalow Road, Jawahar Nagar, Delhi 110 007
1 B, Jyoti Studio Compound, Kennedy Bridge, Nana Chowk, Mumbai 400 007
203 Royapettah High Road, Mylapore, Chennai 600 004
236, 9th Main III Block, Jayanagar, Bengaluru 560 011
8 Camac Street, Kolkata 700 017
Ashok Rajpath, Patna 800 004
Chowk, Varanasi 221 001

Photographs on p. ii, xii and xvi
Courtesy by Sanjiv Arora

MLBD Cataloging-in-Publication Data
A Master and A Seeker : Life of Śrī Maṅgatrāmjī Mahārāj
by Som Raj Gupta
Includes Glossary and Index
ISBN : 978-81-208-4159-8
I. Hinduism II. Saints and Teachings
III. Maṅgatrāmjī IV. Gupta, Som Raj

Published by
Motilal Banarsidass Publishers Private Limited
www.mlbd.com • mlbd@mlbd.com
Printed by Gopsons Papers Limited

PREFACE

The subject of this narrative was a puzzle for the writer, a mystery hard to face, even to bear. He was also a man the ordinary, even, for the sophisticated, less than ordinary – a man born at a village remote from civilization, hard to connect and get to. No means of transport, no rail lines, no newspapers or other means of communications were available there. And, of course, no medical treatment. Poverty abject and dismal, superstitions adamant and stubborn, land barren and unproductive, diseases frequent and fatal sum up the conditioning factors that were to fashion the course and the style of life of one born in that, for very many, scary and chilling atmosphere.

And yet a man was born there that, despite being conditioned by these disabling factors, transcended all these, transcended them at his birth itself. An extraordinary man he was, more than extraordinary, a being superhuman in almost the literal sense of the term. And there was also the Word speaking unto the world, inert and living, through him, the Word that redeems our speech, our human speech, through descending into it. Our speech is a frustration as much as our desire is: it cannot find its being unless and until it turns into the Word, at once the knowledge and the being of the Real, as much as our desire cannot get appeased unless and until it attains to the Being that it ever seeks but never finds. In the Word are appeased both – our desire and our thirst for knowledge.

But the Word comes to be our being and knowledge only in relation to us; it is we who give it the status of the Real and the Bliss. It is conditioned by us, by our teleological passion, by our desire for Being. That passion does not let us pause and consider, pass and consider why we were banished from our Being and Bliss. In other words, why our Word, ***our* Word,** fell into words and our Being into beings. The fall of our God into Creation, Creation ever miserable and sinful, ever disinherited and dispossessed, no Revelation can explain, no Testament and no Message and no Prophet. Revelations discard themselves, the Word turns mute and silent when they find themselves confronted by the question of the fall of God. So the man on the Path finds himself deprived of the Path because the End of his pilgrimage he finds to be ever dying into Creation from which he would escape and flee. With Speech the Revelatory discarding itself, the Man of Revelation has to die with his God into the misery and the pain and sinfulness of Creation. Therein, he finds, lies the glory of God, in His sacrifice into Creation and his own, this pilgrim's, redemption, in sharing in that glory, that sacrificial glory. For, we have lost our paradise not to regain it but to find in our loss the gain and in our Sin the Original our Redemption the Final, in our mortality our immortality. That is what the story of my preceptor's life revealed unto him, revealed unto him not easily but through severe and unbelievable *tapas*, through constant self-burning and self-extinction. We mortals have to pass through many a purgatorial test before we can hope to realize the glory of our fall. We are to see with an equal eye both our fall and redemption, our bondage and liberation. This is what the life of my preceptor teaches us, this is its message, its final testament, the testament of ***samatvam*** or ***samatā***, of sameness.

There have been thinkers and reformers, visionaries and statesmen, even some seers and mystics that have dreamed of a Geist or a Spirit shaping beings into selves, into genuine gnostic beings and the inert into the living and individuals into constituents of the Absolute. They have also dreamed of ideal societies as creative wholes moving towards Being, Being the Absolute. Before Creation every being remains, for these gifted souls, a mere unmanifest potentiality for a fully evolved being and every society, the unmanifest constitutive other of every potential being, a mere potentiality for a genuinely evolved society, in which latter a part lives for the whole and the whole for the part. But all this talk has been a talk about Utopias, more than Utopias, dangerously more than Utopias; for led has this talk to destructive wars and endless oppressions. The first half of the twentieth century saw the devastatingly barbaric effects of these idealistic dreams in the shape of Hitlerism and Stalinism.

Since the eighteenth and nineteenth centuries, there has also been a constant attempt to accept the 'given' individual as an end in himself, sleeping over the transcendental urge in him. Instead of his seeking God as his end, he has anointed himself as God, his desires and passions attaining to the status of norms: ethical, epistemological and ontological. Today the world is fast asleep to the destructive dimensions of this its fidelity, even fealty, to this blind, pernicious and annihilative self-obsession. The teachings of my Master give a stern warning against this suicidal passion that would make one asleep to the real self, the self that is the unknowing witness of our cognitions, of our thoughts, of our knowledge, of our theories and practices, of our discourses, passions and desires. Today, we may be conscious of barbarism implied in the idealistic dreams of a Hegel or a Heidegger but we are blissfully unaware of the latent barbarism of our liberal dispositions, with their thoughtless commitment to knowledge and power and consumer culture. We also in our arrogance have confused, like the aforesaid thinkers, our discourses with reality, all forgetful of the gap that falls between the Real and our knowledge of it. To wake up people from this arrogance, from this ignorance, Gurudeva, my Master the Revered, made a long and strenuous effort, effort that drained out all his physical energy. However, his message was not for the sophisticated elite but for the simple and unsophisticated. For, unlike the elite they were yet to be burdened with the potential decadence of modernity, decadence that was to show its destructive bankruptcy, ethical and spiritual, soon, rather too soon. From village to village he went, from towns to towns, amidst the beasts of prey he did his *tapas*, his ardent absorption in *ātman,* in self the true, to make people aware of the internal way to the Real as against the external ways fabricated by modernity since the days of Enlightenment.

And yet he had to, as reading of this work will show, give up even this urge in him, urge that would save contemporary world from the doom that awaits its gnostic oblivion. Men of sight and wisdom almost always fail to save people from the doom that awaits them; they strive for that purpose only to get disillusioned in the long run. But *prakṛti,* Nature, has its own way to deal with our illusions and deviations.

But to come back to our story and the dilemmas it presented before the writer: Writing of this biography, I should confess, became as a hesitant, even a strenuous and halting task for me. For, I could not decide whether I should act as a mere scribe, a mere Boswell and let the life and personality of the Master reveal its various dimensions: his rustic dialect and way of life, his profound thoughts ever in conflict with his unpolished dialect, the sheen and fragrance of his body and the awesome expression of his face when he was in *samādhi,* a sight that would plumb the beholder into the depths of a self-threatening mystery, a mystery both of life and death. This is what a literary artist would do to satisfy his urge for right and authentic expression. But would that have been enough for me? For, I had to reckon with the descent of the Revelatory speech, speech without a speaker, the descent of the Word into words and the truth It uttered, truth beyond the reach of our speech, speech that ever remains distant from the truth it seeks, is ever spurned by it. But let us not forget that even that Speech of the Word gets conditioned by words when it descends into them, by the relationships and contrasts they embody and the tangles they weave to ensnare every being into them. For, the Word so conditioned speaks to the being fashioned by words (and by forms, their constitutive others), being ever in search of Being. And It makes him strive for that End but only to find after undergoing the despair of a seemingly endless hell that his hopes were vain and his struggles futile, for the Being he sought was Being the ever self-negating. With that realization, he finds Speech the Revelation disowning itself, proclaiming itself as tentatively true but ultimately false. However, this falsehood and its possibilities and promises can only be realized by meticulously going through that Speech, going through it with every attentiveness and fidelity.

So I had to be descriptive, meditative and contemplative as far as I could, I had to be emotional as well as objective, devotional as well as analytical, discursive as well as contemplatively passive. About the aesthetic content of this work I must, have to, speak with every diffidence. I do not know how to translate an Indian country dialect into a parallel English dialect, how to translate the Speech of the Word, which no writer, howsoever gifted or accomplished, can, not to speak of me, me who cannot boast of mastery over creative English. Still I have ventured to undertake this task and would let the reader decide for himself about my success and failure.

This work is about a Master and a Disciple. Why this rude and offensive intrusion by an unworthy disciple? There was the obvious necessity of not only summarizing the contents of the *bānī*, of scores and hundreds of pages of it, into a few manageable paragraphs and pages but also the necessity of explaining and commenting on its contents. Moreover, there was also the necessity of translating, or rather paraphrasing, some of the passages to give the reader a feel of its force and depth, of its images and metaphors. In the Hindi version of this biography, I could let the *bānī* speak for itself but here the impossible task of translating rendered inevitable his intrusion.

Conscious of all my limitations I wrote this biography the way I have described under the impact of an inner compulsion (and also because, I should admit - despite my somewhat rational leanings – that he had commanded me twice in my dreams to write it in English). For years I laid it aside but had to go back to it. For the Master haunted me like a presence and not for days or months or years but for decades. What kind of presence it was, how awesome and intimidating the Prologue and the Epilogue describe in concrete and immediate terms. But I could not think of publishing it because, most importantly, it contains matters relating to me personally, matters in the shape of experiences out of the ordinary, experiences that I would not share with anyone as long as I was alive. Experiences that are to lead to self-extinction can very well result in self-glory if shared prematurely with others, the temptation being very strong and irresistible. Even now, when my life is hanging by a frail thread, I am not completely sure about myself. Yet friends who do not know my experiences have urged upon me to share them with others, including them, for without that sharing no one will know the Grace Abounding that my preceptor was. I am the youngest of his disciples and the very few others that have survived are, for various reasons, unable to undertake the task.

In the Hindi Edition published in 1981, I wrote as a member of the religious congregation the Master had established, congregation called the *Saṅgat Samatāvād,* but this biography is written by an alone in relation with no one, not even with the Alone. Those who do me the honour of going through this work will know the enormity of the difference between the pilgrim that he once was, a pilgrim that with all his pain and anguish could yet cherish some faith and hope and the man now all beret of any faith, of any path and of any destination, And yet he cannot but remain tied to that contradiction that his guide was, For, in his ignorance lay his wisdom, of that guide, and in his fall his redemption. And may not in the loss of his disciple's faith lie the hope of deliverance from the shame that his being is? I am unable to answer this question.

February, 2017 SOM RAJ GUPTA

P.S.: Bcause of the writer's bad health quite a few errors and lapses may have remained undetected and unrectified. The reader may kindly bear with him.

Śrī Maṅgatrāmjī Mahārāj

Table of Contents

Scheme of Transliteration

Vowels	a ā i ī u ū ṛ ṝ ḷ e ai o au
ansuvāra	ṃ
visarga	ḥ
Consonants	
gutturals	k kh g gh ṅ
palatals	c ch j jh ñ
cerebrals	ṭ ṭh ḍ ḍh ṇ
dentals	t th d dh n
labials	p ph b bh m
semi vowels	y r l v
	s as in sun
	ś palatal sibilant
	ṣ cerebral sibilant
aspirate	h

For the reader not familiar with Sanskrit, Hindi or Urdu

a may be pronounced as *u* in but
ā as *a* in *father*
i as *i* in *if*
ī as *ee* in *feel*
u as *u* in *full*
ū as *u* in *rule*
e as *ay* in *play*
ai as *y* in *my*
o as *o* in *globe*
au as *ow* in *now*
ṛ as *ri* in *ritual*
ḷ as *li* in *lick*
g as *g* in *go*
c as *ch* in *church*
ś and *ṣ* as *sh in shun*
m at the end of a word and before labials as *m*, elswhere as *n*

This is only a rough scheme

Hindi or Urdu names or words without the diacritical marks may be pronounced as in English

Śrī Maṅgatrāmjī Mahārāj *with his disciple* Banārsīdās

Prologue

I have lived under his light, under his shadow, under his deathly gaze, under the all-killing presence of his image. He disdained my self, my individuality, my humanity and my world. 'Stern,' 'forbidding,' 'fearful,' 'unsympathetic' are not the words to describe that image. For full three decades, I could not live my days and my nights; he was always there to steal them away, a large part of them, that frail being, that pale face, those intimidating wrinkles and that almost shabby dress. My days and nights were his and not of the people I would relate to or of the trees I would rest under or of the sunsets over hills and mountains I would contemplate, but could not. What I saw there, in the world, appeared more like a dream, what I felt here, within the mind, was all reality: that pale and wrinkled face and its imagined gaze. I call that gaze 'imagined' because that presence was always behind me, somewhat on the left side, to ever unnerve the man in me. In dreams I saw him sitting *before* me, sometimes even speaking to me. His eyes were then human, and so were his gestures and his postures. He was a familiar figure then, unlike that phantom of my waking hours that was so eerie and strange. In the dream, I too was my own self, my own functioning self. I did not have to struggle then for breath and to relate to things. All seemed intact, me as well as the world. Here, in the wakeful state everything seemed to be disintegrating; everything that one could see, hear or touch. My torture alone would not disintegrate; too solid was it to do so, my tearless anguish, the heat in the brain and the burning in my veins, and the stoniness of my feelings, frozen, inhuman feelings. And, of course, the pitiless Presence behind! But could one call that Presence a presence, him that would negate all presence? To another realm of the truth he seemed to belong, not to the realm of the truth to which belonged my hell. To the realm of death he seemed to belong, for, he was the truth that would negate all the truths, not excluding his own. That indeed was his truth, the truth that respects no truth.

I *was* because the pain *was*; *that* seemed the sole dispenser of my truth, that pain, that torture, that shame, not the people around me, or the ground under me or the tall mountains away, far away from me. Their own reality being in question, they could not lend any to me. The pale figure staring me down from behind was not a part of the world – that nightmare – around me; it was not a part of that horror. Nor did it appear like a spirit sent from a world beyond to admonish, to punish or to save me; it seemed the beyond itself, beyond the absolute, a real beyond the real. One could not call it divine, for divinity too, is, in a sense, human; one can at least talk about it, even though in negative terms. But that Presence would despise all descriptions, would spurn all concepts, all epithets: human, divine or demonic. More than man it was, more than God, more than even death. It exceeded the all, that little figure. And yet this Other, this absolute Other, was more proximate than anything else, nearer was it to me than even my breath. For, when I sensed the presence of that Presence most intensely, I found it, my breath, moving *before* me, at some distance from me; too displaced was I then, too disrupted and too de-centred to find it moving within me. A nowhere, I had little affinity, little relationship, with breath, that most proximate among the proximate. It seemed to move on its own, independent of my will or concern. Placed between it and the Presence, I felt that Presence exceed all grasp, all concepts, all understanding. It was a reality in excess, a reality that seemed to exceed the reality of the world, of God, of all that one could think of or imagine. It struck one mute, made one breathless. More than a wonder it was, more than, I should say, death, for a presence it was, not an absence, though a devastation, total and absolute.

Whose image was this, of which man, an image that exceeded the image, exceeded man and exceeded the world? It was the image of a man whom I saw when I was sixteen and who died when I was a little over eighteen. Barely four or five sentences I exchanged with him, unremarkable sentences which no one would ever care to remember. Yet for over three decades, as I said, he did not leave me, held me in his clutches as it were, turning my life and being into hell. So I will relate my first *encounter/s* with him, with the man that was neither educated, nor sophisticated, one who often talked in terms archaic and strange, one who gave discourses that were less than captivating. An embodiment of ordinariness was he, ordinariness totally out of tune with the unnerving aura about him. I remember the first time I saw that contradiction, that disruptive and catastrophic paradox. It was the afternoon of the fourth day of November in the year 1951, a day bright with a soothing, mild sun. An orchard, thick with dense, fruitless trees, with small passages laid for pedestrians appeared along the left side of the road we were walking on, my companion and me. We entered the orchard, following a path that turned right and then left ending up near a well on the right, a little beyond which a small white washed hut appeared. A room and a verandah were all that it could boast of; it did not have room enough for the small gathering of men and women there. Some among them sat in the verandah, some on the pavements on the three sides of the hut, listening all attentive and still to the chanting of verses. The voice that chanted was indeed attractive but not sweet, an old, heavy voice, with overstressed accents.

We approached the silent congregation, my companion and me, and sat among men in the last row. For a few minutes continued the chanting, absorbing, I soon found out, my self into it, and then followed silence, a palpable silence one could say, for one could hear it in the ears. The calm of that silence was broken by the voice of a man that sat aloof near the wall, sat there with his trunk bent a little with a slight quiver in the head. In pale-white was he clad, in clothes coarse and home-woven. In soft and even accents he spoke, in a voice of monotones, with little by way of a rise or a fall. This continued for some time, the soft hum-like monotone, but before long the softness disappeared, a loud and confident voice replaced it, occasionally rising to a pitch this side of a cry. I say this in retrospect, for I can hear even now the pitch, the accents, the softness and the loudness. On that occasion, I took little notice of these things. I was all devotion, all faith then. Even before I had seen him, I believed in him and was ready to surrender my self to him. One of my brothers had lately become his disciple and had nothing else to talk about than his Master. And that was enough for me: his faith, his devotion and his fervour. For me, the words the Master uttered were all divine, the very embodiments of the truth absolute. I do not, however, remember what he said that afternoon. Perhaps I did not understand. The discourse over, the Master asked the gathering to ask questions if they had any. There was no response to the invitation, an aura of awe seemed to envelop and enwrap all. The silence was, however, broken by the ever-articulate brother of mine, his new disciple: They say, he said, that the guru's grace is indispensable for salvation. Does this grace continue to flow even when he has given up his body? Prompt came the reply: That depends on the disciple's *śraddhā,* his faith. No other question was asked.

The discourse over, my brother came up to me and led me to the Master's presence to introduce me to him. I approached him in awe, for his gaze had all come to be fixed on me, on my forehead, I should say, for he was not looking into my eyes. A penetrating gaze I felt it was but it did not affect me because it was not, as I have said, directed at my gaze. I prostrated myself before him and he gave me his blessings without uttering a word. When my brother introduced me to him, he said: 'Ask this youngster not to watch the movies.' I said I won't. That was all that introduction was comprised of. I bowed before him; he responded with a bow touching the ground with his hands. Let me hasten to add that the entire congregation sat cross-legged on the floor with rough mattresses spread over it. A remarkable humility I saw in his eyes then.

I took upon myself the duty of carrying milk to the hut every morning. So, I rose early and went to a dairy to get the milk. The milkman was scarcely awake yet. But he milked a cow for me. With the bowl of milk in my hand, I proceeded towards the hut, full two kilometres away and reached there before the break of dawn. I was and am a timid person and felt the fright of darkness but my adolescent faith was strong enough for the fright of the lonely darkness. I saw the silhouettes of men sitting cross legged on their bed-clothes absorbed in silent meditation in the verandah until the light of the morning woke them up, so I thought. I requested Bhagatjī, 'the noble devotee', to receive the milk I had brought. He asked for my name and identity and accepted the milk with a winsome smile. His head was all shaven but his face was attractive, his voice sonorous, his smile unforgettable. The Master had, I was informed, gone out for his nightly meditation. At around 8 A.M. he came back, walking fast with long, firm strides, took a brief bath at the well and came towards the hut to ascend a few steps that led up to its roof, meticulously swept, with a rough, clean carpet spread over it. A folded black blanket spread near the middle part of the edge of the roof on the left served the purpose of a seat for the Master. On it he sat, all still and silent, absorbed in *samādhī*. What a frail body had he, yet soft and shining like velvet! One could see, vividly and literally, the sunlight gleaming on his feet, his hands and his arms. His face was, however, [something] to see, not to tell. It was a fair face, pale and weak, with traces of the crimson crisscrossing here and there. With the trunk bent down a little and the head quivering, the face appeared to wear an altogether impersonal look. Could one call it 'an impersonal look?' Could one call that look even 'a look?' For, no expression that face wore then, neither the expression of pain nor of pleasure, neither of hope nor of despair, neither of wisdom nor of foolishness. Man had definitely deserted that face, even 'face' had deserted it, the concept 'face'. For what it spoke, that face, could not be identified in our terms. Life seemed to have coincided with death there and death with life. If it was not the face of a living man, neither was it the face of a corpse. It spoke of something beyond all that one can know or articulate. The unknown was it, rather the unknowable, a revelation that was a closure. I saw this all in one moment, saw unknowingly, unselfconsciously. What I say now is only a description of my impression, an under-description rather than an over-description.

Every morning I saw that face, with a brief interval caused by illness, and let that face sink into me. As I said, I had no conversation with him. My daily job was to sweep the roof and clean the carpet, sprinkle some water on it and spread out the blanket-seat of the Master. Others too joined me in this, to me at that time, a holy service. For twenty minutes or so I would look all absorbed on the Master's face and of the depths it revealed, that visible invisibility. After this contemplation, I would go down to cleanse the utensils or sweep the verandah and go back home. My relationship with him was all quiet, my communication, if at all it could be called a communication, was all mute. After full one year, I had a little conversation with him. I had read the *Samatāvilāsa* by then wherein emphasis was laid on the surrender of one's ego of doing to the will of the Lord, the all-Doer. One day, I found myself sitting alone in his presence and, overcoming my shyness, said: What is the difference between my doing and the Lord's doing?

Master: The thought that all that happens is done by God will free you from the ego of doing.

Me: Is the Lord, then, the not-doer?

Master: The doer is He and also the non-doer. Do you understand?

I had not understood but somehow I felt I had. That summed up my entire theological education. On two more occasions I took the initiative of speaking to him, making requests for initiation, one in 1951 and the other in 1952. The first was turned down, causing me great distress, the other was accepted. The second request I think I should narrate. I persistently urged upon Bhagat Banārsīdās, 'the noble devotee,' to speak on my behalf. He had served the Master for fifteen years, accompanied him to remote villages and towns, to fearful forests and solitudes and had recorded the verses that now constitute the *Samatā-prakāśa*. He asked me to go up and make the request myself, assuring me that it would be accepted. Before I could ascend the last step, the Master said, 'Dear lad, d'you watch the movies?' Replying in the negative, I straightway put my request before him. He said that I was too young for that but I insisted. My vocal cords had suddenly become articulate. I was somehow convinced that that was the time for it, for a sudden idea had occurred to me that the Master would not live long. I received a reluctant, tentative assent.

The eighth of December was fixed for initiation. We were asked to reach the hut at 6 A.M., five souls, thrilled and trembling with expectations of a new birth and new life. The Master was punctual to the minute, though he carried no watch with him. When we reached there, he was already there to receive us, back from his solitary self-oblivion during the night. An awesome mystery emanated from his face, as if infinity had covered itself in flesh, as if all the truth had come to reside in it, in one fleeting expression of it. Five persons, as I said, were to be initiated that Monday morning. Before the initiation, the Master said in a soft, barely audible voice, 'Do you all have faith in *It*?' For, that is how he referred to himself, as *It* or *This*, not as *I*. With faith 'absolute' we said in one voice, 'Yes!' This 'yes' did not affect the transcendence that he seemed then, for no human response could it evoke, no expression of reassurance, much less of satisfaction. However, he explained the technique of *yoga* and its various stages, his voice slowly assuming the human ring. After that brief, very brief explanation, he initiated us all into the secret teaching. I had been told, time and again, that after initiation a deep and self-forgetting peace enveloped one, sending the hours and the days on flight. Its duration varied from person to person, with some it stayed for one day, with others for three to four, even to five days. Then it would disappear on its own which no effort on the part of the initiates could revive. When they would request the Master to renew it, he would ask them to earn it for themselves. Borrowings, he would say, could not last long. I had gone for the initiation with great expectations and hopes, but no peace enveloped me, no ecstasy seized me. Rather a sense of dissatisfaction, almost of frustration and irritation occupied me. However, there was one change that occurred within me, a change that I did not notice at the time of the initiation. When, under his prompting, I inhaled the *mantra* he had imparted to us, I felt a movement right within the navel. I imagined that this was the common experience of every initiate, but there I was wrong. It took me fourteen years to realise the meaning of that movement.

I, on my part, waited for the peace and the bliss, 'that foretaste of the absolute bliss to come,' but it was not, it appeared, to be my portion to bathe in the waters of 'the lake of grace' that the Mater was said to be. To me he appeared cold and indifferent, even, perhaps, hostile. There was only one occasion when I could see the love that he bestowed so freely upon his disciples, a love from which I had been sternly excluded. One morning, he asked Banārasīdās to give me some pieces of papaya the latter had peeled. It was bitter, unacceptably bitter. The Master looked at me with a kind look, his eyes all benign, his mien all soft, as if a grace was flowing out of him. With that gracious look, he asked me, 'Is it bitter?' Through a nod of the head, I indicated its taste.'Take it as you would take a draught of medicine,' was the reply. That grace, that look lies more than half a century deep in my memory. But don't I feel as if I saw it only yesterday?

That practically finished my verbal exchange with him. One could not think of a less remarkable meeting than this, if we go by what passed between us by way of conversations. How did it happen that this *encounter* came to have a devastating effect on my personality, an effect that did all but kill me? I will have to tax the patience of the reader a little to describe in brief the state of my life and attitudes before my initiation. To do this, I shall have to go back to the days of my childhood. I was born at Dalhousie, a hill resort now in the Indian State of Himachal Pradesh, a place famous for the beauty of its landscape. But I will first narrate a small incident that happened not at Dalhousie but at Shakargarh, now in Pakistan, a village like town near the borders of the State of Jammu and Kashmir, and at a distance of about 150 kilometres from Dalhousie by the road, but not more than 40 kilometres as the crow might fly. The village gave a commanding view of the Pir Panjal and Dhauldhar ranges of the Himalayas, a long line of snow clad mountains stretching from the left to the right. It was a mild late winter afternoon when the sun was sinking behind me. Before me lay the fields green with the young plants of wheat and those of mustard; here and there were also visible some huge mango trees with their thick and luxuriant leaves. The green spread vast and distant stretching, as it were, up to the hills and the mountains. My eyes came to rest on the snow on the peaks, gone almost pale in the sunlight. A deep and quiet silence seemed to enter my mind, sending a thrill, serene and gentle into my veins and moisture in my eyes. My hair stood on end, the landscape turning into a dream-like appearance, dim and faint, calm and still. A foretaste it was of the bliss that I was destined to experience in the years to come. I was only four/five then. As the years passed by, the frequency of such experiences increased and so did their intensity.

I have already referred to the beauty of the landscape at and around Dalhousie. Dalhousie itself is situated on the last leg of the Dhauldhar range of the Himalayas but opens out to an awesome view of a part of the Pir Panjal range, locally called the Pangi range, whose bluish mountains sink slowly into the plains whereon flows the river Ravi dividing itself into two semi-circular currents.[1] The sun sets there, over the Ravi, transforming its two semi-circles first into silver and then into gold. In the soothing warmth of early summer, the evening transforms the snowy peaks into a breathless sublimity. The entire stretch of the mountains from the left to the right bathes in gold, in crimson, with the blue of the sky turning into yellow green. This sight and the soothing warmth of the summer in my veins often extinguished my thoughts, my being resting on the snow or the glow of the river or the colours of the sky. The sight would often replace the seer, for I was all that I saw. A stillness was out there and within, undoing their distinction, that between without and within. I could not say whether I was there on the mountains or the mountains were in me. All was still, hushed and calm, and remained so until a passing bird would fly past me giving a new lease to my conscious life. Sometimes, a waving tree would break that spell or the gusty wind. Often the sight was more blissful than calm, sending a thrill in my body, in each and every pore of it. On such occasions, my eyes would brim with tears. Then, all of a sudden, the mountains would disappear and so would the sky and so would me. When I came back from such trances, I felt myself overflowing with joy, tears flowing profusely from my eyes. It seemed they had flowed uninterrupted during the trances, for I would find my shirt drenched in them. As for the trees, the mountains and the sky, I perceived them overspread with a light that had never been there before. It made their green, their yellow and their blue shine in an unearthly glow, unearthly because the like of it cannot be found on our earth. For hours I bathed in uninterrupted joy, which neither solitude could disjoin nor the noise of the market place could disturb, not even the noise of running traffic. It was, I may add, not only the sublime beauty of the mountains that suspended all my being; even the silence of the groves, the music of the deodar trees, the lines of clouds or of the rising mist could bring about that suspension, or the distant roar of the waters. I was virtually a creature of bliss born into a world of bliss.

The initiation put an end to all those ecstasies, those blissful oblivions, those trances and transports. I do not remember to have experienced even a trace of them thereafter. Within a few months came my misery, came to choke me, torture me, burn me. I use the words 'choke,' 'torture,' 'burn' literally, for I do not know how else to describe the state of my breath, the pain in my nerves and the burning sensations that I had from head to foot. No sleep came to apply its balm, no appetite to comfort the aching stomach, no hope to release the breath. Fear lurked everywhere: in men, in the trees, in the rocks as if these latter too had a spite against me. I could not speak to people; my heart throbbed with fear when I did. Even of children I was afraid, even of young beautiful girls.

It was, let me inform the reader, in a Delhi grove that I first met the Master; it was there I was initiated into yoga, in the hut I have spoken about. During the first months after the initiation I felt a dreary lack within me but it was not yet the hell that was to be shortly let loose upon me. My examinations over by April 18, 1952, I gave myself up to meditation. But there was only unrest within, a freezing inertness, a heavy dullness, not the joy, the motion and the ecstasy, my companions since my childhood. Within two weeks, the unrest changed into the misery I have just mentioned. Lying on my bed on the roof of our house, I spent the nights gazing at the stars, hoping all the time that my Master would lift up the insupportable weight of the misery, would give me back my lost paradise. The brethren often talked of his grace, of his shepherd-like concern for his herd, his disciples. Divine was he, they said, the seer of past, present and future, the five elements of earth, water, fire, air and the sky at his ready command, mar or make could he at his will. I believed them and so I waited, night after night, for the miracle to happen but vain were my vigils and fruitless my tears and prayers. In those days, our family lived in very straitened circumstances. One day, in utter desperation, I left home early in the morning, unable to bear the humiliation of being unwanted. In the hot and humid sun, I walked barefoot for many a mile, without food and water, until I reached the bank of the river Yamunā, where I thought I would give up my life if my prayers were not heard. Reaching there, I found a large number of picnickers enjoying their food and their songs, not the solitude I had come to look for. I had a sip or two of the muddy waters of the river, swollen with rainwater, and turned back to move away from that throng of people. Barely had I taken a few weary steps when I fell down overwhelmed with giddiness, the discomfort, the exhaustion, the hunger and the thirst proving too much for me. A tear or two flowed out, tears of despair, for I felt that the Master, though present near me, would pay no heed to my suffering and my helplessness.

Some kind people took notice of my plight and sent me back home. I narrate this incident to describe not my circumstances but the crisis of faith that followed. I felt a spiritual humiliation, a humiliation much more cruel than the worldly humiliations, my daily fare. My tears were now dry, my prayers were cries of despair, I felt myself cut off from all relationships, relationships with humans, with the clouds or with the sky.

Meanwhile I got a small job at Simla (now called Shimla) where I thought my mountains, my own mountains, would lend me back their sublimity, the sunsets their glory and the music of the deodars its stillness. But the mountains had turned into huge monsters, the trees into spiteful killers, silence of the groves into a choking, the sunsets into dreary spectacles. My eyes could see their beauty and their sublimity, my ears could hear their music and their silence but there was no room within me to accommodate them, no human room of feeling. All was blank: my mind, my eyes, my ears. I could relate to the world only through eating, for which I developed an inordinate greed, but even that relationship could not last for long. Nothing could be mine, nothing that my eyes saw, my ears heard or my palate tasted. There were occasions when I would put a mouthful of a supposedly tasty stuff into my mouth in order to enjoy it, at least for a moment but the unrest within would not permit me to linger on the taste, forcing me to swallow the stuff with disgust. Eating became a dirty, filthy thing from that time onwards.

People of faith approach sages for peace of mind, for their worldly security, for their future salvation. No one would buy misery, loneliness or despair. The more insightful among them would seek Virgils, Beatrices or Michels to guide them in their pilgrimage through hell and purgatory to their heaven. Few would be ready to live in lonely despair, to strive without hope and pass through their highs and lows without any tangible results. But mortal man is alone, absolutely alone. His journey is a lonely journey, his salvation is the salvation of the alone. There is no guide to lead him, for there is no way to follow. But the majority among us would escape from our despair through our pleasures, our ambitions, our grand projects, personal or social, or through faith, through theories or plain cynicism. The compulsion of drinking the cup of despair is not our portion, not of the majority among us. We have illusions to weave for our comfort, illusions of the here or the hereafter. Can a man who has the painful insight to look through these illusions find his rest in the nowhere, his way where no way is, find grace in his curse and redemption in his fall? That is the question, the momentous question that is going to occupy us throughout this narration. But first we must focus on the Master's own life as it has come down to us through varied sources.

Note

1 I am speaking about the pre-modern shape of the river.

1

Birth and Childhood

Satpuruṣa Śrī Maṇgatrāmjī Mahārāj[1] was born on November 24, 1903 at Gangothian (in the district of Rawalpindi, now in Pakistan), a small hamlet of brahmins who all but had lost touch with the piety, learning and vision of their ancestors. For these latter brahmins reality was nothing else except the act of sacrifice, the cosmotheandric[2] act of sacrifice, in which every being participated, or was to participate, every being from heaven to earth, from god to man and every other creature, the nonmoving no less than the moving. To live that act of self-sacrifice they would participate every evening and morning in the serene death of the day into the night and the glorious death of the night into the day. In that they saw every wisdom and every enlightenment, in that act of cosmotheandric self-sacrifice. From the setting day they besought benedictions and from the dying night, besought them through the divine *gāyatrī.* The more mature among them went further; they sought salvation in Being that was no Being, in that final death of all that is, from heaven to earth and what relates the two, namely, the act of sacrifice.

The brahmins of Gangothian had no such vision of divine-cosmic-human sacrifice. No hymns did they sing to hail the birth of the sun in the morning, of that god of light and life nor did they share in the tranquil calm of his setting, calm cosmic and redemptive. Nor were they children of *pṛthivī*, of earth the extended, as were their forebearers, for expand did they not with her to the horizons and rise did they not with her from there up to the sky and beyond the sky. Broken off had they all bonds of fealty to her, their mother. The countryside around Gangothian alone was *their* earth, that landscape of tiny hillocks, covered mostly with shrubs and rocks, some fields for cultivation and, at a distance, a thick ancient forest, the haunt, these brahmins believed, of spirits evil and malignant. That alone was their earth, nothing beyond that. The genius of the forest, *Pīr* Khwājā, had, it seems, an unappeasable appetite for the meat of goats and sheep, which the inhabitants of the area, Hindus no less than Muslims, took every care to propitiate. This was the notion of sacrifice they had come to have in place of the sacrificial vision of the priests of old. As, for the higher state of Being that was no Being, they could not even imagine it.

It was in that area of darkness that Śrī Maṅgatrām was born but, happily, in a family that still kept burning the flame of ancient piety and meditation. His father, Pundit Gauri Shankar, was the very embodiment of contentment and non-covetousness, those defining traits of genuine brahminhood. The estate manager of a rich aristocrat, Sardar Sujan Singh, he contented himself with the small pay of twenty rupees a month, refusing every raise he was offered. His master would invariably stand up to greet him – such was the esteem in which he held his employee. One cherished wish of the generous man was to gift away a large house to the Pundit, which the latter steadfastly refused to accept. Years later, when the Sardar's only heir died, the Pundit handed over all his vast assets to the government, keeping nothing for himself, despite the express wish of the deceased heir.

If Pundit Gauri Shankar embodied the true brahminic spirit, the Master's grandfather, Pundit Sunderdas, kept alive the tradition of seers and *ṛṣis*. In his youth, however, he had been seized by the war-atmosphere of the reign of Ranajit Singh, who, true to his name, 'the Great Winner of Battles,' had brought under his rule a large part of the north west of India. The young Sunderdas could not resist the call of the war cries of this warrior king and joined his cavalry force. Bravery was the glory of youth in those days and Sunderdas loved to shine in it. He trained his two sons into fine horsemen and felt proud when they too joined the cavalry force of his king. The Pundit, however, received a severe blow of Misfortune when the youths fell fighting in a battle. The tragedy was too hard for him; it spelt the end of his ambitions for glory, for success and honour. Life looked too chaotic for success, too contingent for glory, too meaningless for honour. The security of home appeared of no account, the order of social life all grotesque. He renounced home and his caste to become a wandering monk. His family searched for him long and in earnest, but in vain. It was by sheer chance that his cousins once stumbled into him at a distant town, Sialkot, and somehow persuaded him to return home.

The Pundit returned home but not to the world. He lived in solitude on the outskirts of the village, giving himself up to prayers and meditations. The painful memories would not, however, die down, try as he might; they disrupted his meditations and turned his prayers into tearful sighs. News reached him that a great sage had come to stay in the neighbourhood, barely eight miles away. Promptly, he went to see him to find, if possible, a remedy for his anguish. The sage blessed the Pundit and, before long, he had a son to comfort him in his old age. The sage, it is said, predicted that this son would grow into a wise and noble soul and would have, for a son, a seer of the highest order. The birth of a son might have been a balm for his inner wounds but it could not bring him out of his solitude and meditations. Virtually resorting to the life of a forest dweller, he spent the last years of his life mostly in the solitude of the unfrequented forests of Kashmir, Shabakdar and Banihal. A post-centurion he lived, attaining through his long and fervent meditations the highest reaches of *yoga*. We have to this effect the testimony of no less a person than Śrī Gurudeva himself.[3]

The child Maṅgat was only four when his father died. Before he breathed his last, Gauri Shankar called his two sons by his first wife, Thakurdas and Kishan Chand, to his death bed and extracted a promise from them that they would take every care of their little step-brother who, he said, had a great future awaiting him. Their half brother was, however, a child mystifying in the extreme; too serious and sober he was for his age, with little of the frolic and delight of childhood. Even as a babe he would not cry as babes would. This seriousness was a matter of concern for the family, even of alarm, the predictions of his future greatness notwithstanding. His mother, Ganeshi Devi, was especially distressed, for he was her only son, the sole anchor of her life after her husband's death, the lot of a young widowed mother being what it was in those far off days. Often, too often, she found him, a mere child of five, sitting cross-legged on his bed, his trunk erect, his eyes closed. Perhaps, she thought, a bad dream had waked him up. Or was it something in his head and heart, something wrong there? In a voice of anguished affection she would ask the child to go to sleep, which he would do without a word or delay. But no sooner would the mother fall asleep than the child would rise up again to resume his meditative posture. Her timid and frightened heart had a hope that with the passage of time he would become 'normal' but that hope turned out, as we shall find, all vain and futile.

What was the cause, the secret of this seriousness, this abstraction and meditative sleeplessness, of the love of solitude and of darkness – things that go against the very grain of childhood? The inner life of the child Maṅgat ever remained a closed book for his family and devotees alike. If his biography had been written when he was alive, the mystery that envelops his childhood might have been dispelled somewhat. Since that did not happen, we have to remain content with the few, stray hints that Gurudeva himself threw out when in conversation with the devotees. One such conversation gives us a peep into that inner life:

Devotee: Did the lord ever have a guru?

Master: Dear Child, God alone is *Its*[4] Master. One requires a Master when one is not ripe enough [for self-realisation]. When this body was but three, the Lord blessed *This* with inner wakefulness. Each thing *It* knew, and every, but even the enlightened are not to transgress the limits of mortal life; they too must live within its bounds. Destiny decreed that *Its* last birth be among ordinary worldlings. Of a crude place is *This* a native, of a raw, rough place, barren alike in soil and culture. The Lord ordained that *This* live as they lived. *This* knows not, friend, who is a master and who is a disciple. Distinctions like these obtain in the realm of birth and death. The Lord is infinite, His depth immeasurable. Lost in Him *This* sees neither morning nor evening.

One must dwell on these words with all the leisure one can command. Notice first '*this* body,' the distance from it that 'this' resonates. Notice also the use of 'This' or 'It' in place of 'I.' Each and every thing *It* knew, not *I* knew. Now, the Master is lost in the Lord and knows neither morning nor evening, knows neither time nor space. The Master did not, in other words, know himself, did not know the man that others around him knew him to be. But what about the child and his knowledge of each thing and every? Could his knowledge be like the knowledge of us mortals, knowledge that can only be limited knowledge, with the ignorance of the whole unknown world constituting it? What kind of knowledge it was that he was obliged to conceal it from others? That is the question we must keep on asking, question about the mystery that knowledge was, knowledge that could not be the knowledge that we know of.

Keeping that knowledge to 'himself,' the child went to school. The knowledge that our institutions impart is the knowledge of objects, knowledge that, as the Master's teachings will reveal, suppresses their truth, their being and their life. Why did the child seek this knowledge, this concealing of truth, when the truth shone all bright within him? Not to transgress the limits of mortality was his vow, rather his way. To live among the ordinary as one among them was the command given to him. We shall see, as we proceed, how that knowledge of each and everything too has to be left behind, for that too has to be sacrificed. The Lord, the Vedas proclaim, created the world in order to manifest his glory. His glory consists in concealing himself in the world, to be [a] nothing in the midst of every thing. The ignorant man conceals every thing because he would reveal himself, the man of wisdom reveals every thing because he conceals himself. In losing himself as man, in losing himself as God, in losing himself absolutely, he finds his being true and real, and that of the world.

The school was situated at Dera Khalsa, a village three miles away from Gangothian. The five year old Mañgat covered this distance on foot as did most of his class mates. Schools were rare in the days of the British raj, especially in the countryside, and the people, most of them, destitute. Even those who belonged to what was termed the lower middle class could not afford a conveyance for their children. For the child Mañgat, such hardships were, however, of little account. Indifferent was he to what he ate and what he wore. One morning, to give an instance, he went to the school in a fine velvet jacket to return home in an old worn-out coat, a mere rag. The child had indulged in a little bit of bartering with a classmate of his. Frequently, too frequently, would disappear not only his clothes but even his shoes, a fancy, it seems, he had to walk barefoot. And the tasty, fried delicacies his mother packed for lunch delighted the pallet of poor children, for him their coarse meals were good enough. The school alone was the place for studies for him, not home. As for playing, he was too aloof to evince any interest in it. Mother was uneasy and anxious, the anxiety and the worry changing into alarm when she found her Maṅgat returning late from school. Afternoons would melt into evenings, evenings into twilight, yet the child would not appear. Not before nightfall would he return. Ganeshi Devi could no longer evade the nagging thought that her son was possessed, the thought she had tried hard to evade. Charms and incantations were invoked, insignias hung around his neck. Priests, both Hindu and Muslim, exhausted their store of wisdom but to no avail. The malady increased as months and years passed by. Eventually, Maṅgat the child became 'Maṅgat the Mad.' Maṅgat the possessed was still one among the inhabitants of that village, Maṅgat the Mad was not. You could deal with the possessed, try to free him from the evil grip, but not with the mad; he was the *other*, the absolute *other*, one who lived outside the pale of relationship, of humanity itself.

The modern criterion of sanity too he would have failed to meet as he had failed to meet the pre-modern criterion of those villagers. He neither laughed with other children nor played with them, neither smiled their smiles nor shed their tears. When their greedy hunger hastened them back home, he would sit all alone behind a rock, in a corner of a ravine or under a tree to lose himself into a state of ecstasy, all oblivious of when the sun set and the stars appeared. Full of misgivings, mother would leave home in search of him, but searching a man in that labyrinth of the landscape around was like 'searching a needle in a heap of hay.' In the shades of the Pīr Khwājā, a search was all the more difficult – such was the density of that pathless forest. One may imagine her fears and tremblings when, with a lantern in hand, she would helplessly shout, 'Maṅgat! Maṅgat!' in its frightening darkness. When he would come out of the depths of the forest in response to her shouts, she would, now come back to herself, persuade him, in the name of her love, not to provoke the Pīr. With a soft laugh, the child would dismiss her fears. 'Have no fears, Ma,' he would say, 'the Pīr would do *It* no harm.' The repose, the almost melancholy pensiveness, and the serene disdain for safety that she could read in his face would reassure her and so would the cool of his eyes. That face could not possibly be the face of a mad person nor could those soothing eyes! Her little son was a riddle for her, a mystery that would abide no question. They alone, we hear, find the Spirit that break all ties and discard all props. Here was a mother that nurtured every tie and stuck to every prop. And yet the Spirit, uncalled and unsolicited, would glow within her with all its glory. That, they say, is the destiny ordained for blessed wombs: they live in misery but die in bliss.

For now, however, her anxiety would not abate nor would her fears. Rather, they changed into despair. For, one day Maṅgat did not turn up even at midnight. Not until past sunrise were his footsteps heard. In spite of her long, sleepless vigil, she did not have the heart to get angry with her son. The calm in his face and the peace in his eyes were too deep for her agony and her anger. How could she speak up before that strange paradox that her son was, how could get angry with him? She knew the depth of his love for her, she also knew his forbidding indifference; the softness of his gaze too she knew and also its blindness as it were though his eyes were open and concentrated. And startling was the adult understanding and sympathy that on many an occasion shone forth in his eyes. Her son was a puzzle for her, an enigma beyond her understanding. And yet she understood him in a way, despite her disturbing, even, on occasions, distracting misgivings. How else could she give permission to the child of eight to spend his nights in the open, away from human habitation?

Through rocks and boulders below the village flowed the Trail, a soft murmuring little stream during summers and winters, a swift, angry current during the rains. Along its banks that child of eight would now spend his nights. An hour or two after midnight, when even the creatures of the jungle slept, he would leave home to descend to its sandy bed and spend his nights on a rock along its margin, unmindful of the darkness and dangers of the night. Not until the sun rose would he leave his contemplative seat. A life-long practice of his became these nocturnal self-oblivious vigils. Not for him a roof, whether the nights were humid or freezing, rainy or clear, dark or bright. From those days onwards, few were the nights he spent under a roof.

After completing his four year primary education, Maṅgat had to shift to Kallar, six miles away from Gangothian, to continue his education at the middle school there. He stayed there with a sister of his, Kartārdevī, and her husband, Sāin Das. The new environment saw no change in his life style, the same indifference to food, to dress and to shoes continued. Frequently in the class too he would go into what appeared like moods of abstraction, his eyes closed and his face expressionless. An object of curiosity for teachers and of derision and ridicule for the more naughty among the children, Maṅgat soon turned into a revered person almost, even for his teachers. Often he was asked to speak on matters spiritual and ethical. The seriousness of tone and content of his discourses earned him the nickname of *lāt pādarī*, Lord Bishop. Irony is the 'civilised' weapon of hurt self-esteem but it proved an embarrassment for the inventors of the nickname.

After school, he would not eat but finish his homework and go through the lessons to be taken up the following day. This was an easy, quick affair. His mind was sharp and his memory phenomenal; lessons once read were never forgotten. That explained his success in school, the secret of the first position he invariably secured from class I to VIII, the entire span of his education. Homework over, he would resort to his beloved solitude until late in the evening to take a light, frugal meal, the only meal he took after breakfast. The late evenings he spent in conversation with his brother-in-law who had some inclination towards spiritual matters. When the night fell, he would sit in meditation before he went to sleep, to wake up at 2.00 A.M. in obedience to the call of the open sky and the silence of the earth. When the time came for others to rise up, he would return and go to bed. All humility at home and at school, he did not wish to attract notice. But that was not to be, could not be. His silence was eloquence, his poor looks had a dignity which none could ignore. Headmaster Rāmdās's words were truly prophetic. 'Maṅgat,' he said, 'will be either a *vazīr* or a *faqīr* – a minister or a saint. As things stand today, he seems to be cut out only for a saintly life.'

Each month saw his night vigils prolonged, his intake decreased, his seclusion deepened. He was only twelve when he decided to observe what they called *cillā* – a forty-day period of fasting and meditation, his brother-in-law joining him in the daunting austerities it involved. Food was reduced to almost the starvation point and sleep to barely a step short of sleeplessness. The hard, self-imposed ordeal reduced his body to almost a skeleton, but those that saw him after that *tapas* did not fail to observe a happy, joyous expression in his face, a suffusion of satisfaction that concealed the wreck that the body had been reduced into. Those who lived around, in the immediate neighbourhood, spoke of strange, quixotic notes with a likeness somewhat to those of the flute and the lute floating in the dark air of the night and coming they knew not from which quarter or direction. They also spoke of the unique sweetness of their melody, of those notes, a melody that was not of this earth but of something above and beyond it. The young Maṅgat, however, spoke nothing about them nor did he say anything about what had transformed his melancholy looks into those of joy and ecstasy. In times later, however, he did throw a hint about what had transpired during that penance:

> One day when that forty-day penance was drawing towards its conclusion, *This* asked *Its* brother-in-law about what, in his view, constituted the most significant teaching of the *Bhagavadgītā*. His reply was, 'the part concerned with the *sthitaprajña* – 'one whose consciousness has become stable.' A *sthitaprajña*, he added, looks alike on dualities like happiness and sorrow, victory and defeat, transcending them, in every truth. The description tallied well with the state that prevailed within *This*. That very night, while sitting in meditation, *This* saw a light emanate from this body and pervade the entire room. And then a voice within: 'I whom thou seekest dwell within thee. Of Me thou art not to utter a word, not until you leave thy home. Till that moment arrives, remain you devoted entirely unto Me.'

Of the *sthitaprajña*, the *Bhagavadgītā* has this to say:

When thy intellect rests and reposes unperturbed by the Veda, and stays quiet and stable with thoughts all extinct, then shalt thou attain to yoga, to in-vision of thy truth.

+ + +

When one puts away every desire of the mind,
and by himself stays, sufficient unto himself,
then will rest his mind, stable and in itself.

When sorrows bring him no distress,
and pleasures no desires,

no passion can assail him, and neither fear nor anger,
stable shall he stay then, his mind at rest with itself.
When his love moveth unto no one,
and nothing can make him rejoice, neither this nor that,
when loathing has he none for that which augurs ill,
stable shall he stay then, his mind at rest with itself.

A paraphrase this of II.53, 55–57. Our mind is nothing else than a helpless orientation towards the *other*, that false appearance the mind has set up for itself to become its prisoner.[5] When this blind orientation ceases, mind comes to be free from the grip of the *other*, to stay still with itself, the intellect ceasing to determinate, turning merely into the innocent witness of all that happens or does not happen. The child Maṅgat had attained to this witness self, given entirely to the Me dwelling within him. That Me had still to manifest Himself as his own self and Maṅgat would have to, as we shall see, die into that Me. He had been, since his early childhood, as Gurudeva himself said, the unknowing knower of the all. That unknowing knower of the all had to die into the Me; it was that innocence absolute, innocence totally unselfconscious, that he sought.

Before long, there occurred on a night an incident that revealed the Me, that guide within, as the protector without. A dark night it was, moonless and starless in the latter half of July, the sky overcast with thick layers of the monsoon clouds. Everything the darkness seemed to conceal, the silhouettes of the trees even. The young Gurudeva plunged into it, unaware, in the absence of the stars, of how far the night had advanced. He went out that night not for his usual meditation but to, it seems, leave home, to 'break,' as an Indian phrase goes, every tie and relationship. With quick, long strides he moved in the direction of Chauhan Bahgatan, 'Seat of Devotees,' the place so-called in memory of some medieval sages. Recalling that incident he said to a devotee:[6]

> 'A long distance *It* had covered, when *Its* foot stumbled and *It* found *Itself* falling, all erect, into a deep before, it appeared, Someone took *It* on long, soft arms. That very moment, everything was blotted out.'

The sun was well above the horizon when his consciousness returned to find him on the bank of a stream. It was sometime when he could recall the entire sequence from the stumbling of his foot to the safety of the unknown arms. He looked up and found, to his astonishment, a tall hill before him, and the high summit from where he had fallen down. 'Oh, my Lord! Unconcerned absolute art thou! Yet gentle were the hands that placed *It* here!' Spontaneously these words escaped his lips

For long he kept sitting all alone on the bank of the stream until, by the noon, a man came that way. He asked the man about the way to Chauhan Bhagatan. Getting the information, he took off his clothes to have a dip or two in the waters of the stream and found, to his surprise, no injury on the body, not even a scratch. For long after the wash he sat there, in that unfamiliar place, until the sun sank low in the west. He gave up the thought of going to Chauhan Bhagatan, the time for renunciation, for giving up home, had not, it seemed to him, arrived. He went back home to face the inevitable anxiety, rebuke and reprimand. In silence he heard a virtual torrent of anger and emotion, uttering not a word about what had happened.

It was years when he narrated this incident to the said devotee.[7] Having narrated it, he said, 'This is how time was passing those days. Men of God stick to their way and heed not what men of the world say of them. The two ways never meet, the way that leads to the Lord and the way that leads to the mazes of the world. Impossible becomes for a man of God to deal with the men of the world. His solitary way alone is the way for him.'

A deep melancholy came to seize him. Soon the melancholy deepened into anguish, anguish into a sense of deep meaninglessness of the life he was leading. Studies seemed futile, school a place of desolation, companions a torture and home a place of exile. Alone and dejected he lived, knowing not where to go and what way to follow. He once described his condition of those days in these words:[8]

> When this body completed its thirteen years, a mood of deep dejection came to possess *This*. Winter was in full swing and school closed for the Christmas vacation. *This* came back home to stay with mother. Home gave no consolation and dejection deepened into depression. Solitude was the only refuge and the profusion of sighs and tears the only comfort. 'Be gracious unto me, Thou that art gracious to the lowly, be gracious unto me too!' was the refrain, the constant refrain of *Its* solitary prayers. One day *This* sat all alone in the jungle of the Pīr Khwājā and moved not even when the day was drawing towards its end and twilight was deepening into darkness. Was there any sense, any point [*This* asked *Itself*] in going back home? But of mother then arose a thought, of her never-ending anxiety and worries, which forced *It* to rise and move towards home. Slowly *It* moved, most reluctantly and unwillingly but not beyond the wall near the outskirts of the forest. On that *It* sat again until *It* heard 'Maṅgat! Maṅgat!' in the shrieking voice of mother. *It* left that seat and saw her well inside the forest, all alone with a lantern in hand.
>
> Towards her *It* moved, thinking of the power of the ties of relationships, of these stumbling blocks on the way, hard to avoid and pass by. But then arose, the very same moment, another thought: 'How will you ever pay back her dispensations, ever the giver is she like Providence Itself!' All the way mother kept speaking and *This* kept listening, without a word, without a response until we reached home. An example is it alone of itself, that what they call maternal love. Some loaves of bread she had made and some leaves of mustard cooked in butter-milk. Four or five mouthfuls of that fare *It* took to keep up the form. Otherwise, mother could not have swallowed even a mouthful. "Strange are thy ways, Lord, strange is your *Māyā*, endless is it and limitless, unsurpassed and unsurpassable. If one could only love the Lord the way a mother loves her child!

Who could prevent one, then, from reaching the goal ultimate? Who, indeed could? But lures are there, very many of them, in the shape of names and forms to deviate this being from the straight path, those irresistible charms of His *Māyā*. Such is thy will, Lord, such your dispensation. Let it be so!"

With ideas like these occupied, *This* went to bed and lay down and covered *Itself* with a quilt. Mother was spinning thread, conversing with other women of the neighbourhood, but stayed not those for long. 'You've gone to bed rather early, my child! Are you all right?' 'Sleepy I feel, mother,' said *This* in reply. Soon after, she too went to bed. A few moments and came she near *This* and said, 'What notes are these, Maṅgat, notes that ring in my ears? O sitting again! Lie down and sleep, my dear!'

'You were perhaps dreaming, mother. Where are the notes you speak of? I sat up because sleep eluded me. But sleepy I feel now and would rather lie down.'

It did not take her long to fall asleep. *This* sat up again for meditation, which continued for two to three hours. And then, all of a sudden, there flashed in this very body a light with the brilliance, so to say, of the suns in their millions. Melodies sweet arose of every kind, of pitches low, soft and high with the accompanying beats of the drums without a number. Every moment revealed sights myriad and unprecedented. The external world was blotted out.

And again the voice: 'What light is this, Maṅgat?' How many times was it heard, can't now be said. 'Calm down, mother,' was the only response *It* could manage to give and that too only once. The eyes opened and, lo! the room ablaze with the same glare. *It* closed the eyes for the self-oblivious bliss within. Of the yogic path was revealed the secret all. Fled was all the *Māyā*, every name and form. Grace had dispelled that, Grace that falls on man he knows not from where. A panorama was opened up, a panorama of lives past, one after another. How trivial was all that, a futile fret endless! What the body is and what the soul animating it – all was clear, all was lucid. The goal *It* had sought and yearned for day after day and night after night was reached at last, the goal ever at hand and ever attained! This body was only thirteen at that time, the end near of the year 1916.

Like the waves of the sea arose thoughts thereafter, varied and spontaneous: 'Long was my separation, long my exile, uncounted were the lives and uncountable were the deaths. Whereabouts of Him I sought, of Him, my Love, life after life. Days of distress went by, and nights of dark despair. In hope vain saw I the moon wax and wane, and the months waste and fade out. No beginning had the toil and no end the weariness. But now was come the moment to end the endless.' And, then: 'Mate art thou, the anchor and the co-dweller, eternal though art thou, the indivisible though pervasive.' 'Hail to thee, my Lord, hail to thy Grace Abounding!' And then shrieked the familiar voice, 'Maṅgat, from where comes this light?'

'Why can't you be silent, mother? Go to bed, please!' This is all *This* could manage to say. For, the very next moment disappeared every name and form, all the *Māyā*, all that could be perceived, measured and cognised. Nothing remained except the self-oblivion within. When the awareness returned, *It* found mother fast asleep. *It* went out in the direction of the Pīr Khwājā. A dark cloudy night was that, a virtual invisibility, with the cold at its acme. But no cold was there for *This* nor was the darkness. On their own the feet were treading the familiar path to the Pīr Forest and stopped not until *It* had reached the pool of still deep waters within it. A rough blanket *It* had, half of which became the seat and the other half the protection from the cold. In a trite of a moment disappeared all the cold and the darkness. Grace alone was there, only that remained, the Grace All-pervading. *It* knew not how and when the night ended and gave place to the morning. For, when *It* came to *Itself* the day was shining bright with the sun.

The time for bath was long past. In those days *It* had *Its* bath in the waters of the Trail much before the break of dawn – at 3 or 4 A.M. For nights were spent there, on its bank, not in the Pīr Forest. How *It* entered into the thick of the forest that night and why, *This* does not know. A dip in the still waters there served the purpose of a bath.

Returning to the sojourn they call home, *It* found *Maī* Bhāgavantī[9] reading the *Bhagvadgītā*, as was her wont. *This* sat down on the mat nearby and requested her to read the chapter she was reading all over again, for it seemed to articulate all that

It had seen and experienced during the night and the early hours of the morning. This confirmation made *It* anchor *Its* life, *Its* breath, *Its* very being to the state within. To dwell in it, to get absorbed in it, in that state of truth, of Being, became, from that day onwards, the sole purpose of life and every endeavour.

Once a devotee[10] requested *Māī* Bhāgavantī to narrate what had happened that morning. She said:

> That day Bhagat [devotee] Maṅgat returned home when I was doing the solitary recital of the *Bhagavadgītā*. I don't remember which chapter it was. He, sitting nearby, listened, all rapt, to the recital and was in tears. I was pained and full of misgivings but somehow managed to continue with the recital up to the last verse of the chapter. Recitation over, he said, 'Blessed are you too, my mother! But let not mother[11] know about this.' He entered his room and sat down on a cot, with his blanket spread all over. I asked him repeatedly about what distressed him but he uttered no word, except that he should be left alone.

Three days later happened the unexpected, the not-looked-for absolute. It is best to recall Master's own words about the happening:

> Three days after, while *This* was sitting on the bank of the Trail in the ravine below, words three of the *Mahāmantra* were revealed – *Om Braham satyam*. The next day came: *niraṅkār ajanmā advait purkhā*, and on the third: *sarab vyāpak kalyāṇ mūrat*. Each day, at home, *It* noted down those words.
>
> Thereafter, words of revelation, their depth immeasurable, flowed out spontaneously whenever *It* sat alone in the solitude of the forest but only to melt into the air, for *It* uttered not them before anyone nor ever referred to them. In solitary stillness they pealed and into stillness would they disappear. Only years later when the Lord commanded that *This* go to Ahamadabad on the invitation of the Mahant,[12] many a verse flowed out in response to his questions. Those he took down. Now the Lord prompts you[13] to force them out.

We have to pause to linger on these words. First, the 'Mahāmantra.' 'Mahā' means great, 'mantra' means 'an instrument of thought,' a sacred word or verse. That is the traditional meaning. Some translate *mantra* as the word or the verse that saves, redeems the mind: *trāyate anena manaḥ saḥ*. The latter explanation, which may not satisfy strict grammarians, is, of course, the meaning that 'mantra' has for those that meditate it. They take 'mantra' as '*man-tra*,' '*man*' to think, '*tra*' to protect. A *mantra* is, thus, not an ordinary word; it is the word that protects man. And a *Mahāmantra* is the word or the verse that redeems man from *saṃsāra*, the unending chain of birth and death. It is not the word of a man; it is vouchsafed to man; man can be only its recipient, never its speaker. The Master too was the recipient of the *Mahāmantra*, not its composer. It was the voice of the *śūnya* within him, of the silence within him, the voice that does not prompt man to think and speak but peals within him to absorb into itself his speech and his mind. For, it is in the absorption of the mind, in its dissolution into it, into the *mantra*, that its redemption lies, not in its stirring and its activity. The *Mahāmantra* appeared not to sustain Maṅgat the man but to kill the man in him into his true being. A man who has the rare power that is born out of complete disillusion with mortal life, power born out of a sense of the inevitability of suffering, alone will let himself die into it. Not the man who entertains hope, hope of any kind, spiritual or secular, nor the man who would like to protect himself from the tragedy of life through the enchantment that he takes a *mantra* to be. A man who lives to chant a *mantra* will not be saved; only he will be saved who dies into it.

The *mantra* that saves and redeems need not be meaning-full, yet it often is because man, that son of Eve, cannot have the innocence that absorption in a *mantra* demands; he will, first, think about it, try to understand it, make it a part of his human, communicative speech. So a *mantra* often promises to be open to some interpretation to make its hearer curious about its meaning. To satisfy his curiosity he will carefully analyse the meaning of its words, try to understand the ontology it reveals and expounds. However, a *mantra* has a meaning that ever disowns itself, has a content that annuls itself; it is a recantation of its own affirmation. This annulment and recantation most human beings find too hard and frightening to contemplate. It is in the nature of man, exiled that he is from his own being, to absorb rather than be absorbed. The sin of thinking and of meditating he will have to commit to undo the sin of affirming his being. Not until has he paid much for this his sin will he be freed from it, from the sin of knowing and being. The *Mantra* that was vouchsafed to the young Maṅgat, a *Mantra* of thirteen words to a lad of thirteen years, was the *Mantra* to undo those thirteen years. Maṅgat was not to live thereafter; he was to die into it.

We that would absorb the *mantra* and would not be absorbed into it, have to tread the thorny path of understanding and interpretation to see where our interpretation leads us. First, therefore, the *mantra* in its entirety:

> Om Brahma satyaṃ niraṅkār ajanmā advait purkhā sarab vayāpak kalyāṇ mūrat parmeśvarāya namastaṅg.

The Sanskrit for *niraṅkār* is *nirākāra,* for *ajanmā* is *ajanmaḥ,* for *advait* is *advaita,* for *purkhā* is *puruṣa,* for *sarab* is *sarva,* for *vyāpak* is *vyāpaka*, for *kalyān* is *kalyāṇa*, for *mūrat* is *mūrtiḥ,* for *namastaṅg* is *namaḥ*. A tentative translation of the *Mahāmantra* may read as follows:

> Aum! Brahman is Being formless and nameless,
> The Person a-dual[14] is He and all-pervasive,
> The form verily of redemption.
> To Him, that Lord Supreme, is our salutation.

We shall now attend to the meaning of each and every word. *Om* consists of three elements: a, u and m, o in 'om' is the result of *sandhi*, combination, of **a** and **u**. 'Om' is thus 'Aum.' *Aum* is considered to be the most sacred of the Vedic

syllables though the syllable is not found in the *Saṃhitā* portion of the Vedas themselves. We have to wait for the *Śatapatha Brāhmaṇa* [4.3.2] and the *Aitareya Brāhmaṇa* [1.12.1 and 5.32] to find the mention of the word. In the Upaniṣads it is invested with a deep symbolic meaning; it acquires there the meaning of the *akṣara* of the Ṛg Veda[15] as we find it explained at 10.71.39. I would not, however, pause to explain the Upaniṣadic account of *om* or *aum*; I have done it elsewhere.[16] Here I shall mention what the *vāṇī* has to say about it. *Om,* says the *Samatāprakāśa*, is the *parama śakta.* 'Parama' means the supreme; 'śakta' is derived from the Sanskrit 'śakti' (from the verbal root *śak*, to be able). So *Om* is the power supreme, the ability supreme. It is also *parkāśa ata* (Sanskrit *prakāśa,* derived from *pra-kaś*, to become visible, to shine; figuratively it also means light, splendour; 'ata' from *ati,* going, beyond). So *ata prakaśa* means visibility exceeding itself, visibility going beyond itself. It pervades *piṇḍa-s* and *brahmāṇḍa-s* in their millions (*piṇḍa,* derived from *piṇḍ,* to put together, is the body which is an assemblage, a putting together, a construct, hence destructible, and *brahmāṇḍa-s,* 'egg-s of *brahman*', *brahman* born in the shape of egg/s, into the various visible universes.) So *Om* is visible invisibility, invisibility that has died into the visible universe or universes. And, having died into the bodies and the universes, it pervades them, enters into them as their life and inbeing, yet remaining aloof from them. That is the glory of that Word that it dies to become immanent, and becomes immanent to remain transcendent, the glory of that sound eternal, the sound that is *akhaṇḍa*, the sound that cannot be divided into its constituent notes, the sound in which every note is the all-notes. That Word is *tata,* from *tattva, tat*=that, *tva,* the state of being, that is to say, it is ever itself; it is the subject that itself is its predicate. That *abagat,* that unknown, seers and gods meditate to find it full, ever full; the entire universe, the all, is nothing else than O*m* itself. This is how *Om* is explained in the *Mahāmantra-mahimā,* 'the Glory of *Mahāmantra*'

[*Samatāprakāśa* pp. 414-15]. Elsewhere,[17] the *Samatāprakāśa* describes *Om* in the following words:

Brahman the Word, the a-dual ever,
adored is it by the rarest among the rare.
In that frail, brittle being will it shine,
finds who the *sat-guru*, dispeller true of darkness.

Om, the Word Imperishable, the infinite, the no-other, unsurpassed
that created this visible *formed* entire,
became It without a cause first the mind,
and then fashioned the moving world with *guṇa-s* three.
Of fire, air, water, earth and the sky is the show this entire;
made of these are the bodies all, with different names and forms;
according as the name is so is the form,
so none can know what hide these behind themselves.

This lump is fashioned with a shape without and marrow within,
with the air therein tuning its tunes.
As a, u and m sings that air the Word,
of these three elements finds It as composed,
of Creation the cause, and of continuation and dissolution of the world,
that Protector of all, that Grace of the lowly and of the poor.

From the Imperishable is born the desire for the perishable:
few can know this secret, for sure.
The Primordial Word Imperishable has the head every for Its abode,
therein contemplates It the yogī, forsaking every fever and fret.[18]

Om is the imperishable word, word not in time but out of time, eternal it is and infinite, has no *other* to constitute it, itself it ever is and by itself. That Word created the world, the visible world, first becoming the mind and then the sensible elements of earth, water, fire, air and the sky, thereby fashioning the bodies with different names and forms. We do not, cannot, know anything because as the name is so is the form, the name determining, as it were, the form. When we try to know a thing, we can know only its name, the name as the universal, as the concept. Beyond the concept we cannot go, but the form [the sense-content] disowns, ever and always, the name. And the name too, the concept too, is fragile, there being no *a priori fixed* concepts that would admit of no revision or change. For, the concept through which we cognise a thing is always subject to revision and change, is, in fact, infirm, tentative, revisable and falsifiable. So our understanding of a thing, of any thing, is always an illusion, a mere working understanding for a particular human situation, not an objective understanding. We do not know the *tattva*, or *tattā* of a thing, the thatness of the thing, the thing in itself; we only enframe it in accordance with the framework or assumptions of our understanding. But we are given this body, with a shape without, a form without, and marrow [*mañjā*, *majjā*?] within, and within this body the air sings its tune in the form of speech, articulating the Word in the form of three elements, namely, a, u and m. ['O' in *Om* is, as explained above, the result of the euphonic combination of *a* and *u*]. *A* originates in the throat, *u* is a labial but an open labial, and *m* is a mute labial. The entire ambit of speech the syllable 'aum' encompasses, from its articulation at the throat and the lips and to its end too at the latter. As the word *aum* encompasses the origin, the articulation and silence of speech, so the Word enshrines the origin, the endurance and the end of the world, is itself the moment so to say wherein these three are one, are not the opposites that they appear to us.

To meditate *Aum* is to meditate the origin, the endurance and the end of speech and the *other* of speech, the world. Its meditation implies paying heed to the tumult of birth, to the murmur of life and the silence of death, the glory of coming to be, the struggle bitter of life and the end inevitable of it. In *Aum* is enshrined the song of innocence, the noise of vanity, the cries of despair and the stillness of death. *Aum* is the Word itself, the Word manifest, it is the form visible of the Moment wherein birth, life and death become one, and so do creation, endurance and dissolution of the world. In that Moment, in that self-denying Now lies our truth absolute, of us, and of every other being or thing. Our concepts create distinctions and differences, whereas *aum* is an invitation to their reconciliation. *Aum* is the truth and the word of the truth. In it lies enshrined the knowledge we seek, not in the universals in terms of which we interpret phenomena, concepts which would hypostatize them, reduce them into presences, ignoring altogether the before of their birth and the after of their ceasing to be. If we let all our speech dissolve into this single syllable, it will reveal itself as the Primordial Word, the Name that is the named too. That Word, the *vāṇī* declares, has its abode in the head, therein is it realised by the *yogins*. This point we shall take up when we come to discuss the yogic practice. At this moment, we must attend to the other phrases in the *Mahāmantra* and to what the '*Mahāmantra-mahimā*' says about them.

'**Brahma Satyam**:' *Brahma Satyam*, Brahman is Being or the Truth: This is how the Vedāntīs (*Vedāntins*) describe that *tattva*, thatness, the real as it is in itself. They meditate on the *kathā*, the revelation in the form of the Upaniṣads, interpret it and explain it through many means of cognition, means like analogies, arguments, inferences, etc. After this, a long endeavour, they come to the conclusion that the Real is Brahman, the Expanded One and the Word; 'the expanded one' because it has manifested itself as the world, 'the Word' because it has also manifested itself as the informing principle of the world and each and every of its phenomena. They, the Vedāntīs, meditate Word the unblemished, the Word that ever remains itself, ever remains free of the three constitutive modes of phenomena. Every phenomenon of the world would be itself and yet would go beyond itself, would be something else. That is the paradox about every thing, every being: to remain itself and yet not remain itself. There is also the third mode, the transcendental mode, that of the thrust towards the beyond. Man would not hear the voice of the beyond, the pure beyond; he would always try to remain an ambiguity: he would at once stick to himself and yet disown himself to become someone else, sabotaging thereby the transcendental mode, that thrust towards the beyond. As a result of this perversion, the transcendental thrust turns into the thrust towards death; he that would not go beyond himself is made to go to death. Our mortality is the distortion of the transcendental thrust, distortion created by our passion to *be*. The Word is beyond all these three modes, that of being oneself, that of not being oneself but something else and that of going beyond oneself, transcending every identity, every state of being. It is beyond these three modes because it is the confluence, the coming together, of origin, endurance and end of the world, of its birth, life and death. For this very reason, it has no shape, no *ākāra*, no visible form. It is *niraṅkār*, *nirākāra*, 'one without a shape or a form.' Our words have a shape, an audible form, but it has no audible form. That is why, it is called *niraṅkār* or *nirākāra*. It is liberation, *mokṣa*, itself, liberation from the three modes of being.

The informing principle of the world and its phenomena is this Word, not language or concepts. Linguistic concepts would exclude the before and the after, birth and death from phenomena, they would *presence* these latter. Therefore phenomena, linguistically informed phenomena, never truly come to be, the before and the after and the beyond are always there to put into question their being and reality. The Word as the informing principle incorporates the before as well as the after, the beyond and the primordial, the manifest and the unmanifest to constitute the being of phenomena. In It is revealed the truth and reality of phenomena – truth and reality that is too rich, too deep for a concept to encompass, too evasive for a name to name.

'**Ajanmā,**' 'The Unborn:' Whatever is born and dies belongs to the realm of *Māyā*, to the realm of untruth. The Word is free from birth and death. It is free from these because In It birth, life and death, all the three, come to be one. For us birth is one thing, death another, one is coming to be, the other is ceasing to be. Not [for] the Word.

'**Advait**,' *Advaita*, the a-dual, one without the *other*. All that we know and experience is constituted by its *other*: the whole by the part and the part by the whole, life by death and death by life, the visible by the invisible and the invisible by the visible, the good by the bad and the bad by the good, redemption by bondage and bondage by redemption, God by creation and creation by God. Not so the Word, that home of the present, past and future, of birth, life and death, of coming to be and ceasing to be, of the concealed and the unconcealed, the known and the unknown. It has no *other* to constitute it because it encompasses all the presences along with their negations, their origin, their being and their cessation, their manifestation and their suppression.

'**Purkhā**', 'puruṣaḥ,' the Person: The Word, Word of which *Aum* is the manifest linguistic form, is the Person, but the Person without the *other*. And that is *jñāna*, knowledge, too, knowledge without its *other*, viz., the object of knowledge; It knows but is never known, not even to Itself. And It is the basis, the ground, the innermost being of all that has come to be, but despite this, despite being the basis, the ground of the all, It remains ever itself, unaffected totally by all that It is the ontological ground of.

'**Sarab vyāpak**', the Sanskrit, 'sarvavyāpaka:' It pervades all, that Word, pervades each and everything as ever the same, as itself, in all its fullness; loving none, hating none, unstained remains it ever.

'**Kalyāṇ mūrat**' Sanskrit : 'kalyāṇamūrtiḥ,' 'the form verily of redemption: unsupported itself, the Word is the support of all that is, the power unsupported of any other power.

'Parmeśvarāya : 'For that Lord Supreme:' Let man worship the Word as the Lord Supreme, for that will free him from every fret, every fever, the fever of being.

'Namastaṅg,' Sanskrit: 'namaḥ:' To that Word, to that all-pervasive Lord is my salutation, I take refuge in It, take refuge in It, again and again and ever and always.

So the Word that is ever born, ever lives and ever dies, the Word that is birth, life and death all together – that Word, that seeming contradiction, has become all that is. That alone is the truth, the truth that comes into being only to negate itself. This trio of birth, life and death is also consciousness but consciousness that has no *other* to constitute it as consciousness, it is consciousness as well as its *other*. It pervades the world and yet remains aloof from it, is immanent and yet transcendent. This being which is no being, which is ever alive and ever dead, this unknown and unknowable alone enshrines our redemption, not the anchors that we seek, anchors other than ourselves. And it is the Supreme Lord, that Being that is no-being. To that alone we are to bow; He alone is our refuge, our salvation. The meditation, the worship of the Word is, thus, the worship of birth, life and death as one. Only he who is that moment, the one moment that encompasses the three, will be saved, not he who seeks to save himself.

This redemptive *Mantra* thus recants everything it says; it affirms birth to recant it, affirms life to disown it, embraces death to kill it. For it, for this Mantra, the unknown is the known, the known unknown, the transcendent is immanent and the immanent the transcendent. Other paradoxes too are there and have received our tentative attention. The word for meditation, we may remember, is *upāsanā*, 'sitting near.' If we sit near it, meditate it, this *Mantra*, no concept will remain that will not negate itself.

The Word is not what we understand by the term word, it is also not what ordinary *yogins* take the *nāda* to be: merely a mystic sound they hear within. For, It as A*um* negates *nāda* also, *nāda* as ordinarily understood, that continuum of sound. The sound that originates, endures and is still at the same moment is not the sound that we know of.

This was the revelation, the revelation of thirteen words revealed to a lad of thirteen.

From that time onwards absorption in the self the true became almost the sole purpose of his life, rendering difficult his stay at home. Thoughts of resorting to solitude, to a cave among the hills, came as it were to possess him until they became irresistible. He had heard of a sect of *yogins*, ones with their ear lobes pierced, that lived near a well associated with the name of a legendary devotee, Pūran Bhagat, at a town called Sialkot. Among those he decided to live and left home, telling mother he was leaving for Rawalpindi to spend his Christmas holidays with his half brother. In the evening he caught the train for Lahore and alighted at Wazirabad, near Lahore, to catch the train for Sialkot. He had to wait till morning for the train for Sialkot and spent the night sitting in, to all appearances, meditation on the beams of wood that lay outside the railway station. There he dropped the idea of living among the *yogins* and decided to proceed further southeast. Next day, while staying at an inn at Lahore for the night, he heard a voice from within:

> Thou art born not to live among these *yogīs* but to show the way of the truth to those that are lost in the ways of the world, to show unto them wherein lies the way of purity, and of delusions purge them and of false beliefs. Live awhile as thou hast lived until now and establish yourself in what has been revealed unto you. Vouchsafed not were you this life to give pain unto others.

The command was obeyed and the son returned to his mother and the student to his studies. At the school, feverish preparations were on for an impending and ominous inspection. The nervousness of the teachers was understandable, the fret of the preparations natural, for the inspector belonged to that awesome, 'the chosen,' community of the British officers who 'held dominion over palm and pine' 'beneath His awful hand.' We have to invoke some imagination to realise how Indians in those days loved to obey and to be commanded. Add to this the 'incredible' efficiency of the British officers, the order they had brought into the chaos that India had turned into after the fall of the Mughal Empire. So the school was meticulously cleansed, lessons carefully revised, the pupils were taught every etiquette, every manner of proper behaviour, and were strictly instructed to come dressed in their best. No rustic shabbiness and clumsiness, they were warned, would be acceptable. The headmaster was nervous, the teachers worried and harassed, the pupils, for a change, were understanding and cooperative, for they could see that their teachers too, those stern and formidable men, were like them, their fearful miens pathetic and anxious. The boys were, therefore, eager to make the inspection a success and made it a point to tell their parents or guardians to wash their clothes and get them ironed, if new ones could not be stitched. The morning of the inspection saw the school wear a clean, fresh look, the children bright and self-consciously groomed, the teachers satisfied with the arrangements made, except for Maṅgat who became the eye-sore. He alone had come in his usual shabby dress. For the first time, headmaster Rāmdās lost his cool and administered an angry reprimand to him, who, the monitor of the class, was, he said, expected to be an example to his classmates. All silent, Maṅgat waited until the torrent of angry words had spent itself, when he said, 'Is the Inspector Sahib coming to visit the school to assess the abilities of your pupils, Sir, or the look of their clothes?'

The response would have been taken as an act of impertinence but for what his face expressed and what his voice rang. Instead of a slap (common in those days), the Headmaster gave him only a smile, looking intently, for a moment, at that arresting look, and went away, uttering not a word. The Inspector inspected, first of all, the senior-most Class VIII. The thoroughly drilled children gave the right answers to all the questions relating to their curricula. The Inspector was fully satisfied. Then came the turn of Moral Instruction. He put a question, a general question, outside the curriculum: 'What is the nature of service, whom should we serve, what good does it to us?'

No hand went up except one, which the Inspector did not notice. When he turned to the register before him, probably to write his remarks, the Headmaster said, 'Yes, Maṅgat, what have you to say in response to the question?'

The lad stood up and, bowing to the Inspector, said, 'Everything is doing service to others, is born to do service to others. Man, too, serves others but he does so in order to serve his own interests. To serve his own interests he serves his family, his clan, his friends, serves seers and sages and his country. Even God he would serve with his own self-interest in mind, or do acts of charity or of virtue. Hard is it for him to serve anyone without self-interest. To do acts of service without any self-interest is, however, his paramount duty. To remember the Lord and to serve His creation: that is what Jesus taught, and Mohammed, Rāma and Kṛṣṇa, Buddha and Nānak and other prophets.

'One's first duty is to serve one's elders: mother, father and teacher. Then comes the service of relations, of friends, of one's village and one's country and last comes the service of the entire world.

'Interested service brings to the doer pleasures of the world, disinterested service brings about disinterested joy, joy that never comes to an end. Let the Lord save us from hatred and ill will, let Him bless us with understanding about service the true! For that leads to Him; service the true is, in every truth, service unto Him.'

Having said these words, the lad folded his hands in all humility and took his seat. The Inspector gazed at him in surprise and wonder. For a good many moments not a word came out of his lips. It was sometime before he could articulate his response, in words of profuse and enthusiastic praise. Not for a moment did his attention go to his clothes and appearance.

That very evening, the Headmaster called him to his home and generously offered to meet all the expenses of his education up to the post-graduate level. An M.A. was *the* covetous degree in those days, the sign sure of culture and high education with the prospects of an honoured position in the Government service quite bright. One could, the Headmaster said, serve the country much better if one was educated. His offer was sincere and his advice sound. The young Gurudeva was all grateful for the kind and noble gesture but expressed his inability to accept the offer. 'You,' he said, 'are kindness itself and generosity. But *This* cannot express what is happening within *It*, what flames are burning here! *It* had no intention of coming back here after the Christmas holidays but the Lord willed that *It* remain in your service for some more time. *This* is all helpless before the prompting within. Your wish and command is that *This* prosper in the world, but this mind does not, cannot, move in that direction. My Master alone knows what His will is. Yours is a noble soul, Sir, that has so much concern for *This*, a nonentity. Like unto a father are you to *This*. Never will *This* forget this act of your kindness, Sir, never! But accept your offer *This* cannot. It is not in *Its* power. Please forgive *This*, a mere child!'

With great humility and emotion he bowed down before his teacher and touched his feet and left for home. On the way he turned to look back to find his master standing outside his house, gazing at his receding figure.

With the time for the final examinations fast approaching, the school authorities, anxious to outshine other schools, decided to hold extra classes for Class VIII, the examinations for which were to be held by the District Board. The young Gurudeva was in no position to attend those classes; the call of the Word within demanded all his time and his thoughts. The school authorities accepted his request for exemption from attending the extra classes but requested him to spare two hours a day to guide his classmates, which he agreed to do. There seemed no conflict between attending to the Word and attending to the interests of others. Meanwhile, Headmaster Rāmdās and his own brother-in-law had been urging him to take up tuition of the two grandsons of a religious guru, Bedi Baba Khem Singh. Bedi Baba's family had been for generations bestowing salvation on the faithful, which exalted duty he had inherited along with the vast wealth that the family had accumulated through the way of renunciation! A splendid welcome was accorded to the tutor of the budding saviours the day he went to teach them. A rich table of sweets, nuts and fruits was laid before him. The young teacher did not, however, care to taste anything. The tedium of studies was, however, too much for the young boys. On the fourth day, they invited their teacher to a ride and bird shooting. 'It will be a great fun,' said they.

Pat came the reply, 'Well, the rich and the poor make but poor companions. You are gurus, the guides and guardians of your followers. But your ways are those of the demons. How else could you think of shooting the birds and that too for this wretched palate? Did the great Nānank teach what you do? If you wish to be friends with *This*, you'll have to change your life-style, your food habits, your dress and the way you talk and converse. It will not be possible for *This* to come here anymore. If you wish to continue with your studies, you will have to come to the dwelling of us poor ones. That won't hurt your prestige!'

In the District Board Examination, Maṅgat bagged the first position. Headmaster Rāmdās urged him, once again, to continue with his studies and repeated his offer. But his persuasions failed to change his pupil's resolve. 'The education *It* has already received,' he said, 'should be enough for *Its* purpose. The time has come to complete the other education, the education for which is given this human birth.' Of that education, the *vāṇī* or *bānī*, to use the word that Gurudeva used, speaks in the following vein:

Study the Word, the Word alone,
Dispelled shall be your delusions
And revealed shall be the Benign.
Words shall only puzzle and entangle.

Time fleets away, man,
Long is the way, too long, indeed,
Steep and staggering, up and down!
But once you reach the summit high,
Glory splendid shall sit on you.

Read the Name, the Name alone,
And set you aside every other word;
Your heart will be at rest,
And yours will be the bliss,
The bliss that abides with the Lord,
The Bliss that kills, the Bliss that destroys.[19]

I have tried to be literal, as much as I could. An attempt at elegance would have been disastrous. The Word is to be read, to be dwelt on, the Word unheard and inaudible. Only its symbol is there to dwell on, to contemplate, to sit near, the Name that brings together in one single breath the three 'moments'. That Name which kills you to turn you into birth–life–death, undoing each through the other two – that Name will turn into the Word to change you too into the Word, into the ecstasy that is the death of man and of his world. That is the Name one should dwell on and dwell in, not the words that perpetuate the distinctions of birth, life and death, those our pangs, our miseries and our tragedies.

The day of the final departure from the school was a day marked by solemn emotion. His teachers and classmates alike walked full three miles to see him off. With hands folded he beseeched them, beseeched them again and again, to go back but to no avail. At last they stood under a tree, still and silent, their eyes brimming with tears. He bowed and walked towards home and covered quite a distance. Looking back, he saw them all still under the same tree. Everyone stood there gazing at him.

Notes

1 This is how his devotees remember him. *Satpuruṣa*, Person the Real and *Maharaājji*, the Revered Lord. He was Person the Real because he had attained to his true being and self. And he was the Great Lord because as his true self he had ceased to be constituted by the *other*, that fate of every mortal being.

2 Cosmic-divine-human – ādhibhautika-ādhidaivika-ādhyātmika.

3 I owe details of this information to Om Capoor with whom the Master had a conversation to this effect.

4 I may mention here that the Master always referred to himself as *It* or *This*, not as *I*.

5 This statement is a mere tentative statement. It ignores the complexity of the concept of projection of the *other* for the convenience of the common reader and will receive our focused attention when we come to discuss the philosophy of *Samatā-vāda*. For, the body-mind-intellect is itself a projection and belongs to the realm of the *other*.

6 Bạnārasīdās, a would be disciple of him. We will have very many occasions to speak about him.

7 *Vide* 6 above.

8 To Banārasīdās.

9 His sister in law, much older than him in age. 'Mai,' mother, is used as a term of respect and reverence.

10 Banārasīdās.

11 His own mother, Ganeshi Devi.

12 Rattandās, the high priest of a monastery of the Kabīr sect at Ahamadabad in Gujarat.

13 Banārasīdas. We shall have very many occasions to speak about him.

14 'Advaita' is usually translated as 'non-dual.' Professor Raimundo Panikkar suggests 'a-dual' as a better translation. The suggestion accords well with the 'concept' of *samatā*.

15 And much else.

16 *Vide The Word Speaks to the Faustian Man,* Vols. I - V. The syllable is all pervasive in the Upaniṣads. One has to make an intensive study of those classics to know the meaning they attach to this most famous of the Vedic syllables.

17 The *Samatāprakāśa, Yogacintāmaṇi, p.* 220.

18 I give this rather infelicitous translation in order to bring into focus the meaning of the original.

19 *Vide Samatāprakāśa*, p. 662, 664.

2

Maternal Debt

After his return to Gaṅgoṭhiān, Gurudeva remained lost, almost constantly, in what to us men of the world would appear to be contemplation of the Divine within. He would leave the *'derā,'* 'place for sojourn,' as he called it, at 2 or 3 A.M to sit on a rock on the bank of the Trail and would not return until 10 A.M. Soon after noon he would resort to the dark forest of the Pīr Khwājā to return home after the twilight had long turned into darkness. This forest, as already mentioned, was very dense, the frequent haunt of beasts of prey and, if the villagers could be believed, of evil spirits. There was also a cremation ground on its outer ring. The villagers feared it and avoided it but not so the thirteen year old lad of our story. What they called home was his wilderness and what they called forest was his home. Died had he before his death into death, and death does not die, never dies.

Could there be a man in ecstasy so lost
as to unlock the primal lock,
to open the gate to reach the Invisible?

The swan would be he, flying up with the two wings:
that of the *nirat* and that of the *surat*,
know wouldn't he whither leads that flight.
On *prīta* would he feed and on *prema* fare,
on delight within and delight without;
nothing else would he perceive, his or others.'
Grace would smile upon him,
grace of the one that shows the path straight
to where abides the Veda, the knowledge that reclaims.[1]

The gate is the tenth gate in the crown of the head. Only a swan can fly up there, the swan that can separate milk from water, the truth from the falsehood. Two wings the swan-like-man has to fly with, one the wing of concentrated consciousness, the other that of the dark force that rises from the navel to move up to the top of the head. The flight has to be made in the spirit of letting-be, there has to be no conscious effort to force it up, rather one should let oneself be forced up by it; for it moves on its own, the most swiftly when the least interfered with. When this happens there will be joy within and joy without, joy within because that force will be seen as one's being as it were and joy without because your soul will flow out to every being and every thing. With the flow swelling, all will turn one, there will remain nothing mine or yours because there will remain neither me nor you nor him or her. The man who lets himself be led by the one who knows the straight path, alone can traverse that path, not he who himself would forge a path for himself. For, that path, the one he would forge for himself, will be a crooked path, contaminated by lust, greed and pride. The path straight would lead him to the Word that would silence all speech, the Word with no *other* to constitute it.

Moment after moment I wait for his coming,
for the coming of my beloved, one and sole;
cared I not for the ways of the world,
and caring not for them, I found the home
I long had sought, the wonder wherein dwells the Wonder.

Dissimulations have I given up, dualities and cunnings,
prop-less I live, without a support or a link,
with each moment a discovery, each day a revelation.
Of the unapproachable path would Maṅgat speak
for a rare of the seers to guess and know.[2]

Man can find the home he seeks, this exile from his own being, by waiting for the moment of revelation. The price is heavy, the path difficult because it is the path of waiting, not of striving. Striving, of course, is there but only until the dark force wakes up in the region of the navel. Afterwards, too some striving is necessary until it comes to reside and stay between the eyebrows at the 'root' of the nose. From there on the path of passive surrender starts, the path most hard to tread; for man will not let things happen before him, not easily; the doer in him will always interfere, will always intrude, to stand in the way of the benign darkness that would lead him to light. The dark force is the guide, that is the guru true, that is the saviour but only when you do not offend it with your presence. It will, if you offend it, turn into the visible, that invisible, into false and premature visions which cannot but augment the ego of the pilgrim, making him feel that his findings on the way are his final goal. This way, men will undo themselves: the righteous, the strivers, the *yogins* and those given to spiritual endeavors. Only a rare among these can find the straight path, the path of passive surrender, of self-extinction.

Men of the world do not easily tolerate the presence among them of a man as radically different from them as was the young Gurudeva. Self-complacent and arrogant, they have no eye and ear for what they do not already understand. So it was but natural that his ways should invite sarcasm, ridicule and censure. The honourable titles of 'an idler,' 'a parasite,' 'an eccentric,' 'a mad cap' and the like were freely bestowed upon him. His solitary meditations were a mere obsession in their eyes, of the man whose continuous sittings had spared not even the rocks; even they, as they put it, had been erased smooth! Some among them, the more timid, feared him, for they thought he had tamed the evil spirits into ready obedience. How else could he escape the wrath of Pīr Khwājā? He talked to them even while walking alone, was ever in communication with them. That was their explanation of his absent-mindedness, of his self-forgetfulness.

Vilifications, obloquies and derisions notwithstanding, his fame could not but spread among the people in the surrounding villages. The Muslims called him 'Pīrjī,' the holy guide and master, and the Hindus 'Bhagat Maṅgat,' Maṅgat the Devotee, or just 'Bhagatjī,' the Noble Devotee. This homage and reverence did not, however, impress the family. After giving up his studies, he had not cared to prepare himself for any profession, which was a matter for worry among his relations. The strict principles of his father had not left the family in easy circumstances. Earning a living was the clear imperative and could in no way be postponed. Many a time, Pundit Thakurdas, his elder brother, tried his best to make him aware of his obvious duty and so did his brother-in-law, Pundit Sāindas and other relations. He would listen to their advice with mute respect but would not say what he intended to do. Years passed away but he kept to his ways, with no thought of the morrow. Eventually, even his mother had to remind him that he had to do something for a living. Timid were her reminders and hesitant, for she knew, in the heart of her hearts, that it was only his care for her that had prevented him from leaving home for ever and taking to the life of a renunciate like the *ṛṣis* of yore. Others could be emphatic in their advice but not she. His silence on the issue made her deeply apprehensive.

Five years passed away, full five years, with no change in his life style. One day Pundit Thakurdas came from Peshawar, where he worked as a clerk in the office of the

Military Engineering Service. Ganeshi Devi asked him to take Maṅgat to Peshawar and get him some job at an office. The Pundit invited Gurudeva to Peshawar, did his best to persuade him to come there but with no success. His long, well-meaning speech could evoke no response, except that of an irritating silence. So, in total exasperation, he told mother to make him understand the things. The officers in his office were, he said, happy with him and would not turn down his request. There would be, he added, no difficulty in getting him a job. The ultimate decisions, of course, would be his; he perhaps knew best what was right or not right for him! He left for Peshawar, annoyed, washing his hands of the entire affair. It was now the turn of mother to persuade him to go to Peshawar. To console her, he agreed to do her bidding and followed his half-brother to Peshawar. It was the year 1922, full six years after he had left school. Pundit Thakurdas, true to his word, got him a job at the Military Engineering Service Office. Two or three months later he got him a regular job at the office of the Controller of Military Accounts.

The system of education the British introduced in India was primarily meant for recruiting Indians for small administrative jobs. In those days, the days we are talking about, India was largely illiterate. Jobs were few and fewer still were the persons qualified for them. To be a clerk of the lowest rank, which they called 'lower division clerk', one had to be a matriculate, had to have at least ten years of successful training in education. Gurudeva was not even a matriculate, but the British officers had great discretionary powers and could employ, if they were satisfied, even under-qualified persons. It must be said to their credit that they generally used their powers with true discretion. The officers must have been satisfied with the abilities of the young man, which, as we know, were extraordinary. With the job secured, the family felt relieved, for his future was now secure, even though the pay was small. What else could be done for a man who would not study, despite his abilities and his keen intellect? He had to reconcile himself to a hard life!

They did not know that Gurudeva had accepted the job to free his mother from her anxieties, not to make his future secure. Except for attending office, his life-style continued as before: the same silence, the same less than Spartan diet, only a step short of starvation, a little rest in the evening, followed by almost a nightlong self-absorption. At the office, he would not participate in the conversations the clerks would indulge in to while away the tedium of their jobs. Their crude jokes could not invoke even a trace of a smile on his face. He would attend to his work, despite many a mild provocation and ironical hint. The calm on his face was invulnerable, his detachment intimidating, his bearing all serious. The ardent fervour of his meditation had made his body soft and his complexion shiny. Many an expression would appear and disappear on his face like on the surface of still waters. There were moments, many of them, when he would be lost in himself, his eyes closed and his face frighteningly impersonal, the files lying open before him. An awesome silence would then envelop the room, his colleagues gazing at him in wonder and amazement that bordered on dread.

These withdrawals could not fail to rouse the curiosity and interest of his colleagues. During lunch hour they would put to him many a question which he avoided to answer in the beginning. But the questions became persistent, the tone of asking serious, with a clear ring of sincerity and respect in it. So he had to talk to them, speak of the spiritual possibilities of man, of his destiny and destination. In the conversations on these matters, his voice would assume varied tones, intonations and rhythms. When he woke up from his contemplation, his voice was soft and calm, when he was in 'normal' moods it had a ring of authority and certainty, the pitch often rising to persuasiveness and persuasiveness into a commanding eloquence. His colleagues were so much impressed by these dialogues that they would often visit him at home, without a notice, much less an invitation. So irresistible was the inner prompting to be near him that they would not care for ordinary formalities, not even for the inconvenient timings. He became an object of conversation among his colleagues, among the other employees, among their neighbours and acquaintances. A local celebrity in the making, no doubt!

They loved him, admired him, respected him, revered him. Even the British officers came to know the curiously extraordinary ways of their new recruit. A perceptible change crept into the atmosphere of the office. Dullness gave place to seriousness, frivolity to sobriety, worldly concerns to spiritual inquiry. The drab look of files and books of accounts stood in sharp contrast to what occupied the minds of the clerical staff. They were anxious to go to the office to feel the soothing effect of his proximity, to hear his voice and observe the changing expressions of his face, his total withdrawal into himself and the marvelous process of waking up from his self-oblivion. It was but natural that they should, whenever they found an occasion, start some conversation about the matters that occupied their minds, about his 'trances,' his understanding of life and its purpose, if it had any. Some were there, however, who out of religious prejudices or plain vanity, did not like the attention paid to him, and lodged complaints against him to the officers that Maṅgat was ever busy with his spiritual discourses and did not pay attention to his work. However, no shortcoming could be found when his work was examined.

Colleagues turned into friends, more than friends, intimations they sought from the deeps within him whether at office or on the way home. Lives and teachings of various seers and sages were discussed and the contents of ancient scriptures and the symbolic meanings of mythical legends or icons. One day after office, discussion started about the life of Prahlāda, a legendary character described in mythical works called the *Purāṇas*. His father, the legend says, proclaimed himself God, which claim his son, a young lad, declined to accept. The differences became sharp, the conflicts bitter and the father, an arrogant king, gave orders that Prahalāda be tied to a red hot iron pillar; let his God, the king said, save him if He could! The order was obeyed but the son came out of the monstrous ordeal unscathed and unscarred, Agni, the god of fire, turning all-benign to him. This, in brief, was the story, the truth of which was strongly questioned by some in the group. No one, they said, could survive that ordeal; stories of this kind were mere creations of sick or hypocritical minds. In silence he heard the heated dispute that followed. Eventually, the matter was referred to him. 'Men of God,' he said, 'do not, will not, display their miraculous powers, they have neither the will to do so nor have they the vanity. Miracles are happenings, not conscious actions. Times come when they find themselves in difficult, impossible circumstances; then *Prakṛti*, Nature, herself comes to their aid to do the undoable. Sometimes some pigheaded people too come into their contact, those that have not the ability to perceive or to understand. To give rise to faith in such hard hearted people, to make them link their life and being to the Lord, men of God turn gracious to them and do things which are out of the ordinary and the understandable.'

Some among his associates did not agree with what he said. One among them said, 'There can be no such devotee, not these days, nor can there be a miracle of this kind.' In response to this observation he said:

> Even if miracles were to happen before you, you would not have the true faith. They will evoke only amazement and applause from you. Learn something from what the prophets of old did, the gurus of old and those they call Incarnations of the Lord. Never did they deviate from their allegiance to the truth, never did they forsake that anchor, that breath of their life. O you lovers of the Lord, leave the poor men of God to themselves, provoke them not! In that lie the good of all, their joy and

happiness. Do you not ever be arrogant unto them! Humility alone should be your bearing in their presence.

A *tandoor*, a baking receptacle, hot and flaming, lay nearby. The man who had expressed his scepticism about miracles said. 'Look at this *tandoor*! If someone were to put his hand or foot into it, sure it is that it will burn. Put your foot into it and see what happens to your devotion! All this talk about miracles is plain nonsense. They are mere fictions to please the credulous; gross distortions are they of the actual happenings.'

The discussion was getting spirited but it came to a shocking halt when everyone saw that a foot of his was already in the *tandoor*. One among them rushed towards him and forced his foot out of the burning flames. Not a hair had been burnt, not a nerve had been injured. A breathless, openmouthed astonishment, a stunning amazement, was writ large in their eyes and their expressions. All silent they stood; their body language spoke of the shattering of their ways of thinking, of their views, inherited or acquired. Awe-struck and speechless they fell at his feet, seeking his forgiveness for their sense of friendship for him, the innocent liberties they had taken with him, for, in a word, taking him for a human being, a man among them, one belonging to their own species. For, sublime he appeared, more than man, a being sent they knew not from where to admonish them, to chasten them, to show them the way and the path. Seeing their astonishment, their oppressive awe, their breathless wonder, Gurudeva said in a voice almost unrecognisable:

> You love the Lord. Obstinacy does not behove men of this sort. Nor does self-assurance. The past events are not mere fabrications that could be trifled with. Take them seriously, consider them cautiously and take a leaf out of the lives of your revered forefathers. Those who have given up everything for the sake of the Lord, are poor and deprived because of their ardent seeking for Him, can make or mar alike. But as companions are you now, so entertain no fears. But be heedful in the future. Let

this happening remain confined within you, let there be no mention of it anywhere to anyone. The will of the Lord was such that this had to happen. Maybe your life and being will get oriented towards the truth, maybe you will have the faith that saves and redeems!

The event turned them into devotees, mute and obedient. Awesome became his presence, holy and sacred, which one could, if repentant, revere and worship but not get familiar with. As for Gurudeva, the occurrence made him inward oriented, almost completely. All conversations stopped, all inquiries, all questions and answers. He avoided human company and resorted to solitude as he had done at Gangothian. It was, however, too much for those who had seen the event to keep it within them as a secret not to be revealed. They were bound to speak about it to some, with the result that the news spread among many, prompting them to have a glimpse of the man of miracles. Whatever the effect the happening produced on its beholders, it became a misery for him, forcing him to resign his job and leave the town.

His companions turned devotees went to his house to request him to take back his resignation, but Gurudeva was not open to their persuasive effort. They, his colleagues, knew that he did not need a job; one that could command the elements had no need to serve wretched mortals. All that they sought was his nearness, his proximity. Men of the world sometimes get deeply attached to those who have no concern with it. That is the strange paradox about narcissistic humanity.

His boss too asked him to take back his resignation, impressing upon him that a job of that kind was hard to get, it might not fall his way again. To this well-meant suggestion, his reply was, '*This* can serve only one master, not two.' The boss was an Englishman, the conversation was being carried on through an interpreter. 'If you, Maṅgatrām,' said the boss, 'remain here, I will see to it that you rise in your career and life.' Gurudeva folded his hands and asked the interpreter to say to him: Let the Sahib kindly say what he had found that he would give to this servant of his! Hearing this reply, the boss could just smile a response. Nevertheless, he refused to accept the resignation. Gurudeva, however, had made up his mind: he had decided not to attend office from the first day of the following month, whether the Sahib accepted his resignation or did not. So one day at the dead of night he left Peshawar for Gangothian. The term of his service was less than a year.

Mother was naturally happy to see her son, thinking he had come on leave. However, her happiness changed into grief when she came to know that he had resigned his job, but not a word of censure or of sorrow came out of her lips. For years had she borne with the burden of his ways, in silence and apparent patience, now too she did the same. The relations too took this action of his as irresponsible, the result of a diseased thinking. He, on his part, ignored their opinion, for he had come back from Peshawar fully determined to snap off all interactions and social relationships. Communication with others had resulted in his being provoked into showing his miraculous powers, an act he found to be a stumbling block in the way to his goal.[3]

The dangers and the pitfalls of associating with the men of the world had now become fully obvious to the Master. So, he resorted to solitude to give himself up to silent meditation, give himself up to it almost exclusively, saying goodbye to all thoughts of his safety and interests. Pangs of hunger seemed to have almost disappeared, so had the torments of thirst and so the heaviness of sleeplessness. What could be the explanation of this phenomenon, incredible as it would seem to those who never have had an opportunity of seeing him in person? A stray remark he once made would perhaps give us a hint to understand a little of this mystery:

> Once the true being of the Self manifests itself within, there remains no consciousness of the body at all. If for a moment or so it happens to revive, then the body appears different from oneself, a shadow as it were. No interest remains then for its remaining or not remaining.

A twenty-year old young man is not supposed to be a solitary monk, disinterested in everything that those at his age are necessarily interested in. The maternal instinct could not possibly bear this disinterestedness especially in the times when the bonds of family life were strong, when individuality could not be imagined outside the ambit of those bonds. Mother suffered in silence and for long, her suffering eventually ending up in illness. Other relations too were worried about his future. His half- brother, Pundit Kishan Chand suggested that Maṅgat should establish some handlooms. The British had seen to it that the prosperity they enjoyed as the result of the Industrial Revolution should not reach India. So the business of hand-weaving was quite popular among the not well to do in those pre-industrial days. Consequently, the suggestion appealed to mother who urged her son to take up the business of weaving. He accepted her suggestion, taking it to be an order as it were and established some handlooms at a small town called Sagari, a four-mile distance from Gangothian. Some weavers were employed and the weaving started, with results, as could well be imagined, disastrous. For born was he to weave another kind of garment to clothe him with the glory that should be described in the words of the *vāṇī* itself. That *vāṇī*[4] *is*, however, untranslatable, at least for me, so I would rather paraphrase it.

> My body decays naked and exposed,
> Give me a mantle to reclaim me from time,
> the inheritance mine and sinful
> from birth to birth, from death to death.

Of restraint be its warp and of truth the woof,
patience be the weaver and love the weaving shuttle,
with breath the mind stretch it,
and dispassion weave it thick and tight.
And let the Name trade it,
and with love the desolate measure it.

To pay its price none was there
on earth or in heaven or in the ethereal sky,
none to wear that dazzling glow,
beyond his ken and beyond his speech.

There will be one to buy this cloth, one alone will he be,
the man true, won over to death.
At the confluence of the three[5]
will he wash the mantle,
to wash off the maladies three.[6]

Let his guru stitch the mantle,
joining together the two, the *surata* and the *nirata*,
consciousness intent and the dark one unconcerned.[7]

Discrimination will be his needle,
and passive opening up the stitching thread;
fashion with these will he the wrap
of yogic ardent fervour.

That will be the garment of *nirvāṇa*,
that will be the Word, that garment indivisible.
A rare one will wear it, on the guru his mind intent.
To that self-extinct Maṅgat will ever bow,[8]
for immortal will be he out of ashes sprung.

The young man who was trying to weave a cloth that would clothe him in the glory of the no-being that is the true being could not, as was inevitable, succeed in the business venture he had been made to undertake. Soon, too soon, the result became visible: no work, no sale, only a loss after a loss. Things came to such a pass that no money was left even to pay the workers' wages. As for the 'entrepreneur,' he always waited for the evening to suspend that mess for the next day and spend the night in the real work, the only work that could be called worth undertaking. Eventually, the mess turned into utter chaos and the work had to be stopped – forever. A few things he distributed among the workers and other people around, the rest he left them where they were and went back home. It was left to his half brothers to dispose of the things and the gadgets; he never visited the place again.

The routine of his life regained its earlier rhythm, the days passed by in the Pīr Khwājā and the nights along the banks of the Trail that wound its course among the ups and downs of that landscape. Dawns brightened into mornings, mornings into days, the days melted into evenings and evenings into nights. The moon continued to wax and wane, the seasons came to bloom and to wither and the years came to disappear. Rains fell down and storms came to uproot and destroy, but nothing could make him change his ways. A little past midnight he would go out for his solitary 'meditation' to return at 10 in the morning. An incredibly light meal followed by a little rest prepared him again to resort to the shades of the Pīr Khwājā. No relationships he had, no dealings with the world around him. His relations, brothers or sisters, too snapped off all links with him and withdrew the financial help, saying, quite legitimately in a way, in their way, that no purpose could be served by helping 'a born idler.' So things were getting really difficult at home, the prospect of starvation becoming a real possibility, rather a high probability. At last a day came when mother told him that she had nothing at home to cook for the following day. But let the incident be narrated in Gurudeva's own words:

> One day when *This* was getting ready to go out for the night, mother told *This*, 'Maṅgat, nothing is here for tomorrow. What shall I cook for you?' *This* said in reply, 'Let the morrow come, mother, that will be the time to give thought to what we shall eat.' Saying this, *It* went towards the waters. When the time for

> returning home arrived, mother's words of the evening came to the mind. As for *It*, hunger was no more a problem to reckon with. For the sake of mother alone would *It* swallow a few mouthfuls of food. Well, *It* left for the *derā* and, arriving there, repeated her words of the evening but before *It* could finish the sentence, she said, 'I brought some mustard leaves from the fields. These have I cooked in butter milk.' 'Let that be our fare for today, mother,' was *Its* response.[9]

While narrating this incident, a smile came to appear on that face, a human smile that seemed to transform the visible invisibility that his face was into a face human, the face of a man who could feel like us mortals, feel the bond of filial relationships. He concluded that narration with the words, 'Those leaves of mustard boiled in butter milk had a unique taste, the like of which was never experienced thereafter.'

How this man that had transcended all ties and relationships and all the desires of the senses and the mind could speak in this way, in this *human* way? His distance from what was human in him was indeed a miracle, but a greater miracle was his love for what was human in others, a phenomenon to see was it, not to describe. Perhaps, love is possible only for him who is [a] naught, for only as nothing can he be every thing and every one. That is why, this aloneness absolute could live at home, could eat for his mother's sake, could enjoy the food she prepared and remembered it for years, even though he lived all withdrawn from the senses. So, the man in him was still alive, despite his death. That is the paradox, this account will, as far as possible, try to contemplate, if not to resolve.

There was, however, the hard fact of the straitened circumstances, for his mother if not for him. So, something had to be done for that, done without a delay. But where was the man in him, the living man, to do that something, where was the room, the space, for thinking about what he would eat and what wear? For, there was no body to clothe and to be fed. Yet he who is not is every one else, he is *Vaiśvānara*, All-beings. So, He that was All, had to do what the man in him could not, do something for the sake of the mother that had given birth to this man that had crossed the very bounds of humanity, had reduced to nonsense its very definition.

It came to happen that his thoughts went on their own accord to herbs and roots. He had seen, when at Kallar, his brother-in-law extracting medicinal drugs out of them and knew the curative effects of some among them. He brought a book of indigenous medicine from him and rapidly glanced through it and prepared some medicines, following the instructions given therein. He was not certain of their efficacy, could not be, given the fact that he knew nothing about medicines or about the traditional account of them. Yet he administered them to some poor patients, mostly his acquaintances, with no thought, no idea of what they could do or bring about. The surprise of the surprises for him was that the patients got cured and would come to thank him. The phenomenon encouraged him and he started administering 'medicines' to whosoever approached him with the result that the number of people who came for cure increased manifold. Within six months their number swelled to such an extent that he had to fix up a regular time for them.

Was this act of fixing the time for the patients a return to the world, rendering his resignation from the job at Peshawar futile and unnecessary? For, this meant, as did the job at Peshawar, disruption of his yogic way of life, much longer, as it turned out to be the case, than before. A time comes in the life of every genuine *yogin* when he has to give up the joy of contemplation, of self-forgetting, give up the bliss that falls to the lot of a man when he ceases to be man. For the sense of distinction between the joy of self-oblivion and the misery of being situated in the world and among mankind persists hard in *yogins*, forcing them to remain ever self-absorbed. So the next step, the hardest one, is to give up this sense of distinction, to see alike the bliss and the misery, to give up the thought that there are such things as bondage and liberation or fall and redemption. Most of all, to shed the striving for the latter, to give up all *sādhanā*, all 'striving for the goal' and to live in the spirit of *honī*, of happening, not of doing. A true *yogin's* pilgrimage is done for him; he does not have to do it himself. So Gurudeva had to give up his strivings and live as others live, subject to death and decay, with no thought of his own salvation. So what seemed a means of livelihood was really the *sādhanā* of the highest order, that of perceiving as one the world and the self, the *sādhanā* for *samatvam*, for sameness.

The medicines he administered to his patients could hardly be called medicines even according to the traditional system. They consisted of common herbs and essences of ordinary stuff of common use, like aniseeds and dry ginger, and yet they produced incredible results. What were considered incurable diseases by modern system of medicine in those days, diseases like tuberculosis, were cured by these things, which, by no stretch of imagination, could kill the bacteria responsible for those diseases. So he became, before long, a great physician in the eyes of the villagers who had, most among them, neither the awareness of nor the means to afford modern treatment. It was but natural that those near and around him should get jealous and shower curses and abuses upon him. 'How this novice, this ignoramus absolute,' they declared 'could be a physician? Let those who go to him for a cure get their graves dug, for sure is it that they will not come back alive!' Such was the praise he received, such the fame and such a name! This criticism had, however, no force against the plain facts. Patients in large numbers continued to pour in, from villages far away and distant. He would examine them from 9 A.M. to 4 P.M. He would also visit those among them who were too ill to travel, charging no fee and accepting no hospitality from them. On many occasions he had to go to distant villages to 'see' his patients. Miles he would cover on foot rendering impossible his reaching back home on time. So on returning, he would sit on the rock along the Trail, his usual seat, and spend the night there itself to return home at the right time – 9 A.M. There were times when it would get dark on the way itself. On such occasions he would select some solitary place for his 'meditation' but would see to it that he reached home at nine, where he knew patients would be waiting for him.

While dispensing medicines to his patients, he would invariably give them a precaution or two, precautions that would make any physician smile, traditional or modern. He would say: 'Abstain from meat eating and drinking and be straightforward in your dealings; while measuring out things for your customers measure them right, while weighing out things to them weigh them right and see to it that no word of deception or falsehood escapes your lips.' A sound medical advice, no doubt! And especially to those for whom life meant little else than the acts and things he would ask them to refrain or abstain from. Another characteristic of this medical practice also we should not fail to mention: he never asked for any payment, in cash or in kind. Some among his patients would leave behind some cereals or some fresh vegetables they grew in their fields; they had no cash to offer. Some among them, when cured, would leave some money too. But the majority of the villagers lived in utter poverty and destitution. Many were there who could not afford proper diet, not to speak of purchasing medicines. For people living [or breathing] in such unhappy circumstances, he would provide food too in addition to medicines. And nurse too would he them, cleaning them of the bodily filth.

The medical 'practice' was, thus, more a service than a profession, for the majority of the patients received their treatment free of any cost. The few that paid for it paid according to their own wish and will. His mother and he himself lived mostly on what their little, almost barren, fields would yield with a little supply of the milk their cow gave. Very little of this earning was spent to meet their other needs, bare necessities we should call them. Whatever remained after it had been spent to meet the needs of the poor patients was spent in another, extravagant, way. Come the day of the full moon or the first day of a lunar month, or come some other festivals, generous gifts of fruit were distributed among the patients and the villagers, things that were rarities for them in that area of unproductive land. The service he rendered to the people and the generosity of his gifts made him extremely popular among the people far and near; they respected him, revered him, almost worshiped him. But his relationship with people at large remained confined to only this kind of disinterested service; no discourses on spiritual matter would he give them. He truly embodied what the *bānī* says about the characteristics of a physician:

> Let him be forgiving and generous of mind, his life anchored absolutely to the Spirit Immanent, suffering with those that suffer; a partaker of their pain and their anguish should he be. Equipped this wise, let him embark upon his practice. Let him diagnose well and prescribe well the treatment, taking every care he becomes not vain of these his abilities, for his entire endeavour should he take as ordained by the Spirit that sustains. Only then will he qualify for being a *vaidya*, a healer, true and unstained. Let him serve with no interests of his own in mind, with no thought of self or fame. Maladies hard will disappear at his mere approach and touch and an ideal will he become to reach and emulate.
>
> And let him be compassionate to all that live, be they humans or beasts, cure them with care but with no greed in mind. Flee away shall every disease when acts he this way and treats. Let him take every care [of his patients], care in spirit this, and let him give light doses of drugs, his own life anchored to the Lord. Victory shall he have over every wrong and every disease. He shall diagnose when the light shines within him, the light of the

> Spirit, not before its advent. And serve shall he with no desire in mind. Splendour of the Spirit will come to clothe him to burn away affliction every. The Full he will find within, the Infinite, of That will he become the food, of that Full in him. With acts like these, with thoughts like these, will he become the cure itself, the soother and the comfort. This is the word true of him they call Maṅgat.[10.]

Modern medical science, with all its enormous limitations, has shown some truly spectacular results. Therefore, no modern-minded person will believe that a man like the one presented in these preceding lines could be a dependable physician; you need, he would say, careful training and education to qualify for that position. The qualifications mentioned above are altogether different. A man, the description says, must die as man, so to say, to become a healer, no training can truly equip him for that purpose. With this rider however: he should turn to the function of healing only when thoughts of healing arise spontaneously in him, arise as revelatios rather than as decisions. I would term that healing and that cure a miracle but the miracle of the Sustaining Spirit in him, not of the individual they called Maṅgat. At Peshawar the man still lived to be provoked but here the man was absent, only the Spirit was active.

For his mother and sisters, this grace of the Spirit that would turn the *yogin* into a *samadarśin*, one who sees all as one, bondage as well as liberation, was a mere medical practice, a successful practice at that. It gave rise in them to the natural desire that he should now marry and live the normal life of a prosperous householder. But knowing what he was, knowing his ways and nature, none had the courage to express this desire before him. One day, however, mother summoned up her courage and, aided by other relations, expressed her desire more by way of a hint than an express statement. Gurudeva was always affectionate towards his mother, soft-spoken, considerate and respectful.

But that day he spoke in somewhat harsh and stern terms to close the chapter forever. 'Two swords,' he said, 'can never be placed in one sheath.' A well known phrase is this in India, often used by seers and sages, to mean that the ways of the world and the way of God are sheer opposites and can never be reconciled, a view which practitioners of easy spirituality of these days often dispute. He had, he continued, other things to do, things ordained for him by the Lord. If he entered the way of darkness, as his mother suggested, he would fail in his purpose and his mission. The mother in Ganeshi Devi, however, was strong and she continued to pester him whenever she found an occasion. So came the final warning to her, '*This* stays here only to serve you. But if you pester *This* again, *This* will leave home forever.' So the matter ended there. No one took it up again.

In the month of March of 1928, mother died, without a sign, without a symptom of the impending event. Her departure from here to the hereafter was described in these words to a devotee, Om Capoor, by the Master himself:

> This body had completed its twenty-four years when news came that a niece [of his] had died. Mother asked *This* to go to Rawalpindi to attend the ceremonial rituals. This *It* refused to do but had to give in to her persistence. The day was spent among the relations, the participants in the rituals, but at night *This* went to a small stream, the *Lai,* that flows through a forest on the outskirts of the city. In that forest *It* spent the night in *tapa[s],* in self-burning. There at Gangothian mother was all right during the day but as the evening approached, her head ached with an accompanying discomfort. Her term was over and she breathed her last shortly afterwards. A man was sent to Rawalpindi to break the news. A nephew [of his] came searching for *This,* and said that his grandmother had passed away.
>
> The time was 1 P.M. Two thoughts arose at this tiding. The first was: For the sake of whom *It* lived at home is now no more. Why go back there now, for what purpose? The ancestral property these will distribute among themselves, brothers and relations. So cross over to the other bank of the stream and move away

wherever these feet may lead! Then, seconds after rose another thought: Won't it be better if things should start from Gangothian itself rather than from elsewhere? From there should these begin and then from elsewhere. Theirs is the privilege first, of those that dwell there. The second thought prevailed. *It* said to the boy, 'Go you to the bus stand, *This* will follow you from here itself.'

So *It* went back to Gangothian and cremated the body in accordance with the prevailing custom. Other rituals *This* refused to perform, for they, *This* said, were mere frauds. Brothers felt annoyed and declared *This* to be a shame for the family and performed all the rituals lasting for ten days. They urged him to accompany them to Rawalpindi but *This* refused, despite their repeated attempts. *This* also told them that with the death of mother all relationships between *This* and them had ended. They would be welcome if they liked to visit *It* but they would be guests like other people, nothing more and nothing less. *It* continued to stay at Gangothian, communication with people [re]starting there itself. Years later, *This* went to other provinces too. *This* avoids sticking to one place, even one seat lest people should start worshipping the place or the seat, as is the wont of the worldlings.

He did not, let it be emphasised, start talking about man's spiritual needs immediately after mother's death. He continued to stick to his old ways, much more than ever before. Nearly all his time was spent in solitude, with little articulate communication with anyone, of matters spiritual with none whatsoever. Remained he absorbed there in the silent depths within him, silent depths that would often peal into words, into a fount of *vāṇī* that would flow uninterrupted for hours on end but only to disppear, as before, into the air. Never for once did he think of reducing it to writing. That was not the function of the Berefts, he would say, this writing down the speech without the speaker. Some day, he thought, a man in love with the Lord might stumble into it to take it down, if that were the will of the Lord. So the solitude came to relate to the world through the speech that none spoke but that everyone could hear, if he happened to be nearby. For the redemption of the people the Word descended in the form of words, so that the words may lead them to the Word. But the time, the time as we of the world reckon it, had not yet come for its dissemination. But can one say, could one ever claim, that the words that melted into the air went all useless? We will not make any attempt to answer this question.

Man is born in debt and lives in debt. He lives in debt to the elements: to earth, to water, and to fire, air and the sky. He lives in debt to his mother, his father and his teacher and to humanity. He is indebted equally to non-human species, to animals and to the birds of the air. And to gods and to the Ultimate Truth. His being is more than cosmotheandric and so is his debt. He lives in the world of the elements, lives situated therein, he is constituted by men, birds and beasts; constitutive *others* are they of him. He lives indebted to gods for his orientation towards the beyond, for the call it makes to beckon him on. And there will also be the call of the ultimate truth because no beyond ceases to be the beyond unless and until man dies into Being, the Ground of all that he can perceive, conceive, imagine or aspire for. Gurudeva had paid the debt he owed his mother by serving her all those years. Humanity he was also serving by alleviating their pain and their suffering. But to serve mankind through alleviating their suffering is not enough. For man's being is oriented towards transcendence; just to remain what he is, is to vegetate, to die as it were. Men of the world often pervert this transcendental thrust into ambitions and desires and move on from one miserable state to another. They pass this thrust on to the states of affairs before them and, instead of transforming themselves, they would change their circumstances, perverting the call for sacrifice into the call for violence. So one, who has seen through the illusions that desire weaves before us and has a genuine concern for the well being of mankind, has to wake them from their dreams into the truth, make them aware of their possibilities and their real, inner urge.

The time had, therefore, come for the physician to turn into the saviour but the urge was still not there. For that purpose the man in him had to die totally and absolutely. So gradually were given up the medical duties and solitude became his home, the flowing of the *vāṇī* therein being his only contact with the world. Food intake was reduced to an alarming extent, crossing the limits of credibility. His total intake of cereals in a month amounted to one and half pound. A small loaf of bread he would take every day with vegetables cooked in butter milk supplemented, for dinner, by a small bowl of vegetables or *dāl,* i.e. pulses. Occasionally, he would take a glass of butter milk, say, twice a week. That was all he took in those days. His sister-in-law who made the loaf of bread for him would, on certain occasions, increase the quantum of flour but he would reject the excess. She was much older than him in age and loved him as a mother would love a son. But in this matter her wishes proved of no avail. His spirit of renunciation was breaking all bounds and so was his disinterest, his dispassion. A prelude was it of the things to come, a preparation for them.

Notes

1 The *Samatā-prakāśa,* p. 664. *Surat* means consciousness. Some take this word as the colloquial form of the Sanskrit *śruti,* hearing. If the latter meaning is accepted, then the word *nirat* would mean the *Nāda,* the Sound or the Word. But some experience and contemplate the Word not as *Nāda* but as *śūnya,* the void. In that case *nirat* would mean the *kuṇḍalinī* or what the Vedas call *agni,* Fire. Cp. *The Samatāvilāsa,* Ch 8. 5.2. This work has since been translated into English bearing the title: **The Radiant Sameness**.

2 *Ibid.,* p. 664.

3 Modern world, despite this narration of the incident, would still repeat the objection of the person who had provoked the young man of God. We believe that the laws of Nature only science can understand and manipulate and that too only to an extent but not our wishes or desires or so-called spiritual powers. If, however, our scientific knowledge cannot exhaust the depth of a given object, even of a small, seemingly insignificant thing, can it ever touch the deepest deeps of the human psyche – that subjective counter part of the so-called external world? We must remain, we mortals, humble enough not to pass judgements on things which we do not, cannot know. Let us not commit the mistake of equating reality with our knowledge of it. Our self-enclosed arrogance must give way to open-ended humility, humility open to the voice of the depths hidden within us and to the mystery hidden within what we see and hear and touch.

4 *The Samatāprakāśa*, pp. 1215-16.

5 The confluence of the *Iṅgalā*, the *Piṅgalā* and the *Suṣmanā*, the three yogic nevers.

6 The physical, the godly and cosmic.

7 See Note 1 above.

8 Literally, bow to his lotus feet.

9 As narrated to Dev Raj Gupta, a devotee of the Master.

10 *The Samatāprakāśa*, p. 1243.

3

SAHAJA-SAMĀDHI

It was the rainy month of August of the year 1929. Gurudeva happened to be at Rawalpindi. One afternoon, he resorted, as it was his habit when in that town, to the solitude of a forest nearby for the purpose of 'meditation'[1] on the banks of the Lai that gently murmured through its thickly shady interior. Moving towards the place where he would sit for his *tapas*, he saw on the way a *sādhu*, a monk, just a little over thirty, sitting under the shade of a tree, fully absorbed in writing. Spontaneously, he proceeded towards the tree and stood still before him but the *sādhu* was so absorbed in his work that he did not notice the Master's presence until some words, to him startling and strange, roused him from his self-absorption. The words were, 'My mind, Mahārāj, Adorable Lord, is ever restless, imaginings numberless assail it ever; an endless distress are they for me. I do not know how to shed this oppressive burden, to come out of this labyrinth of torture. Is there no one to show me the way I seek? Or has this land of seers and sages become totally bereft of them?'

Immediately the monk raised his head, his writing all ceased, lines of astonishment writ large on his face. The words had startled him, for they reflected, precisely and literally, the very thoughts that were troubling him at that time. How on earth could that total stranger articulate these, his own very thoughts? The rustic dress the man before him wore showed him to be an ordinary villager, one among the innumerable that visited the town every day. But there was something in the face that arrested the monk's attention, mesmerizing him as it were. What followed could best be described in the monk's own words:

> When I heard his words I found them expressing my own inner feelings and thoughts. The man before me could not be an ordinary person, the man that could divine what was passing in my mind! I looked up to see who he could be, looked at his face and found my attention all fixed on it. I stood up and spread out a piece of cloth on the ground and, with hands folded, requested him to take his seat thereon. When he graciously acceded to my request, I said, 'Like a gem hidden in a coal mine are you, Lord! I see in thee one who has become the Truth itself.'
>
> 'I came here only to ask of you a few questions. From the countryside do I come. Occasionally, I visit this place in search of someone who could show me the true path.'
>
> 'Desert me not, my Lord. Whatever your habit might show you to be, my soul tells me loud and clear that I am in the presence of a perfect *yogī*.'
>
> 'Be kind enough,' said he, 'to answer the question I put to your revered self. That will give me the consolation I seek. Be you gracious to me.'
>
> 'My Lord Gracious,' said I, 'conceal as you may what you are, but I cannot accept you as you tell me you are. An ordinary man you cannot be!'
>
> Saying this, I caught hold of his feet and said, 'How can I, in what way, believe that the questions that you were gracious enough to ask me were *your* questions? For when the Lord showered his grace upon this servant of his, these very questions

were troubling me, these very thoughts, these very tortures. Let not the Lord bring this broken hearted man to test. This his servant had imagined that this great land of Bhārata, this land radiant with holiness, is now empty of the seers and sages that once roamed in numbers here. But today, after having seen the Lord, my faith returns to assure me that even now this land is a land blessed. For the light still shines here and the waters that wash one of mortality flow still in abundance here.'

'Wherefrom have you come, which is your native place?'

'With a mind open shall I reveal everything before the Lord. I, with a companion, left the *derā*[2] in search of a man who had attained to the truth absolute. From Ahmadabad in Gujarat to Rameshwar, from there to Bengal, to Bihar, to the United Provinces up to Haridwar and Rishikesh we two wandered, and from there on to the Punjab. Practically, the whole of India we covered, we two, exhausting all our resources and energy but found no one whom we could accept as our guide and master, who could show us the path we sought, and the truth we would attain to. We lived among many saints, *sādhus* and monks, the heads of monasteries and guides of legions but everywhere found nothing else but greed, fraud and deception. My companion went back, dejected and in despair and my own condition is hardly better.

Desponded I sat here, my life wasted and of no purpose when the Lord came to restore my faith. Indeed my sense of despair had deepened to such an extent that I was seriously thinking of putting an end to this futile life, this dreary and helpless crawling towards death. On the other hand, my empty pocket also made me think of finding some means at least for the return journey. With this confused state of mind I sat here, deciding neither this way nor that when I heard in clear and articulate terms my own thoughts and feelings. Now I should in no way, says my mind, leave these holy feet, for here alone I shall find, it says, what have I yearned and sought for so long. .. And the wonder of wonders is that now that I am in this condition, the Lord himself has come to reveal himself to me. In what way could I ever find him and recognise him? I feel myself blessed today. At long last, I have found all, the all.

His effusions over, a fount of *vāṇī* gushed out from the lips of Śri Gurudeva. Rattandās – for that was the name of our unhappy interlocutor – was at that time a disciple of the head of a monastery of the Kabīr sect, named after a famous saint of medieval India [to be anointed, later on, its *Mahant*, its head]. He was suffused with the *vāṇī* (or the *bānī* as it is called in the colloquial language) of Kabīr, listening to it every day, morning and evening. That day he felt as if Kabīr himself had come to recite his *vāṇī* before him, such was its force, such was its rhythm and such the depth of its meaning. His long and arduous pilgrimage was, it seemed, going to be fruitful. So without much ado he straightaway requested to be initiated. 'But can you,' he was asked, 'repose your faith in *This*, for without it you cannot move forward?'

'Today I have found the anchor I sought, the refuge I yearned for long. There is no other anchor for me, there is no other refuge for me.'

Having said this, he clung to the Master's feet and left them not until he was initiated into the secret path of *yoga*. He was the first disciple. Bowing before his refuge and Master, he requested that he be allowed to live with him.

'*This* cannot,' came the reply, 'take anyone along with *It*.'

'Then may the Lord allow me to take him to Ahamadabad, to the seat there of Kabīr.'

'That also is not possible yet.'

Then the would-be *Mahant*, the would-be head of the said monastery, asked for the Master's address. 'You have got,' said the Master, 'what you wanted, so why care about *Its* whereabouts?' Nevertheless, he told him the name of his village and its location and invited him to visit the place in a week. With words of blessings on his lips, he departed, Rattan Das following him a long distance to see him off. Coming back to the foot of the same tree, he thought of his future plans. But soon he noticed a change within him, setting at naught all his worries about his future. He recalls:

> Soon after the initiation I found myself lost as it were in joy, in an ecstasy of it. For four or five days I hardly knew myself. I remember I went to the market place to buy something. To a shopkeeper I mentioned the name of the thing I wanted. Then I knew not where I was. I knew only the yogic process going on within me, that alone. The shopkeeper had to call me many a time before I could know what he wanted me to say.
>
> I waited anxiously for the end of the week to go to Gangothian and have the *darśana* of my lord and master. Happy was I, my mind at rest. If this state remained constant, my destination, I felt, would not be far away!

For full four days Rattandas was in a constant hypnosis as it were, but then the ecstasy ebbed away, slowly but surely. He strove hard to revive it and drink in full the joy of life but the fount from where it flowed in such full current seemed to have dried up. For hours he sat in meditation, bringing his mind to focus on his breath and flow with its controlled motion but the effort proved useless, the striving a waste. His unhappiness returned and so did his anxieties and worries, his restlessness and his anguish. But hope was there, hope of the revival of the joy and the ecstasy. He was anxious to ask Gurudeva about this his fall and counted every moment of waiting for the end of the week. For he was confident that the moment he touched his Master's feet, the fount would flow again to slake his thirst.

At the end of the week, he left for Gangothian. There was a bus service that led up only to a place called Chowk Pandauri. The rest of the six mile journey had to be done on foot. Arriving at his destination, he came to know that the Master was away in the nearby forest for his 'meditation.' So he waited for his arrival outside the village under the shade of a tree. A bright sunny day was it, fiercely hot and humid but Rattan Das stuck to his chosen seat, silent, thirsty and patient. Gurudeva returned but rather late that day. From a distance he had recognised the Mahant, so he went straight to him. The Mahant stood up, all respect, and prostrated himself before him. Śrī Gurudeva took him home and made him have a good meal.

Many questions he put to the Master, cleared many of his doubts and dispelled many of his misgivings. All the answers came not in the form of ordinary human speech but in that of the *vāṇī*. His mind was now clear, the way straight and the guide infallible. But where was the joy, the elation, the forgetting of the self, the joy of being [a] no-being as it were? It seemed to have melted away, leaving not even a trace of it behind, except its memory and the pain of its loss. He had come to the Master's presence with the hope that it would revive and the way to the bliss supreme would open up for his asking. From bliss to bliss he would move to the final Bliss. He requested for grace so that the tangles of the world should no more make him the wreck that he was. But that was not to be. Said the Master:

> Do not ask for unearned treasure, you of a gentle soul! Strive and struggle for the bliss you tasted, earn it by yourself. You were heart-broken, forlorn and without a hope. You had to be provided an anchor to which you could tie and relate your breath and your life. Your doubts had to be cleared and your unrest composed. So you were vouchsafed what you now ask for because the Lord had so ordained. Now a long way lies before you, the way of strife and struggle to make that bliss a presence, an eternal presence for you. Wait in patience for its return. Find *This* within you, for *It* abides there within your heart. The blessing you seek will always be there with you, not for a moment will it desert you.

Rattandas took a watch out of his pocket to make the offering that an initiate makes to his guru. For he had nothing else left with him. 'Be kind enough, Lord,' said he, 'to accept this trifle as the offering of a man poor and lost.'

'The stars of heaven are always there to show the time. On travel you are, so keep it to yourself, it will be of much use to you. Abide in what has been revealed to you. That alone will be your offering true. Spend the rest of your life striving for the goal, the ultimate goal of all that has come to be.'

Once again the disciple received his Master's blessings and left to start a new life.

The Master's life style, to resume our story, remained as it had been before. With one change, however: In January 1933 he held an open *yajña* wherein were invited, apart from the locals, people from all the villages around. Ever since he started his 'practice' as a physician, he had been spending his earnings mostly in looking after the well being of the poor and deprived. Many a poor man he supported, many were helped in meeting the expenses of their daughters' weddings. But only the giver knew of the gifts and the receiver, no one else. We already know the liberality with which he distributed fruit on days held auspicious by the Hindus. Yet his incredibly austere life assured that this generosity should not exhaust his savings. So whatever remained after his – in the eyes of his relations 'irresponsible' – liberality had to be got rid of. And what better way of spending it than in a *yajña*? The *yajña* became an annual event from that date onwards. At its completion, he would become almost a pauper, with no savings left with him. Everybody was invited, rather beseeched to attend the *yajña*, the poor and the rich, the low caste and the high caste, the Hindus and the Muslims. A splendid affair used to be that *yajña*, 'extravagant' would be the more appropriate word to describe it. All the traditional delicacies were prepared, and prepared in excess; there would be *kheer* and *mālapuas* and sweets in addition to *halvā*.. The last was distributed, not in packets or plates but as measured out in shovels. The poor villagers, starved of delicacies, ate, each one of them, the *halvā* in kilogrammes and would pack a much greater quantity of it to carry home. For many days they feasted on *mālapuās* and *halvā,* heating them a little. Seeing that excessive hospitality, the people of Gangothian thought that 'Bhagat Maṅgat' had amassed quite a wealth. That was why he was so liberal, didn't know how to save it and, in their own phrase, 'digest it.' Was there ever a brahmin who knew how to 'digest' his wealth?

'Yajña' is a Sanskrit word, meaning sacrifice. The concept of *yajña* is a highly complex one. Even in the most ancient work of Indo-European literature, the Ṛg Veda (1.164.35), we find the concept already deeply symbolised. The verse in question calls *yajña* the centre, the *nābhiḥ*, of the world, and the altar, where it is performed, as the utmost bound of the earth. In the ritualistic portions of the Vedas, called the Brāhmaṇas, the concept acquires, as we mentioned earlier,[3] a cosmotheandric dimension. Prajāpati, the Lord of Creation, sacrificed himself, say these texts, into the world and died in the process; now creation has to sacrifice itself back into Prajāpati to revive him, to give him back his life. Creation is nothing else than the act of sacrifice, the act in which God participates and so do creatures, inert no less than living. Thus it is the act of sacrifice that these texts would implicitly lay emphasis on, that being the *centre* of the world, not, as Jaimini their interpreter would explicitly proclaim later, God and creatures. The concept acquires a still deeper meaning in the Upaniṣads in continuation of what the Ṛg Veda says at 1.164.35. This is not, however, a place to dwell in details on the Vedic concept of sacrifice. Here I shall confine myself to what the Master has to say about *yajña*, rather what the *vāṇī* says about it, the speech that can have a hearer but not a speaker.[4]

The *vāṇī* draws inferences from perception. There are rivers to flow for others, there are trees to bloom and bear fruit for others, there is the sky to accommodate all, there is the air to give life, and there is fire to warm up and cook. And there are animals to give wool and milk, to pull and to carry. There is the destructive aspect of all these elements too, and along with creatures that support and serve man, there are also creatures that kill and eat other creatures. As for man, like unto the beasts of prey is he born, born more to serve himself than to serve others. That is his curse and that is his bane. Not that the other aspect of Nature is absent in him, the aspect that makes him live for others. But that aspect he has to augment and nurture. Unfortunately, man, the natural man, would often snatch than give, undo others than sustain others.

To protect himself, to serve himself and to enjoy himself: this suicidal formula seems to sum up the essence of his life. But what is that 'himself,' what is there in him that he would serve and protect? Self-negating is his life, life that consists in thoughts, feelings, sensations or relationships. In these would he find his being, his self, in these ephemeral shadows, his quest turning all futile and useless. For, this way, this suicidal way, man can never come to be himself, never come to live, really and truly. A semblance remains he, a mere name attached to phenomena that never pause to receive the name. That is his tragedy, of this creature who would seek being through no-being.

Yajña is there to make him live, to make him share in the life and being of all that he finds other than himself: all the creatures from the humans to the non-humans, from the living to the non-living, from the seemingly infinite world to what is beyond the world, from the known and the knowable to the unknown and the unknowable. In sum man cannot, for the sacrificial vision, come to live, truly live, without becoming one with all that is, all that was or could be, all that was not and could not be. He has to be the past, the present and the future of all that is and also what is beyond the past, the present and the future So, man is asked to give away all that sustains his thoughts, his feelings and his sensations to sustain others. Thoughts, feelings and sensations can make of him only a frail, elusive semblance of an entity, of individuality, but would never make of him the living Man, Man the All, Being the All. Even animals, as we said earlier, should receive his care and attention; even inanimate things should receive his love and regard. For, without flowing into these latter, he cannot give up his sense of identity with sensations, with the body. The act of sacrifice demands that man self-submit to the *other* rather than make the *other* self-submit to him. Let him, therefore, self-submit to the *other* instead of making the *other* self-submit to him.

Life the true means the end of narcissistic thoughts, of desires for self-gratification and laying aside the coil of sensations. So whatever fosters love for the I-sense, for sense-gratification and for embodiment should be offered to others. This way will man be free from the choking evils of individuality and will come to be truly alive. And so too will those that receive his gifts, his care and concern, if they emulate his way and vision. If the receivers nurture their self-love, they will be doomed to destruction. Harder indeed is to be a fit receiver than a generous giver. That is why, service of a seer is considered to be the best *yajña*, for service rendered to him neither feeds the vanity of the giver nor does it water the covetousness of the receiver.

However: This kind of *yajña* may loosen the ties of thoughts, desires and sensations but it cannot free man from consciousness. And without the sacrifice of consciousness, man cannot become the all-Men, cannot become the all, for there will always remain the *other* to constitute consciousness and negate it, however 'unreal' or 'scarcely felt' or inarticulate the presence of that *other* may be. But who will remain to do the act of giving up of consciousness when thoughts become passive, when feelings become faint and sensations vague to the point of being scarcely felt? How does the final act of sacrifice get performed in the absence of the performer? That is the question the answer to which the Master's life will show forth, but in due course.

For the time being, however, *yajña* meant basically service of *human beings*. No offerings were made to the fire and, through the fire, to gods but only to human beings. This *yajña* implied two principles: simplicity for oneself and liberality or service for others. The concepts of simplicity and service will be explained in their fullness in due course; it is enough to say here that unless and until one denies the pleasures of life to oneself one cannot serve others, cannot perform the *mānuṣa-yajña*, sacrifice unto man.

Performance of *yajña*, noviolent yajña – for eating of flesh is a taboo in *Samatāvāda* – performance of non-violent *yajña* had started but, with all the preparations and expense it involved, Gurudeva's solitary meditations were continuously on the increase. The service in the form of medical treatment too stopped – finally – in the month of November 1935. However, communication with people, communication in terms of spiritual discourse, did not resume, despite all the hectic activities associated with the *yajña*. One cannot relate, truly relate, to the world until the man in one is dead finally and irretrievably.

Then came the moment of a radical change in his life, in his external life, for from that moment onwards he became a man ever on the move. In the month of March 1938, he thought of going towards Kashmir, with the intention of doing *tapas* in the solitude of its dense forests. He went to Rawalpindi to catch the bus for Kohala, a small town on the way to Kashmir. The bus, as it turned out, was empty and he occupied the front seat. Presently a man came and asked the driver to get the seat vacated for him. Then came another man and he too made him vacate his seat for him. Passenger after passenger came to repeat the rude act with the result he had to vacate many seats, one after another. The cause of this behaviour was nothing else than his plain, simple dress and his silent gentleness. A man had been noticing this behaviour of the passengers for a long time. A relatively prosperous man he looked, his habit and the gun he carried on his shoulder showed his class. He felt outraged at this behaviour, for those were the days of acute tension between the Hindus and the Muslims with the air thick with the talk of partitioning the country into two parts: one for the Hindus and the other for Muslims. [The demand for carving Pakistan out of India was formalised that very year]. The passengers, who had misbehaved with Śrī Mahārājjī – for that is how his disciples later came to call him, 'The Revered Lord' – were Muslims and the man with the gun on his shoulder was a Hindu. With a voice shrill with anger, he said, 'It is a matter of great regret that everyone here has been so rude to him. What right anyone has to make him leave his seat? He is not travelling free that you should behave so arrogantly with him!'

None could utter a word in reply. Śrī Gurudeva said, 'Please don't be cross with them, you gentle soul! What difference does it make whether you sit on the front seat or on the rear one? To reach the destination alone is the purpose here.'

Karam Chand – for that was name of the gentleman – requested Śrī Gurudeva to sit along with him on the seat he was occupying: the demeanour of the Master during the entire happening had made him curious to know more about him. So he said, 'Who are you, Sir, and where are you going?'

'*Premī*, Blessed Devotee of the Lord, *This* is only a *faqīr*, a bereft. *It* has heard about a thick and unfrequented forest at Hilsurang in Poonch[5] where one can do *tapa[s]* undisturbed by intruders. Nearby they say there live some brahmin families too. Since you are an inhabitant of that area, you could do *[This]* the favour of introducing *This* to those among them whose dealings are straight and spotless. They could send *This* a few mouthfuls of food once a day.'

In those days of easy relationships, people in India, especially at villages and small towns, saw nothing wrong in asking strangers about details of their place of birth, their parentage, their schooling, their jobs, even the pay they received. Karam Chand too put some of these questions to the Master to which he gave replies as far as he could. During the conversation, the Master mentioned his school at Kallar. This information made Karam Chand ask him more questions, for he was posted at the post office there during the days of the Master's schooling. He could also recall one of the young Master's visits to the post office to collect the money sent in his name, the recollection rousing all the more his interest in the strange person sitting by him. How that young boy came to be a renunciate, a sage and a seer, he wondered. However, the words of introduction over, Gurudeva resumed his silence, uttering hardly a word on the way. Absorbed in the depths within him, all oblivious seemed he of the passengers and their frequent boarding and alighting, of Karam Chand's curiosity and of the look of the landscape around. A silent astonishment possessed the latter, the awesome aura of the person sitting by him making of him a mute spectator.

Afternoon was about to melt into evening when the bus reached Kohala, a small town situated on the bank of jhelam, the place where met two roads, one to Srinagar and the other to Rawalpindi. On the other side of the river were the frontiers of Kashmir and Poonch, nearby, a little above on the hills, was the border of the district Hazara of the Northwest Frontier. About two kilometres above on a hill was situated a small village, Jalamada, surrounded with hills on every side, lines after lines of them. Lush green were the lower among them and thickly covered with trees were the higher, trees of varied shades of the green, here light, there dark. Behind that delightful scenery of hills after hills stood the sublime beauty of the eternal snows of the mountains. A little more than a kilometre below flowed the majestic Jhelam making a curve that would force every traveller to pause and stare at its shape and shine. In the silence of the night its music could be heard far away and far above on the hills around it. The landscape of Kashmir would not, even on its utmost borders, tolerate the ordinary appearance of the land on the other side of the river. Unique is the beauty of this land, it is not for nothing that they call it heaven on the earth.[6]

Karam Chand took Gurudeva to his own home at Jalamada. For full two days, he declined every request for a meal. On the third day, he agreed to take a small loaf of bread. The apparent reason: he had to satisfy himself that the man earned his living through straight and honest means. But, I would say, only apparent. He did not require two days to test the man, a minute, as many would testify, would have been enough for the purpose, even a fraction of a minute. The truth is that there had developed in him a disinclination for eating, an unpleasant task was it for him, though unavoidable. Anyone who saw him eat or drink could notice lines of aversion on his face, lines bordering almost on disgust. He had really lost all appetite. But he would not blow his own trumpet, would not show it to the world. So he continued to take a little for the sake of form. This would naturally sound incredible but this life story will reveal very many incredible phenomena, which, but for the fact that many perceived them, would appear so to any man of sound commonsense.

The search for a proper place for *tapas* or *tapa* [the Hindi equivalent of the Sanskrit *tapas*], self-burning, taking on oneself all that mortality would force upon man, began. But Hilsurang, despite its thick and leafy forests, did not have any spot that could be called suitable. Accordingly, the inhabitants of Jalamada requested him that he do his *tapa* at Jalamada itself, especially Rāmadittā ['the Gift of Rāma'] and Sevā Rām [one who delights in service, is lost and absorbed in it], for impressed had been these two with the person and the words of the Master. So the search for the *tapobhūmi*, the spot for ardent meditation, commenced, a few of his admirers assisting him for the purpose. Below the village was a lush green spot, where once stood an orchard, but divested it had now been of most of the fruit laden trees, except a few here and there. Reaching that spot, Gurudeva paused and stood still and silent, all lost in thoughts (or no thought!), with eyes closed and the body almost frozen into stillness. The devotees too stood silent, none had the power or the will or even the desire to disturb that silence and that silent figure, so awesome was the aura and so holy the dread. After full two hours, Ramaditta broke the silence and said in all humility, 'Mahārājjī, if the Lord so commands a hut could be built here. Today we give up this place for the holy purpose. A sacred place will it be for the times to come.'

The request evoked no response, the stillness and the silence continued, as if nothing had been heard, nothing noticed. A good deal of time passed before he spoke but in words strangely soft and slow, audible only to those that stood most proximate to him: 'This is the place, this is the spot where *ṛṣis* of old did their *tapa* in times ancient. There should be a spring of water too here.'

The words sent a thrill of joy and wonder among the devotees. They begged of him that they be allowed to construct a hut there. A rock stood overlooking the place where the hut was constructed. Gurudeva asked them to dig up some earth behind that rock, from where gushed out a spring of water, clear and fast, making the spot look more beautiful than before. At this very spot the seers of old had lived doing fervent ardour, burning away all that they were and theirs in *Agni*, the light eternal that burnt fierce and destructive within them. In that spot, where creation had died into God and God into creation, began the *tapas* to redeem the *tapas*, to redeem man and to redeem God. The date: March 23, 1938.

All the devotees were forbidden to enter the hut except for Seva Ram. Every morning he would carry half a litter of milk with some leaves of tea boiled in it, the Master's sole intake for the entire day; the twenty grams of cereals that he used to have earlier too were given up. After his morning bath under a spring of water that gurgled a little below the hut, he would remain, all the twenty-four hours, lost in *samādhi*. This ardent fervour, this *tapas*, soaked away almost all his blood, reducing his already frail body into almost a skeleton. You could, those who saw him then report, count virtually every rib of his and every vein. The pale complexion had become still paler but the wonder of wonder was that weakening, that paling brought out a strange, arresting glow in the complexion, overspreading the pale on it, or transforming it.

For five and thirty days went on that *tapas*, that fervent ardour, that absorption in *samādhi*. One night at the early hour of 2 A.M., Seva Ram was awakened from his sleep by a voice that sounded like that of the Master. He was sleeping on the roof of his house in the open to escape from the oppressive heat of the summer, almost at its zenith then. The place of *tapas* was at quite a distance. How could Mahārājjī, with his frail body, wake him up from such a distance? he wondered. Speculating about the possible cause of the call, he proceeded towards the hut, with a lantern in hand. He found the door a little open and entered the hut and prostrated himself before his Master, the lantern dispelling the darkness within.

'All welcome to you, *Premī*! Have been put to a great trouble and inconvenience!'

Seva Ram looked up but could not bear the transcendental radiance emanating from that transcendental face. He directed his eyes towards the Master's feet, amazement and wonder overwhelming him. In the meantime, other *premīs* too arrived, for they too had heard the call. They too saw that splendour and light and the peace resting on that visage, but peace informed by an incomprehensible and impersonal melancholy. There was hope in them, there were fears and there was the desire to look into that mystery, to plumb the depths that seemed immeasurable. But none could speak, could not even think of speaking. Silence absolute was their response to the not-event-able event before them. Gurudeva asked them to sit down, apologetic about the trouble he had given them.

'We await the command of the Lord for which he was gracious enough to call us to his presence,' said one of them.

In words soft, slow and barely audible said the Master, 'The purpose has been attained, the goal achieved for which was undertaken this sitting. Today, the term of the stay here too is at its end. To tell you all this has been given this trouble at this unusual hour.'

Seva Ram: We do not feel troubled, we do not feel inconvenienced. Blessed are we that we came to behold the Presence before us!

Gurudeva: Noble *Premī,* at the break of dawn, *This* will bid you farewell. What should *This* do to repay the trouble *This* has given you? A poor one is *This,* no possessions *It* has, no means of recompense. Yet bid *This* do what you will.

Seva Ram: May not the Lord speak about the trouble! We never felt it, never knew it.

Master: O.K. *Premī,* be kind enough to prepare some *prasāda,* gift of grace.

Immediately Sevā Rām went home to bring the *prasāda*. The dawn was about to break when he came back with it.

With his own hands, Śrī Gurudeva gave to each one present there the gracious gift in the form of *halvā,* the gift of grace which sets the receiver on to the path to redemption. Such is said to be the power of that consecrated food. Meanwhile the dawn had brightened into morning.

And then said he: 'The time for departure has come. Your permission, *Premīs, This* seeks.'

Seva Ram: Let not the Lord add another sin to our life!

Gurudeva: *Premījī,* for fourteen years has *This* been in search of it, that what has come to *It* today at this place. This is the spot where during the days of the Vedas the sage Sanakādika did his *tapa* and this Jhelam that flows a mile down flowed then here itself. The future too will see this place sanctified, and the Lord will shower His blessings on you all.

Devotee: If this is the sanctity of this spot, then this slave of the Master would put a request before him.

Gurudeva: Noble Premī, *This* deems Itself not as different from you. Say your will and your wish.

Devotee: Mahārājjī, this place has been sanctified with your presence and was sanctified by the *tapa* of the *ṛṣis* of old. If the Lord permits, let there be held a *yajña,* holy sacrifice. Let others too be blessed by the holy Presence as we have been.

Gurudeva: Much will you have to spend, and much to endure!

Devotee: Mahārājjī, you the Lord Blessed himself will do all. What have we in us to undertake that blessed act?

With the permission granted, the devotees busied themselves with the preparations for the *yajña*. The people in the neighbouring habitats were informed and so were informed those at Kohala. The fourth day of the lunar month of *Jyeṣṭha*, according to the Hindu Calendar, was fixed as the date for the *yajña*, the day that fell in the third week of

May. A large number of people came to get a glimpse of the man who had done the thirty five day long *tapas* on the strength of a mere glass of milk-tea – many who tilled the soil, many who worked as labourers, many who owned shops, and many among the faithful from amongst the Hindus, the Sikhs and the Muslims. But no highbrow intellectual, for no one was there in that area, and no one from among those that administered or ruled. The poor came and those that belonged to what is called the lower middle class. Among them came too two young persons, just past their teens, who had, later on, the high privilege of serving the Master for long, one until the Master's *mahāsamādhi*, the final absorption in what *is*, the other until his own death. One was Banārasīdās, who came to be known by the epithet, *Bhagatjī,* the Noble Devotee, and the other Thākur Dīvān Singh. Companions were they two, more than companions, more than friends, what one willed the other did. The Sanskrit *sakhā* would the better description, *sakhā*, the same-named, and, for this reason, sharing in the same being. Both bowed low before the Presence and sat down, all devotion and silent. Gurudeva was not in *samādhi* at that time and sat, all awake, under the shade of the tree near the hut. Looking at them, he said, 'Wherefrom come you two, *Premījīs*?'

Banarsidas: I know not wherefrom do I come, Great One!

A smile appeared on the face of the Master but soon he withdrew into his self, his eyes closed, the face turning into the awe-inspiring enigma, the desertion blank of all that could be called human. For long did Banārasīdās gaze on the Presence that was naught, and speaks thus about what he saw and felt then:

> The body was weak and frail, so weak and frail, so destitute of flesh that one could see every rib of it, every bone and every vein. Even then the mind was so fixed on it, so absorbed, that I could not think of leaving the place, did not have the feeling and will

> for doing so. From the depths within depths in me I could hear as it were the voice: 'O Banārasī, here is your anchor, here is your support! From here alone will start your way, way the true. Your peace is concealed here, your bliss dwells here, their secret and their being.' For the first time I knew what peace is, what tranquillity is. Never had I known it, never felt. Lost was I in thoughts like these, when the eyes of Mahārājjī opened; from the deeps of the deeps he was coming up, from the depths of *samādhi*. I felt as if he was attracting me towards him, dragging me towards that presence. 'Premīs,' said he, 'go you now, for the day comes to its end.' Having uttered these words, he was lost again. Darkness was descending upon the hills. But we, both Dīvān Singh and me, could not move, could not leave that Presence. Again his eyes opened and he asked us to go. But we lingered on for some time more and then prostrated ourselves before him and left the place....

The day of the *yajña* arrived. Every devotee, with no exception, worked with dedication, with devotion, with feelings of joy and tranquillity despite the long labour lasting for days. There was no sign of weariness, none of tiredness or a trace of it. Fresh and energetic they worked, from one to all. Followers of every religion participated in that *yajña*. There were Hindus busy with making offerings to the sacred fire, the Sikhs to do the continuous, uninterrupted recitation of the Holy Book and there were Muslims to read the *suras* and verses from the Quran. When the Hindus had poured their offerings, they came to him with a request to make the final offerings; the Sikhs came to request him to offer the last petition, and the Mulims to say the last *namāz*, the last prayer. He heard them all, the Hindus, the Sikhs and the Muslims and uttered these, his words:

> *Premīs* of the Lord, the last offering has already been offered here, the last prayer said, the last *namāz* performed. Complete your rituals and rites and then assemble here so that something could be said about, some contact made with that which IS.

They completed their rites, said their prayers, offered their final *namāz* and assembled to hear the words of the Truth. Of bondage he spoke and of freedom therefrom and of the way that could lead one from one to the other, from bondage to liberation. Of the inevitability of suffering he spoke, of the pain and anguishes of life, of the tragedy that it is. And of the way that could bring about the end of that suffering, that pain and those anguishes, the end of the tragedy we call life. If they wanted to live the life true, live it here itself, life free from every fret and fever, they should take to the life of simplicity, to reduction of desires and wants and live as the Lord willed them to live, with their own will surrendered unto His will, for it was in that, in His will, alone lay their peace. His body was weak, alarmingly frail, but the voice was firm; the conviction of the truth of what he said overpowered the weakness of the vocal cords and of the lungs. The words were simple and colloquial, the language like that of the non-learned. No high quotations were there, no high flown sentences, not a ring of what they call eloquence. One could not distinguish the style from the content.

Many among the audience sought refuge in him, requested and beseeched for a place, as they put it, at his feet, to be accepted as his disciples, to be set on to the path that led to the truth he spoke of. Two among them, Baṇārasīdas and Dīvān Singh, dedicated their entire life to his service. That was the result of one short 'discourse,' a living confirmation of the truth of the ancient saying that it is the guru that chooses the disciple, not the disciple the guru. A seer gives *upa-deśa*, he simply points out, he does not give discourses, does not move to and fro, as the Latin etymology of the word would suggest. Only the thing stands out when he speaks, not the word or the speaker.

But to resume our story: The *upa-deśa* over, he gave his blessing to the assembly and asked the *premīs* to distribute the *prasāda*. By that time the sky had come to be overcast with dark clouds, sending down rain in torrents, threatening to spoil the preparations made with hard and sustained efforts. Seeing their anxieties and worries, he said, 'Take this too as His grace.' To the comfort of the devotees, the rain ceased before the things could turn uneatable and the distribution started. Those who served the guests were appeased as were those who were served. For days the devotees had worked hard and the day of the *yajña* was particularly taxing. But where was the fatigue and where the burden? With affection they served, with love and with humility and with devotion as if the guests would do them a favour by accepting their hospitality. With heads bowed, their hands folded, they made requests, repeated them, to each one of the guests, to take something for their sake, their satisfaction, even though he/she had had his/her fill. Such was the spirit, such the atmosphere that prevailed in that *yajña*, and, as many would affirm, in the *yajñas* to follow.[7]

The congregation dispersed, the day melted into the evening, the sun going down behind 'the mountain of setting.' The guests made obeisance to the Master, one after another, each receiving his benign blessings. Those who had served them, till then fasting but satisfied, looked long at the departing rows of people, for love had gushed up in them even for those they never knew personally. People love individuals, but here they loved the crowd. Each one among the crowd, each stranger seemed their *ātmīya*, the sharer of their being, their self.

Bidding goodbye to the *saṅgat*, the devotees presented themselves before the Presence. 'Saṅgat' is the colloquial form of the Sanskrit '*saṅgati,*' going together, going towards the same goal, attaining to the right, the real, end. In the presence of a seer humanity attains to, turns into, *saṅgat*, into *saṅgati,* feeling a deep sense of existential and ontological[8] affinity with others, rather of existential and ontological identity with others. To be in his presence is to be in presence of one's being, one's truth. That is why, association with a seer is termed *sat-saṅga*, association with one's truth, one's being. So no one among them thought of rest, despite the long and hard exertion. The Master recommenced the *upa-deśa* before the devotees quoting chapter and verse from the *vāṇī*-s of many a saint of medieval India, but not a word of his own *vāṇī* was mentioned, not an inkling given of the fount that flowed within him. They heard him with attention, rapt and concentrated, till it was 1 A.M., the time for his awakening into or, if you will, of his absorption in *samādhi*. Until that moment, none among the audience ever thought of sleep, it seemed to have fled from their eyes. They could think of the time and sleep only when he asked them to take rest. They lay down in the *kuṭiyā,* the hut, itself, going home at that hour was unthinkable. Here they lay down to rest and sleep but Śrī Gurudeva went down towards a forest nearby for his solitary *samādhi*. His days belonged to others, but his nights were his own. What was that state, that being, that life which he became one with in the solitude of jungles?

We know the revelation he was vouchsafed when he was a mere lad of thirteen. Full two and twenty years had passed away since that time. What distances had he covered since then and what did he find now which he had not found then? The revelation, we know, was the revelation of the Truth and Being, of the Anchor and the Ground of man's being and of the world in Which birth, life and death had become one moment. But it was a revelation of that Being in the form of Thou. He was yet to rest in that Thou, had to lose himself into It. Now the I and the Thou had merged to turn into ...[?]. None can say what became of the Thou and the Me then. From that state, the *Taittarīya Upaniṣad* says, speech returns, along with the mind, finding it not – *yato vāco nivartante aprāpya manasā saha.*

We may turn to the *vāṇī,*[9] to the word without the speaker, to get a glimpse of, merely a hint of, what was found in that moment when he called the dwellers of the tiny hamlet Jalamada to his presence. The passage I wish to refer to is loaded with dense symbolism, that of the Islamic as well as that of the Hindu scriptures. So an interpretive rendering of it will alone be possible, not its translation, which only a seer could accomplish. The reader will forgive me for this attempt to reduce the sublime, the absolute sublime, into the ordinary, maybe less than the ordinary. That it might turn bathetic in my rendering of it is my worry and fear.

> Sitting on the earth, with his consciousness established in the sky, shall he find the knowledge that burns up all and blows out all, from the earth to the sky, from consciousness itself to its content and intent.
>
> This *tana*, this growing and expanding body, is the *masjid* [mosque], the place to make the *sajadā*, obeisance. And *prāṇa*, breath, is the carpet whereon to do the *namāz*, to make the call true to the invisible and the unapproachable. Offering of the self-hood, of the me and the mine, is the obeisance. When the sense of me and mine attached to the body has been given up and breath has mingled into the all-blowing air without, then let that man-cosmos make a call to the beyond, to the invisible and the unapproachable. When thus dies the man-world into the unknown and the unknowable, then alone will he find the secret of That which sustains, will find it in this his very body.
>
> There will remain then neither the guide nor the guided, neither the teacher nor the disciple, for will he have forgotten then that there ever was the Prophet and the Message. With the sense of the master and of the follower gone, of the Prophet and what he said and taught, let him kill his mind and rise up to the top of the fort, the flag of victory to pitch and fly thereon. He who lives thus, he alone is an *ārif*, one who sits above all that is, above the earth, above the obeisance, above the breath and the cosmos, above his calls and prayers, above the relationships between the master and the follower, the messenger and his message.
>
> For every moment of breath in him will he utter His Name, utter it in silence and in solitude, the Name turning into the sound immortal at the top of the fort, of the body. There will remain no awakening for him, no dreaming, no sleeping; neither will remain birth, nor life nor death, neither the beginning nor the middle nor the end. The states these three will he have then transcended

> to rest and get absorbed in the Fourth, the state where birth, life and death become one, where the beginning, the middle and the end of the world turn into one moment. From that he will move on to the Fifth, the deep and profound one, the hardest one to reach, the state which has no support, no base to depend on. For the *base-less* base is it of all that he has left behind: what he saw, dreamt of and forgot in his sleep; his birth, his life, his death, and the origin, the duration and the end of the world, and of their merging into the Moment Eternal. But rare among the rare will he be, he who can undertake this pilgrimage from the state where nothing ever comes to be to where in not coming to be every thing and every being comes to be. Who can say what that state is, who can think of it, will ever try to imagine it?

That was the state he attained to, the state beyond becoming and being, beyond man and his *telos*, beyond the world and god, beyond time and beyond eternity. But was there a ***he*** to attain to that state, and more importantly, can we call what he attained to a state, and, still more importantly, was there such a thing as attaining or the one that attained?

With utmost hesitation have I paraphrased, with some explanation, mere eight lines from the *vāṇī*, undoing its rhythm and the voice of authority it has. A narrator poor cannot relate what the seer saw. Could I revive that symphony, that song and that movement, to borrow a little from Coleridge, the English poet, I would have conveyed to the reader an echo of the voice that one hears in the original. But that *vāṇī* is itself its speaker, it has no speaker, neither man nor god. To add a speaker to it in the form of a translator is to destroy it, to deform the revelation into a discourse.

Notes

1 Meditation here means self-oblivion, a holy trance and not conscious meditation.

2 'Derā,' the place of sojourn. Men and women of the world live in *gṛhas*, the *sādhus* in *derās*. *Gṛhas* are what have been seized. That is the word for houses or homes. A *sādhu* lives in the world as a pilgrim, his home is only a place for temporary stay, whereas men of the world live as grabbers and in 'the grabbed.'

3 *Vide* Chapter 1.

4 The thoughts that follow are based on verses scattered in the *vāṇī*. See, however, the *Samatāprakāśa*, pp. 309-15 and 365-67.

5 A province of the then State of Jammu and Kashmir.

6 This is all I could extract by way of description of the landscape from Bhagatjī and some devotees from Jalamada. I wish I could give a more concrete word-picture of it. I dare not describe the landscape as my imagination paints it before my eyes. I wish I had a fiction writer's license

7 The description given here is based on what the participants of the *yajña* reported to the writer, especially the Bhagat. In his memoirs also he briefly mentions the scene in question.

8 Sharing in the being or reality of others. See Heidegger.

9 *The Samatāprakāśa*, pp. 235-36.

4

The Teacher and His Disciple

After the *yajña*, the Master stayed on at Jalamada for a week. A number of men would arrive at 9 P.M. from Kohala and other neighbouring villages to enjoy the proximity of the person the like of whom they had never seen before. Those of Jalamada would offer them a rich hospitality. All of them came after having had their dinner but the spirit of hospitality of the hosts was such that they could find no escape from it. After this after-dinner they would sit near the holy Presence, their apparent overeating never interfering with their wakefulness; no dullness they would feel, no sleepiness. The time would fly away without registering its presence and the hour of midnight would come without a notice. An hour after the midnight, the Master would ask them to go back home. Jungles enveloped in the darkness of the night fell on their way, the luxuriant trees darkening all the more their darkness. But they felt no fear of the jungles and their darkness, the benign image of their Master replacing all their thoughts and feelings

A week passed away, flew away rather, when Rāmdittā, 'the Gift of Rāma,' came from Nakhetar Gaon to take the Master there, his native place. The Master consented to go there but only for a few days. But the few days were too many for the devotees of Jalamada. They walked, all of them without an exception, full three kilometres to see him off, the frail Master on the back of a pony, these walking behind on foot. On the way flowed a small stream called the Batoke; near its bank the Master stopped to ask his *premīs* to return, for a long distance had they covered. With eyes brimming with tears, they consented to return, Banārasīdās crying helpless as it were. Seeing their sorrow, the Master said with his usual calm and composure, '*This* is not away from you. Find *It* in your hearts. Break the worldly ties gradually, step by step. That is the way.' They prostrated themselves before him, one after another. The Master mounted the pony and moved away at a swift pace. But they remained there, as if tied to the ground. Not until he had disappeared from their sight did they return.

A few days later he returned to Jalamada. The time for the annual *yajña* at Gangothian was not far off, so he decided to go back there. The devotees, of course, were anxious to have a glimpse of the place which had 'given birth' to their guide, their guardian and a form visible of their own innermost being. For nothing short of that was he for them. So they waited impatiently for the day of the *yajña* to tread the ground of his birth, to besmear, as the Indian phrase and practice go, their foreheads with its dust. As for Banārasīdās, the future Bhagatjī, the very course and direction of his life had changed. Unhappy he lived and forlorn, running a shop at Kohala, that of tobacco, the forbidden thing. His condition was like that of a pure vegetarian condemned to sell meat, the very sight of a customer nauseating him. All the time he thought of his guru and of living in proximity to him, this exile from himself, spending most of his time in meditation or in writing letters to his Mahārajjī or waiting for his replies. In those days, Gurudeva often wrote his letters in the form of *vāṇī,* which Banārasī would sing in his sweet sonorous voice, again and again and again, or muttered it to himself. It was evident that running a shop was not his vocation, could not be.

Rains came to slake the thirst of the dry land, parched by the merciless sun of the Indian summer. The earth quickened back to life, a lush green carpet of the green covering it. The leaves of trees glistened fresh and bright and the forbidding dark of dense forests turned light and fascinating. With these transformations the rains brought the inevitable diseases and epidemics too and the killing fevers. They stalked the plains of the Punjab with deadly cruelty and fatal end. Banārasīdās too fell a victim to the seasonal fever, its intensity beyond the control of the poorly qualified local physicians. So he left for Rawalpindi to get himself treated at some modern hospital. But that was only a pretence, that journey to the city, for the very next day he left for Gangothian, the last place for any treatment. But he forgot about his malady, his pain and his fever the moment he reached the *rohānī durbar*, 'the Spirit's Court,' the term the more sentimental among the devotees used while referring to their Master's abode. He had all but lost his appetite but the Master made him eat more, much more, than he could ever eat when in his normal health. The protests were vain, for more one ate at the *guru-durbar*, he was told, the better would it be for one.

The following day too he was made to eat more than he could and fell asleep soon afterwards. For an hour and a half he slept . When he woke up from his deep and sound sleep he found Gurudeva fanning away the heat from him. Perturbed and distressed he sat up and took away the fan from the Master's hand. There can be nothing more sinful, nothing more dreadful, than to make the guru serve a disciple, for a guru is greater than the gods, higher than even God. That is the belief, the faith and the tradition that no one could ever think of violating. So imagine the state of Banārasī's mind, when he saw the unthinkable. He could only say, 'This way... .' The sentence could not complete itself, his voice choked with emotion, his thoughts bewildered by the sight. How could he pay back the debt, he wondered, how could he unload that sin off his heart? He sat at the feet of the Master, his tearful eyes directed towards the ground in shame, in fear and in awe. When he did look up, he found the Master gone deep into *samādhi*, the disciple brimming with devotion, fervent and self-effacing.

Before long the Master came out of the deepest of the deeps to say, 'The giving and the taking have to be completed. What *This* received in the lives past *It* has to give back, so have you too. That is the law unalterable. *This* would not like that *Its* disciples should serve *It*. Jesus, you know, washed the feet of his disciples. Different is the way the seers act and behave. What are you thinking of?'

Devotee: This slave of yours would find some room in the corner of your blessed heart. All the time would he wait upon the Holy Presence, at the gate of the Lord's abode.

Gurudeva: Where will you find the mettle, the heart for this? To live in the service of the dwellers in the nowhere, of those that have only the Lord as their abode, is not an easy affair; it is not a matter for your mind to decide and your will to endure. Go back to your mother and serve her! She must be anxious about you.

Devotee: How hard are the ties that chain one to the world!

Gurudeva: A lion, they say, can break open his cage. Summon up that courage and strength. If the Lord wills, the way will open up on its own.

Having said these words, obliquely encouraging and hopeful, the Master left for the Pīr Khwājā Forest, Banārasī following him. A beautiful place was that despite its solitude and, almost, frightening silence, the trees covered with green leaves, the birds chirping occasionally from among them. The Master sat under a tree thick with leaves, the place replete with thorns, but he neither cared to clean it nor spread a piece of cloth or something else to save himself from injuries. Soon he was lost in *samādhi*, oblivious of himself and of the forest and the thorns, the same [no-]expression on his face, the same awesome [no-]Person peeping out, the same Absence, the same [no-]being. Bhagatjī, the Devotee Noble, had seen this sight many times before. He knew that the Master would not come back to his human self for long, so he left for the pond of still waters at some distance to wash his clothes. The Master had still not come to be 'himself' when he came back, so he prostrated himself before that blankness and sat nearby for the man in Him to revive.

A deep silence permeated the forest, but forgetful of even that, he was lost in the Silence Absolute, the Bhagat gazing awestruck on that no-being, that presence-absence. Some time passed this way, when, to his utter surprise and amazement, the young Banārasī saw words flowing out of the lips of the Master, his eyes closed, the same no-expression still overspreading that face. The flow of words sent a thrill through his body, his hair standing on end, a joy overflowing from each and every pore of his body, light to the point of being scarcely felt. He took out a notebook from his pocket and started taking down the *bānī* in pencil. When the surge of words had flowed itself out, the Master's eyes opened and he saw what Banārasī was doing. 'What are you doing?' said he, 'Such acts will render you unfit for life; they will not let you remain what you are. No abode will remain for you, no resort; you will just be swept away. Go back and live and act as men of the world do! That is what you are born for.'

Devotee: I know not, I understand not why I feel a peace overspreading my being in the Presence, why do I feel this delight. Would to me that I lived forever at these feet and went on writing down these blessed and redemptive words that flow out of the blessed lips! Such is the depth of this peace and such the intensity of this delight.

Gurudeva: Hard is this living with *faqīrs*. But now recite what you have taken down.

The Bhagat recited:

From birth to birth have you moved, from death to death. Countless have been these, your births and deaths, in millions do they count them, sometimes low and sometimes high. Deep indeed has been your agony and deep indeed your delusion. How will this process end, this process of going up and going down, from one span of tragedy to another? Not until have you seen your truth and that of the world, seen their ground and their in-being will this end. But on your own you shall find them not, the ground and the in-being, for your finding has concealed them, your search for them, your very desire to know and be. You will have to find a guide, you with mind deluded, the guide true to your truth, to your being. His very sight will end your journey hard without an end, the very sight of him, of the guide true. For his truth will be your truth too, his being will be your being too.

Inhaled he the Name and exhaled he the Name and stopped not until his breath came to a standstill, revealing the secret of birth and of death. With that dawned the vision of the origin of birth and of the end they call death, burnt he himself into it, into the vision that made him ever born and ever dead. Even then his pilgrim continued. Restrained then he himself and kept he himself apart from this process of life dying into death and of death living into life. A witness thereof remained he, a bare seer, unconcerned either with one or with the other, or with their coming together. Hard he strove for this, for this distancing from that revelation, that marvel.

> All darkness was then dispelled from him, all attachments fell away, aloof he was from name every and form every, this once inhaler of the Name and its exhaler, of the Name at once proper and universal. Above did he sit from *Māyā,* that naming and enframing. And yet he had an impulse, this being with no impulse, the impulse to redeem all, for that is his being, to make all as one with him, to let nothing remain the *other*. For as long as the *other* abides, abide too shall he. And that he will not permit, for die must he the final death. That is his last impulse, to interiorise all, to be the all, to be each and every being, to die with each and live with each. For that will be the end of his own death and birth.
>
> In the Word alone will his mind abide, the Word no one can see, no one can hear, neither within nor without. The body will not remain for him nor will there be the mind. . . . Forgetful of them, he will abide in the Word, his Self. In that alone will he be an adept, in abiding in the Word, his Self, not in words, in sights and sounds. He will speak then a speech that takes no side, neither of truth nor of untruth, neither of this nor of that, for ambiguities there will be no more for it, ambiguities that make one's being and of all that one perceives. His speech will be truth itself, for no dividing line will fall between the word and its referent, his speech will be its own referent, for Being itself will it be, this his speech.
>
> That, verily, is the definition of the guru true, of the guide true to the truth: in his speech alone the word and its referent become one to turn into the Word. He sees with the eye equal all beings, be they high or be they low, for these are the distinctions not in the Word but in words. His knowledge will be of *samatā*, see will he all as one and the same, will see them with love, see them as one with himself. For that is what love is. There can be no caste for him, no clan or family, only the Truth does he behold, only That and nothing else, him they call the guide true to the True.[1]

Many other verses had been taken down, those too the devotee recited, recited with fervour and emotion, with a voice quivering and eyes brimming, sometimes overflowing, with tears. 'Great has been' he said, 'your grace, Lord, no bounds has it. Daily shall I recite them and live the joy I lived today, and the thrill and the ecstasy.'

'How much can you take down and how long?' came the reply. 'Your writing will end, your energy all exhausted, but this fount will flow endless, this grace abounding of the Lord. Days without a count have passed by and nights without a number, days and nights of this effusion of ecstasy and of revelation. The glory of the Lord has no end and no end can be of its celebration.'

For about ten days the Bhagat stayed there, his malady forgotten, his fever gone. But the peace could not last, not for long, neither did the joy nor the ecstasy. The Presence turned into a presence, a human presence, the ties of the world resurrected to make him remember that he was not alone, an alone before the Alone, but a being among other beings. The Bhagat had no choice but to ask for permission to go back home, remembering there was his mother worrying about him. So he departed, Gurudeva's elder sister accompanying him up to Rawalpindi. A long distance the Master walked with them to bid them farewell which, in the words of Bhagatjī, happened this wise:

> On the way, many a time I prayed to the Lord that he return home. But he continued walking, despite the requests, which he set aside with an indescribable affection. We went on until we reached the local school where all of us paused under the shade of the tree nearby. The Lord bowed before his elder sister. This slave of the Master touched three times the blessed feet. Going away became a difficult fare then, the ties were too strong for words, too deep for the ties of the world. Only the Lord spoke: 'Premī, you'll get late for the bus. So on you move.' Weeping helpless I took his permission and walked on. At a distance I turned back to see the Lord standing under the self-same tree. Of his overflowing grace I thought then, of him who had broken all our human ties.

The *yajña* was, comparatively speaking, a grand affair that year. Earlier, people from the surrounding villages alone participated in it. Now the number of the devotees had swelled a lot; from Kohala they came in large numbers, from Jalamada and from other villages of Kashmir. The *yajña* was held on Sunday, the twenty-fifth day of October. On Saturday itself preparations were afoot. The water was to be brought up from the Trail below, which the devotees did in drums big and large, placing them on their heads. Many cleansed the utensils; others made dough of the wheat flour. Huge fireplaces were dug in the earth. On one side *pūrīs* were being fried, on the other were cooked vegetables and pulses. At still others they prepared the sweet delicacy, *halvā*. The whole night was passed in making these preparations in the dim light of lanterns, for electricity had not reached the Indian villages by then, modernity was a distant thing. By eight in the morning preparations were complete. The Master had left for his solitude at the hour of midnight itself and returned at 9 A.M. He cast a long, penetrating look at the preparations and then occupied his normal seat.

With the break of dawn, *saṅgat-s* in numbers came with the rhythmic beats of *manjīras* and drums. Śri Gurudeva gave them an *upa-deśa* for about two hours after which commenced the holy feast. Before the food was served, Gurudeva stood near the preparations for about five minutes and sprinkled a few drops of water on them. He gathered a shovel-ful of *halvā* to indicate to the devotees the quantum they were to serve to each of the guests. The public kitchen seemed inexhaustible, for about two to three thousand guests were served and in a matter of about two hours. When the guests were gone, carrying large quantities of the eats with them as gifts, the Master tried to serve the servers the way he had served them the preceding evening. He had first put a garland of flowers around the neck of each one of his disciples and then, bowing before each one of them, had requested them to take the meal he had served.

But that day the disciples refused to let him repeat his way of hospitality; they placed a plate of the preparations before him and requested him, all humility, to partake of it. A half of a *pūrī* with two spoonfuls of *dāl*, pulses, he took.

That was his breakfast, his lunch or dinner, call it whatever you like. 'All that was taken by the assembled *saṅgat*,' said he, 'was taken by *This*. This, verily, is the truth. Now you, too, please, take your meal.' Then did the devotees take their meals, which for them were his *prasāda*, his grace. A large quantity of preparations still remained, despite the numbers and despite the extravagance of serving, and, to say what should not be said, the gluttony of the guests. The kitchen was really open, open to the public and all open in resources. What survived that virtual loot was distributed among the people of Gangothian; each home was flooded with food and delicacies.

Next day the devotees presented themselves before him, before 'his divine presence,' for the time for their departure had arrived. To each one of them he gave the *prasāda* in the shape of fruit and food, a turban and a gift of two rupees.

Astonished at this parting gift, one of them said, 'Gracious Lord, this place is for giving, not for receiving. Isn't it?' 'The *saṅgat* is verily the Lord, wherein dwell all beings. To Him is to be offered all that is His,' was his reply.

Banārasīdās too had participated in this *yajña* with his friend and companion, Thākur Dīvān Singh. Before this *yajña*, a few months earlier, his mother had passed away, her death causing him great grief. To assuage his sorrow, he had presented himself before the Master, who had spoken to him in these seemingly unfeeling words, 'The bonds of him who would seek refuge in the Lord fall off on their own. Take every event as ordained by His will, and remember your death. You will act rightly if you ever remember that you are only a mortal. In that alone lies your good, in this remembrance. There is no heroism like the one that frees you from this recurring cycle of birth and death.' Thereafter had flowed out the *vāṇī* calling upon him to see through the illusions of happiness and hope, see through the tangles of meaning one imagines into life. The words had their impact on the devotee, disillusioned he felt with every hope and ambition.

After the *yajña* all the devotees left for their respective homes but for Banārsīdās and Dīvān Singh, the two 'inseparables.' It was not in the nature of the latter to express his opinions or chalk out plans. His opinions would be the same as those of his friend and so were his plans. After a week could the two get the Master's permission to leave. The Master accompanied them, as earlier, up to the school and stood under the same tree where he had seen off Banārasī before. What he felt and saw, the would-be Bhagatjī describes in these words:

> The Thākur, his grandmother and I sat at his feet, tears streaming out of our eyes, rendering impossible any speech on our part. '*Premī*,' said the Lord our Master, 'Grieve not, for many occasions will come when you will have opportunities enough to do the service you so fervently wish to do.' Great heart was needed to seek his permission to leave but the permission was sought and was granted. I said, 'Let the gracious look fall on us poor too!' Saying this, I raised my eyes and lo! the wonder and the amazement. I could see, clearly see, moisture in his eyes. My hair stands on end whenever that scene flashes before my mind. 'Go, *Premī*,' said he, 'Lest you miss the bus. You will be posted about the coming programme. You may, if convenient, come here before *Its* departure.' With these words of affection ringing in mind, we moved forward, but looked back again and again until he disappeared from our sight. Only then could we direct our steps towards the bus stand.

Banārasī had no choice but to return to Kohala and open the detested shop. But before long another tragedy struck the family: his elder sister, who lived at Kohala, too, died, making him feel most poignantly the instability of all that we seek and love. His shop too had remained closed for over two months; no interest was left in him to resume the dreary work of selling and buying the hateful tobacco. The image of the Master followed him continuously, whether he was awake or asleep. Seeing no meaning, no purpose in the wretched life he was leading, he decided to close down the shop. He gave away all his wares to his brother-in-law and left for Gangothian. The Master, as his letter had informed him, was leaving for Ahamadabad on the 17th day of *Mārgaśīrṣa* of the lunar Hindu Calendar, falling towards the end of November or the beginning of December. With hope he went there and with anxiety.

The very next day Gurudeva left for Ahamadabad, covering first the ten-mile walk on foot to the Mandra Railway Station, Banārasī accompanying him. At the Mandra station, he requested Gurudeva to let him accompany him to Ahamadabad, which request the latter declined to accept, saying that he was still a boy, unfit for going out of home atmosphere. 'Look,' he added, 'on your way of life! This care for your looks and appearances! And the cut of your hair! As if you were some British gentleman! This style of life and the desire to live with *faqīrs*! No, this cannot be, simply cannot be!'

Banarasi's plans seemed to have gone awry. He had given up his little business to spend the rest of his life 'at the blessed feet of his Master.' The words of the Master made him feel abashed and embarrassed. When Gurudeva was waiting for the bus for the town called Gujjarkhan, the Bhagat left him on some pretext, went to the market place and got his head shaved. Gurudeva was amused by the look he bore, the shaven head and the shirt and trousers of the typical British style of those days! In reply to his question about this antic, Banārasī only repeated his request, to which he received the same earlier reply, 'Living with *faqīrs* is not what you imagine it to be. It will be an extremely hard and stern task.' 'Maybe,' said the determined would be attendant, 'this polluted mind and intellect will get purified in the company of the holy Presence. Let the Lord be gracious enough to accept this petition of his slave.'

Before the Master could say anything in reply, the bus came, and the two entered it. Gurudeva went to his sister's and the disciple to the market place to buy some coarse cloth woven on handlooms and got stitched a kurtā (a loose shirt) and a pyjama to complete the process of shedding his style of life. Gurudeva laughed to see him in his new dress but did not agree to take him along with him, saying the time was not yet ripe for what he had asked for, some other time, maybe, that might become possible.

Nothing could be said further, no reiteration of the request rejected so unequivocally and firmly. He sat silent and dejected, holding back his tears. Gurudeva made him have a meal and gave him a shirt, (kurtā), a pyjama and a turban and asked him, 'Take this, child, this *prasāda*, this grace.' The Bhagat could not think of accepting these things, for people, he knew, made offerings to their Master, they didn't accept gifts from him. So he said a 'No' many a time. 'Whatever the guru gives,' he was told, 'accept it without a question. You do not understand what it means and can effect.'

The train was to leave half an hour past midnight. The Master's sister and his noble disciple went to the railway station to see him off. Only one ticket was bought in obedience to the command of the Master. The train arrived punctual to the minute and the Master entered an apartment, the Bhagat going in to touch his holy feet. He came out and the train started, gaining its speed and, before long, its moving lights were lost in the darkness of the night. The tears, held back with effort, flowed down the disciple's face. With hope he had come, giving up all his belongings and means of livelihood, but the hope proved vain. There seemed no purpose left for him, no way and no direction. The whole day had passed in dejection but the presence of the Master had kept it within him. But now with his disappearance, disappeared all self-control, and he wept helpless like a child. All attempts by Devakīdevī, the Master's sister, proved of no use; his despair was too deep for words. Devakīdevī made him stay at her home for two days to console and encourage him but succeeded only in changing his tearful despair into a silent pain. He returned to Rawalpindi, counting his days, for each day was a burden and each night a fright. Despite promptings from his relations, he could not bring himself to do anything for himself. For hours on end he would do his yogic meditation but the atmosphere around him was too worldly for the purpose, too distracting, too discouraging. The only thing that consoled him was the letters he received from Gurudeva, which arrived at regular intervals. They alone sustained him, showing a faint glimmer of hope.

Months passed by but he could not chalk out a plan for his life or devise a means of living. Spring came to replace winter, breaking the seeds into sprouts, and sprouts into plants, and, at last, ripening the corn into gold and overspreading the fields with the flowers of mustard. The festival of *vasanta* too came to celebrate the reawakening of the earth, of brightening of the sky, of the renewal of life. As the fields wore the yellow, so did the people. Yellow kites flew high in the sky, those symbols of man's aspiration for triumph over the limitations and compulsions of earthly life. But the would-be Bhagat's soul would not stir up with the stirring up of the earth. Aloof he remained from the earth and her songs, and those of men and women and birds and beasts when they, all exultant, joined in joy the earth's celebration of her coming back to life. He lived as if in exile, far away from his home, the Master's feet. In the meantime, he received, written in the Master's own hand, as many as forty strophes of verse. One among them seemed to point out the way for those who can no longer feel at home in the world, for whom the earth turns into the Other, a place of exile and lonely despair. Again, the authorless Word would not accept a conscious translation, only a rendering of a part of its meaning.

> The spring, says the Word, has come. It is the time, O Man, to remember the Murāri, the slayer of the demon in man. Remember

him that slays the demon in you, for that will redeem this rarely vouchsafed human birth. And remember, remember the speech of music, the music that will reveal what this body of man is. For until then, until you hear not that speech of music, you will not know what this human body is. Here come and depart those that move and those that do not, stays here none, neither the living nor the inert. Desire burns all creatures and so does hope, be they born of wombs or of eggs, or spring forth from the earth or breed in waters. Spare they none, the hope and the desire, consume these all the creatures four-fold. Unreal is the body and unreal are its pleasures, out of delusions are they born, out of thought the perverted, both the body and its pleasures. A disease is this, a malady deadly, this they call desire or hope. Nothing can appease his hunger, of this ever hungry being, nothing can bring hope to this one-without-hope. No effort, no endeavour, no thought and no wisdom. So link yourself to the Truth, find the way to It, find the way to that place where blossom waits not for the spring to bloom, the blossom whose dazzling splendour will burn away all, from the beholder to the beheld, from man to earth to heaven. On that blossom will hum a bee, its humming all pure, for devour will it every shape and form. All will melt into it, into that sound that sounds where nothing is, where has been blown out thing every and being every. With all your awareness dead and gone, no more will desire burn you and no more hope. That will be the grace your guide the true will bestow upon you. Let you live as He wills you to live, be a witness mere of the body, of the mind and what sustains them, distance yourself you from these! That is the writ of the Immortal Person, heed it you, heed it well! Your tensions will be at rest and your conflicts firm and relentless. The bee will be intoxicated, finding the land where abides the Truth.

Seek the guide true that will make you *that, that* which ever is *that*, only itself and nothing else. For that is the drink of Immortality, prepare it ever, prepare *that* that ever remains itself, ever remains *that*. Your mind will come to be itself, will be lost in its self, when it comes to meet with Word the True.

The Word of the Vedas meets there with that of the Śaivas.[2] A bank is laid there to plunge into that confluence, the bank where groves bloom in full and forever, where spring does not come

> because it ever is there. There the mind comes finally to rest, on that bank and in that confluence. Maṅgat has seen the path to *that*, the path that makes one wonder [makes one wonder, for, ever nearby, it is never seen, ever familiar, it remains ever unknown].[3]

How many thoughts are enshrined in these words! A being of earth, a being placed and contextualised, man finds himself informed by the Other and ever alienated from himself. Never, not even for a moment, does he come to be himself, his overweening passion, the passion to be himself, ever remains unfulfilled, turns in the end into a tragedy absolute. So when earth stirs up into life, remember the slayer of the demon in you, the demon that makes you a sharer only of the joys of spring, rendering you forgetful of summer that will parch, and of autumn that wastes and of winter that kills.

You sing with joy, sing the songs human but you do not know the music that is hidden in your speech. That music you are to hear, for that will reveal the Being that dispenses life to your body. And when will you hear that music? When you do not seek to live, do not seek to die, when you live as life wills you to live and die as death wills you to die, when your life ceases to be a striving, when it turns into a mere event, and you a bare witness of the event. When, moreover, you let your breath exhale and inhale you with itself, when all tranquil you find yourself distanced from your eyes and ears. When you find yourself thus distanced from your eyes and from your ears, your thoughts will come to a standstill, you will not think of what your eyes perceive and your ears hear. A seer of the eye will you become and a hearer of the ear. In the ear then will sound a hum like that of a bee, a hum that will turn before long into a sound scarcely distinguishable from silence, a sound of silence as it were will it become. With the hum turning into silence or sound of silence, the silence ringing palpable in your ears, your thoughts of things without will end and so will end your desire for them, and with that will end your mind, that orientation towards the things outside.

As the hearer of the ear you become the hearer of the redemptive silence, as the seer of the eye, as the eye of the eye, you turn into the ecstatic seer of an enchanted world. The ordinary, the most ordinary thing will turn celestial, the familiar will become the mysterious, the old the new. The beauty that the season of spring can dispense to the earth will then appear a pathetic, poor thing in comparison with that celestial beauty. The barren, parched and thirsty land of summer will be no less fertile than the lush green of the rains, the luxuriant spring will be nowhere superior to the bare and bald autumn. And cool will be the heat of summer and warm the cold of winter. The earth will not remain the earth that we know of, it will turn into a land of magic, will wear the beauty of a dream and the impalpability **of the transcendental.**

So the bee, the mind, will sing in joy and perceive in ecstasy. And these will cause the death of the eternal spring, these, its joy and its ecstasy. So, let man be aware, palpably aware, of the tragedy that our life is, our being is, for only that can save him, that awareness, that palpable awareness. If he does not have this awareness, he will fall back again into the state of orientation towards the world, the distance between him and his senses will be annulled and he will find the world, once again, as the frightful and killing *Other*. If, however, he keeps himself in check and restraint and does not exult in the joy that results from distancing from the senses, he will find all forms and shapes melt into Nothingness. That will mean the end of all concepts in terms of which we cognise the things of the world, identify them as such and such, perceive them as such and such. If desire no longer comes to assail us, we will find our thought process almost suspended and ourselves distanced from the ethereal beauty revealed by the eye, from the sound of the ear and the peace of the mind. We will turn into breath, mere breath, will, all unconsciously, become one with it.

Concepts, however, will only turn unmanifest in that state, they will not die down. The world outside will have only been forgotten but it will not have died down finally and irrevocably. So, one must keep up distance from the joy and the ecstasy. When one succeeds in doing this, one no longer breathes; breath moves on its own *before* one, not *in* one. A moment will come, if one continues to remain steadfast in passivity, when the motion of breath will almost cease, when it will turn into a mere quivering, a flicker as it were. That will be the moment when the two ways will come to coalesce, the way of yoga and the way of the Vedas, the way of heroic endeavour and the way of passive endurance, of letting-be. The way of Śiva or yoga too turns into the way of a quiet fading out, the way of *presencing* death, when one becomes the passive witness of breath. For, it is by stepping out of breath that one becomes the Word, the unknowing witness of the still breath. What the Upaniṣads call the unknowing witness, witness innocent of himself, the *vāṇī* calls the Word, the Word that speaks unaware of its speaking. Consciousness of the self is the death of the self; similarly consciousness of the Word is the death of the Word. This obviously calls for an explanation and analysis, which can hardly be undertaken in a biography in any details. However, a brief analysis will be undertaken in the course of our analysis of the doctrine of ***Samatāvāda* and the ontology of the Word.**

Notes

1 See *Samatāprakāśa*, p. 608. A paraphrasal rendering is this, with some explanation added.

2 Or, the revelation and its traditional understanding of it.

3 *The Samatāprakāśa*, p. 195.

5

The Starry Pastures

The Master stayed at Ahamadabad up to February 1939 where two revelations descended, namely, *Yogacintāmaṇi* and *Cirañjīva-goṣṭha.* On the way back home, at Pachamari, another revelation manifested, which was given the title: *Amarakathā*. When he arrived at Gangothian it was but natural that the Bhagat should be the first to present himself before him. He recited, at the Master's command, the *Amarkathā*, made some corrections as directed and recited the *vāṇī* that the Master had written to him in his letters. He had rewritten the entire *vāṇī* in his beautiful handwriting. This pleased the Master, but who, he asked, would read verses like those?

'The drink of immortality,' said the devotee, 'flows out here, in the form of these verses, and in a language which everyone can understand, even those who never have had any education. This divine speech will save many a being that is lost in the mazes of the world.'

Not for long did he stay there. Silent he came and silent he went, keeping his desire to himself, the desire to spend his life as an attendant of the Master. The patience and the silence could not, however, sustain themselves for long, for within two months, in April, he presented himself again but could not summon up the courage to express his wish, thinking of the inevitable rebuff. So in four days he sought permission for going back.

Gurudeva: Where would you go, *Premī?*

Devotee: Mahārājjī, I know not where I shall go. The Lord dwells in all and knows the in-being of each and every being. We are ignorance itself. How can we know what we have to do and how to do? I came here with the thought of spending the rest of my life at these holy feet. But my Master is the Lord and it is his command that will be obeyed.

Gurudeva: Say clearly what you want?

Devotee: May the Lord let this servant remain at his service during the time of the ensuing *tapa*.

Gurudeva: It's no use staying with *faqīrs*. Do and live as men of the world do.

With these words, he granted him permission to go but added in the same breath, 'Shortly will you know about *Its* programme.' A ray of hope gleamed in Banārasī's mind, for he could hear a ring of a yes in the no. So he bowed before the Master, almost reassured. As before, he looked back, while walking away, to find the Master standing still in the verandah. A reluctant going back was it for him, his home was no longer his, had nothing in it that could evoke his interest. He thought of going back to the Master but the call of home, he found, had not yet become fully silent, it still had some force, some power.

Soon after his arrival at Rawalpindi he received a letter informing him that his Lord and Master would visit him the following day before proceeding to the mountains for the coming *tapas*. This was beyond his expectations, beyond his dreams. Not a wink of sleep could he have during the night; all the night he was only thinking of the Master and his grace and the joy of bidding the final goodbye to the ways of the world.

The following day, he went to the bus stand to receive the Master and bring him home. Blessed was that time for him, that moment, and also for his never failing friend and companion, Thākur Dīvān Singh. In a short while, the three left for Kohala and from there to the hut at Jalamada. A few days were spent there, the Master giving discourses to his disciples and others. One day, however, the Master expressed his intention of staying in some forest for *tapas*, for the time for it, he said, was drawing near. Casting a look at Banārasī, he said, 'Now, what is your programme?'

Devotee: Let the Lord be gracious enough to let this servant be at his service during the *tapa*. This alone is my wish, even though I know for certain that I am not fit enough to make this request.

Gurudeva: Do with diligence and with regularity what has been revealed to you for meditation. That alone is the true service of the Master, that alone, nothing else. Let your energy be spent on it, your mind absorbed in it. You have never lived in the jungles before. Full of danger are they and frightening. Beasts of prey prowl there. One's life is never secure there.

Devotee: Where dwells my Lord and Master, can there be a fear of the jungles and the beasts?

Banārasī thought that the Master would readily grant his wish but that did not happen. He remained mum, saying neither no nor yes. That afternoon a decision was taken that by the end of May [the sixteenth day of the month

Jyeṣṭha, according to the Hindu calendar named after the king Vikramāditya], a search would start for a place appropriate for the *tapas*. A day before the time of departure, the devotees of Jalamada again held a *yajña*, those people who by no standard could be called well to do. But such was the depth of their devotion for the Master that they would not let him go without the open feast for the people of the area.

An extensive search started two days after the *yajña* in the vicinity of places like Domel and Muzaffarabad, the latter town now the Capital of the part of Kashmir under the occupation of Pakistan. There were dense jungles around these places but not the kind of solitude and silence the Master wanted. Next day, Garhi Habibullah, a place in the district of Hazara in the North West Frontier, was chosen for the search. The day was spent in *sat-saṅga*; it went on late into the night, except for a short interval when Gurudeva went out to fix the place for his *tapas* at night. Accordingly, he asked the devotees to go to bed, which they did without a question, for tired and exhausted they had been all, including Banārasīdās who had so ardently prayed to the Master to let him stay with him during the hard *tapas*. He too was in need of rest, wanted it but could not, despite his sleepiness, help wondering how the Master could sit cross legged for as long as eighteen hours and then spend the night all awake in *tapas*. How could he serve him, wherefrom get the energy and the power to pass the superhuman ordeal? His train of thoughts was, however, interrupted with the words, 'Banārasī, what are you thinking of? In an hour you'll accompany *This*. Get some sleep till then.'

The Noble Devotee lay down and was fast asleep almost immediately. After about two hours, he was made to wake up and follow the Master into the thick darkness of the night. Other devotees were lost in deep sleep when the two left them, the Master in front, the disciple following him. A stream flowed near Garhi Habibullah, a bridge joining its banks. Crossing it, Gurudeva plunged into a deep ravine, covering quite a distance at a swift pace, when he ordered Banārasī to go back to 'the place of rest' and come back in the morning. He himself went still further down.

Completely dark was that night. Banārasī had brought a lantern with him but a strong puff of wind blew the flame out. What was his condition at that time is best described in his own words:

> I was helpless, for, I knew neither the place nor the way that could lead me out of the forest and the night. As long as the Lord was with me, neither the darkness had frightened me nor had the forest, nor had I any fear of falling down into the swift stream below. What was the Lord's will in throwing me into this situation? I wondered. As if the fearfulness of the place itself was not enough! And now that pitch darkness, where nothing was visible, neither what was before nor what was behind! I almost froze with fear, knowing not how to go back. Just one wrong step could prove disastrous. Add to this the clear possibility of becoming a feast for some wild beast. My nervousness changed into terror, I virtually trembled with fear. Never had I felt so insecure and so fear-stricken. But, then, in a flash as it were occurred a thought: 'Why this fear, my mind, why this agitation and nervousness? Can there be a fear for you, you who have taken refuge in the Great One? Sure is it he will protect you from every danger, he that is ever gracious to the lowly and the poor!' This thought gave me some relief, but only *some* relief. I resumed my walking, reciting the *Mahāmantra* to myself. It was, as I said, thick dark, a test of my nerves. I saw some frightening appearances, which, I soon found, were nothing but the projections of my own fear on to a tree. Whatever courage I managed to summon up was, however, washed away by the noise of the waters below. But continued I to walk, keeping before me the image of Mahārājjī. Near the bridge I found five or six tall strongly built men with guns on their shoulders coming towards my direction. When they came near, I uttered the Islamic greeting: *slāmālekum*, 'peace be unto you!' They responded to my greeting with the same prayer for me and went their way, silent, without inquiring about me.

> Reaching the *ḍerā*, the place of sojourn, I sat down, all silent, on the bed, for sleep had deserted me. The very first day was a day of test, hard and stern. But then a thought occurred: 'How free from fear are the Great Ones! What a life, what sublimity, the very embodiment of transcendence! Infectious is their fearlessness ... !' The entire night passed away in wonder and in awe. In the morning *Premī* Sevā Rām and Premī Bodharāj asked me, 'Whereto did you follow Mahārājjī?' My reply sent a wave down their spine. 'No one,' they said, 'goes there even during the day. You went there and came back too, alive and well!' I could only say that the gracious eye of Mahārājjī was always directed towards us. Where was the occasion for fear? But I know that I only concealed my own weakness with these reassuring words.
>
> With the sunrise, we all went to the place where I had left the Lord. There we saw the Holy Presence lost in *samādhi* under a tree in a field. All of us bowed down in reverence from a distance waiting for the moment for his descent from the transcendental heights. When we found him awake from the *samādhi*, we went near him and prostrating ourselves before him sat down respectfully at a small distance. 'This place,' the Lord said, 'is very calm and quiet but the people here are cruel and blood thirsty. At midnight some persons, armed with guns, passed this way and asked, 'Who are you?' From this side was given the answer, 'A *sāin*[1] is *This One*. *This* sits here to remember Him.' Hearing these words, they saluted and went away.'

Next day, the Master said, 'Let tomorrow be the day to depart far, far away from this place.' Many places in the vicinities of many a village and town were considered but none were found suitable for *tapas*. In the end, the Master decided to go to Nikhetargaon, the village he had visited in 1938 on the invitation of Rāmdittā. Nikhettargaon was situated at a height of 5,500 feet above the sea level and was surrounded by lofty hills and mountains. At a distance of about eight miles from the village and at a height of 8,000 feet was a forest called Baragali, dark and thick with not a single habitation for miles around. An ideal place no doubt for *tapas*, but for the disturbances caused by tree-felling then in progress. Accordingly, Gurudeva proceeded towards the summit of the mountain, a small plateau-like place, absolutely silent and remote from humanity with forest-covered mountainous landscape all around. The place and its awesome solitude immensely pleased him. The forest-lessee got a hut built in barely two hours, with a hole dug into the earth for fire and two trunks of trees so placed on the open side as to serve the purpose of a door. Even in that month of June, when the plains below lay scorched and living beings felt scalded as it were with the heat, this plateau was severely cold; you simply could not do without a fire, even for a while.

The following day, the devotees that had accompanied the Master left the place except for Banārasīdās. He had, we know, pestered the Master long for permission to stay with him and Gurudeva had reluctantly conceded to his repeated entreaties. On the third day, however, he asked Banārasīdās to go back, but the latter refused to be put off. With hands folded he entreated that he be allowed to serve the Master during the *tapas*. Gurudeva said, '*Premī,* it is hard fare to stay in jungles. Occasions may arise when you may have to go without food. Add to this the constant danger from wild beasts. You are still a boy and never had an occasion to stay with *faqīrs*. Disabuse your mind of the illusion it's a smooth affair, this staying with them. But stay if you must! God bless your noble resolve!'

Having said these words, Gurudeva went into *samādhi*. For long did he remain immersed in his depths, the young Bhagatjī gazing awe-struck at that familiar but forbidding presence and demeanour. When what we humans call 'normal consciousness' returned, Gurudeva remained silent for quite some time. Then said he in soft low tones, 'Think out on your own what you have to do from morning till evening and from evening till morning. You'll have, no doubt, some trouble in the beginning but things will smoothen themselves out shortly. Do unto *It* only what you are asked to do, never press *It* for unnecessary eating or otherwise interfere with *Its* programme. At the mealtime, wait not for *Its* coming back from *samādhi*: just go down to have your meal and bring the tea for *It*.'

The young Bhagat accordingly chalked out his daily routine of activities. Early in the morning, he would walk over two and a half kilometres down to a spring to have a bath in its icy cold water.[2] He would then collect a bucketful of it, wrap the bucket in a piece of cloth to protect his head from its bitingly cold touch, and carry the bucket for Gurudeva's brief bath. After that he would again walk down almost two kilometres to have his meal at a kitchen where food for the forest labour was cooked and prepare tea for the Master. This tea was the Master's sole intake in twenty-four hours and consisted of one and half quarter of a litre of milk and an equal measure of water. This three-fourth of a litre of the water-milk mixture, so to say, he would take at 9 A.M. After having the tea, Gurudeva often went into *samādhi*, and the Bhagat into the jungle to collect wood for fuel. When he returned, he would always find Gurudeva lost in the awesome depths within him.

Here too, in that dangerous solitude, the Word pealed into words but not, as before, to fade into the silence of the sky. Daily would Banārāsī see that miracle, see Gurudeva, his eyes closed and oblivious of the world, sing verses for hours on end, without an interruption. Banārasī had, we know, seen this phenomenon earlier too. Then it had struck him with wonder and awe, but now he felt elated and thrilled, with tears flowing down his cheeks.

Five or six days passed away in a happy trance, so to say. One day, however, he thought of taking the verses down and put the request before the Master at the very first opportunity.

'Would the Lord permit me to take down the verses he has memorized?'

Gurudeva smiled his kind and soft smile and said, 'Ever old is this affair, ever new, this peal of *prakṛti*, of that Creation before Creation, that primal doer.[3] The voice of Nature arises to mingle into its air, its breath. This being remembers not what it says. What d'you think of these numbers that flow out anew this way?'

'I think the Lord first composes these verses and then recites them from memory.'

'O you Innocent! *It* is not a maker of verses. Of God-intoxication is this flow and of divine ecstasy, absolutely spontaneous and unpremeditated. No thinking is involved in it, no conscious 'making.' In that state even an illiterate man will sing, unwearied, the glory of the Lord. Whatever gets uttered here will ever be replete with wisdom, will be revelation itself. As the verses (*āyat*-s) revealed themselves to Mohammad and the Vedas unto the *ṛṣis*, so does this *bānī* (*vāṇī*), this speech. It will be some time before you come to understand all this. Take every word that manifests itself here, as you'll take the word of the *Bhagavadgītā*. Now things are out of *Its* control; the ecstasy and the bliss will not be contained – irresistibly is it flowing out into these strains. Who knows what the Lord wills by prompting you to act the scribe? He alone can count the number of verses that have mingled into the air of the jungles all these years. *It* is indeed surprised by your persistence. *It* tried to resist your will, but that was not to be. Compelled is *It* to sojourn here in this wilderness. Of Kabīr's *bānī*, revelatory speech, how much came to be actually written? Kabīr himself said:

> Sixteen billion verses of wisdom did I utter, and yet remained concealed the Word within. The Word, O Dharamdās, would not come out. Verily, I tell thee, again and again.

'A mere fraction of Kabīr's *bānī* came to be recorded. Serve the world, as much as you possibly can. Some beloved of the Lord may, someday, chance upon it, upon this speech without a speaker. Thus may your life find its purpose. Now, what do you understand of this affair?'

Devotee: Now do I understand how these verses resemble those of Kabīr, Dādū and other sages. They too must have uttered them as the Lord does.

Twilight was slowly descending on the mountains and the forest, enveloping them in its fold. Banārasīdās fanned the fire into flames, lighting up a warm glow in the hut. Gurudeva asked him to recite some bānī [*vāṇī*] of a saint. Accordingly, Banārasī recited from memory some *vāṇī* of Kabīr, Sahajobāyī and Dayābāyī.[4] Recitation over, Gurudeva said, 'If you want more of such numbers, then take them down.'

The young Bhagat immediately improvised an inkpot. He had with him an old notebook, with many leaves torn out. There was no arrangement for a light in the hut, no lamp, no lantern. So he fed the fire with some more fuel. Flames leapt up bright and smoky, giving out enough light to read and write. Gurudeva went into *samādhi* and the flow of *vāṇī* started, continuous and without a pause. There was no hesitation, no brooding or waiting for the 'right word.' As water flows out continuous and uninterrupted from a snow-fed spring, so was the effusion of those rhythmic words. Try as he might, the pace of Bhagatjī's writing could not synchronize with the pace of the *vāṇī*. In a short while his fingers got numb. With a timid hesitation, he requested for a natural speed of dictation. Gurudeva opened his eyes to find the *vāṇī* recorded rather poorly.

He then dictated with the eyes open until the scribe picked up the requisite speed, which he did in barely three days. He also improvised some system of shorthand, which often dispensed with vowels. From the fourth day onwards, the dictation would continue past midnight, often up to 1 A.M. At that time the mountains wore a look of dread: they presented a series of outlines rearing their ominous heads into the depths of the sky. The oppressive silence of the landscape was often disturbed by the varied sounds of the wind that blew now softly and now with a terrific speed. Occasionally the place shook with the roars of wild animals, whether tigers or leopards Bhagatjī could not tell. Frequently the sky got overcast with thick clouds, with their deafening thunders and fearful lightning. That was the time and that was the place the Word had chosen for its peal. When the flow of revelation came to a stop, the Bhagat would rub Gurudeva's legs and feet, benumbed by continuous sittings – for almost 24 hours each and every day. Only then would he lie down for a few hours of sleep. But not Gurudeva, who would remain lost in *samādhi* until the sun rose to bathe that wild place with its soft light.

One evening, Gurudeva asked the Bhagat to go to bed rather early. That night the clouds had gathered into a thick blanket in the sky and rain fell in torrents interspersed with flashes of lightning and peals of thunder. All was dark without. But Banārasī did not seem to notice its non-human look and appearance. He went to sleep, peaceful and happy, for full two hours when Gurudeva woke him up and asked him to feed up the fire.

Rubbing his eyes, the young Bhagatjī, true to the name he was soon to be given, woke up and fed the fire into bright and warm flames, a cosy contrast to the dark cold that poured on the mountains without. 'Take up your pen,' said the Master, ' and take down the effusion of the Lord's rapture!' Immediately he sank into *samādhi* and the Word pealed out into words.

> On his own the Lord has appeared, the killer of the demon in man, has appeared in this my body, and in a form wondrous and playful;
> In the flame high up-leaping a treasure opens up of gems that flash and surpassing burn;
> Alive shall he die unto himself and unto the world that but catches a glimmer of them.

> There sounds the *nāda* that sounds not in time nor bound by space, and thither shines a splendour as if had risen suns in their tens of millions.
> In a hole in the sky flows the fount of nectar where abides the Word infinite, killing of his beholder the mind and desire.[5]

This is a paraphrase of a few of the lines that flowed out that night. The other lines have not been paraphrased because of their dense symbolism, which no rendering can convey without a detailed analysis and commentary. So I postpone the discussion of their content until I come to discuss the being of the Word and its expression in the form of revelation and the relationship of the revelation with our ordinary human language and discourse. Here we have to stick to the narration of events and of the phenomenon of the spontaneous flow of the *vāṇī,* the revelatory speech.

So to return to our narration: When the flow of the revelation stopped, Gurudeva came back to 'normal consciousness.' He asked the young Bhagat to go to bed and read out the verses the next day. That, the devotee soon found out, was his normal practice: to go back into the silence of *samādhi* after the divine creative energy had spent itself out and ask the scribe next day to read out the *vāṇī* to know the contents of those verses, for during the time of the dictation he was not conscious of what he uttered. In this respect, the following conversation between the Bhagat and Gurudeva (Thatta, November 1941)[6] is quite revealing:

> 'Lord, the divine speech flows out mostly in Hindi, whereas you never learnt this language; you learnt only Urdu.'
>
> 'Words come out as my Lord wills. *It Itself* is surprised whenever you read them out. *It* does not know when a particular verse was uttered, **nor does *It* know whether it was the right sort of thing or not.** *Premī,* this being has no choice or will of *Its* own. Stern, indeed, is the command of my Lord. *It* has no say in what He wills *It* to say. It is for the good of the living beings that the Eternal Word is revealing Itself in words. My Lord's grace

manifests itself in accordance with the needs of the time and place concerned. It can descend as easily and spontaneously in Sanskrit or in English as in Hindi. But *It* has no option in the matter, no choice; *It* has to present unto you whatever flows out on its own. Preserve it if you like. In the times to come the country will evolve this kind of simple language. The mixture of dialects that you find in the *bānī* is in accord with the needs of common people. Seers instruct people in the language they use and understand. And seers of this order are born in every time and clime. Mohammad was not the last prophet nor were the [Sikh] gurus the last gurus. Divine glory will manifest itself whenever people give up the right ways to follow the wrong ones, whenever they come under the grip of *rajas* and *tamas*, of the desire to acquire and enjoy the things of the world and of the passion to remain immersed in them. The voice of the *sat-puruṣas*, of the Truth-become-s does not fail to reach the good people – it matters not where these seers stay, near the people or away from them. For, that voice intermingles with the atmosphere and finds its way into the hearts of the good – unobtrusively and without their conscious knowledge. And the good people, under its influence, do good to the world at large. The thought of *samatā*, of sameness, has reappeared in a new form in this *bānī* (*vāṇī*). It will have its impact in due course of time, not now.... Only those who are established in the truth can awaken the world into the right way. The country that deviates from *samatā* will not survive nor will the laws that do not accord with it do any good to anyone.'

Another conversation regarding the manifestation of the *bānī* that the Bhagat had with the Master on those solitary heights themselves is also instructive:

'The Lord speaks out words of divine revelation continuously and uninterruptedly and pours out scores of verses in a matter of a few minutes. But while correcting a small mistake I inadvertently commit, he takes as much as two or three minutes!'

'When the divine rapture pours itself out, the intellect comes to be inoperative, does not think in terms of the dualities of right or wrong. In that state of wakefulness, no wrong word can possibly get uttered. Only your carelessness or inadvertence causes certain mistakes to creep in. ... It is only when the intellect gets oriented outwards and emerges out of the state of oneness with the Real that it starts thinking about linguistic or other problems. When the intellect is merged into the Word, spontaneously rise up right thoughts and on their own the revelatory words, no thought-activity, no thinking goes into their making. Nothing remains concealed in that state, neither the world nor its Creator. Hidden secretes open up – with absolute clarity. But knowledge of the things of the world is not the right sort of knowledge; it does nothing but ill to man. That is why findings about the world are not heeded to. Only the thought that soothes the unhappy into peace is revealed ....'

We have to linger on these words to clear up many misunderstandings that are prevalent among the faithful. First, the man that utters the *vānī* is not the Word. He is as much a recipient of it as are other human beings; he too has to understand it and to reflect upon it. He can, of course, enter into the source of revelatory words easily because he can, whenever he likes, go beyond his senses, his mind and his intellect. Only the seer that succeeds in embracing that death, death of his senses, his mind and his intellect, can become, the *vāṇī* declares, the seer of the truth, the seer that does not know that he is the seer. That seer alone is the Word, the Word that speaks without knowing that It speaks. Only that Innocence is the truth as well as its revelation. That alone manifests itself in the form of the *vāṇī*.

So the faithful should understand that their saviours and messengers and their gurus have two selves, one self is the Word, the other is the human person. They should not confuse the two. Every prophet is the messenger of the truth when the Word speaks in and through him, but not when the man in him speaks. The man in him shares, to an extent, some limitations of human nature. Every guru can commit mistakes, does commit them, can be calm or disturbed, patient or restless, depending on the factors of his birth and training. His personality is not the Word for he becomes the Word when he dies into It. But before his body actually comes to fall, he will move from one state to the other, from the Word to the man and from the man to the Word.[7] Of course, the man will be extraordinary, more than extraordinary, for one who attains to the Word cannot remain an ordinary man. The life of Gurudeva is an example of the truth of this statement. But that does not mean he had no human limitations, that he did not, on occasions, commit mistakes or that his opinions were always revelations. His opinions were profound and deep but not infallible. His actions were amazing, wonderful, dazzling, a challenge to the limitations of human nature. But still it was human nature that he embodied, though human nature the extraordinary and transcendental, but, nevertheless, human nature. Christians should never feel embarrassed by the last words of Jesus, for it was the man that cried and felt forsaken by God, not the Word. That was the moment of final death of the man into the Word. And let us not forget that it is the Word that is the Son, the Prophet, the guru, and not the man. The reader may excuse me for this rude interruption in the narrative; it was necessary to dispel many misunderstandings that crop up among the faithful, leading to fanaticism and all the evils related thereto.

The unknown became the known in the *vāṇī,* revelation, not the unknown knowable but the unknown unknowable. That from which speech returns along with the mind finding it not – *yato vāco nivartante aprāpya manasa saha* – was itself turning into speech. That was the miracle that was occurring in that terrible solitude, in the thick forests where death roamed free, whether it was day or night, clear or cloudy. And blessed was the man who heard the revelation and acted the scribe, the man who did not hear the Word but who did hear its voice, its descent into our human speech that otherwise ever remains distant from its referent, that chain of mere signifiers without the signified. Man is a creature fallen from his being; his voice rises but only to come back to him, reaching not to the One it is addressed to. But he will not find himself such an exile if he finds himself in the presence of a seer who has not only heard the Word but has become the Word, has died into It:

> The very truth will come unto you and the very being of being when you come into the presence of a seer blessed, his holy presence and sage. Of the holy great is this glory great, thus Kṛṣṇa sang unto Dhananjaya, of every contest the Winner.
> Blessed is the seer, blessed is his company, blessed the grace he showers upon you. The mere dust of his feet will undo thy sins, a million ten of them. Such is his glory and of his blessed presence and compassion.
> A sharer great is he, sharer of the Good, the man that serves a seer true. Sins of his a mere look will burn, look the blessed - sins of the now and of the fore.
> The seer is the Creator that dies into creation, the seer is the Sustainer that dies with creation, the seer is the Destroyer, the Death that redeems. The visible form is he of the Invisible, that home immortal of the homeless mortals.[8]

In the morning Banārasī read out all the twenty-six lines of the *vāṇī* he had been dictated to at the night, a few among which were presented in a paraphrase above, beginning, 'On his own the Lord... .' After his and the Master's bath, he went down to the camp of the tree-felling labour to have his meal. But he found, to his dismay, that the meal had not been cooked. Nor could he find Parmānand, the son of Rāmdittā, who used to look after the cooking. It was getting late, so Banārasī decided to cook himself his meal and took a tin and an empty sack to cover it in order to fetch water from the spring about 400 metres down. On the way he saw a huge tree being cut, a thought flashing across his mind when he approached it: 'If this tree falls upon me, not a bone will remain, all will be over.' His eyes were fixed on the tree, all unaware was he of the path – a virtual bed of dry and dead leaves. Heedless of the slippery leaves he walked on, sizing up the size of the tree. So his foot slipped and he found himself sliding down the slippery slope that led to a deep ravine below, the tin and the sack thrown aside, the sound of the falling tree deafening his ears as it were. For two or three minutes he continued slipping down until he reached a spot free of dry leaves, the slipping coming to a halt. Motionless he lay for a few moments before he stood up to find, to his astonishment, that he had received no injury. But soon he found his foot bleeding profusely, a sharp point of a dry hard stick having pierced into the flesh. He looked up and saw the tree lying precisely on the spot from where he had slipped. There stood some men, saying, 'A fortunate one indeed! A fortunate one indeed!'

'How gracious of Mahārājjī!,' said he to himself. 'Death was the wage fixed for my past sins which he, with his grace, reduced to this trifle of an injury. How kind are you my Lord and Master, infinite is your compassion, O You who are nothing else than the Lord of the universe Himself!'

He rubbed away the blood and pasted a layer of earth on the wound, found out the tin and the sack and brought water from the spring to the camp where he made two loaves of maize flour and ate them with salt. Thereafter he prepared tea for the Master. On the way up he thought of the Master's annoyance, for the time for the tea was long past. Reaching the hut, he placed the bowl of the tea before the Master, poured a few draughts of it into a small cup and offered it to him, keeping his gaze fixed at the latter's feet, daring not to look up. 'How hard,' said the Master 'is it to live with *faqīrs*!' Looking up, Bhagatjī, that noble devotee, felt as if the Master was unhappy at the delay. Nervous, he looked towards the ground. But the Master's words conveyed something else. 'Grace too,' he continued with a broad smile on his face, 'remains with those that serve the *faqīrs*, follows them as if attached to them.' The kind and compassionate look brought tears into the eyes of that Devotee the Noble. 'Never can I,' says he, 'forget that look, that kind and gracious expression of it! It often haunts me, bringing before me the entire episode of the falling of the tree and my slipping down the slope. To serve a Great

One is possible only when one becomes a sharer in the Good, a great sharer in It. I did not deserve this privilege. It was only out of his grace, of our Divine Master, that he gave this undeserving one the opportunity to sit near his feet.'

It was on this occasion that the Master narrated to him the incident of his own slipping down the hill at Kallar.[9]

After the Master's tea, the Bhagat washed and cleansed the utensils. Seeing him doing so, Gurudeva said, 'Who knows how long, for how many births, have you been thus cleansing the utensils of the Truth-becomes! This staying here of you may have been the result of that cleansing. Render this service in every earnest now, with every care.'

Soon there arrived the forest ranger, its guard, along with some devout Muslims and their priest. Entering the hut, they saluted the Master with utmost respect and humility, including the priest. Gurudeva asked them to take their seats. 'Could we be of any service to the Great One who has only the Allah as his succor and support, and no worldly possession?' said the priest.

'To think of one-self as different from others, to look upon them as *others* is to be a non-believer; it is to deny the Truth that the Lord is. All that you see and experience is the manifestation of that Marvel, that Being. To worship Him is to see that Pure One, that Transcendent One, as immanent in each and every being, in each and every thing. That alone is His worship true. See Him everywhere, in each and in the all. Confined is He not within the walls of a temple or a mosque; these are only places for worship. Study the scriptures, immerse yourselves in them, be the scriptures the Vedas, the Bible, the Quran or the Holy Book [of the Sikhs] in order to make you pure and an abider in the truth. Let a man who devotes his life to these revelations free himself from every hatred and every complaint against others, let him refrain from these so that he may have the supreme insight into the Truth that is One, that has no form.

Let him know that Being through the insight pure and supreme born out of his giving himself up to the revelation dispensed to him. Let him be free from sectarian thoughts, for they bring about his ruin and end. Let him free himself from these and see the Infinite, that dispenser of life to every being from man to an ant. He it is that makes them alive and move. "The whole world is His manifestation": let this be his principle. Let him end, erase, the sense of me and mine. For, with its death, the death of me, will he know the Living Spirit in this body; that will bring about his liberation from the embodied form.'

'Holy Master, what is the meaning of liberation?' said the priest, 'Your words suggest that one is compelled to be born again and again until the death of the sense of me and mine. We do not know of this, this going and coming.'

'As long as there is desire in the mind, as long as it continues to spring up, the malady will remain, the malady of going through happiness and sorrow, pleasure and pain. And that is possible only through a body, not without it.'

For about two hours the priest went on discussing matters relating to bondage and liberation, fall and redemption and other matters relating to the goal of life. After this long conversation, he said, 'It was nothing but the grace of God that brought us to the Holy Presence. It was indeed ordained that we be blessed today.'

With profound humility and a sense of reverence, the priest and his associates left the hut, moving backwards, showing their respect for the Master.

The evening was approaching, the inside of the hut getting almost dark. Like on other days, the fuel was fed into the fire to dispel the darkness. With the coming of the night, the Master went into *samādhi*, the fount of *vāṇī* opened up, the faithful scribe scribing it as fast as he could. When the creative force had spent itself out, the Master descended slowly and gently into his human self to become outward-oriented. When he became fully conscious, he said, 'Enough has been revealed here. Other matters may spring forth at some other time and other place, if the Lord wills so.'

It was getting very late, the night had advanced much. The noble Bhagat was feeling very tired and longed for sleep. So the Master asked him to go to bed but before he obeyed him, he put in a request, 'Let the Lord bless us with couplets in the style of Tulasīdāsa's'.[10]

'Don't be greedy! Take rest and go to sleep.'

The Bhagat rubbed the Master's feet for some time and then went to sleep. In the morning, when he came into the presence of the Master, the latter placed before him some leaves of paper and asked him to read out what was written thereon.

Bhagatjī found that the couplets he had requested for were written on the pages before him, about two hundred of them. He read them out in his usual way. The first among them read like the following:

> The seers call ye to meditate the Lord; in that lies the meaning and the essence of life, in remembering His name. For the reservoir of bliss is He. Bereft of His name, let not an hour pass, let not a moment.
>
> Like the shadow of the clouds will melt into nothing this world and whatever is and happens here. So earn the wealth of the Name, the Name only few can know and find. Know it from the guru true that leads you to the Truth.
>
> This transient world is a false appearance; a dust inert is it, a wave mere of the mind. So meditate the Name so that your mind may cease to desire and to stir.
>
> Eight million and four hundred thousand is the number of creatures. Among these, man is the best and supreme. Only he, he alone, can meditate the Name in which are enshrined treasures all.

For years without a count, for thousands of them, have you been striving to be happy. But that always eluded you, the happiness you sought, and all the years passed away, all the births, futile and in vain. Never fell to your lot the joy true, the joy you have been ever striving for. Pleasures without a number you enjoyed, but could you ever feel a moment of rest when there was no fret to trouble you and no fever to torture you?

Empty handed you came and empty handed will you go, leaving behind all that you called yours, for nothing will go with you, nothing will accompany you.

Like a ripple is your life, restless and ever on the move, ever changing and never coming to be itself. Know this as the truth of your life; know this, you who they call the gifted and the glorious.

Like unto a tree on the edge of a river is your life. How long will you be patient, how long can you be safe? A wave has to swell to sweep you all away.

Like the fuel thrown into fire does your life burn. In no time into ashes will it be reduced. That is your life, into nothingness a burning. Maṅgat has found it such, a mere four-day tumult and despair.

These couplets were later on included in the *Samatā-prakaśa*, the collection of the *vāṇī* that flowed out of the hidden springs within the Master's soul. They were given the title: *The Chapter on Dispassion.*[11] For, that was the tenor of the entire *vāṇī* the Master had written in his own hand. This last point may raise a doubt: if the *vāṇī* is the revelation of the Word, its swelling forth, making the man in the seer its mere medium, could not *The Chapter on Dispassion* be termed a composition in the usual sense of the word? We have also mentioned earlier that there was a time when Gurudeva often sent his replies to the letters addressed to him in *vāṇī*. The *vāṇī* in the letters too could be considered as falling in the category of composition, of poetry as it is usually called. Was this *vāṇī*, then, a composition of the man or the voice of the Word?

A conversation between the Bhagat and the Master about the manifestation of the *vāṇī* during this *tapas* itself will throw some hint in regard to the matter in question.

> 'When and how does the *bānī* (*vāṇī*) that the Lord utters comes out so spontaneously and so rapidly, without any interruption?'
>
> 'When the Word manifests itself within man and the *buddhi*, the faculty of knowing, gets established in the sky, that is, in the skull, it, the intellect, understands the truth about each and of all. Who is the doer, and who is the living being, what is his origin and what is his end, what is bondage and what is liberation, what is right and what is wrong: it understands all these matters, ever and always, not for a moment does it lose knowledge thereof. **Verse and prose are of no account then; it can express all these matters whatever way it chooses, whether in the form of spontaneous verse or in the form of prose**. Whether it becomes outward oriented or inward oriented, it remains ever immersed in the Truth that knows only itself and enjoys only itself, for knowledge too it is and also bliss. The mode of expression in verse is chosen so that the glory of the Lord may not be distorted by mind-oriented beings [as they can easily do with prose writings]. **For a true seer there is no difference between the living and the inert, for all are the same Brahman, Its manifestations**, all that is inert and all that lives. But distinctions have to be drawn for instructing people and the limits and framework of their understanding too have to be kept in view.[12]

There was a frequent reference to the *Nāda*, Sound, in the *vāṇī*, including the couplets of dispassion. Banārasīdās became curious about it and said to the Master, 'Mahārājjī, you have glorified the *Nāda* in several ways: it sounds as thunder, shines like tens of millions of suns. A little rumbling in the stomach can be heard outside; the heat the one sun emanates is hard to bear. How is it possible to bear the light and heat of the suns in their millions? And how is it that the roaring thunder of the Word remains inaudible to others when it, the Truth-become say, resonates in each and every pore of their bodies?'

The reply was:

> The Word and the light thereof are beyond the reach of the mind, of the intellect and of the sense organs. The *buddhi*, the faculty of knowing, can know it but cannot express it.
>
> When that faculty, the *buddhi* [from *budh*, to know] gets identified with the body, it experiences heat and cold [and other dualities]. When it is lost in that Supreme Thatness, the *That* which ever remains itself, of which nothing can be predicated except itself, there remains neither heat nor cold. For, beyond the three modes of being is that Supreme Thatness: the mode of remaining coincided with oneself, the mode of *tamas*; the mode of changing, the mode of *rajas*, and the mode of transcending both these modes, the mode of *sattva*. Nothing remains of the *is* there, nothing of becoming or process or change, and nothing of the urge for transcending the states of *is* and becoming. That is your self, your true being where not a trace of these three modes of being remains, the modes of *tamas*, inertia, of *rajas*, of change and transformation, and of *sattva*, mode of self-transcendence. Heat cannot scald it, air cannot dry it and water cannot moisten it.
>
> As to your other question as to why the *Nāda* remains inaudible to others, the answer is: the power and ability of the Truth-become enables them to keep it within the confines of the body. Only they know this secret. A man who has reached this state ever remains lost in it whether sitting or standing, eating or not eating. Sleep, lethargy and hunger – the three defilements – come to an end with the manifestation of the Word. The Truth-become eat a little merely to escape from the gaze of the people of the world and in order to retain their normal human functions. Pretence has no room here.[13]

After telling Banārasī what was the *Nāda*, the Master took his cloak off his back and asked the Bhagat to place his ear on it. What happened to him is best described in the latter's own words:

> With misgivings and fear I did what I was told to do. I heard the continuous resonance of the secret *Mantra* into which the Master had initiated me. From the lower part of the back arose sweet and beautiful melodies, a symphony of them, to rise upwards.

> 'May I continue to hear them for ever!': that seemed to be my only wish, my only desire. For as long as my ear remained in touch with the back, my mind became still, bereft absolutely of every thought. But a moment later, Śrī Mahārājjī pulled me apart. But now certain I was, absolutely certain, that what the *bānī (vāṇī)* revealed was the truth. There remained no room for any doubt on that account.

What was it that he heard, what form of the Word? Not, for sure, the Word that is the home of all that is, the Word a *yogin* realises or, more accurately speaking, becomes one with when he has escaped from the hold of desire, thought and sensations and from the peace of innocence and of the stillness of the Void. That Word he had not heard. He had heard the melting of the *Mantra* into sounds beautiful and sweet – sounds that calmed his mind into stillness. He was made to distance himself from the senses and all the orientations of the mind towards them and their objects. A glimpse he was shown of the way he was to traverse, not of the destination. He did not have the power to distance himself from the bliss that accompanied the music and the words, did not have the power to step out of them. So he was not allowed to remain in that state, for to glory in it is the sure way to fall, the primrose way to it. This, I believe, is implicit in the words of the Master that he uttered immediately after this incident:

> Earn this on your own, by your own effort! As long as you do not attain to this state through a sustained meditation of what has been revealed to you, you cannot come to abide in it. You have to go after it actively, seek it and strive for it; it will not come to you, will not be gifted out to you. You may get a glimpse of this state for a minute or two through the grace of your teacher, but from where will you get the ability to guard and absorb it? So earn this treasure, guard it well and reap the real joy of the life vouchsafed to you. Be an example unto others. But thick and tight is the net that *Avidyā-Māyā* has woven for man. Hard is it for him to disengage himself from what he sees and experiences. So ever keep in mind that what you see and experience will not stay, nor will stay this body of yours. Orient your *buddhi* inwards

through the dispassion that this thought of the transience of all that you are and behold will give rise to and augment this inward orientation by a sustained meditation. That will reveal unto you, this dispassion and this meditation, that you are only That. As long as you do not have this realisation, you will not be freed from your bonds. It is only when mind, breath and the Name become one that you will have the concentration to know *That, That* which is ever itself. Remember what Guru Nānak has to say in this connection:

> Combine these three into one, the mind, the breath and the Name, and hear then the Sound that rings with friction none. With these three absorbed in It, you will not remain to see either day or night. All shall have been lost in the *śūnya* of *samādhi*.

'There are,' said the Bhagat, 'all kinds of passions to possess and distract man, there is desire, there is anger, there is greed, there are stupid obsessions and the sense of me and mine. Enemies are they of one who would strive to attain to that state. How to kill these beasts that obstruct one's way up? Should one get rid of them one by one or of all of them in one go?'

'Resist,' said Gurudeva, 'these thoughts! Only look at all that happens before you, all the coming and the going that constitute what they call the world, look at all these as occurring under the will and command of the Lord. Let this alone be your thought: 'Thou alone art, only Thou. Thou art the doer and Thou art the undoer. Only Your will is done, only Yours!' Suffused with this thought, lead your mind from here to there, from its orientation towards the world towards *That* which is ever itself. You will reach *That* through the meditation taught to you, through a sustained concentration and effort in that direction.'

Surrender of one's will, one's sense of doership, is indispensable for yogic contemplation. As a first step, one must actively equalise the inflow and the outflow of breath **with help of the Name vouchsafed to him by a seer who**

has become one with the Word. When this has been accomplished, then the man on the path turns a mere passive witness of its motion from the atmosphere without down to the navel and from the navel up to the atmosphere. This long attendance upon this Name-breath motion leads to the rousing up of the *kuṇḍalinī* in the region of the navel until it comes to stay at the root of the nose between the eyebrows. There one hears the Nāda, with joy one hears it and in ecstasy. One must keep aloof from that joy, one must not exult in it. For exulting in it will resurrect the ego and one will slide back into *buddhi,* into the mind and the senses and their correlative *other*, the external world. The paradise will be lost, not to be regained. All hell will then be let loose upon him.[14]

Is there a way out of that hell for this fallen being, for the being forsaken and spurned by his inmost being? He must, he has to, endure all, all that happens to him, his failures, his humiliations, the wretchedness of his body and the sinfulness of his mind, and above all, its madness. For mad will he be, a man that lives without a hope and a purpose, and breathes not to live but to sigh and grieve. A frozen being will he be, a being who can relate to nothing, neither to living beings nor to inert things, nor to the beauty of the sunset or the glory of the sunrise. But this does not mean that he will be a lost soul. For the *kuṇḍalinī* will continue to work its way up, will continue to knock at the tenth gate located in the crown of the head. He will be unable to do any meditation but meditation will continue to be done for him. Not until the tenth gate opens up will his suffering cease and the Word appear, appear not to give him bliss but to absorb him into Itself. What will remain then, what survive? Only That which ever is That, of which nothing can be said or predicated. No man will survive that merger, no God, no word and no Word, no *other* and no self, and no oneness because there will remain no many to constitute that oneness.

Theoretically speaking, man can avoid this infernal way to redemption, this lonely journey through inferno without a guide. He can pierce the tenth gate by losing himself in the *Nāda* provided he does not enjoy it, does not glory in the bliss that he turns into. Theoretically, then, it is possible to move on from bliss to Bliss. But only theoretically! For it is virtually impossible for man not to enjoy the bliss and desire to stay there forever and, in the process, bring about his fall. Our exile from that paradise is a must, is inevitable, given the obstinacy of our selfhood. It is easier to be patient in suffering than in bliss, it is easier to remain humble for an ordinary man than for an extraordinary man. In this regard, the following words of the Master should be heeded to carefully:

> Only a rare man, gifted with a rare power of discrimination between the truth and the untruth, tries to free himself from the bondage of desire and action. And a rare man among the men endowed with this gift can attain to the goal of not-doing – the man ever given to yogic discipline, to bringing about confluence of the mind, breath and the Name. Only he can attain to the bliss of ever remaining self-same. Performance of sacrifices, great in extent and number, cannot put an end to the malady of *vāsanā*[15] in man. Nor can *tapa*, purgatorial self-purification, **nor can mere sustained meditation, that confluence of the mind, breath and the Name**. Nor can, for that matter, service of others and emaciation of one's body through self-denial. A man may do all these acts to one's heart's content but *vāsanā* would not die down in him. On the contrary, these virtuous modes of life will degrade his consciousness into self-consciousness, bringing about his fall. His self-consciousness will make him ego-centred and ego-oriented to glory in his ego and its joys and pleasures. He will thus fall down from the state of peace that he attained to, never for a moment able to relive it or re-find it.
>
> Hard did he strive to free himself through these ways but all the efforts he put in and the hardships he went through for the purpose succeeded only in increasing his *vāsanā*, increasing it manifold. This, verily, is a strange phenomenon that the right way should lead to the wrong end! One requires a deep insight

> to pass through these hurdles, the insight that can tell the truth from the untruth, and also an instruction from one that has become the Truth itself. **Only these two, insightful discrimination and the grace of a Truth-become**, can make one *vāsanā*-free and establish one in the bliss called the self, the self that has no *other* to constitute it. Strive as much as they can, the pretentious will not attain to this state.
>
> *Tapa*, knowledge, contemplation, meditation and other means are there to free man from *vāsanā*. That alone is their purpose, freedom from *vāsanā*. But they turn fruitful only when one has *viśvāsa* in the truth, when one's very breath is anchored to it, one's being and life. It is only the man who lives for that truth, is totally dedicated to it and lives for it and by it that can succeed, through these means, in reaching the goal. Otherwise, all will be vain, all the strife and all the effort. Instead of purifying man's mind, these means will only bring about a furious intensity of *vāsanā* in him [the way sure to his doom].[16]

'Viśvāsa' is often translated as faith but the term *faith*, as it is generally understood, is related to the mind, to the belief one has in someone, a god or a prophet or a man, or in the words of scriptures. But 'viśvāsa,' derived from the root *śvas*, to breathe, suggests more of existential dependence than attitudinal self-surrender. A pilgrim to the truth is not merely to have faith in his teacher, teacher that is the Word itself, his being, his very breath is to be anchored to the latter; take the teacher away and you are no more. He constitutes you, makes you, is your being and your life. Without this kind of what one may call existential faith, and not mere attitudinal, one cannot reach the goal. For, the way opens up many a state of bliss and joy and of even supernatural powers, which are bound to make one self-conscious unless one has the life of his guru to serve as one's ideal. Otherwise, the way will be confused with the destination, the journey with the end, and that will make one de-anchored both from the world and what they call their God. In this regard, the following words of the Master sound a clear warning to the man who would seek to redeem himself:

"'The Name is, verily, the *Seed-Mantra* that is gifted out to a disciple by a teacher that has attained to the goal, has reached it – the *Mantra* that equalises the inward and outward flow of breath. That Name is to be meditated intently with one's life and being totally surrendered to the guru; he, the guru, alone is to be one's refuge and support. With every moment of his life thus dedicated to his preceptor should the disciple concentrate all the thoughts and processes of mind on the Name-breath. Let him become a mere consciousness-of-the-Name. This exclusive concentration on the Name-breath is termed meditation on the Name or *yoga*.

If a man receives the Name from someone who has not attained to the ultimate goal, from someone who has not gone beyond darkness to light, he will find it hard in the extreme to attain to his end. For, without the ideal of the guru before him, the guru that has striven for and reached the truth, he cannot hope to attain to the state of the Good. One finds many a pretentious guide these days, initiating all sorts of people into the path of *yoga*. The end-result of this relationship can be a mere business transaction, of giving and taking, not redemption. Initiation by an imperfect saint can neither bring about redemption nor can it orient one's mind fully towards the real end. Let no one have any doubt in the matter.

If the guru self-sacrifices, so will his disciple, if he is pure, so will be his follower. The guru's dispassion will be *the* dispassion for the latter, the guru's abiding in the truth will be *the* abiding in the truth for his devotee, and his meditation will be *the* meditation for the latter. His example, that of the guru, alone will make the disciple emulate it and free him from all the polutions to turn him into a fit recipient of the truth. When the guru himself is a mere prattler and his teachings all stained and deviating, the disciple too will become a like of him. Every seeker of the truth should know that only the guru that is the Truth Itself can fashion a disciple into the Pure.

When one is fortunate enough to be initiated into this path of *yoga* by a guru the perfect, one's *buddhi* readily imbibes the qualities embodied in the guru to give itself up, with [relative] ease, to the meditation of the Name to purge itself of all stains and blemishes. And free thus from its stains it will attain to *That*

> which is stainless-ness itself. It will attain to the state desire-free, the very state supreme that the guru attained to through his strivings true.[17]

Many a person-on-the-path gets lost on the way, notwithstanding the ideal set by his guru and has to drink the bitter cup of poison to die into immortality. Not for many is the way to die in ecstasy into redemption. For most, for almost all, the way lies through death. Such is human nature. For, the guru, the person of the guru, despite all his superhuman qualities, is a man. The temptation to emulate his qualities for the sake of self-glory often becomes too great to resist. Not until a man has suffered much and borne much, not until he has been shattered by the great and colossal tragedy of life will he give himself up to what the guru has revealed to him. We shall find many an instance of this misfortune in this account. Even the Noble Disciple, Bhagatjī, will have his share of human frailties. For not until, to paraphrase the words of the Master, one gives up all hope from hope, will one find the way.

It is necessary to keep in mind this instruction and warning of the Master to escape from very many illusions and false notions about the path of yoga, a path like, to invoke one of the most famous Upaniṣadic phrases, the edge of a razor [KaṭhaU 1.3.14]. But let us return to our story. The Bhagat referred to some other teachers of yoga who taught methods that did not involve the restraint of breath. It is unnecessary to refer to those methods but the reply that he received is instructive:

> You may wrench out your eyes, seal your ears with lead, sew your mouth into silence but the mind will not come to get concentrated. Mind is active because breath is in motion. Until breath is restrained, one will never reach the truth, try as he may for ages. **Yes, faith and belief can make one virtuous but one cannot go beyond that.** Ever since the discipline of yoga was revealed, the great ones attained to the truth by equalising the incoming and outgoing breath through the Name. This is true of

> the East as well as of the West, of the Hindu seers or the Muslim renunciates. There is only one yoga-path to reach the goal of the truth. Those who are ignorant of it continue enunciating useless theories...
>
> Fortunate are you that you can perceive the flow of *bānī* (vāṇī) with your own eyes and have the privilege of noting it down. But meditate! Meditate! For as long as the *Nāda* does not sound within you, you will not know what contemplation is. And as long as contemplation is not done, the state of *samādhi* will indeed be far, far beyond your reach.

Continuing in the same strain, he recited a verse of Guru Nānak Deva: 'Impatient be you not, Shah Sharāf, for not without many a pounding will the paddy turn into rice.' 'A disciple was this Shah Sharāf,' explained he, 'of Guru Nānak, impatient, like you, to reach the goal. Nānak told him that he would be pounded as paddy is pounded into grains of rice. He too would have to give up much, suffer much and undergo much. All interests would he have to renounce, all desires would he have to give up! Completely bereft of these he would have to be. But he did not have dispassion enough to bear even one stroke of misfortune. So let him move on step by step, let him not take a jump. Let him be patient.' 'As for *This*,' he continued, 'there remains no more accounts to settle, all ledgers have been closed and thrown into the waters deep.'

The Bhagat was curious to know about the accounts that had been settled finally. The Master postponed the reply, asking him, instead, to suggest the title of the *vāṇī* he had recorded. When no answer came forth, Gurudeva himself suggested four titles, namely, *Prabhu-bānī*; *Nirmala-bodha*; *Prāṇa-vidyā*, and, lastly, *Nikhettar-parbat-goṣṭa*. The Bhagat chose the last one and it was accepted. 'Nikhetttar Parbat' means 'Nikhettar Mountain.' The mountain was given the name after the name of the village Nikhettar. *Goṣṭa* is a Sanskrit word meaning 'going of the cows.' Away from civilisation was that dangerous mountain forest, away from human habitations, where no pastures were for cows to graze in. Which, then, were the cows that gathered there, and who were they that performed the ceremony of 'going of the cows' there? The word *'go'* does not merely mean cow, it also means speech, a ray of light and senses. The cows, the senses, experience their respective objects through the two eyes, the two ears, the two nostrils and the tongue; the eyes perceive shapes, the ears experience sound, the nostrils experience smell and the tongue is the organ of both taste and touch. These seven cows, these cognitive organs are outward oriented and ever remain unappeased because they fail to find what they truly seek to find, unknowingly seek to find, namely *Sat*, that is Being. But instead of that Being what these cognitive faculties come to find is a world which is merely an objective correlate of these, their own projection as the Other, their constitutive other. But in the Nikhetar Parbat, in that wilderness, they could graze in the pastures of the truth, the truth they had ever sought. Suffused with the truth became they there, and appeased was their longing for it.

The word 'Nikhettar', however, is problematic. It could well be the colloquial form of the Sanskrit 'nakṣatra', derived from *nakṣ*, to come near, to arrive, to attain, to approach, to arrive at [*vide* Monier-Williams]. *Nakṣatra-s* means the stars, which, according to the Chāndogya-vision, *approach* the moon to merge into it during the bright fortnight. The word also means the *moon* because the latter too attains, according to that very belief, to the status of the stars, disperses into them during the dark fortnight. To move to the *other*, to become the *other* is the fate of all that would be themselves. The senses as the cows, however, *approached* that *parbat*, that mountain, but not to continue the process of moving, moving of one to the *other* and of the *other* to one. As the seven stars ever move around the pole star, that ever firm star that never merges into the moon, so the seven cognitive senses [stationed on the face] too revolve around the eternal light in the crown of the head, the *parbat* of the yoga symbolism. The cognitive organs that are outward oriented become oriented towards the Word to become the Word Which has no *other* to cognise as the senses have, in Which all is one, the name and the named, the self and the not-self, consciousness and the object of consciousness. There is another meaning of '*go*' to reinforce this symbolism. Besides the meanings already mentioned, '*go*' also connotes the *suṣumna* nerve, the yogic nerve through which the *kuṇḍalinī* reaches the crown of the head to merge into the Word there. And who were, we asked, the performers of the ceremony of the *goṣṭa*, going of the cows? They were the mind, the breath and the Name. These brought about the merger of the senses into the Word that has no *other*, into Brahman, the self without a second.

This interpretation, of course, will be in order if the 'nikhettar' is considered the derivative form of 'nakṣatra.' But it could also be the derivative form of 'niḥ-kṣetra,' a place bereft of *kṣetra*, that is to say, bereft of land, place, etc. So 'Nikhettar Parbat' would then mean 'The Mountain of the Nowhere.' The place [the crown of the head] where the Word thunders is the place without place, the place that cannot be described in terms of spatial relationships. The senses go there only to lose themselves and also their *other*, the world of space, the world external. And nowhere is also beyond time. So on that mountain was accomplished the pilgrimage of the senses to the height[s] of the nowhere, the nowhere where there is neither time nor space. The yogic symbolism remains intact even when the word is read as '*niḥ-khettar*.'

Now, the other titles: '*Prabhu-bānī*',[18] the Lord's Word. But 'prabhu' means the Word, too, according to Indian lexicographers. So the Word of the Lord is the Lord Himself. It was the Word that had thundered into words in that mountainous wilderness. The other suggested title was '*Nirmala-bodha*', Knowledge Unblemished; unblemished because it involved, unlike our knowledge, no concealing,

concealing of Existence or Being that permeates all that we behold and perceive. In dealing with things we forget, sleep over, that Being, their informing principle. To complicate the matter still further, we also, while cognising a thing, conceal from ourselves the unknowing and the unknowable depths within us, the depths we call or miscall the *ātman*, the self in us. So knowledge unblemished is knowledge unconditioned by concealment of Being without and of the silent depths within. As long as we *know*, as long as we know the *other*, concealment will remain, the blemish will remain. It is only when our concepts, thoughts and senses die down, that knowledge true will arise, the knowledge that knows only itself, has no *other* to constitute it. The third title '*Prāṇa-vidyā*,' meditation of breath, has already received our attention. This *vidyā* too leads to the Word. So, all the titles suggest the essence of the revelation that descended on those high mountains. It is now time that I paraphrase some of the lines that uttered themselves in the dead of nights at that height and in that solitude to confirm and reiterate what we have just said about the titles given to the *bānī* in question:

> Even when alive shall he find deliverance, he who knows this meditation, this way of union with the Truth. There is a land which no one can attain to, a place without a parallel, where walks the Word beyond the reach of the senses. Shines there not the sun, nor does glitter the moon, but without either a flick or oil burns there bright a light. Śiva is the oil that burns there, Śiva, the Death Redemptive, and the flick is the calm in death.
>
> With the calm consenting to burn with death, light eternal glows in night no less than in day. The five do the auspicious worship of it, all the cognitive senses, with wonder struck at the sight of that light. The way up leads to the west, from the west it moves on to the east, where it finds the lake where bathes the mind to find the Lord of the meek. A marvel indeed is this sight, the sight of the Lord of the bereft and meek. This movement up is from the earth to the sky, strikes it a fear among all that live, be they men or be they beasts.

Brimmed with waters becomes the dry lake, swans fly on to it on its edges to rest. A tree springs up there, on those its shores, a rootless tree bereft of branch, and bare of leaf. Without the coming of spring it blossoms and bears fruit without the blossoms. Who will know what means this account, this tale strange and quixotic? Yes, he will know it that has followed the guru, he alone and no one else.

There the sun merges into the moon and the moon into the sun; behold this wonder, this marvel the matchless! The Unconditioned comes and the Conditioned goes, but there do they meet, in that land of marvels. Supreme is this meeting and supreme is the bliss to watch it, this their meeting, of the sun and the moon.

The Unconditioned consumes what the Conditioned fashions up, the Conditioned dies because it would fashion and would set up.

A lady comes from the land where no one goes, comes to drink in deep both the Conditioned and the Unconditioned. Consuming them both she moves up to the sky; that is her way, the way reverse that no man can tread, except the one that is his guru's slave. The lady has no face and no body, but with her sought union the seers and sages, with that lady without either a face or a body. Without the vocal organ she speaks, revealing truths that none can measure, and without the eyes she sees the world, that living into death and dying into life. And walks she without the feet, all-knowing she walks the all-knowing to pervade. Within all dwells she, that lady from nowhere, but none knows her, that lady all-knowing. For bodiless she pervades the body and the cosmos, and fierce becomes she without a rhyme or a reason.

With the meditation revealed by the guru true, the mind, the eclipsing one, comes to an end, and with its ending shine out the pores all of the body, each and every one among them. Unfed will he be appeased, for mouthless eaten will he have the world, the one of mind extinct.

The meekly one shall descry this knowledge hidden from every eye, he that follows his guru true but asks him questions none. Lost shall he be in That which without a ground abides .... The

way to knowledge is the way reverse. Let seers consider it well.
Maṅgat laughed when he found an ant eat up a hill.[19]

I have rendered 'agama nigama deśa anūpā' as a land that no one can attain to, a place without a parallel. This could well be rendered in a different way if the initial 'a' in 'agama' is read as the long 'ā.' Then the sentence would mean the 'unique place revealed both by the Vedas and the Śaiva tradition.' The five senses would be the seven orifices in the face, performing the five sense-functions, those of seeing, hearing, smelling, tasting and touching. The tongue, we know, can both taste and touch. The movement up is the movement of the *Śakti* or of the *kuṇḍalinī* which is roused at the navel by the meditative confluence of mind, breath and the Name, and rises up to the place between the two eyebrows, and from there to the top of the head. There it is absorbed in the Word transforming itself and the body below into the Word and also what the body perceives and is stationed in, the world. So, all becomes the Word. From That emanate the *buddhi*, the mind, the senses, the body and their *other*, the world. But when the *kuṇḍalinī* gets absorbed in the Word, then all will turn into the Word. All fear this all consuming *Śakti*, this force but not he that gives himself up to it – he becomes the Word Itself. There in the Word comes to an end the before and the after, the precedent and the antecedent, the blossom and the fruit, the seed and the tree. All is present there in one moment, the past, the present and the future, the moment in which the eternal sun merges in the waxing and waning moon and the waxing and waning moon in the sun eternal. Eternity is time in the Word and time is eternity. The qualified turns into the non-qualified there, the non-qualified into the qualified.

Before the coming of the lady from the nowhere, the Unqualified consumed up the qualified, turning every determinate thing into naught, into a nothing; it disdained the latter, rejected it, spurned it. But that lady from the nowhere, the *kuṇḍalinī*, consumed up the qualified and the unqualified, the interpreted and the uninterpreted, the subject and the predicate. When the word and the referent became one, the signifier and the signified, then sprang forth the bliss that every being seeks, the bliss he is ever deprived of. He becomes *That* which ever is *That*, *That* which has no *other* to *place* It. It ever remains Itself, this That; this subject is its own predicate. To us men of the world, it might appear a nothing, or an abstraction, but not for him who has seen all merge into *That*. *That* is infinity itself, is, in the language of the Chāndogya Upaniṣad, *bhūman* itself, fullness itself. The imagery of the latter half of the passage would suggest the richness of that which is ever itself. We fear it because to us it appears our death. But one who has died into it will find the all in each, the hill in the ant, the ocean in a drop of water, the infinity in a grain of sand. I have put in dry terms what the passage suggests. One must linger on its words to have a feel of the ecstasy. The paraphrase (infelicitous paraphrase, at that) is only a paraphrase, the genuine richness is the *vāṇī* itself, which too is a pale rendering of the actual realisation. All expressions fail to show forth what the joy of dying into the Word is, where dying is the Word, where joy too is the Word, where the dying one also is the Word and where the life that appeared death too is the Word.

The passage I have paraphrased was one of the twenty such passages on the nature of the Word. The number of other passages dictated came up to eighty in addition to the 200 verses on dispassion. To paraphrase other passages was not considered feasible here because the density of the symbolism might get too heavy for a biography. An illustration alone should do here, though the gist of other teachings of the Master will be given at the appropriate time, of the other dimensions of his vision of life and of reality. We have now to return to our narrative.

The time of the *tapas* was drawing near its end and the

Master asked the Bhagat that he should inform Ramdittā accordingly. The following morning the Bhagat went down to the camp to prepare tea for the Master and deliver his message to Parmānand, Rāmdittā's son. But he found, to his shock, that the young man had gone out to distribute mutton among the labourers. His meal too had not been cooked. So he made two loaves of bread and took them with tea and left the place with the tea for Gurudeva. That very moment Parmānand came back and beseeched him not to tell the Master about the meat. Banārasī went back, served the tea to the Master, cleansed the utensils and sat down to read out the *vāṇī* he had recorded the preceding night. All this he was doing in glum silence, invoking an enquiry from Gurudeva: 'Why this silence and glumness? Did you have a quarrel with some one?'

The Bhagat narrated all that had happened. The narration hurt the Master deep, a distressing anger seized him. 'Why did you,' he said, 'serve the tea to *This*? You should have come back immediately, why did you cook your meal and prepare the tea there? That could have been taken at Jalamādā! Demons are these that we have stumbled into! Let there be departure from here tomorrow morning! Hand over all these things to the person concerned at the camp. From here let's proceed towards Abatabad. No need to linger on here anymore.'

Having spoken in this strain of distress, the Master became silent. The Bhagat saw the Master's eyes brimming with tears. He regretted the moment he narrated the cruel incident. As commanded, he did not go to Rāmditta's after this incident. The lessee requested the Bhagat to accept his hospitality and at his place he prepared tea for the Master.

When Rāmdittā came to know of the incident, he started, without a delay, from Nikhettar Gaon to the hut at the mountains but only to receive a reprimand the kind of which he had never received in his life. With a piece of cloth wrapped around his neck, the sign of repentance, he bore the torrent of angry words, his requests for pardon intervening regularly. He took a vow to give up eating meat from that very date. In the evening, he received a command to leave the place. 'I have to,' said he, 'do penance hard today and will spend the night at the holy feet.' 'It is the first time,' he continued after a pause, 'I have been reprimanded thus in my life. I have seen *sādhus* moving from place to place, eating all this stuff and making us too eat it. But the Master has ostracized me, has spurned me. None has the guts, none has the power to summon up some courage to say a word of protest against what the Lord utters.' And then in a vein that could lighten the somber atmosphere, he added in a low, soft tone, 'Hard indeed is our predicament, there is no way to escape from these clutches!'

The last sentence did succeed in making the Lord smile a little. Said he, 'Free are you set from these clutches! Those teachers that are little better than thieves ask you to eat what the demons eat. But you deserve only the likes of them. What would you have said if a teacher of that kind had given you a piece of his mind the way it was given today?'

'Mahārājjī, we are *kṣatriyas*, to the class of warriors do we belong! A little anger is an affront for us. A word like those of the Lord would have meant his expulsion from my home. He would have been warned never to show his face again, respect though we every saint and every seer.'

'Why don't you do the same here?'

With his 'ears in his fingers,' he said, 'O my God! Forgive! Forgiver! In the name of my ancestors all I seek thy forgiveness. Over a year have I seen the Lord, his ways, his style of life! Death I see incarnate in thee. To hell will I repair if but a word of anger escapes these holy lips. Today, I have come to seek refuge in these feet, to make a humble request to the Lord to initiate me into the secret way. Earlier, my mind was not yet ready for this, but today it says that the Lord alone is my stay and my refuge.'

'What does your mind bid you do?'

'Tomorrow will this servant say what it tells me to do.'

For long he spoke in this strain expressing his devotion to the Master. Seeing the state of his mind, the Master asked the Bhagat to recite before him the *vāṇī*: 'On his own the Lord has appeared...' He was also told the time of the descent of that revelation. Having listened to those words, Rāmdittā could only say, 'Blessed Lord, deserve we not to sit near these holy feet. Only the Master's grace can save us, only his forgiveness. No other hope is there for the likes of us!'

'Disconsolate he wept, his pride and arrogance having been washed away. Many a time the Master reassured him, but there seemed no end to his weeping, no end to his sighs of repentance. Eventually he prostrated himself before the Master, and said, 'Mahārājjī, let me confess I thought you a young fervent soul and thought myself all wise. Self-opinionated have I been even before this divine Presence. Forgive me, Lord, for this folly! That alone is the prayer this slave makes to you, forgiveness alone he begs of you.'

Needless to add, Rāmdittā was initiated into the path of yoga the very next morning.

For thirty days and two that *tapas* had gone on on those starry pastures; very many nights of thunder and lightning the Word had been invoked to speak to man. Now had come the time to descend from the Mountain of the nowhere where cows had come to low with the Word. The Master decided the date for bidding goodbye to that dangerous solitude. Rāmdittā, however, insisted that there too a *yajña* should be held but the Master gave permission only for a *sat-saṅga*, keeping in view the condition of the weather and of the situation of the place. The sixteenth day of the lunar month *Śrāvaṇa* was fixed for that purpose, the day that fell approximately in the last week of July or the first week of August of that year, 1939. The audience consisted mostly of Muslims from the villages around Nikhettar, some Hindus and, of course, the entire labour force employed for the felling of the trees. This is the gist of what he said:

> Every being is enframed in terms of name, form and attributes. Enframed thus he is made to act, act under the compulsive force of desire and hope. Therein lies his bondage: in name, form, attributes, desire, hope and action. To liberate himself from these bonds he has to worship One God. But as long as he is concerned with preserving the body and its looks, he cannot free himself from desire. And as long as desire rules his life, he cannot worship the One God, he can worship only images called bodies, his or of others. It is only when he seeks the Spirit, the Spirit that makes the body alive, can he become the worshipper of the One. But desire is always there to hold every being under its sway and force him to act - every being, be he a Hindu, be he a Muslim, a Zoroastrian, or a Christian. And acts lead to profit or loss, to happiness or sorrow. And these keep him ever restless, desire for one and aversion for the other. No one can give himself up to the One but only up to images – bodies – as long as desire keeps springing up in him. The Messengers and the Prophets, the gurus and the Incarnations and those who attained to the Truth, the Great Ones, taught the world what the truth is, what the way to it is, what to do and what not to do. One must follow their teachings if one would liberate oneself from these shackles. Your true joy lies in following their teachings, of the Messengers and the Incarnates. It is no use worshipping their forms, their bodies .... .

The Islamic message could not perhaps be better summarised.

The same day he descended from those heights. On the way he met the devotee, a Muslim, that used to supply milk for the Master's tea. Bowing low before the Master, he spread out a piece of cloth on a flat rock and meekly requested the Master to rest there a while. Taking his seat, the Master said, 'The *faqīrs* are happy with you, Faqirkhan! Very happy with you! Ask for what you desire.'

'Let the Master lift up a prayer to the Lord that He bestow faith upon this His servant.'

"Why don't you ask for wealth and a happy family?'

'With God's grace life's business is going on. One should not ask from those who have given up all for the sake of the Lord the things of the world. Faith is all, with faith comes all.'

'Let the Lord give unto you the faith pure and unblemished. Banārasī, give him two rupees for his children.'

Meekly accepted he that small gift. Touching his forehead with it, he said, 'All-rich have I become today!'

Notes

1 One who has nothing but God as his support and shelter.

2 There was no question of bathing in that water.

3 Notice the *vāṇī* is the peal of *prakṛti*, not the voice of Brahman. The ambiguity involved in the statement needs our constant and close attention.

4 Saints of Medieval India were all these, Kabīr, Dādū and others.

5 *The Samatāprakāśa*, pp. 738-39.

6 *Vide* Ch. 9.

7 *Vide* the *Samatāvilāsa*, p. 635; also, *The Radiant Sameness*, p. 564.

8 See the *Samatā-prakāśa, Vairāg-aṅg*.

9 *Vide* Chapter 1.

10 A medieval Hindi poet. Among his works, the *Rāmacaritamānasa*, his epic on Rāma's life, is the most famous.

11 *Vairāg-aṅga.*

12 The *Vāṇī* is the utterance of the *buddhi* when it gets established in the skull to hear the Word which Itself is a manifestation of Brahman. Its understanding, that of the *buddhi,* relates to distinctions like bondage and liberation, good and bad etc. But these distinctions are not the ultimate truth. The ultimate truth is the truth of *samatā,* of sameness. A true seer sees no difference between Brahman and Māyā. For him *prakṛti* and Brahman are one and the same and so are the living and the inert. However, as long as man finds himself a mortal being and in bondage, he has to worship the Word as the ultimate reality itself and believe in the *bānī* as the expression of the ultimate truth and self-submit to it. Un-self-conscious self-submission will transform the *bānī* into the Word and dying into the World will lead him to the state of *samatā.* The worship of the expression, of the living symbol, will lead to the truth. Before this self-submission and this death, his formulations of Brahman and Māyā as one will be an act of blasphemy, of hypocrisy and wickedness. Only for the completely innocent, rather innocence itself, there is no difference between Brahman and Māyā, between Brahman and the Word. For a thinker, thinker the honest, there is no escape from distinctions woven by the duality of *Avidyā-Māyā.* The matter will receive our attention when we come to consider the ontology of the Nāda. See Chpater 9. The *bānī* is redemptive because it recants all that it says and proclaims. For a detailed discussion of the matter in question, consult also Preface to the *Radiant Sameness.*

13 Thus the Master's words quoted earlier, words to the effect that the *buddhi* comes to know the truth of everything, when it gets established in the Word should be interpreted the way described here. It is not intellect, as we understand it, intellect that is inconceivable without concepts, thoughts and sensation that can 'understand' things; it is the *buddhi* as one with the Word that can truly know, can redeem its name, 'the knowing thing'. As long as we seek to know and cognize the *other,* it will remain unknowable because the *otherness* of the *other,* its very unknowability, is the condition, the precondition, of our knowing and cognizing. And as long as I speak and articulate about something, that something has to remain other than my speech, and hence something beyond its reach. Even the plainest thing

will elude my grasp and mock at the inadequacy of my speech. My knowledge will ever remain ignorance, my speech a blasphemy. My knowledge will redeem itself only when it turns into Being and my speech when it turns into the Word, for there alone the gap between knowledge and its *other* and between speech and its *other* will be bridged, not as long as I seek to know and to articulate. Even the Word, as we shall see at Chapter 9, will disown itself.

14 I will relate in the Epilogue how hell is let loose upon one and the purgatorial suffering one has to undergo and endure.

15 'Vāsanā,' derived from the root *vas*, to dwell, means desires, thoughts, impressions and ideas sedimented in a being as the result of his modes of life in the past births. *Vāsanā* it is that determines the mode of one's life in one's present birth, its force inexorable and not to be set aside by conscious efforts. How to undo its effect and free oneself from it the quotation in question will presently explain.

16 *Vide* the *Samatāvilāsa*, pp. 305-6. *Cp. The Radiant Sameness*, Sayings 41-44, pp. 293-94.

17 *Ibid.*, pp. 556-58; also *The Radiant Sameness*, pp. 508-09.

18 Let us remember that the Master used the word 'bānī' instead of the Sanskrit 'vāṇī'.

19 *The Samatāprakāśa*, 887, pp. 723-24.

6

In the Midst of Fanatics

Once again the Master started the process of wandering from one place to another. From Nikhettar Gaon he went on to Jalamada, from Jalamada to Kohala, from Kohala to a place called Navānshahar in the district of Abtabad in the North West Frontier of the British India before its partition in 1947 into Independent India and Pakistan. From there on he went to Taxila (Takṣaśilā), once the seat of a famous University before the advent of Muslims and other invaders. Tere he saw many a ruin and the museum where can be found exquisite works of plastic arts, famous throughout the world for their artistic style and beauty. **[There are of course many who would question the use of the description 'exquisite works of plastic arts.' For these art critics the blend of Greek and Indian styles of arts speaks more of decadence than of richness**]. A whole history of a civilisation in miniature is that museum said to be, a civilisation that arose out of the contact between the Indians and the Greeks. There were, of course, many other things to see and examine which a connoisseur would like to linger over for days on end. For, the height and decline of a phase of Indian civilisation, the phase that emerged during the period when Buddhism had reached enough of its height to turn into a potentiality for decline, comes alive as it were in that museum. But how did Gurudeva respond to these things during his very short visit there? 'Where have they' said he, 'disappeared, those that made these things? How much effort and toil must have gone into the making of these things! What pleasure they must have given to those who made use of them! Now remain neither the makers nor the users. Strange indeed is the *Māyā* of the Lord!'

A look, a gesture, a demeanor an artist would capture in stone or on a piece of metal – a look, a gesture, a demeanor that catches in a moment, in a fraction of it, his entire vision of life, even, on occasions, almost the world view of a civilisation. Men and women of culture and knowledge spend years on reading and interpreting a smile, a gaze or an expression generation after generation, century after century but the depth does not come up to the surface, the meaning refuses to become explicit. That richness, that depth humanity treasures, civilisations protect to enrich themselves, to have a relook at themselves, their past haunting their present to guide them into the future. Many are there that relive the past to live the future, to see in recollection the projection, in memory imagination. To art critics of this sort, Gurudeva's response might seem a facile generalisation, a trivialisation of a civilisation, a refusal, maybe an inability, to see the meaning 'inscribed' on the stones or on the metals, to see the life breathing in these inert and lifeless things. Of course we know, one might demur, that the artists pass away and so do their connoisseurs or users of their creations. We also know that works of art too decay and perish, they cannot withstand the ravages wrought by time. Still we cherish them, treasure them, preserve them as the inspiring heritage of mankind; we see in them our past enriching our present, sometimes forcing it, our present, to revise its outlooks and orientations.

The Master's remark enshrines however an altogether different response. Man knows he is mortal but he would immortalise the meaning he finds in life. Where he cannot stay, his understanding, his interpretation, he hopes, can or would. But it cannot because all interpretations, all understandings are illusions at a most subtle level; they are desperate attempts to conceal the fact of our mortality, our first and last truth, the truth that we would not face. That is the meaning of the last sentence of the Master, 'Strange indeed is the *Māyā* of the Lord.' Where the living being cannot live, he will make an abstraction live! Let us not forget that even art is not free from abstractions, it is only an attempt to reconcile the idea with the image, the abstraction with the concrete.

One may, however, object that reconciliation of the idea and the image involves much more than my rather simplistic account would suggest. In our day to day life, this reconciliation, it is true, never comes to be possible. The sense-content or the image would not remain confined within the concept and the concept would not find the sense-content adequate enough to embody it. We do not find any object, to use the Platonic language, embodying perfectly any *eidos,* the informing principle, the eternal archetype of any class of things. But in art experience, we do find, many would claim, a reconciliation between the idea and the image, not, to be sure, in the sense that we find the image embody perfectly the concerned concept but in the sense that we find in that embodiment the concept exceeding itself. We feel as if all the concepts, the constitutive *others* of the given concept, too had come to dwell in the presentation before us. That is why we come to stay still with the presentation before us, a presentation that seems to encompass the beyond itself, as if the entire unknown world had come to stay for a while in it. We become absorbed in the presentation before us because it has no beyond to limit it. That, some would say, is the explanation of the disinterested joy that we find in the experience of such a presentation. That this disinterested contemplation is still an escape from our mortal predicament, is possible only because we would not countenance the end of both the concept and the image and also of their reconciliation, is borne out by the following event.

Coming out of the Museum, the Master saw a peon doing the duty of a guard at the gate. 'How much,' he asked, 'do you get as pay?'

'With the Lord's grace, twenty two rupees a month.'

'How do you manage things with this amount?'

'The Lord Supreme is the sustainer,' said the man with hands raised in thankfulness.

A smile appeared on the Master's face and he asked the Bhagat to give the man two rupees.

The Buddha found redemption in ego-extinction, the artists in question tried to capture the calm and serenity of that no-person to sustain their own persons, however expansive or in excess of themselves. So did his followers who worshipped him through these expressions of the inexpressible. Even while talking about extinction of the self they asserted their expansive selves through these their acts of creation or contemplation. What did the peon do, that guard of the guardians of the inexpressible? He knew his penury, the deficiency of the means of a simple, bare living, yet he gave himself up to the will of the Lord, the One God that remains when all else perishes. To his perishing he gave his consent, owned up to his mortality, did not move towards death but let death make its presence felt. For to live in insecurity and uncertainty, to live so with all willingness, alone was his way; his was not the way of the faith that cries for security. Nor was his way that of the aesthetic connoisseur that would forget his mortality in contemplation, in the contemplation of the beautiful or the sublime. Can those that would experience 'purpose without purposiveness,' would taste the pleasure of disinterest, ever think of doing so when their simple needs are not met, when every day is uncertain and insecure? This is what the peon could do, remain disinterested in the face of insecurity and uncertainty. One can truly know the sublime and be the sublime only on the dangerous 'mountains of the nowhere', not in the secure atmosphere of a museum or an art gallery.

From the museum the Master went straight to the railway station, the Bhagat going to the temple, their shelter during the preceding night, to fetch their luggage. A malarial fever had seized him only a few days back. The fever had disappeared but had left him weak. So to carry a trunk and a holdall[1] was a difficult and tiring task, the toil making him a little breathless and his face flushed. Totally exhausted he felt when he reached the railway station. He unloaded himself of the burden and tried to sit down on the floor as fast as he could. Before he could take his seat, he felt as if things were getting dark and indistinct, his energy all gone, even the energy to sit down. 'Why don't you,' said Gurudeva, 'sit down? Your face too is flushed! What's the matter with you?' The Bhagat could not help pointing out to the heaviness of his burden.

Instead of showing any concern for his trouble, the Master went into *samādhi*. When he came out of it, he said, 'Well, Child, let the Lord bless you with understanding and insight! Inscribed on His threshold is your name. Go shall you there, willing or unwilling. No escape is there for you. Remember, never goes waste the service rendered to a *faqīr*. So grudge it not, let your heart and mind be ever open, in weal or in woe.'

'Where and how my name is inscribed I don't understand. I don't have the ability to understand. Nor do I know how to serve ungrudgingly, with mind and heart open.'

The response came from the Word Itself, for the Master spoke merged in It. Hearing those words of the Word, the

Bhagat's heart melted into tears. He did not have the calm or the presence of mind to record what said the Word to him. When the man in the Master resurrected and noticed the state of the Bhagat's mind, he said to the latter, 'Weeping is of no avail. Weigh and consider what the world is, what your origin is and what your end is, and the whereabouts of your parents that fashioned you.'

In the meantime, the train arrived and they boarded a compartment. 'Like the railway travel,' said the Master, 'is the journey to the Real. Take care of the Name as you take care of the ticket here. Smooth will be your way then.'

In about twenty minutes the train arrived at Panjasahib,[2] a place of pilgrimage for the Sikhs. Devotees without a number came from far and wide to get a dip in the holy waters of the pool there. Seeing the throng of the devotees, the Bhagat said, 'In hundreds of thousands pilgrims come here to bathe in these waters for their salvation. Can liberation come this way?'

'A dip in water,' said the Master, 'will not free you from the cycle of birth and death. The Truth-become establish such customs to make people come together. Coming together frees people from many an ill. Bathing here can only wash the dirt off one's body, it cannot wash away the stains of the mind. That can be done only through the confluence of the mind, breath and the Name. The places, the dwellings of the seers of the truth often become holy places for the people of the world and they make it a point to visit them for one purpose or another. That is their way.

'This place has a long history. In times ancient it was the seat of the sage Pāṇini. Young scholars came here to learn grammar from far and wide. As many as ten thousand students did their studies at a time. This pool was there at that time too. Thereafter the Buddhists settled here. In their times the great university of Takṣaśilā was established. What they now call the city of Peshawar was the seat of the sage

Parśurāma. Jamrod once had the *āśrama* of the seer Jamadāgni. With the change of the times, places too change, new shapes they acquire and new appearances.

'Here occurred a dialogue between Guru Nānak and the grand old saint, Valī Qandhārī, between the one who had become one with the Truth Itself and the other that had at his command varied kinds of supernatural powers. The man of powers proved helpless before the man of the truth. From the clutch [*pañjā*] of the latter, he had no escape. Nānak became his refuge and master, and he the Guru's humble follower. The shape of the clutching hand was inscribed here during the days of the king Ranajitsingh. On the way to the battles he chanced to stay here twice. The landscape appealed to him and he knew its history too. Under his orders stones were laid along the margins of the pool. This was his way of reviving Hinduism. The powerful do leave their marks behind. As to the story that Valī Qandhārī hurled a stone from Qandhar which Nanak took in his hand ***(pañjā)*** undoing the supernatural force – this story is a mere fiction. The faithful often weave such myths but these can do no good to the people. Good comes about only when the teachings of their masters are followed faithfully [not through mere ritualistic gestures]. This is how the world changes. Times will come when even this its shape will also disappear. Things never stay to remain themselves. Change is inherent in them. Only the formless self is ever itself, only that and nothing else.'

After this conversation, the two went back to the orchard where they had spent the night. The Master asked the Bhagat to have his meal at a *ḍhābā,* a pre-modern version of a modern restaurant, a shop-like establishment, small and plain, where food is cooked and served. It was a long time when the latter returned. The reason: Most shops served meat, it took him long to find a vegetarian *ḍhābā*. The conversation however had a different diction. Banārasī said that most shops served *mahā-prasāda,* the *great* gift of grace from a holy man or seer. When asked to explain the meaning of the term, he said that the people there termed mutton as *mahā-prasāda*. The clarification upset the Master a great deal. 'In the shrine,' said he 'they take a dip in the holy pool. Outside they pour ashes on their heads, provoke the deadly nemesis. This is not what Men the True taught; this is the way of those who have only their desires as their guides. They, Men the true, sacrificed their lives for the establishment of the Way, their followers sacrifice the mute beings to satisfy their desires. That has become their way and their life. Wine and meat will, one day, be their undoing. Let's leave this place at once. It is a sin to stay here.' To reach the bus stop it was necessary to go through the market place, which the Master refused to do. Through another way they reached the road that led to Rawalpindi and waited, outside the town, for the bus.

At Rawalpindi one devotee of his, Lakshman Das, took him to his home. Hospitality is ingrained in Indian culture. *Atithidevo bhava*, welcome a guest as you would welcome a god, is the commandment of the Upaniṣads. And if that guest turns out to be your spiritual mentor or a sage or a seer, then hospitality exceeds every limit. Some would serve eleven dishes, some twenty-one, others may exceed even that auspicious number. A genuine seer may partake of only two or three mouthfuls of food but there is no let up to the cooking; the kitchen becomes the focus, the centre of the entire household. The inevitable happened that day too, for a long cherished wish of the devotee was being fulfilled that day, the wish to have the Master as his guest. Gurudeva, however, took only one mouthful of the food served. He asked the Bhagat to make it a point never to accept an invitation in future. 'What a waste of effort!' he said. 'The hospitality of saints has turned into a nuisance. Eating means self-ruin, not to eat an offence to the hosts, to hurt their feelings.' The devotee and his family made repeated requests that the Master partake of something more but he refused, saying, 'Distribute these things among yourselves.'

That indeed is the way of the world! People would seek to please even those who have given up everything with the things they love and cherish. They would not follow the way of their Masters; they would rather wish that the latter be like them. A relationship of give and take alone can they understand, not the relationship of giving up. In a passage of the *vāṇī,* there is an explicit comment on this kind of relationship.[3] The passage reads as follows:

> Hard to tread is the way of *dharma*, difficult to find and hard to walk! Let no one choose this way to the truth, for death will be his companion sole and alone.
>
> The guru you have found lives on love; drinks in he that flowing out, but lure would you him with mere food and drink!
>
> The price you would not pay, his measure you would not measure. And yet you would be a sharer in his share. Your effort will go waste, your hard difficult striving, for seek would you the *vastu*, that ever abiding one, where it is not.
>
> Your very life the guru demands, less than that will not move him, for all forbidding is this relationship. The secret hidden will not open up if devote will you not your very self unto him. The giving and taking will be settled then. ..
>
> Let the guru be your sole guide in this world unstable and transient, let him be so until your life flickers out. Blessed will be your fame and blessed all will be you.[4]

From that day onwards, the Master lived mostly on tea. The decision saved his disciples from what he considered an unnecessary trouble but proved, eventually, harmful, rather disastrous, for his already frail health. We shall, however, return to the consequences of his decision at the appropriate time.

After the *yajña* at Gangothian that year, the devotees beseeched him to, as they put it, sanctify their respective village or town with his presence. But he declined their invitations. There were other people who, he thought, had a right over him, so he decided to go to a place unknown to him. Spontaneously, he thought of going to Matore, famous for the Islamic shrine there. In the vicinity of the town was a village Bamyālān, situated on the slopes of a hill. He proceeded towards the top of the hill but avoiding the regular path that went through the said village. The way he chose was a steep, slippery ascent replete with bushes and thickets and stones and pebbles. Anywhere and every moment one could slip down to almost certain death. However, he managed to reach the top of the hill, an uneven expanse of earth, barren, dreary and dusty, a few straggling trees softening a little its cheerlessness. The winter sun was about to set to augment its inhospitable look and herald the coming of a fierce cold night. After a little search for a suitable place in that waste and desolation, the Master decided to spend the night under a tree.

From the village below, a man saw him wandering on the hill and got curious. With another man accompanying him, he reached the place to find, to his astonishment, that the man under the tree was no other than the man he knew at Peshawar as Maṅgat Rām, the same person whom fire had 'dared not' burn. What could be the state of his mind to see the same transcendental person sitting on the bare earth littered with pebbles and stones can easily be imagined. Hīrānand was his name.

His astonishment subsiding, he bowed with respect before the Master and said, 'How did the Lord arrive here? There is but one way to reach this place and that way lies through our village!'

'*Premī,* the Lord is there to show the way. His grace led this being here.'

Hīrānand beseeched the Master to accompany him to his home and stay with him. 'If the Lord,' he continued, 'wishes to stay in solitude, a hut will be made for him. He has only a thin sheet of cloth and a blanket. One cannot spend nights in the open in this freezing cold.'

'The Lord's grace will smoothen out everything. Let there be no worry on that account. The stay here will last only up to the end of Magghar (Mārgaśīrṣa).[5]

Hīrānanda repeated his request again and again but to no effect. He went down to the village and came back with a large number of people to repeat the request with the same persistence but in vain. 'Let there be,' they were told, 'no concern about the winter cold. Were it a matter for concern, *This* would not be here. Lost is *This* in the Love Divine. You have all come here out of concern for *This*, that very concern will be protection enough for *It*. Appeased is *This* with your noble feelings. No need is there for anything else.'

But they still persisted with their request. To them then he said, 'If this persistence continues, in spite of reassurance, then *This* will have no choice but to leave this place at once. Solitary *tapa* is the purpose of coming here. Let that be done undisturbed. Please make sure that no one disturbs *It*, neither you nor anyone else. Only one amongst you will do some service here. Now the night is approaching, so please go back, all of you, men, women and children. After the *tapa* you will have an opportunity to participate in *sat-saṅga*, only then, not now.'

So they all had to go back to the village. They obeyed his command and did not try to disturb him. Only Hīrānand was permitted to do some service to the Master. Early in the morning he would carry a pail of water for the Master's bath and at 9 A.M., a bowl of tea. That alone was his intake during the time of the *tapas*.

Bitingly cold were the nights, with icy cold winds blowing on the hilltop. With a piece of cotton-cloth and a blanket for protection, he continued the *tapas* in the open with nothing except the bare earth for his seat. Ever since he was twenty-five, he had not had a wink of sleep. And since his boyhood his nights had mostly been spent in the open but here the excess itself had been exceeded. It was in the fitness of things that his fame should have spread far and wide. Many wanted to have a glimpse of the man that could undergo such hardships for *tapas*, turning the mythical legends into a fact. But the people of the village would not let them disturb him.

Matore, as has already been mentioned, was famous for its shrine, its high priests enjoying great prestige and influence and their decisions and decrees almost the status of the law. Fanaticism has often been the mark of the clergy, and those of the shrine in question could be no exception, given their power and position. The presence of a Hindu saint in their neighbourhood was an affront to their 'dignity,' a stain on their 'purity'. If some infidel of a saint committed the mistake of straying into their area of influence, death was the punishment reserved for his trespass. The fame of Gurudeva touched them to their quick, letting out the demon in them. His fate was sealed as far as they and their will were concerned.

One late evening, when it became dark, seven men proceeded towards the hilltop with axes in their hands. No detailed account of what happened to these seven murderers is available. Only a hint of it was given to a disciple, Bhīmsen, when he inquired of the Master about this incident. 'When,' said he in reply, 'those men were at the distance of about eight feet from *This*, fear seized them. A step ahead seemed death to them. They did try to move further but could not. Helpless, they went back. Three attempts did they make, night after night, meeting the same end.'

Three attempts were good enough to wash off their cruel fanatic insensibility. They went back to the clergy and reported what had been their experience. The clergy became unnerved and realised, perhaps for the first time, that their piety and faith were but masks for the sinfulness and the darkness they carried within them. Repentant and trembling, they went to the Master along with the seven murderers. Falling at his feet, they said, 'A sin great and heinous have we committed against the Man of God. In repentance deep we approach these holy feet. Let your mercy, your grace, be on us sinners, let us be forgiven!'

'Devotees of the Lord, no sin have you committed which the *faqīrs* should forgive.'

They narrated the entire incident of the previous three nights, begging forgiveness at the end. Having heard their account, the Master said, 'In the eyes of *This* all is the same, *Its* own self does *It* see in every being, living or non-living.'

'Great Master, in ignorance great was this sin committed. Never again will we do such a thing, never again!'

'Does the Holy Quran teach what you do?'

'No, Sir! It is only our misguided willfulness that prompts us to do such acts.'

'Act as the Holy Quran commands you. Remember in every being dwells the Self-same One. So give up these distinctions between 'us' and 'they.' Look alike on all and seek the wellbeing of all.'

Again they fell down at his feet, the clergy and the murderers. Until the partition of the country, they never failed to attend the annual *yajña*. With a touching devotion and humility these proud men of religion served 'the infidels' there.

Years after, a devotee of his, Amolak Rām, who too had the privilege of serving the Master long, asked of him if he wore fearful forms when those murderers approached him. Gurudeva's answer was: 'No, *Premī! Faqīrs* would do no such things. They ever remain absorbed in Brahman, unaware of what others do or not do to them. But there does emanate a kind of current from them that affects adversely those that approach them with evil intentions. Their own mind projects such forms before them.'

The incident increased his fame all the more, from village to village was it talked about, especially among the Muslims. All pressed Hīrānand and his associates hard to let them have a 'vision' of the transcendental soul. Under this pressure, he put the request of the public before the Master. 'What will they get by looking at *This*? They do not, would not, do what they should and must do. That is the way to redemption, doing what they are instructed to do, of no avail will be a mere sight of a *faqīr*.'

At the persistent requests of Hīrānand, Gurudeva spared a Sunday (the twenty-fifth day of *Margaśīrṣa*) for the *sat-saṅga*. Followers of many faiths attended it, the Muslims, the Sikhs and the Hindus. The Master gave a discourse to the gathered assembly. This is the gist of the *upadeśa*, that 'pointing out:'

> Deisre burns every being, without a let up. Of desire is the reservoir this perishing body, body composed of the five elements. Greater the desire, deeper will be the misery. Smaller the desire, smaller will be the misery. Every spiritual effort, every such endeavour has only this end in view: to find liberation from desire. Through earnest and sustained endeavour one does come to put a restraint on it. Spiritual endeavour or effort means meditation on the Name vouchsafed by the Man True, by one who has become one with the Truth itself. That Name should become the sole refuge and resort of the man on the path. Only that can take you beyond the pale of desire, this meditation of and refuge in the Name. Frail and uncertain is the term of one's life, one does not, cannot, know when the breath of life may desert one. So give yourselves up with devotion to meditation of the Lord, take refuge in Him, live as He wills you to live. A blessing and priceless is human birth. Waste will it go if you live bereft of the meditation and vision of the Lord. For, burn you will in desire, life after life without a count, without an end. They attained to the happiness true, those that the Lord loved, attained to the happiness that ever appeases and fulfills. And they, when called upon to redeem the people of the world, spent all their lives for that purpose. Full is his life, perfect is it, the life of him who has stilled his desire. They alone are the guides,

they alone are qualified to be so, those who have killed desire to find the Lord within them and everywhere.

Men and women of the world live divided into many sects and many faiths. But those that the Lord loves have only one way to follow, the way that leads to the extinction of desire. That is the message and the command they bring from Him to the world, the message and the command that man put an end to desire. They alone know the truth, not those who live as slaves of desire. Fortunate are you all that you are participating in this *sat-saṅga*, in this association with the Truth. Make your life pure. That will be your grace unto *This*. Be the true guardians of your ideals. From sins will you be protected, from cunning and from conduct evil if you share in the *sat-saṅga*. Study your scriptures with care and with a pure mind. Pay heed to their words and learn to live as you are directed therein to live. That will be the way to know the Way, know the faith true and the conduct true.

The *upadeśa* over the time came for the distribution of *prasāda*, the gift of grace in the form of fruit and other things. There were some among the Hindus in the gathering who were hesitant to receive it. For, had it not become impure by the presence of the Muslims? Noticing their fanatic disposition, Gurudeva said:

Why this hesitation, what is the meaning of this reluctance? In the eyes of the *faqīrs* all are one. Give up such stupid thoughts and beliefs! Can there be a greater folly than hating other people? Think about it!

The reprimand had its effect. All hung their heads in shame and accepted the gift, repentant and grateful. The Muslims were deeply moved by these words of the Master. It was beyond their imagination to think of a Hindu preacher speaking in this vein. An atmosphere of intense tension was in the air in those days, the tension that eventually led to the division of the country into two parts: the India of today and Pakistan. After this *sat-saṅga*, the Muslim population of Matore requested for a *sat-saṅga* in the town itself. But that was not possible:

> In solitude has this life been spent, away from the habitations of people. You like and accept the words of a *faqīr*. That shows the goodness of your hearts. Make your life pure and sweet and serve your fellow beings. The Name of the Lord is the most precious thing. Lose yourselves in that Name and, losing yourselves therein, seek to find the truth. Follow in your life what you have heard today. The Lord wills that *It* should stay here for another week. After this *tapa*, a *yajña* will be held at the village below. Be kind enough to participate in it.

They requested then for another *sat-saṅga* at those solitary heights. But that too was not possible. Said he:

> For *tapa* stays *This* in solitude here. That has to continue. This place is away from the town. Coming here will be inconvenient. But stay *It* will at the village for a week after the *tapa*, if that be your wish. You will get an opportunity for *sat-saṅga* then. A *faqīr* should not be pressed much. Next Sunday is the day of *sam-melana*, of congregation. Do come to participate in it.

At the said *sam-melana* the small hamlet on the slopes of the hill virtually overflowed with people. A large number of them came to attend the *yajña* from far and wide. At half past ten in the morning, Gurudeva spoke in these words to the participants:

> A functioning complex is this body-mind-intellect complex. Ever and always does it function, ever and always is it active. In his ignorance, this *jīva*, this living being, confuses these functions as *his* functions, imagines himself as their doer. This confusion, this, his, self-identification with those functions is the cause of rebirth, an endless process of this ever recurring malady.[6] When this body came into being, its size was small, and so was its understanding. It could not distinguish between the right and the wrong. With its growing grew the disease of desire, a disease that proved terminal. Youth came to fulfill desires of the mind. Every effort was made for that end but all went futile and useless. Whatever thoughts arose in the mind became the motivating force behind all actions and struggles. There were moments of happiness and unhappiness, of gain and loss, of health and disease. At their mercy he lived, helpless and miserable.

> Remember, this ever-perishing body is a disease, a disease unfathomable and deep. Strive, therefore, to free yourselves from this great disease [. ..]. Where are those that brought you into the world, where have they disappeared? As birds fly away from the trees their habitats, so flew away those from this world, their garden. So endeavour well to liberate yourselves from this net of illusions and try to find the truth, to find *That* which is ever itself. Find out *that* which makes this body live and move; find out that force, that power. Reap out something for yourselves from this body which never stays as itself and will, one day, disappear into nothing.
>
> To free you from this disease there is the way of meditation on the Name. That makes the mind still, makes it find appeasement eternal and endless. For, no attraction will remain for the man stilled and appeased thus, no charm in what the nine apertures in the body could offer him. Meditation on the Name makes one stable and go beyond the three modes of being, that of *tamas* [dull inertia], that of motion and activity and that of transcendence. It is only then that this being comes to rest, having gone beyond the range of these three modes. Only a human being can find the way to that state where there is no *tamas* (inertia), no activity [*rajas*] and no transcendence [*sattva*].
>
> Gentle souls devoted to the Lord! What will you get out of this body and the pleasure that it can offer, this body that will not stay for long? Please have faith in what the Great Ones have revealed unto you. Devote yourselves to meditation on the Name, spare no effort to succeed in it. Let that be the focus of your life. An ocean of misery, verily, is this world. From death to death you will have to go, finding no end to this process. Be kind enough to turn this misery, this life, into true joy and be the guardians of the generations to come![7]

The *yajña* over, the Master was forced to extend his stay at the village for another week. Here descended the revelation that was given the title *'Vijñāna-mātrā.'* Someone from the village itself scribed the revelation. *'Vijñāna'* means knowledge; *'mātrā'* means a measure. So the title means a measure of knowledge, a glimpse of it. Now what kind of knowledge it was, and why only a *mātrā* of it, a small measure of it, can be understood if we pay heed to what was actually revealed:

> Open the door that opens out to the sky and behold the Flame without the shape of a flame. Halt before it in worship true and move not until you burn with it, for the shore of the shore-less world is the Flame, beyond the world, beyond your life. Listen, ye of blessed souls, listen to what speaks Maṅgat unto you.
>
> Base has none the Man that speaks. Within these bones, within these veins, within this flesh and within this skin abides the Man that blessed you be. *Prāṇa* do they call him - breath, your life, do they call him. Know you what he knows; know it, that knowledge, to dispel your knowledge false and all the net it has laid out for you.
>
> *Prāṇa* the still does all, all that happens and all that is done. This shall you find, this contrariety, this vision that disrupts all thoughts and views. He is it that will lead you to the Lord and to the end of your miseries all, for eater is he and the eaten too, the food itself and its consumer too. So seek him, at once the truth and its knowledge true, the scabbard one with the rapiers two.
>
> Of *sat-guru* perfect is this the glory that through the path contrary he leads you to the truth. Bind together the incoming breath and the outgoing breath, the breath you inhale and the breath you exhale, and all intent contemplate the splendour bright. Bliss is that light-in-excess, supreme is the bliss and measureless the excess. Have faith in full in the guide full, and behold that light to become that light (*samādhi*).
>
> In own home yours will you live, not in the home of death as those who earn not the Name shall do. The flow of breath is the flow of nectar; beyond the world will go the man that all intent dwells on it. You drink the poison without while the drink immortal flows full in you. Death will be the wage of this your neglect.
>
> All was vain, all was pain, all that you found, all that you lost. You counted these and lost your life. What did you find in the end? Yours is not this city. Never will it accept you, gifted rich though you be.

> Awake you, therefore, and remember the Name and give your heart to it, give it in joy, in pleasure great. In your mortal home immortal waters wave, behind the secret door they wave. A seer of them shall open the door and there shall you behold them, hidden in your home. The Speaking Ones are they, the Immortal Ones, waters those that wave behind the gate. Let the Name possess you and all that you think and feel, and cured shall be you of delusions all.
>
> Let given up be device every other, gifted rich though you be. For all is an illusion, the world entire, world of sense and thought. No thing is yours, and no one, and of no thing are you, and of no one. False are your relationships, and false is your joy in them. The Name alone is your joy, the Name true that resides in you and resides in all. With intent pure seek the being of breath. That is the teaching of your teacher, the final teaching of the final teacher. Within you lies the chest of bliss, of your sins the killer. For bliss the dense is he, that Speaking One, the Lord, the Nameless with hurdles none.
>
> This body must you search, this brittle jar of clay, and at the immortal fount will you drink. Death will not come near you, your fevers all come to rest. Verily, Maṅgat speaks the truth unto you.[8]

The senses do not lead you to your truth, nor can your mind or intellect. Behind the senses is the mind and behind the mind is breath. That is a measure of knowledge, a little measure of it weighed out to man. In that lies hidden all knowledge, in breath that we pay no heed to, with no idea of what our breath knows. So man has to be breath, has to live as breath, not as the mind–sense–body complex as he does. This he can do only when he conjoins breath and the Name. When, guided by the Name, man flows with breath and, eventually, as breath, he will find, first, the door open out at the navel, then at the heart, then at the throat, and later between the two eyebrows. From there he will rise up to reach the crown of the head where, breaking open the tenth gate, he will behold the Word there, the speaker true, knowledge true, bliss true and consciousness true. In other words, speech will find its true being there, so will *buddhi*, the faculty of knowing, so will the mind that seeks bliss. But when speech merges with the Word, the *buddhi* with Knowledge and the mind with Bliss, what will remain of them and of the Word, Knowledge and Bliss? No one can say. For us men of the world it is death, for a seeker of truth it is the confluence of the name and the named, for the unhappy and the wretched it is to be lost in bliss.

But this is only a measure of truth, a little measure of it. But that is all we can know and say. That is all that even the Word can say, Knowledge can reveal and Bliss can give. The truth, the being, the bliss are but appearances of the goal and the end. That remains ineffable, the goal and the end. One can only die into that, one cannot revive to 'know' it or describe it. So all revelations are only revelations of a trite of what truly is. Even 'what truly is' is a measure of it. The other meaning of '*mātrā*,' of measuring, namely, enframing the truth in terms of intelligibility, is a concealment of it. Revelations redeem themselves by disowning themselves. In that lies the secret of their truth, in disowning the truth they proclaim.

Notes

1 A rough cotton mattress with slender ropes tied around, not the holdall as is normally used.

2 'The Hand Revered.'

3 *Vide Samatāvilāsa*, pp. 442-43 and *The Radiant Sameness*, pp. 50-51.

4 Your fame will not make you vain as it does in the case of those who are not blessed by a perfect seer, whose guide is their own mind and its formulations.

5 The month falling in November-December.

6 I have modified these three sentences to make them intelligible. The recorder's rendering is defective.

7 The discourse [its summary] is full of many a paradox that the recorder of the given passage did not fully comprehend. Some gaps too have been left in it to puzzle an attentive reader. In *The Radiant Sameness,* the author's translation of the *Samatāvilāsa,* I have tried to explain such paradoxes, as far as I could. Interested reader may consult the index in the said book.

8 *Vide* the *Samtāprakāśa,* Strophe 237.

7

Descent of Samatā-Jñāna

From Matore we now move on to Chinari, a small village like town in Kashmir, surrounded by tall hills, and reverberating with the music of the Jhelam, one of the tributaries of the Indus, that flowed a little below it. On the slopes this side of the river was situated the village, a little above the road that went along with it towards Srinagar, the summer capital of the State of Jammu and Kashmir. Chinari now forms a part of the Pakistan-occupied area of Kashmir.

On the tenth day of June 1940, Gurudeva arrived there, along with Bhagat Banārasīdās and Sevā Rām of Jalamādā, the same Sevā Rām that was the first to respond to the Master's call a little past the dead of night. The sun had already sunk low in the west, and, for lack of any other accommodation, they stayed for the night at the rest house attached to the temple there. The temple priest, a chain smoker, learning from Bhagatjī that the Master was a seer, said, 'Holy One, no one will listen to you here. Meat-eaters are they all, drunkards and gamblers. No one will make you any offering.' Whatever his motives, what the priest said was not entirely untrue. For, the majority of the inhabitants of Chinari had little or no understanding of matters relating to the Spirit. A weekly offering at the temple, a ritualistic worship of the idols, and some rituals on certain days considered auspicious – that was all that meant *dharma* or religion for them. Reflection was not for them, nor any consideration of good conduct nor any concern for culture. The young knew no restraint, the old had no dignity. The sole occupation of the majority of them was to earn and to spend. Perverse and mean, hedonists and niggards, careless but calculating – that was the stuff many among them were made of. Their ideals were the courtiers of the State that had neither the faith of the past nor the responsibility of modernity. A pathetic and cheap imitation of that decadence they represented.

Because of its situation, Chinari was a relatively prosperous village. The hill-men sold their products to the traders there, who sold them to the tourists at a good profit. That should explain their tendency to ape the courtiers in their own crude and clumsy ways. How could they possibly listen to the words of the Master, words that spoke of the tragedy of mortal life and the necessity of standing apart from what one did or what happened on its own? They would have sounded strange to them, those words, unheard of and 'bizarre'. So they did not come to listen to the Master, despite the individual invitation given to each and every shopkeeper to attend the *sat-saṅg[a]*. The temple priest saw in the Master a competitor in his 'business.' He let the people 'know' that the Master was a patient of tuberculosis, a deadly and almost incurable disease in those days. Looking at his frail body, the people were easily taken in.

The Master chose a hut a little above the bank of the river for his stay. Its owner was one Gokulshah, one of the few people who had some interest in what the secularists call religious matters but what the faithful term discrimination true and proper. Added to it was the virtue of hospitality towards strangers. But he too did not respond to the invitation. To make them open up to the deeper dimensions of their being, the Master decided to hold another *sat-saṅga* and sent Dīvān Singh, at that time his attendant, to request each one of the shopkeepers to participate in it. Some did respond to the request, but not many. At the end of the *sat-saṅga*, the gift of grace was distributed. One among the audience requested that he be allowed to bear the expense of the gift.

To this his request, the Master gave the reply, a smile lighting up his face, 'At Kohala was distributed the very blood of the *faqīr*, you people have received only the gift of grace. Why this distance, why this hesitation, when the *faqīr* has come here to give a new life to each one here? Free, of course, are you to follow your will.'

But never remains totally unheard the call of the Word. For even in that area bereft of thought and culture some souls were there to respond to it. On the morning of the third day of their arrival, when Gurudeva, the Bhagat and Dīvān Singh – the last having come to join them – were deliberating about a suitable place for the forthcoming *tapas* in the vicinity of Chinari, they saw an old man coming in their direction. A long, grey, white beard almost covered his face, his clothes were shabby and age showed its presence in his limbs and expressions. On his head he carried a container of milk and in his worn out cotton shawl [a gross misnomer for that simple, rough and worn out covering] were bound some pieces of wild fruit. To the Islamic faith he belonged, that embodiment of age and destitution. Bowing before the Master he said, 'Revered Master, be gracious enough to accept this poor offering!'

'For whom did you bring these, thou Blessed Elder with a Blessed Soul? Who asked you, who told you?'

'In the market place I heard about the Presence that remembers ever the One God, takes no meals that ever appeased one. The One Lord, it seemed, commanded this heart, "Go and pay respect to the Revered One." So, came I here under the prompting of my own heart. Thy grace I pray for, thy blessings.'

Receiving the blessing and saluting the Master, he departed. With the milk was made the Master's tea and the wild fruit served as breakfast for Banārasīdās and Thākur Dīvān Singh. The Master did not, as a rule, accept gifts from strangers. That he did accept the old man's gift could only be due to his perception of the latter's sincerity and purity.

Only a few people of Chinari, as already mentioned, showed some inclination to attend the *sat-saṅga*, the rest remained indifferent. So, on the invitation of a disciple, he left Chinari after a week for another place, Naradhajian, seven miles away. Naradhajian was situated on the heights of a hill on the other side of the river. There was no regular bridge to connect the two banks. One had to cross its swift current with the help of an iron rope, sitting on a crude seat hanging on it and manipulated manually on both the sides. Nervous people found it difficult to use that device, for a look down on the turbulent current would send a shiver of fear through their bodies. After crossing the river one had to negotiate a steep ascent through a beaten track in a thick forest. Naradhajian, a beautiful vale of two to three square miles, had only one house and one shop to boast of, the property of the devotee. Remote from every sign of civilisation, the vale was surrounded by dark hills spotted with houses here and there of Muslim shepherds, a streamlet racing through it. It was on this streamlet at a hut at some distance from the said devotee's house that the Master and his associates stayed for the *tapas*. His nights, however, continued to be spent in the open a few hundred metres away from the hut on a rocky seat where descended the revelation called, *Nirbandha-Jīvana-prakāśa*, 'The Revelation of Life without a Bond.' The descent of this revelation has a small incident behind it. Two of his devotees from Kohala came with a request that the following of the Master should have its own name. The Master was not in favour of giving a name to his following lest it assume the form of another sect. Countless sects had already beleaguered the country with conflicts and tensions, even, on occasions, violence. But the devotees said they were requesting for a name that should please all and should create unity and not divisions among the people.

'No doubt, the name,' said the Master, 'will appear, *Premī*s, but how many will understand its meaning? But the Lord's will be done!'

Four days later, Gurudeva suggested four names: *Samatāvād[a]*, *Samatā-satsaṅg[a]*, *Samatāsamāj[a]* and, lastly, *Saṅgat Samatāvād[a]*. The devotees chose *Samatāsamāj[a]* but, eventually, *Saṅgat Samatāvād[a]* was preferred. After pronouncing the name, the Master said, 'Higher than this name, *samatā*, no name appeared before *It*. Three times did it appear. Without *samatā*, there will be, there can be, no change in people's life, ethical or spiritual, no improvement. The word and thought of *samatā* has now mingled in the atmosphere. Slowly and gradually will it show its effect. With the spirit of *samatā* as their basis, the country and the world at large will move towards the right direction. No other way could be found. The rest will be decided by your *prārabdha*.'

Having said these words, the Master addressed the Bhagat, 'Banārasī, let the Word put Its seal on this name. Come here after the *sat-saṅga* in the evening. Take down then what the Lord ordains to be revealed.' By 'here' he meant the rocky seat where the Master used to spend his nights in *samādhi*.

Before the dictation, the Master asked Banārasīdās to write '*Samatātatta-vicār*' ('*Samatātattva-vicāra*' in Sanskrit). '*Sama*' means 'the same,' *tatta* or *tattva* 'thatness,' '*vicār*' or '*vicāra*' 'thought.' 'The Thought about what Sameness is' would be a literal translation of the title.

> *Samatā-jñāna, samatā*-knowledge, says the Word, is the primordial anchor and the home original. In it finds the becoming world its being, in this vision of the Alone by the alone. Without a beginning is this knowledge and without an end - this origin of the world and its end, this ground of it and its being. Of bliss is it the flow, this knowledge, and of pain the end, the pain that is life and the pain that is death. No activity stirs up in that vision, no unrest of it and fever. Unique is this knowledge, this matchless wonder. Ever liberated is this knowledge, liberation itself indeed is it, no trace of coming to mark it and no trace of going to blot it.
>
> The ground of all is that *samatā*-knowledge, Brahman itself is it, that Word unknown, and the power to soothe but not to hurt. Life of beings is it and the Word that pervades every place and spot. *The* way is this, the way that leads beyond the distinctions killing of the high and the low. Alone is it and ever itself. In the waters it flows, and in the inert it stays, flows as itself and stays as itself. To the other shore leads a bare touch of it.
>
> Before the beginning of the beginning was this knowledge; as wonder has it entered the world and as wonder does it stay therein. The final end is this, Maṅgat, the cessation this of sorrows all.[1]

Knowledge that we know of is the knowledge of distinctions. The *other* is always there to constitute all that we know and perceive, *other* in the form of phenomena, known and unknown and in the form of their supposed background, the world, that place of phenomena. There is the further distinction between a thing and the knowledge of it and between knowledge and the knower. But neither the thing we know can be pinpointed, nor can be the knower, with the result that the relationship between the two that are not, the relationship called knowledge, must, inevitably, remain indeterminable. We can, in other words, know neither the thing before us, nor its contextual background, the world, nor do we know what we are, nor can we determine the meaning of the term 'knowledge.' Knowledge of distinctions, the knowledge we know of, is, therefore, termed, *avidyā*, ignorance.

But there is a knowledge, says the Word, that is not afflicted by these distinctions. That knowledge alone is knowledge the true, that knowledge the same and of the same. Obviously, the why and the how have no place in that knowledge, for there is no before in it and no after, no cause and no effect. And yet it is termed knowledge, this darkness to us, to us who can know only what never is, who ourselves are naught and whose knowledge too is naught. This 'darkness' is the support, the primal home of all – all that ever would *be* but can never come to be. Things come to be themselves when no distinctions remain to constitute and negate them, no object and no background, no knower and no known. What is this knowledge and what is this bliss, this being of every being? What is this stillness, this wonder among wonders, this ground of all that is and could be, this Word, this Life, this All-pervasive, this Self, this Sameness that is at once the origin and the goal, this quenching of our thirst, quenching absolute? Let us pause a little and reflect on these questions. Victims of *avidyā,* false knowledge, that we are we cannot escape this kind of reflection, not until we come to realise the futility of all reflection, realise the futility of all reflection through reflection itself.

When we know a thing, we know it as informed by a concept/concepts but concepts that are not self-existing or self-sufficient but are constituted by their *others*: concepts rise out of oppositions and contrasts, they themselves are oppositions and contrasts; they are what they are through being what they are not. Our knowledge is, as we said earlier, a network of such concepts, concepts into which has been written their negation. There is also what is called sense-content, sense-content that cannot be cognised without concepts. Concepts make the sense-continuum cognisiable for us by hypostatising and entitising it.[2] So the world is a network of negations, sense moments intruding one into another, concepts informing them and spurned by them, concepts constituting each other through negating each other, and, in the process, negating themselves. And yet this interfusion, this universal confusion can be cognised or conceived only by one who finds himself stabilized into a being, for without this his stay he cannot think of, imagine or experience the world as the network of affirmation through negation, as informed by self-negation. One can, in other words, cognise, become aware of self-negation only by disowning it, not by being it. One has to, in other words, identify oneself with some phenomenon and, through this identification, add the characteristic of stability to it to experience the 'mirage' of entities that the world is, mirage because things experienced by a being situated in their midst never come to be themselves. Nor can become itself their percipient, despite its seeming stability.

This IS character of the phenomenon one identifies oneself with is not, however, confined to that phenomenon alone; it pervades all that can be thought of. Even the negation inherent in things cannot be cognised without positing the IS character of those things, even temporality or duration cannot be cognised without that permanence. IS pervades the world, the world that is not, pervades each and every object in it. But the moment IS is sought to be cognised, it does not remain itself, it turns into is–is-not ambiguity, into the Is ever on the move, ever a negation of itself. So there comes a divide between the IS and what we know of it, and the gap can never be bridged, though the IS is present everywhere, constitutes every being, even concepts and language, the two indispensables for any cognition. Is is our ontological ground and not the world, the world interpreted-deinterpreted in terms of self-negating concepts. The world suppresses the IS; *This*, *That* or *It* suppress the world; what we find predicated of the It or

This or That suppresses the It, This or That. Our entire knowledge is thus a veil, a concealment and ignorance. No perception, no thought, no intuition can lead us out of this web and this estrangement. And no methodology or system, however precise, rigorous or systematic.

Does this mean that we are condemned to remain banished from our being, our truth? There are moments when we withdraw from the images we have identified ourselves with and stand apart from them in serene detachment. Images rise before us to melt into each other, eventually to melt into the calm that we turn into, the calm that is calm because it is not. It is at such moments that Is and every interpretation of it, along with the self-negation that goes with every interpretation, come to be one – to undo themselves in the process. For Is can be Is only so long as there is one to know it and there is a knowledge or interpretation of it. When the two melt into each other, Is and its knowledge, there can survive neither Is nor knowledge nor one that knew of it. Yet this their meeting, this extinction of knowing, is knowledge the true; knowledge that is *samatā*. For here come to be reconciled all distinctions and all conflicts. No sense-content remains to resist the concept, no concept to impose itself on to the sense-content. No affirmation asserts itself to prove its negation, no object stands out to suppress the world, and no world remains to disrupt that object. Knowledge tends to turn in that serene nothing into reality itself, words into the Word. In our ordinary moments of knowing, we affirm but only to negate. But when we do not hypostatise a fleeting image by identifying with it, when we disown it to disown our being, then alone Being comes to own us up, Being that comes to be Being by disowning itself. We become the IS when we are not and, consequently, the IS too is not. That is the state of *samatā* that one attains to by provoking our death, by *presencing* it. And that knowledge is true knowledge that does not affirm itself as knowledge.

Three hundred strophes, each containing as many as nineteen lines, with each line consisting of two units, followed by a couplet, flowed out in the darkness of that night, revealing, in details, the vision of *samatvam*, of sameness. Next morning, the Noble Bhagat, read out those verses before the Master to let the man in him know what the Word had rung forth. The Master touched a foot of his faithful disciple and said, 'Settled at last are all the accounts, the giving and the taking. Into the waters have been thrown the ledgers all.'

The act embarrassed the disciple in the extreme, flushed with shame was he. With emotion he fell at the feet of the Master, tears flowing down his face. 'The Guru bows down before the disciple, for that is his way, the way contrary,' added the Master. All this was Greek to the disciple. He only gazed at the Master, all amazed and confused. A smile appeared on the Master's face, a soft and passing smile. 'Don't be surprised, *Premī!* This relationship is not new, life after life have we met, you and *This*. You are dumbfounded because you know not that relationship whereas all is present before *This*. That is the difference: *This* knows, you don't. The accounts between the two are now being settled, finally settled.'

'What kind of relationship has been there between the Master and me?'

'With questions like these provoke not the past. Just let your life run out its course. All shall you know when you know within yourself the knowledge true. Pride will seize you if the hidden is brought up to the surface. And this service that washes away all the stains will not remain to do the washing.'

After a pause the devotee said, 'How this *buddhi,* this knowing faculty, which has deviated from its nature, will ever know this secret, this wonder?'

'Gradually will you move towards that state, slowly and step by step. Serve and meditate with no desire in mind, no ambition and no hope. Haste is of no avail here nor is anxiety. Let the writing be resumed.'

Another hundred *pada*s, strophes, were revealed, which the devotee took down. On the request of Bhagatjī, verses came out revealing the nature of action and non-action *(karma* and *niṣkarma)*, *Maṅgalācaraṇa*, a prayer for the auspicious beginning of the *sat-saṅga*, and *Īśvara-mahimā*, 'In Praise of the Lord.' What was revealed regarding action and no-action might be summarised and interpreted as follows:

Karma (Sanskrit: *karman*) should not be equated merely with action, human or animal. Karma is nothing but the play of the three *guṇas*, the *sattva* (the transcendental thrust), the *tamas* (the state of remaining coincided with oneself, remaining an entity) and *rajas*, the struggle between the two, between the *sattva* and the *tamas*. Thus *karma* is nothing else than *rajas*. The *sattva* would not let me remain a Me, an I; it would not rest until it has negated me, and also all that I perceive and behold, the world before me, the world known, unknown and unknowable. I would not self-submit to the dictum of the *sattva*; rather I would resist this transcendental thrust in me with all my might and would rather change the things around me to make them favourable to me or adjust myself to them. I would make every attempt howsoever desperate to sabotage the transcendental thrust in me into activity, into *karman*. Every thing, subjective or objective, shares in this threefold *karma*. Names change and so do their forms. To be ever active, to be aggressively ever active, is their nature. *Karma* is the essence of all that one perceives and experiences.

But there is also the living being that perceives this play of the threefold *karma*. All that happens, happens within the realm of *karma*, the *jīva*, he who lives, should, as a seer and witness of that happening, have nothing to do with it but he somehow attributes all that happens in the so-called subjective sphere on to himself, the other happenings he superimposes on to what he calls the world. His individuality is a superimposition on to his true being and the world is a superimposition on to the true being of the world, though the distinction between the two, the individual and the world, too is a creation of this superimposition. The sense of *me* comes into being through the superimposition of a limited sphere of phenomena on to his, the *jīva's*, being, the other phenomena, the constitutive *others* of these phenomena he superimposes on to the being of the world. The being of the me and the being of the world are not, however, two beings: they are interconstituve dualities, the me the constitutive *other* of the world and the world the constitutive *other* of the me, the me in conflict with the world and the world in conflict with the me. This way man becomes a mortal living in a world that is alien and hostile to him to live a life that is nothing else than dying. This act of superimposition is also a form of *karma*. *Karma* can be done by the being of man, by his self, when it is already identified with the *buddhi*-mind-body complex, not by the self as it really is. Yet the *buddhi* itself cannot do this act of superimposition; it requires the self to do this act. This original ambiguity is well brought out in the following words from the *Samatāvilāsa*:

> When the *jīva*, he that lives, finds himself imprisoned in the thought that he is the doer of actions, when he imagines himself as such, he cannot but get anxious about the results of what he imagines to be *his* acts. This anxiety about the results of 'his' actions makes him happy or unhappy depending upon the nature of the results contemplated. Inevitable results of his imagining himself as a doer are these, this anxiety and deliberation about happiness or unhappiness. Deliberation of happiness and unhappiness fills him with desires of many a kind, desires to bring about a happy state of affairs and avoid an unhappy one. And desire results in deliberation of varied

acts and projects to fulfil it, making him ever restless and apprehensive. This unrest and apprehensiveness conceals from him the state of bliss that his being is, his real being called *samatā*, sameness, is and reduces him into a being of desires, a being given to incredible stupidity and egoism and to a fret with no let and no end. (2.1, p. 27)

'Every living being, every embodied being, is a prisoner of doership, be he a creature noble or ignoble, endowed with traits called good or with traits called evil. Whatever state of being he identifies himself with, in accord with that he acts and endeavours and reaps the fruit of his actions. Not a moment of rest this reaping lets him have, a moment when he could come to be himself and abide as himself.' (2.8, p. 30).

If a being is born as ever and already a prisoner of doership, then what sense is there to say, as (2.1) seems to say, that it is he himself that becomes a prisoner of 'I am the doer' illusion? The *jīva* is *samatā* already conditioned by this illusion; he does not exist, as a *jīva*, prior to this conditioning. Should we, then, put the matter in clearer, conceptually clearer, terms? Should we not say that it is the superimposition of the *karmas* (*karmans*) on to the self that brings about the rising of the *jīva* and all the resultant tragedy of mortal life? The thought expressed in these terms would, no doubt, be 'clearer' but unintelligible. For, without the *jīva* there cannot be superimposition of *karmas* on to him. It is true that *karmas* have an existential priority over the *jīva*, but this priority is dependent on the *jīva*. Without the *jīva* there can be no *karmas*, as without the *karmas* there can be no *jīva*. The expression, 'When the *jīva*, he who lives, finds himself imprisoned in the thought that he is a doer...' brings out this primordial ambiguity in simple, non-discursive, terms.[3]

The first step towards freedom from this tragedy, this inevitable movement towards death, nay, this dying itself is *vicāra*, discrimination. One has to know that one's self, one's true being, does not belong to the sphere of action but is a mere witness of it, a bare witness innocent of itself. One has also to know that the true being of the world too is not what the world presents itself to be, a spatial and temporal chain of relationships, but the being bare of beings, the existence bare of existents. So, one has to move oneself from the status of consciousness-of to bare consciousness to find existents as existence itself. This *vicāra*, however, cannot turn into a perception, or even into a conviction through discursive reasoning. For, discursive reasoning is constituted by concepts, concepts that are world-related, that is to say, related to the realm of ignorance; abstractions from the world, they also constitute the world. Therefore, the first step, the true step, towards this distancing from *karma* is to resort to *sat-karmas*, good actions, actions that lead one to one's true being. The actions that lead to the state of no-action are *yajña*, sacrifice, charity, truthfulness and service of others. '*Yajña*' does not mean here, as we have already learnt,[4] the traditional ceremonial sacrifice but flowing out of the confines of one's narrow self into *others*; it means, especially, sharing in the pain, the suffering, the anguish of others. Unless and until one can live the pain, the agony and even death of others one cannot be said to be a *yajmāna*, sacrificer or a *yājñika*, a performer of sacrifice. To be a genuine sacrificer or a performer or priest of sacrifice one has to give one's belonging to others, share them with others and relate to others through truthfulness. A truthful man surrenders his self to the other, lives at the other's mercy, all insecure and defenceless. With this meek innocence he has to serve the cunning world, which knows only how to serve itself. So he has to return respect for humiliations, comfort for discomfort, good will for ill will, openness for fraud and deceitfulness. This is how he will perform what is called the *mānuṣa-yajña*, sacrifice to mankind.

Another sacrifice too he has to perform, sacrifice to the elements and to non-human living beings. His sacrifice to animals consists in abstaining from meat eating, tending them with care and affection and abstaining from inflicting pain on them. To the earth, water, fire, air and the sky he has to sacrifice through leading a simple life. Let him be a visitor to the world, a traveller. Let him not become the centre of the world; let the sky become the centre, and the air and the water and the earth. Let him look at them, contemplate them, live with them and as them. If he opens out to them and lives with and as them, the entire world, the entire cosmos will enter into him, the difference between the body and the world coming to an end. The mortal will become the cosmos, will become *Virāj*, to use the Upaniṣadic term.

This contemplative abstinence comes to be possible when one associates with the truth-becomes. Not until one perceives Existence in their face, rather that which is beyond both existence and non-existence, and not until one sees in them the living example of *sat-karmas* will one be oriented to the latter. I need not focus on this aspect of the *sādhanā* because this biography itself will reveal what a *sat-puruṣa* is. When a man has done the good deeds, has sacrificed himself unto the elements, has taken refuge in a Great One, his actions will turn into actions without desire; they will become events, they will no longer remain actions, actions done with will and choice. With his will and choice extinct all innocence will he become, all passivity. He will not know that he *is*, for there will remain no *other* for him to constitute him. This is the state when, says the Word, the *me* turns into the Self, the words into the Word, the world into Brahman, the *Absolutus*, the Alone, relationships and distinctions into *samatā*. But the last word, the false word, we can speak about it is that it is the wonder among the wonders, the ineffable, the indescribable, the Nameless. The only legitimate thing we can say about that state, legitimate for us creatures of illusions, is that our thirst is quenched there, our hunger appeased, our desire fulfilled. But all this is *our* talk about the state of *niṣkarma*, non-action, and our talk can only move towards that state but cannot find it, cannot reach it.

Needless to add, to reach this state one has to contemplate the confluence of the Name, mind and breath, the contemplation described earlier. This meditation has however to give place to complete self-surrender, for the earnest striver has to turn into a calm endure-r, into a passive anonymity to let things be what they will or can. There remains no doing then, only happening, and, then, the cessation of happening. For, there can be no happening when there remains no one to witness it. That remains the ground of all happening, that witness. Without him/it nothing can happen, nothing can be, nothing can die, without the witness that abides in the world as being or existence.

The *vāṇī*[5] that manifested that night runs into several *pada*-s, strophes. This is only an interpretive summary of it. My apologies for the rude intrusion of interpretation, which could not be avoided owing to the complexity of the thought enshrined in the verses. So concepts had to be substituted for images, discursive thought for experiential expressions. I also regret the employment of the Vedāntic terminology in some of the sentences.

After the Word had spoken, the Master said, 'This *vidyā*, this revelation, is for all mankind. Supremely blessed will be he who reads it with care and devotion and turns his life into an embodiment of what it says. And as long as the sun shines and the moon glitters it will remain intact, this revelation. And age after age generations to come will celebrate your name.'

The Devotee Noble bowed down before his guide and Lord, and said, 'This being, given over to every stupidity, has found a refuge at the holy feet. That is the result of Mahārājjī's grace, of that alone. He it is who has brought me out of the confines of a cave, as it were. My speech fails and falters. No words can I find to sing the glory of my Lord and Master. Knowledge have I none, nor have I the power to think and judge. Thy grace alone can make this birth of mine bear its true fruit.'

When Banārasīdās was speaking in this vein, the Master asked him to read out the first strophe of 'In Praise of the Lord.' It was two hours past midnight when the Bhagat recited it in the glimmer of a lantern:

> Doer art Thou of every action and the Creator of the world entire, worship Thee I from moment to moment, You that are the Witness and the Man Infinite.
> Again and yet again Thee I worship, for of the lowly and the helpless art Thou the Lord Gracious, the honour of the dishonoured, guardian ever of theirs and of all.
> With but a digit Thine hast Thou fashioned the world; bound to the despised art Thou, Thou the giver supreme. In ways many I hail Thee, in ways many I hail Thee!
> Guard Thou the whole universe, sustain Thou it and uphold it.
> Remember Him you all, remember that Govinda, that knower of the senses, that One to the all gracious.
> His glory sing the Vedas four, and so do the wise and the seers.
> This world is Thy play alone, let Thou be my refuge and my support, in Thee let me find them, in Thee ever seek them.
> No thought have I to guide me, no light to show me the way, no door would open up for me. Bereft of understanding do I come to You, a beggar at Thy door. Give me devotion unto Thee; that is the alms I beg of Thee, that alone is my prayer unto Thee.
> Let my mind flow unto You, let it flow day in and out, be Thou benign unto me, for benign to the deprived You ever are. Let no stains blot my understanding, no trace of them let ever there be.
> With a thousand mouths sings the *Śeśa* Thy glory, that Serpent Coiled at the navel, sings he Thy Name ever and ever. But endless, inexhaustible, is Thy Name and glory, beyond the reach of that song. How could I then sing it, when sing can't it he of speech itself the lord? Ground art Thou of every singing, and of every singer the being, beyond their reach and beyond their ken.
> Undo my sins, in them do I drown. Let me have the thinking true, let me remember Your Name, let me find my happiness at Thy feet, there alone and there.
> The age of darkness is there around us, of horrid darkness and deep, of the holy is lost the sense and lost is the way to it. Now,

filthy cunning is the way, and foul fraud the support.
In times blind like these Thou alone art Maṅgat's hope, his Refuge sole and Saviour; take away all his desires false, desires for the phantoms false.[6]

After having recited the verses, the Noble Devotee bowed again before his Master and made a request for what they call *caraṇāmṛta*, the nectar of the feet, water touched by his toe. This act of him will undoubtedly put off a modern reader. For we of this age have been nurtured on the notion of the dignity of man. To drink water of this kind can only be a degrading thing for us. For no man is, for us, great enough to purify one through these degrading rituals, we would protest. This protest has every force in it, every justification but only until the point of time one has not come across a true seer. His body is, in every truth, a revelation and a disclosure. The body, they say, is the house of the Lord, His temple. The truth of this statement can be realised only by one that has seen a true sage. He is not a man among men, emphatically he is not a man. For, one cannot find the man in him when he is in *samādhi* or when he wakes up from it. I have heard many people talking about the human person that Gurudeva was, the smile that often spread over his pale face, the expression of love that gleamed out of his eyes, the tender words he spoke, words that touched the heart deep and profound. They saw in him a father, a friend, a counselor and a consoler. A being human almost to perfection! But that man was not the guru, not the guide unto one's being and truth. Then who was the guru in him?

The true guru, of course, is the Word but for a devotee the body is the guru, the body that shows forth the Word, shows It forth either as the silence of *samādhi* or as the articulation of the *vāṇī*. And it is especially the body in *samādhi* that is the guru for his more perceptive followers, for that is the body that negates the very concept of the body. He who has had but a glimpse of that wonder among wonders cannot but find it all holy, all transcendent and all redemptive, all saving. No word is equal to that silence, no revelation can rival it, no exposition, no thought, no human conduct howsoever sublime or noble. For, nothing is as sublime as the death of man when the man is alive. Let us pause at this paradox, let us try to imagine it, try to relive it. I am, of course, anticipating many things that are yet to come. As for me, I know only guru the transcendent, of his human self I have little knowledge and experience. And it is on this no-man that I will focus, while not ignoring the human 'encounters' that others had of him.

To this request of the faithful disciple said the Master, 'You say you have no understanding! Wherefrom did you get it to make this request?'

'The Lord[7] alone makes our vision clear, it his prompting that made me make this request.'

A month he spent at that place, remote from civilisation and inhabited, at a distance, by shepherds belonging to the Islamic faith, people simple and straight, who would not think of looking down upon other faiths, despite their illiteracy and lack of sophistication. In that solitude in the midst of the dark hills his time passed mostly in *samādhi*. This silent communion could not but have its impact on the inhabitants of those dense jungles. Even the people of Chinari could not but pay heed to this unheard of miracle. So, many from among them came to his presence, covering, on foot, the steep seven-mile ascent through dangerous jungles. They fell at his feet, begged him to forgive them and their folly and sin and made a fervent request that he return to Chinari. Easy to please, given to forgive, he consented to return there, and stayed there at the same hut on the gurgling Jhelam, for full eighteen days, a boon unexpected for those who had, in their view, erred so deeply. Every day a *sat-saṅga* was held, in which almost the entire town participated: men, women and children.

On the eve of his departure, a *sat-saṅga* was arranged, the last one, which people from the neighbouring villages too came to attend. When the time came for departure, a mood of pensive and silent melancholy seemed to have enveloped every one, nothing of the enthusiasm, of the joy of conversion into a new life remained. They looked at the figure of Gurudeva with a sad, unhappy look. Noticing the mood of the moment, the Master said, 'Ill is this *faqīr*, Pemīs, contagiously ill! Whosoever comes near *It* will imbibe *Its* illness. Think well, think with all seriousness before you approach *This*! The Lord bestow upon you the insight to know what disease is and what health is! For your good alone did *This* come here, for that end alone.'

The words went deep into their hearts, mute they sat with tearful repentance. For these creatures had, just a few days back, mistaken the physician for a patient, physician because he had come to cure them of the disease they called life. To break that silence, that embarrassment, Gurudeva asked Banārasī to recite some *pada*, strophe, from the *bānī*. The gift he gave to the people assembled there had this to say:

> Poison shall one reap when poison does he sow. In the hope in poison wastes away his life. The nectar he ignores, the Name, that immortal drink, to grieve out the day and the night, not a moment's rest, rest in himself, falling to his lot.
>
> In turmoil useless ever lost, of time a prisoner, his delusion unending, distortions endless will he fashion in the mind. Bitter will be his cup and everlasting his grief.
>
> His wealth will be a burden, his family a misery, empty handed will he go, leaving all behind, his vast wealth of no use, of no avail his riches.
>
> All would he make his, nothing short of all, but death will claim for itself whatever 'all' he has. A penny to a penny he adds, but a destitute he goes, his life a tale of sin, and his mind a weaver of it. The weaving will not cease until he lives for the Lord and dies into the Name.

> Forgetful of death, he lost his way and, adamant and willful, enjoyed the pleasures of the sense; motley shapes he gave to the heap of dust, forgetting that dust will but go back to dust.
> Of little account is his life, but great is his pride, while here can stay back neither kings nor heroes, ...neither those that cure nor those that are ever young, neither the wise that revealed the truth nor the yogīs in *samādhi* lost.
> Whosoever came, came only to go, without an end moves on the wheel of time unknown. Time spares none: neither the Creator nor the Destroyer, nor will remain the all-Pervasive to support and preserve.
> A term is allotted to every one, to gods as much as to men. Away shall pass the earth, and pass away the air, waters will not stay to flow nor the sky to contain, nor will remain fire to burn, nor mothers to suckle their broods. There is time for every being, a term allotted to it. Only the Lord remains, the Truth, the Measureless, the unknown Unknowable.
> Of the essence of time is the world entire, in change from moment to moment. Only the Lord mine, O Maṅgat, is the truth, beyond the more and beyond the less.[8]

After the recitation of the voice of the Word, the Master took leave of the audience, standing, his hands folded. He blessed them all that had come to assemble there, and they in turn bowed down before him. The Master with the Disciple Noble ascended a *tonga*, a small two seated carriage, drawn by a horse. The *tonga* moved away at a leisured pace. The people of Chinari, who had been so indifferent to him, looked at it with tearful emotion. Not until it had disappeared from their sight could they think of going back.

From Chinari he went to another village, Hattian, six miles away, from there he moved on, after a four day stay, to Jalmada and, from there, back to Gangothian as the time for the annual *yajña* drew near. It may be noted here that the Master lived mostly outside the villages. His message of the Spirit was not reserved exclusively, even mainly, for the elite. Well-intentioned people these days think of the poor in terms of only alleviating their poverty, a laudable thought indeed, but will that and can that do? Do they require only what are called the necessities of life and comforts, or something more? Many would argue culture could wait, you cannot teach people the deeper truths of life until they have a reasonable standard of living. But deeper truths are not something that a well-fed man can find in his leisure. In misery one finds them, in tragedies deep and disruptive. There are no comfortable ways to salvation.

Notes

1 *The Samtāprakāśa*, p. 342.

2 Pure duration cannot be cognised as pure duration; it can be cognized only as a succession of sense-moments. There has also to be a cogniser that stands apart from succession of those sense-moments to connect them into a series of those moments.

3 Cp. *The Radiant Sameness*, 2.1 p. 23 & 2.8. p. 25. Also *cp* the notes appended to these sayings.

4 Vide Ch. 3.

5 *Vide the Samatā-prakāśa*, 440-464, pp. 359-77.

6 *Vide the Samatāprakāśa*, 440 -467, p. 378.

7 The Master.

8 See *The Samtāprakāśa*, 359-77.

8

The False Guardians

After the annual yajña, the Master again went into solitude at a place called Shahpurkandi, once 'the town of a chieftain' but now shrunk into a village, its glory gone, its fort and palace in ruins. Within the fort, then the property of a rich man of Lahore, was a bungalow from a close vicinity of which one could get a view of the awesome beauty of the landscape. Below the bungalow flowed the crystal clear waters of the Ravi of those 'premodern' days and beyond them lay a vast stretch of fields and plateaus, of land uneven and hillocks that gradually rose to turn into forest covered hills to fade, eventually, into the blue of the mountains and their snowy peaks. Behind the bungalow was a room, plain and simple, evidently meant for the servants of the rich owner, and around these two, the bungalow and the room, lay the ruins of walls and pillars giving an occasional glimpse of their architectural design and of the carvings wrought thereon. It did not take Gurudeva long to decide to live in the midst of those ruins and that beauty. But as for the shelter, he chose, as could well be expected, the simple and unpretentious room. Cereals had already ceased to be a part of his diet; here he denied himself even fruit and vegetables. A cup of tea in the morning and another cup in the evening alone consisted of his daily fare. He remained in *samādhi* for almost all the twenty-four hours of the day, interspersed by the peal of the Word in-between. The villagers thought of the ruins of the fort as a haunt of ghosts and witches, so no one came to disturb him.

Here ascended, in those ruins, *Jīvagati-siddhānta, Sat-nāma-prabodha-mārga, Sat-anurāga-sarovara, Mahā-mantra-mahimā* and *Samatā-nidhāna*, the last work a collection of sayings in prose. The *Mahā-mantra* revealed itself, as the reader already knows, when the Master was only thirteen; it has already received our contemplative attention and so have, by implication, the ideas expressed in the *Samatā-nidhāna* during our discussion of the concept of *samatā*. *Sat-anurāga-srovara* has also, again by implication, received our attention, concerned as it is with the disposition of devotion to the Truth. We may, therefore focus in brief our attention on the two: *Sat-nāmāprabodha-mārga* and *Jīvagati-sidhānta*. So, first, the *Sat-nāma-prabodha-mārga*, 'The Way to the Realisation of the Name True'.[1]

Name, we are often told, constitutes our being but name the common and not name the proper which is only a label, a pointer. It is through a concept, that mental counterpart of the linguistic name, that a particular thing can be known, not independently of the concept. But concept also is multi-referential; it denotes a class of things. And a class is unthinkable without the individuals constituting it. So, neither common name nor proper name can be my name, nor for that matter can be common-proper name. For, if the common name is unthinkable without the proper name, it cannot constitute the latter nor can, for the same reason, proper name the common. Two unreals cannot become real through combination. So my real name has to be a name which is at once common and proper. And a name of that kind cannot be found in our experience. And yet we are ever in search of our real name, it is our need, our paramount need.

As far as society is concerned, a category or a concept is enough to sum me up. However, that clearly is not enough for me. For, I would be myself, would have the feeling of being myself. But I am born to be a dependent identity, an identity defined not only in terms of relationships but also in terms of contrasts. Divided against myself I am destined to live, as a mere *dvandva*, a mere duality, a conflict of opposites. The Other is always there to haunt me, Other in the shape of human and non-human beings and also in the shape of Nature, the so-called external world. Given this predicament, predicament inherited, I perversely try to seek my identity through differentiation. I would dominate others, would be a master in order to differentiate myself from them. From one category to another category would I move on – from 'the master' to 'the respectable and powerful' to 'the scholar' to 'the writer' to 'the scoundrel.' A fake identity I would set up for myself, an identity in the grip of unending unrest and anxiety, with tragedy absolute my ultimate portion, the true name, the name that constitutes me, is truly my being, ever eluding me. For our language, of us social beings, can only classify-declassify us, can only lead us from one category to another category or sub-category; it cannot find the name that we ever seek. We have to go beyond our being the social and its language, language of relationships and contrasts, to find our true being and its truly constitutive name. The *Sat-nāma-prabodha-mārga* reveals to us the way to find that name.

We have to, says that the *bānī*, distance ourselves from our speech, from our desire and from our intellect, from these three abodes of false names. What is there behind, interior to, these three, namely, our speech of relationships and contrasts, our desiring mind and our intellect that determinates--de-determinates phenomena, external as well as internal? It is the motion of breath. We have to focus all our attention on this motion, on it alone; no other thought, desire or percept should distract our attention from that motion. How can we accomplish this seemingly impossible feat? This can be done, says the Word, when man equalises the outflow and the inflow of breath, through a *Mantra* given by a seer who has become one with the Word. That is the name, that gift of the Word, that will lead the man so gifted to the Word Itself, to that source and end of all that has come to be. In That comes to be healed the divide between the name and the named, between the class and the individual, between the universal and the particular, in the Word that resides in the crown of the head. In that alone one finds or becomes the Name that is one's true, native name, one's being and one's self.

So the true dispenser of the name at once common and proper is a seer, a Word Incarnate, and not one's parents or priests. For, it is he who gives you the name that will turn into your true being.

The Master chose, we know, the humble room instead of a suite in the bungalow, the way to it lying, as noted above, through the ruins of human power and wealth. Inhuman was that way, a threat to man and his *human* being, a haunt of ghosts and witches, as the wise men of the village would assure you! The way and its destination indicated the *jīva-gati, gati,* the way, the movement and the goal of the *jīva,* of the living being. The way to our being lies through the ruins of all that we have achieved and striven for, through the death of the human person in us, through the terror and agony that ruin and death are for us. Beyond the ruins lay the humble room, symbolising the way we should live in the midst of the ruins that we mortals are destined to live in, the way of humility and meekness. The healing waters of life, however, flow deeper than humility and poverty as did the waters of the Ravi deep down the humble room. When destiny has reduced man to a ruin and made him learn enough not to seek his lost vanities again but to live all subdued and chastened, he will be called upon to be oblivious of his poor and meek self as much as he is of his proud and vain self. The man in him has to die down, completely and irrevocably, to bathe in the waters of immortality. The waters of the Ravi below and, beyond the waters, the long and vast stretch of green plateaus and fields and the sublimity of the mountains and their snows – the entire sight presented as it were a symbol of our destiny and pilgrimage. The waters that wash away our stains flow deep within us, in depths that are deeper than our human self. It is only when we have washed ourselves in them that we can breathe the true breath of our life and perceive its sublimity. That is the way to our life, to our being and to the joy and beauty that dies not with the death of *our* pathetic joy and beauty.

So, The *Jīva-gati-siddhānta*[2] 'The End Established of THAT WHICH LIVES', commences with a couplet about the true goal of man and then, immediately thereafter, on the actual end of our vain life and its ambitions. Victims of time we live, oblivious of our own true being, ever trying to *be* where we cannot *be*. No prop can make us come to be our true self, neither our body, nor our thoughts nor our intellect, not to speak of the possessions in terms of which we measure the value, the truth, so to say, of our being. In bondage we ever live, in bondage of the three modes of being, of *tamas*, of *sattva* and of *rajas*. These three determine our nature, our nature determines our actions and those actions, in turn, fashion our nature with no end to this process, taking away every hope of deliverance from this vicious circle. So we move on from one state of coming-to-be to another state of coming-to-be, the passion for being ending in our death, death that gives rise to another frustrating journey towards being. That is the end destined for us, the end nowhere, the end that is tragic in the absolute sense of the term.

That end is apportioned to us, us victims of desire and action, because we forget our true being, the true being that can redeem us from this our inevitable tragedy. We meet that end because we hear not the Being that speaks in all, the Word that is Man the True. Blind and deaf we live, forgetful of that Lord undecaying and immortal, that Being that is ever the same, that Being that is sameness itself. It would not stick to Itself, that Being, nor would It change nor would It transcend, that Call from gate the tenth. Invisible and Nameless is That, the Word that dwells in the all without being the all. Brahman the higher and transcendent is It, that Passive One untouched by activity, that Life of the world, that One without a second, without a beginning, without a sign, without a colour and without a title. That is our end, our true redemptive end, that Lord Supreme about which the Vedas can speak only as 'Not this, Not this.' He is the Self, He is Brahman, He is Speech, He is Silence, He is the Name and He is the Nameless, and yet He is none of these. His names are countless, and countless are His forms. As no-Cause He dwells in all, this Cause, dwelling as Himself and in Himself, without a prop and without support – that life and death alike of the world, that Being Ever-the-Same. The name true is the way to that Name True, to the Word that is no Word, to the Silence that is no Silence, to the Self that is no Self. Where one is and is not, where one speaks and does not speak, where one is oneself and is not oneself, where all is one, being or no being, the Word and the no-Word, the name and the nameless - that [state?]is the end of man, his true redemptive end.

If man's bonded being is nowhere and so is his liberated being, what is the difference between the two, between life-in-death and life *in* death? The bonded state, says the Word, is the deviation called the sense of being a me or an I. This I-consciousness is the primordial bondage. From I-consciousness springs desire that prompts one to act justly or unjustly. Action leads to I-am-the-doer sense and that to identification with a body. Identification with the body leads to social-relationships, to the state of being that is fashioned by others, to a state where you are and look as the others would like you to be and to look. These social relationships create distinctions between the high and the low and the resultant tensions and conflicts. Sexuality, anger, resentments etc. inextricably inhere in the social being that man comes to be as an embodied being. All frauds, all acts of injustice, cruelty and greed breed in the being called a sociality or communality. In truth, to be born is to be in bondage; one cannot escape these phases of bondage when one is born into the world. Name and Form, the three modes of being, actions and perceptibility – all these constitute the state of bondage. Hope is bondage, thought is bondage, the senses are bondage, religious belief is bondage, and knowledge is bondage and so is power, power created by cruelty and sustained by it. In desire is man born, in desire he lives and dies, be he a king, or a beggar, be he a man with a family or one gifted and learned. ***Even guides, teachers and gurus, those who tell truth from untruth, redemption from fall are victims of desire***. Even they live in bondage. The whole world moves inflicted with desire.

The Word alone is free, the Truth that has no shape and no form. That alone is free and no one else. And it is Its name alone, the name of the Nameless, that can lead you to your self, self that is not, to the word that is silence, to the silence that is the word, to the base that is baseless. Immortality is owning up to your mortality; it means *presencing* death before you ever and always. Our hell will be our heaven, our fall our redemption but only when we live and die with all, each moment, each conceivable and not conceivable fraction of it. For, it is only when I am not that my bondage will turn into freedom, my curse into blessing, the *other* into the self, the self into the *other*, the alone into the all and the all into the alone. But we profane the Truth when we use these terms. Our descriptions are all blasphemies, our prayer a sacrilege, our homage an insult. They are so because we are there to pollute them, to degrade them, to blemish them. We are the sin, we are the curse, we are the bondage and we are the fall. When we are naught, then misery too is naught. *Māyā* will turn into Brahman, speech into the Word, the not-self into the self, bondage into liberation, ignorance into enlightenment when I am absent from the scene. Self-sacrifice is the essence of *tapas*. And that comes to be possible when the the Name, mind and breath come together to turn into stillness. To be simple in appearance, to be self-restrained in eating, to be innocent in thought, to be a servant unto others, to be open and truthful, to find one's refuge in the seers and follow their instructions - all these are a preparation for bringing about confluence of the name, mind and breath.

However, the confluence of the name, mind and breath is difficult to bring about without *sat-vicāra*, right thinking. '*Vicāra*' is derived from *vi-car*, to move in different directions. So '*vicāra*' means to think about a thing, examine it thoroughly, to look at every aspect, every facet of it. One can do this kind of thinking only if one does not have any interest – theoretical, conceptual or practical – to prompt it. The Narcissus in man has to die to do this kind of thinking. He has to be and live every point of view, which eventually will lead to no point of view. *Sat-vicāra*, true thinking, ultimately ends up in thinking in innocence, in simple, disinterested ob-servation rather observance[3] of what occurs before and in man. Some may object that passive observance or observation of this kind is impossible; there are always some considerations or interests behind our thinking and observations, some conceptual or practical framework. Bereft of that framework our thinking will be chaotic and our observations confused and confusing. The unacknowledged assumption behind this thought is that it is man, man the Intersubjectivity – that brings about an order among phenomena, that he is the dispenser of meaning, that he is the, to use a phrase that was much in fashion sometimes back, interpreter and that the world is nothing else than an interpretation – an intersubjective interpretation. But there is a before and an after, here and there; there is birth, life and death, and, most of all, there is a given, instinctive struggle against the ravages caused by time.[4] Man does not have to devise a framework, theoretical or otherwise, for observing these, he is born into these. That there is a struggle between decay and his desire to preserve himself is evident to every man, sophisticated or unsophisticated. There is also violence, the transfer of the forces of death operating within a being on to others. That the battle between Thanatos and Eros is eternal is a truth no one can deny, despite one's reservations about Freud's formulations of it.

So the first step towards right thinking is the acknowledgement of our mortality, acknowledgement living and genuine; we are not only to think that we are mortals, we must *presence* that mortality before us. For only death, as I said earlier, can be a genuine *presence*, not the objects that serve as props for our own being, fake props for fake being. They can never come to *be*, nor can we, their dependents. So true thinking consists in not only observation in passivity of what happens before us, not only in the awareness that we are moving towards death but also that death is there in every moment, in every conceivable moment of our life. We must live that death, find it a presence, we must cease to be a form among forms, a shape among shapes.

As shapes among shapes, as beings related to others, we tend to forget our ultimate loneliness, forget that we have come to be in order not to come to be, that each and every moment enacts our death, death of the sense of our respective identities. When realisation of this truth comes to acquire an experiential depth in us, we tend to stand apart from our thoughts and desires, the reports of the senses and even the motion of our breath. It is as this innocent witness of our being that never is being, it is as this unobtrusive and passive witness of our tragedy that we let happen what happens and do not turn it into actions, *our* actions. If we try to know what that witness is, we will inevitably fail in our attempts. Only the confluence of the name, mind and breath can lead us to that witness, witness innocent of itself, not our thinking: practical, theoretical or scientific. True thinking cannot be the product of communicative discourse, nor can it be a theory-laden observation; it is observation in innocence, bereft of all self-interest. To think [truly] is to turn into a recipient, a passive recipient of what comes to happen to man; it is dying, not living, and through this dying becoming [a] witness of dying. But this is not an easy thing to do, for man's natural thinking is narcissistic; it is anthropomorphic and flows from 'man the centre, that so-called measurer of everything.' This self-interest, this narcissism has to die before one can qualify for being a thinker in the true sense of the term. To acquire that qualification, one has to let *sat*, Being, pervade one's entire being, let the being that is not become Being that too is not. All our ethical actions have to be directed towards that end, to the erasure of our self-interest, self-love and selfhood.

We in this age tend to envisage ethical conduct as enshrined in only social relationships; there is no ethics for us outside those relationships. Man, we believe, is essentially a sociality or communality and his ethical conduct cannot transgress this ontology. Now, being *with* others easily turns into being *for* others, for some select others, those with influence, power and intelligence, and those who have the means to orient all social projects and activities towards serving their own interests. I need not dwell on these unpleasant facts of our contemporary cultural scene for the present. All that I wish to say in the present context is that genuine ethical norms are never the products of the history of social relationships, norms that could be called universal and ever applicable. Our customs change and so change our usages: products are they of various cultures and their epochs; these do not make true *dharma*, the right conduct – the *dharma* that could satisfy our sense of *the ough*t and our aspiration towards it.

Wherefrom, then, can we receive the Law that can appease our transcendental thrust, our sense and aspiration towards *the ought* as against our aspiration towards the apparent and fake *is*, if cultures are there to fail us invariably? The answer is: Only from the Word, from him who has died into the Word and speaks not as a man but as the Word. He alone can give the call, the call that disowns all states of being man would identify himself with in order to *be*. The so-called righteous cease to be righteous the moment the norms adopted by a particular culture give place to norms adopted by another, succeeding culture. But the paramount duty remains intact in every phase or facet of cultures, the duty of accepting one's portion of mortality. Death will come and man must grapple with this truth, must let it confront him, this his real, final goal. He is not to invent the fictions of historical process, of a collective *Geist*, of pragmatic considerations, or episodic norms of *epistemes*, to name some of the bewildering norms invented in modern times. The eternal conflict between life and death has to be recognised as *the* truth about being-with-others; we are not to let our theories and so-called norms to sleep over this deadly conflict. **So in order to die as a being and to become a witness of its dying**, one has to adopt a conduct that leads one to distance oneself from the senses, from the mind, from the intellect and from breath too. For, that is the real way to genuine death. What we term death is not the real, ultimate death.

To attain to that end, the first duty of man the embodied being, the being living among and along with others, is, the Word proclaims, not to live in terms of give and take but in terms of giving. *Dāna*, giving, is his first duty. But that is not possible without a check on his greed and hedonistic inclinations. To give to others he has to deny much to himself, has to give up all unnecessary and vain desires. This denial is not possible unless one sees an example thereof in the person of his *guru*. So the Word-become *guru* is the indispensable guide through this inferno of desire. When its fury turns mild and soft, man steps back from the senses and his mind and becomes inward oriented. His next duty is to give up concepts, to step back from the intellect. This he can accomplish only if he has given himself up to the word of his *guru* or teacher. That alone, that word alone, becomes his preceptor, the maker of his precepts. When that happens, his guru will initiate him into the contemplation of the Name, mind and breath to become their witness. Then will end the torture of his ego-sense, his I-sense, when he turns into that innocence.

A man whose I-sense has ceased to be and with the cessation of the I-sense has ceased to be the doer in him – a man dead to himself would not, of course, absorb the *other* into self the subjectivity, as would some Idealists, British or Buddhist. He would not reduce the so-called matter to the so-called mind. He, the man dead unto himself, will just live with all, die with all, will be born with all, suffer with all and be happy with all. And yet he will neither live nor die nor suffer nor enjoy – for distant will he remain from all these occurrences of birth and death, a bare witness he will be of these events, witness who does not know that he is a witness. A mere passive letting-be will he be, a mere innocence will he be, innocence that knows no distinctions. Innocence alone, we may say – for we humans cannot but speak - is *sad-dharma* and the real undertaking – that is the way to the truth, to the aim and goal of our life. For, this disposition of passive letting-be leads to innocence absolute, which the *yogins* term as *samādhi*, or the Word, men of wisdom as Brahman the All, the ontologically disinherited as the Self or Man, and men of thought as Being and the unhappy as bliss. These terms however are self-disowning terms for the man who has attained to his Being. Even 'Being' would make no sense [to him].

One cannot get immersed in the spirit of this kind of *sad-dharma* unless and until one does the right *karma*, the right act, the act that leads to the truth, the truth that abides beyond the sense-mind-intellect-breath complex that man imagines himself to be. Thus only a *mumukṣu*, the seeker of release from the embodied state of being, is the true man of piety, the true *sad-dharmin*.

This way longing for liberation alone is, for the Word, the true *karma*, the true desire and the true striving, for it is the *karma* that puts to an end all *karmas*, all desires and all strivings. It is in this state of his being that man surrenders his will or tries to surrender it. They say that surrender of the will is *the* thing, surrender of one's will to that of the

Lord. The *vāṇi* too, in the section on *sat-karma*, speaks in the same vein, or seems to speak in the same vein. But the true surrender of one's will, if we take into consideration its teachings in their entirety, comes to be possible only when man attains to the state in which all that one is and beholds is revealed as nothing but suffering, suffering absolute. With this qualification, however, that to know our hell as hell implies distancing oneself from it. To be the witness of hell is altogether a different thing than to be in hell.

And it is in this state of the witness, the witness of the senses–desire–intellect that one comes to live as breath and eventually as [a] witness of breath. When breath flickers before the witness, when it comes to be almost still, then it turns into what some term the all-pervasive upward breath, into *agni*, fire, of the Vedas and the *kuṇḍalinī* of the *yogins*, to strike at the tenth gate in the crown of the head. It keeps on striking at that door, the door ultimate that opens up to bliss the absolute. This the Word will reveal in the next section of *jīva-gati-siddhānt:* namely, *Ānanda-sarūpa-sādhan-nidhān* [Sanskrit: *Ānanda-svarūpa-sādhana-nidhāna*], 'On the Nature of Bliss and the Way to It.'

As language is separated from the Word, is a restless orientation towards it, so is desire a separation from Being. Until it attains to Being, desire will ever remain a frustration. And since nothing in the world ever comes to be a *be-ing*, desire for things remains a frustration. Not until name and form come to be one, not until they turn into the Word can desire find its fulfillment, its appeasement. That alone is bliss, that becoming one of the idea and the image, of the subject and the object, of the name and the named, of man and the world, of past, present and future and of life and death. There alone abides bliss, the real, genuine bliss, in nothing short of .that unity. The yogic way has many lures to distract. There is joy to distract one when one is distanced from the senses, when language turns into what is called *Nāda*, sound. There is a deep, holy calm when one is distanced from thoughts. There is stillness deep and profound when one finds oneself distanced from breathing process. There is a danger lurking in this joy, in the *Nāda*, in the holy calm, in the profundity and the mystery of the witness and its – of the witness' – stillness in the midst of the riot of thoughts, senses and breath. The danger lurks in the form of enjoyment, in celebration of these states and in expression thereof. Enjoyment within and recognition without cause the yogin's ruin, his fall from the states he has attained to. One must, one has to, resist these temptations on the way.

It is, however, not merely intensity of our effort or intensity of our sense of distance from our goal, surrender of our will and realisation of the tragedy of our worldly life that will lead us, says the *vāṇī*, to the Word. Since our effort often turns willful and makes us proud of it, we have to remember the deep tragedy that every thought is and every moment of breath is. The *vāṇī* in the present context refers to these temptations, elsewhere it sternly warns us against them. We have already quoted such a warning from the *Samatāvilāsa*.[5] But vain beings that most of us are, we cannot resist the temptations. We who have tasted the fruit of the tree of knowledge cannot but lose our paradise to undergo all the woes that go with mortal life. It is only when our purgatorial suffering has burnt up all our vanity and selfhood that we will be led to the state of *real paradise*, paradise where fall and redemption become one, and so do hell and heaven. However, these observations should not be taken to mean that there cannot be pure souls who can reach the goal without the curse of self-hood inflicting them. But such souls are rare, they are, as the phrase goes, born liberated as it were, born as already attained to the Word as it were.

A true seer lives at two levels, as the Word and more than the Word and as a man but greater than man. We must now come down to man the mortal. As a man

Gurudeva was a *tapasvin*, one given to *tapas*, to solitude and to incredible abstinence not merely from pleasures but from what may be called bare necessities. It was natural that he who had reduced himself into a no-body should become the talk of the villagers. If the people of Shahpurkandi had no fears of ghosts and witches, they would have all flocked into his presence merely to get a glimpse of the incredible phenomenon that he was. Notwithstanding those superstitions of theirs, there were some sensible persons in their midst that came to the fort and could not but be impressed by the look and demeanor of the Master. They requested the Master that he visit the village to show the redemptive way to its people, steeped as they were in ignorance and false beliefs. Out of compassion for these people, Gurudeva went to the village and gave a discourse wherein he urged upon them to shed such beliefs. Indeed, so widespread were such beliefs in our countryside in those days that he had to write a full chapter of the *Samatāvilāsa*[6] to explain the falsity of such beliefs.

The divide between the Hindus and the Muslims had, in those days, gripped the entire country, from cities to towns, from towns to villages, especially in the northern part of it. Already the demand for the partition of the country had been formalised and presented as the precondition of the independence of the country.[7] The World War was on and the British rulers were occupied with it but they made it certain that the divide should get sharpened. So the two communities hated each other as never before. Thoughtful people in both the communities understood the danger inherent in this divide and wanted that the two communities should learn to live together. The basis fabricated for the divide was religion, not the way of life. For, that had very many things in common. Some Muslims who knew the shallow foundation of this divide came to the presence of the Master and requested him to give a discourse at the local mosque. The Muslims came to attend it, the Hindus and the Sikhs. What he said to that common audience could be summed up as follows:

The world is a manifestation of Being, Being one and only. [Ignorant of the true nature of that manifestation, ignorant of the fact that the distinction that we draw between the One and Many is not, truly speaking, real] beings wander here aimless, unaware alike of the way and the goal. So [out of compassion for these lost beings] some souls, beloved of the Sole Lord, come to this ever-changing world to show unto these souls the way to the Truth. Age and after age they come for this purpose. What they proclaim as redemptive principles of life come to be, as the time passes, mere customs and usages, bereft of the purpose behind those proclaimed principles and laws. External signs never bring about one's salvation, be they brahminical, or those of the renunciates or of the *yogīs* or be they those that the Sikhs adopt or the Muslims or the Christian mendicant friars or the clergy. The sacred thread will not save you, nor the emblem on the forehead, nor the shaven head, nor the uncut hair – the obligatory sign of a Sikh – or the rosary that the Muslim and Christian holy men often carry with them. Nor, for that matter, the ear rings some *yogīs* display. These constitute no faith, no religion, these mere signs of identity. Everlasting rest can fall to the lot of only that person who lives those principles, follows the path shown by the blessed of the Lord. No fanaticism, or even a trace of it, can touch the souls that follow the ways shown by the Blessed Ones. Where fanaticism abides, there never can abide devotion to the Lord, surrender of one's self to Him.

Jīvas, living souls, live for themselves, ever and always. That is their way innate and natural. When their self-concerns find obstacles in the way of their fulfillment, they hold others responsible for them and nurture enmities that result in conflicts and violence. This is the way of the world. Against this way, the miserable way of the world, prophets and teachers of every religion have shown two ways to deliverance from that misery: the way of disinterested action and the way of contemplation of the Supreme Being. One is the way of self-surrender to the Lord, of living as He ordains you to live; the other is the way of distancing oneself from every desire, every thought and every act. These two ways alone are the ways of the men given to the service of the Lord, devoted to Him. When the ego thus burns up every will and desire, it dies into the Lord, becomes one with Him:

> I became Thou and Thou became me;
> I became the body and You the life in it.
> So none could say thereafter:
> I am one and Thou another.

May the Self-born Lord bless you all with the faith blessed!

Caste is the Achilles' heel of the Hindu society, a divisive and exploitative curse, its scourge and its undoing. There are castes within castes, clans within clans; there are the high and the low, the touchable and the untouchable. The high idealism of the Upaniṣads, the spirit of renunciation enshrined in the *Darśanas,* the philosophical visions; the critiques of Buddhism and Jainism, and, to add to the list, the teachings of medieval saints could not undo this evil, an evil that eventually reduced the Hindu society to the status of slaves. The way natural to slavery, the way of cunning flattery, threatened to become the way of life for the Hindu community but for the reformist movements that arose from time to time in the medieval and modern phases of its history. It is hard to imagine another high civilisation so obsessed with its own destruction. The cultural elite among its people practised, generally, *ahiṃsā,* the virtue of non-injury. The Upaniṣads initiated them into this virtue, the *Darśanas* encouraged it, some of them making it an obligatory duty, the *Yogasūtras*, for example. Buddhism, Jainism and many a medieval saint tried to convert it into a universal ethical principle, to be practised alike by the seekers of truth and the common people. When ***ahiṃsā*** became the cardinal virtue, so to say, and when liberation from life, that embodiment of *hiṃsā*, of injury, became the ideal, those who would command and rule, invade and conquer found little to sanctify their ends. Societies, however, need the *Other* to be cohesive. This is the unhappy truth about them, the truth that their cohesiveness is the gift of the enemy, be it in the form of an alien society or in the form of hostile Nature. Here aggressive enmity against the alien was discouraged, so people directed their destructive instincts against each other, directed them consciously and with a perversely easy conscience. A social masochism became the characteristic, the defining principle as it were of the Hindu society, an all-pervasive masochism. This was amply illustrated by the way the people of Shahpur-kandi behaved with each other, those caste-fanatics.

The brahmins of that village, unaware of or indifferent to the social forces operating in those days of the struggle for freedom, stuck to their old arrogance and self-conceit. To despise others, to look down upon them was their sacred duty! They would readily accept gifts and fees from those of the trading caste, they had no objection to it, but they would not eat the food cooked by any member of that caste. To feed a number of brahmins on certain auspicious occasions was, however, a sacred duty of those of the warrior and the trading castes. So, invitations were extended to them, with, on the part of the traders, remarkable humility and earnestness. The brahmins would accept the invitation, go to the homes of the traders, turn their womenfolk out of their kitchens, consecrate the latter with sacred rituals and *mantras*, cleanse them of every trace of 'filthy lucre' and cook food for themselves and, as a gesture of grace, for the hosts and other guests. For, purified would be all the partakers of the holy food, a part of which had been offered to the sacred fire, the divine *Agni*, at once the priest and the god! As long as the brahmin cooks cooked food, no member of another caste, even of the higher castes, could pollute the kitchen with his/her presence. When the food was ready, it was consecrated with sacred rituals. The first partakers of it were, of course, always the brahmins themselves. When they had had their fill, the kitchen and the food were handed over to the householders concerned. Seeing this hypocrisy of the 'learned' brahmins, Gurudeva gave them a piece of his mind in stern and hard terms. 'What is this imposture,' said he, 'this pretence? You accept their gifts, their foodstuffs and other things, and their money but you would not eat the food cooked by them! What chains have you forged, what shackles, you that call yourselves brahmins! Your writ prevails unquestioned, of you brahmins. Ages have failed to undo it and so have saints and seers. You continue to stick to your old notions of the touchable and the untouchable. Only the rule of the law will set you right some day!'

'An old, immemorial custom is this,' said a Pundit, 'which we find difficult to break, neither does it die down on its own by the weight of circumstances. Only the grace of seers like the Lord can dispel this darkness. We cannot, dare not, question what the Lord commands. None here can do this, will think of doing this.'

'Love you must all, you that love the Lord! Never for a moment think of anyone as untouchable.... This divisive disposition will bring about a ruin you cannot imagine. May the Lord make you wise!'

When the trading community was administered this kind of fare, it should not be difficult to imagine what treatment was meted out to the lowest caste, called the caste of the *śūdras* in the traditional literature. Gandhi called the lowest among the lowest, the 'untouchables,' *harijanas*, men of God,[8] in order to undo the evil of untouchability and started a social movement against it. The evil, however, proved to be too deep rooted and Shahpurkandi presented a typical example of it. On the Master's next visit to the village in February 1942, a brahmin devotee put a question before him, 'In what way should the *harijanas* be treated, Mahārājjī? We accept the gift of money from them but we do not perform their wedding ceremonies. We do not attend them.'

'This caste system has brought this country to utter ruin. Outsiders came to rule this country because of the social divisions it generated. They welcome the *harijanas* into their fold but you spurn them with contempt. You may not, if you like, partake of their wedding feasts nor may you enter into marriage alliances with them. But what prevents you from reciting the ritualistic *mantras*?'

'Today itself,' said one among the brahmin devotees, 'a wedding is to take place in their community. They requested us to solemnise the marriage but all of us, without exception, refused to accede to their request. Our elders do not give us the permission. Let the Lord tell us what we should do. The *harijanas* have threatened to convert themselves into the Islamic faith if we don't consecrate the marriage. What is our duty in these circumstances?'

'Let there be no delay, *Premī,* not even a minute's. Give not your ear to what your elders say. Perform the ceremony but do not accept any fee from them. Do it without any self-interest. And let there be a relationship of harmony among all. They remember Rām (Rāma), they remember Krishan (Kṛṣṇa), with all sincerity they do so. And yet you despise them, treat them as the outcasts! What good is in this your behaviour, what justice?'

In obedience to the Master's words, two brahmin youths went to the habitat of the *harijanas*. There they learnt that a pundit from another village had solemnised the marriage according to the Hindu custom and rituals. The youths told the *harijanas* that they had been urged by the Master to perform the marriage ceremony. Next day, a large number of them came to pay their homage to the Master. One among them said, 'Mahārājjī, what is our fault, what is our sin that you all spurn us, would not allow us to come near you? Don't we remember the names of Rām (Rāma) or of Krishan (Kṛṣṇa)? The Hindus have received more protection from the harijans (*harijanas)* than from those of the upper castes. How many upper caste Hindus were there among the five chosen ones of Guru Govind Singh?'

Looking at the pundits gathered there, the Master said, 'Listen you to these words and give an answer, if you have any. These are the days of enlightenment. The British have done some good; a good deal of this evil has been eradicated by them. The fast unto death of the venerable old man, Gandhi, too is bringing about some harmony. The acrimony that Jinnah[9] has generated by the demand for carving out Pakistan out of India too will wake you up from your slumbers. Assure them that they will not have to go through such humiliations in future!'

The pundits, in one voice, gave them the assurance. This pleased them and they left all grateful. 'Terrible times,' said the Master, 'are approaching. Your rigidity will not allow any end to this divisiveness. No happy relationships will it let flourish. These are the people that render you the services without which no society can sustain itself. You flourish at the cost of their labour, you who style yourselves as the guides and teachers of society. But you were given this status, that of the teachers, so that you may decide what is true and what is not true, and instruct the *kṣatrīs* (*kṣtariyas)*, the rulers, the *mahājans (vaiśyas)*, merchants and land-owners, and the *harijans {harijanas)*, the working people, the distinction between the truth and the untruth, between the right and the wrong. You were to spend your life in *tapa (tapas)*, in self-denial and meditation and burn your self into the light of the truth. Others served you to let your contemplative *tapa* continue uninterrupted. The *kṣatrīs (kṣatriyas)* were to dedicate themselves to the protection of the Land and the people and the *mahājans* (*vaiśyas*) were to serve the Land by donating their material possessions. In addition to these services, that of instructing after self-burning, that of protecting at the cost of one's life, that of serving the country through wealth, there were other sundry services which were reserved for the *harijans (harijanas)*. Feet walk on the earth, clean or unclean. Can you do without them? Can any society sustain itself without these workers? But you hold in contempt even those of the merchant caste! The days of your arrogant self-complacency are over. Be aware of the changes that have come about. Teach now the lesson of harmony, of coming together. May the Lord bless you with wisdom unblemished!'

The pundits asked for his forgiveness and gave a solemn promise that they would, from that day onwards, change their ways and their attitudes.

Notes

1 The reader may kindly bear with some repetition. The ideas expressed here are unknown to most modern readers and warrant persistent re-emphasizing.

2 *Vide* Ibid., 416-27.

3 Roughly, giving oneself up to a thing before one, without the desire to understand it or manipulate it. From Latin *ob* towards, *servare*, to attend to.

4 That concepts are required to know, to be aware of, even these 'given' phenomena is not to be denied. Concept–sense-contents are *dvandvas*, dualities. And so are concepts and empirical objects: they are interconstitutive dualities. Here, however, one is asked to give up all empirical thinking as much as one can. One is to do thinking as innocently as possible. *Pāramārthika*, real, innocence, is the end, *vyāvahārika*, practical, innocence, is the means.

5 *Vide* Chapter 5.

6 At the time of writing the essay in question was an independent composition. It was only later that it was included as a chapter in the *Samatāvilās*a. *Vide* Chapter 11. Also consult *The Radiant Sameness*.

7 *Vide* next footnote.

8 The term 'harijana' is no longer in use among those that constitute the political class. The community in question calls itself a community of *dalits*, community of the oppressed, downtrodden and exploited. The *dalits* question even the sincerity of Mahatma Gandhi in undoing the evil of untouchability. With some obvious exceptions, the political class, on the whole, has accepted the term with a deeply troubled conscience, for they cannot forget what the country owes to the Mahatma.

9 Mohammad Ali Jinnah, the leader of the Muslim League, the party that fought for what it called the rights of Muslims. The League believed in the theory of the two nations, that of Hindus and that of Muslims, as constituting the British India and for this reason demanded partition of the country on that basis. Jinnah wanted that all the Muslim dominated areas should constitute Pakistan. His demand was met, though only partially.

9

The Fount Among the Ashes

Gurudeva was now a man ever on the move. 'Man' would, however, be a misnomer, a gross misnomer. A man would believe himself to be an identity, a human identity with a character, a being with a name. A seer who has disowned his human identity and flows with breath to become the Word that is not the Word has no identity, no fixed character, no identifiable being. His 'ever on the move'-life reflects his being as a constant disowning of itself. That kind of life he now lived, a life that stays not to be itself. But the paradox is that wherever he went, he left an everlasting effect on many a person of the place concerned. A short visit, a brief glance, and, on occasions, a mere lingering glimpse of him were enough to make many remember him virtually every moment of their life. Many are there who would bear witness to the truth of this statement. When I say, 'every moment of life', I mean precisely, literally what I say. That is the miracle that has remained an enigma for them, a mystery they can neither fathom nor understand, much less explain. From Shahpurkandi he went to Lahore, from Lahore to Gangothian for the annual *yajña*, from Gangothian to Kohala, from Khoala to Chinari and from there to Gopītīrtha, seven miles away from Srinagar. Here descended *'Atha bhakti-mārga,'* 'The Way of Devotion.' For two and a half months he stayed at Gopītīrtha, virtually in *samādhi*, for the revelation, *'Atha bhakti-mārga,'* is relatively small in size. His attendant there was Thākur Dīvān Singh, the Good Friday of Banārasīdās, a man totally given to devotion, an example verily of it. We shall speak about him at some later time. The Thākur became a victim of the terrible riots that followed the partition of India, so nothing can be said about the happenings during the Master's stay at Gopītīrtha.

After the annual *yajña* of 1941, Gurudeva decided to go to Thatta, a town situated some miles this side of the mighty Indus in the district of Kembalpur. The decision was the result of an earnest request on the part of an old invalid who had heard much about Gurudeva but was unable, because of his bad health, to undertake the hardships of a long journey. The Master reached Thatta, along with Banārasīdās, on the seventh of November at about 5 P.M. The town presented a ghostly look, its markets closed, its streets deserted, the houses looking more like forts than homes, but not a soul could be glimpsed therein nor was heard a human voice. Inhuman could be called that place, absolutely inhuman, but for the presence of the armed Nepali Gorkhas at the gates of those structures that had the silence of the tombs about them. The reason for this deathly look was the proximity of the fierce tribesmen of the North West Frontier of India, whom the British, with all their power, could neither control nor tame. They resisted every intrusion of civil society in their midst, stuck to their way of life that could be summed up in two words: murder and revenge. Even during daytime they would not hesitate to leave their habitats to invade the town to plunder and to kill. Evenings and nights were, of course, dear to them, as dear as they are to the beasts of the jungle. For, that was the time when they would be agile and active. The Gorkhas that guarded the houses were made of a different stuff. Second to none in courage and bravery, they had the virtue of loyalty and mildness (I am speaking of those pre-modern days when the decadent individualism of today was yet to assert itself). The Pathans feared them as much as they feared the fierce but open hearted Sikh soldiers, for, one to one, they could be, these Nepali guards, more than a match for any tribesmen, with all their wildness and their cruelty. But they too, those wild Pathans, had, as many accounts show, their ethics. If once they accepted you as their friend, they could, these accounts show, go to any extent to protect and save you.[1] But an enemy was the pre-condition as it were of their being, he was their constitutive *other*. They hated 'a man without an enemy' almost as much as they hated their enemy.

Banārasīdās found out, with a little effort, the whereabouts of the home of their host, Chanan Shah. That old invalid came out of his house and walked on foot to the presence of the Master, despite the discomfort the exertion caused him. He made a request to the Master that he spend the night at his home, the very next morning he would help him to find a suitable place for his *tapas*. On the way, he talked about the insecurity of the place. His account received the response, 'Talk not about insecurity. The Lord is there to protect you here and elsewhere. Every being finds out some way or the other for his safety.'

At 2 A.M. the Master asked Banārasīdās to open the door and accompany him. The huge door, closed with strong bolts, bars and chains, opened producing a harsh and creaking sound, waking up a confounded Chanan Shah. It was hard for him to believe that the Master and the disciple should think of going out in that dark night regardless of what he had told them. But there was no way to protest before that silent, overwhelming bearing and deportment. So he closed the door behind them. A deep and pitch darkness enveloped the town, bereft of any system of streetlight. Gurudeva moved on with his usual fast gait, the Bhagat following him through the blank desertion of the streets. In a short time they were in the outskirts of the town, spotted with dunes, now turned into bare dark outlines, and with heaps of stones and earth, and shrubs and wild plants, all shrouded in darkness. Reaching a place away from every habitation, he asked Banārasīdās to make a blanket-seat for him and leave for the host's home. Banārasīdās had spent months and months in the wilds, where roamed and roared fierce beasts of prey but the fear that the human beast can cause in man is of a different kind. Needless to say, his going back was not a welcome experience but he had become strong hearted, his stay in the jungles had fashioned him in that mould. So he went on, remembering all along the guardian of his being, and, reaching his destination, knocked at the door. Chanan Shah was still awake, confounded with astonishment; he could not understand, could not imagine, how a man could stake his life with such simple, routine indifference. This one sight was enough to make him a devotee of the Master for the rest of his life. In the morning, he and Banārasīdās went to the spot chosen by the Master for the solitary *samādhi*. Chanan Shah was aghast to see the spot but the Master was deeply pleased with its solitude. The place was not, however, suitable for a prolonged *tapas*, for a pond of water there served the needs of some people. During daytime, it could not provide the solitude the Master needed. Accordingly, a search was made for some other suitable place in the surroundings of the town but with no success.

After a two day search, the Master decided to move on towards the Indus, about sixteen miles away from Thatta. On the way, about twelve miles away, lay a small town, Sagari, with a vast, dense forest ahead. Gurudeva entered the forest on horseback,[2] Banārasīdās and another devotee,

Rāmachandra, following him on foot. The Master and Rāmachandra went ahead, leaving Banārasīdās a little behind. On the way, he found the road dividing into two paths. With some hesitation he made his choice for one of the two and hastened ahead, anxious to overtake Gurudeva and Rāmachandra. He had covered only a short distance when he found his path leading to a small hamlet. There he inquired about the way to the Indus but, to his dismay, he found that no one there could understand a word of his. It was mystifying in the extreme, this their lack of comprehension of the language well understood not only at Thatta but nearby at Sagari too. Nor could he understand their language. So he hastened back as fast as he could to the very place where the two paths met with the road. There he found Rāmachandra coming back in search of him. He had strayed into the people who were a terror to the citizens of Thatta and who took it as an insult to obey the law. A wave of fear ran down his spine and his body was wet with sweat.

They followed the other path through the forest and reached the summit of a hill with some rooms built on it, three, to be precise. Below the other side of the hill flowed the Indus, with its vast stretch of calm waters extending up to a distance far and long. Beyond those mighty and quietly moving waters lay lines after lines of hills; on this side was a wonderful topography of hills and plains, the hills, at some places, suddenly ending up in the plains and the plains rising up to the hills at a step as it were. No human habitation could be seen there, none whatsoever except a few houses two miles away on this side of the river. A silent, vast expanse of breathless beauty presented itself to the eye. The summit was a place of pilgrimage, and the three rooms had been built for the pilgrims. On the day of the full moon and the new moon and the other days considered sacred, the Hindus went there to have a dip in the waters of the Indus. The ancients had declared that place holy. The believers believed them, the non-believers did not believe in the word of the ancients but they could not help believing in the holiness of the place. There could possibly be no soul, no living and breathing soul, that would not find itself elated and blessed in that solitude, with the calm it breathed and the beauty it revealed.

One of the three rooms was under the occupation of a *vairāgī*, 'one who has turned his back on the pleasures of the world.' Alone he lived there, far away from civilisation, in the proximity of the jungles and the wild beasts and wild men. When the three reached there, the *vairāgī* was cooking food. He did not care to speak to anyone, much less extend a gesture of hospitality. He left for Sagari after taking his meal. Banārasīdās and Rāmachandra, after a dip or two in the waters of the Indus, engaged themselves in cooking their meal, whereas Gurudeva started writing something on a piece of paper. In less than fifteen minutes, the Bhagat reports, he handed over a sheet of paper to the *premīs* wherein were written the verses that may roughly be rendered as follows:

> End hast Thou none, my Lord, Thou Creator of this spectacle wonderful, the spectacle of the world that stays not to be itself, though Maker real art Thou, with every power endowed. To Thee I give myself up, ever and always.
> Seen have I Your Nature, O Maker thereof, seen have I It, Thy Power, brims It with Thy Presence full; in the lands I see It, and see It in the waters. With joy I feel It, my mind appeased in full. Fled is my desire all.
> Manifest art Thou within every being, though colours have You none and forms no either. But who can ever get a glimpse of Thee, or remember Thee or contemplate Thee save he who has received Thy grace benign?
> Swift flow the rivers, their waters inexhaustible, for years in millions flowed have they. Such has been the game You have been playing. With flowers of the wild will You charm the world. But glory Thine decreaseth never, Thou Lord and Being true, Thou Giver of bliss, Thou God of gods that dwellest full in the waters as You do on the earth.

To the tortured You bring comfort, to the wounded You apply a balm. A giver You live in the world, dispensing Your life away as rivers dispense their waters. In losing it You find it.
You give Yourself away to make others happy, with the ashes of the burnt up world You smear Yourself. Thus have You found the place of rest for You.
Like unto a servant You roam in the world to bring them the Good the creatures seek. As their end and purpose You come, to chalk out their way and their hope.

Your life, O Friend, is an affair of a moment, a play that lasts not more than an hour. Seek then the life blessed and blissful. Let others be your care and your concern, no more shall you stray, no more shall you wander.
Serve your Master true, live with the straight that have hit the mark, and give to the Name your mind entire. Let your body be theirs, and theirs your mind and possessions, of those that are other than you.
Wash clean your mind of every stain every moment, every fraction of it. Die in body and in mind, die into the truth and into the meaning supreme.
Remember, this human birth is the rarest of the rare, priceless is it, its glory immeasurable. Seek therefore thy Good as long as you live. For, the end will be a separation and a parting, and dust will return to dust.
Meditate the knower of the senses, meditate him every time and in every act, your heart set in the truth. That, say the seers, is the striving true and so do proclaim the Vedas too.
Act well unto others, do them every good, and bathe you in the springs of love. Your wounds will be healed, says your guru, the scars you received life after life.
For that alone is the *tīrtha*, the bathing holy and true, this your service unto others without a hope of a return. In humility Maṅgat bows unto him, to him that unto others in service dies.[3]

In less than fifteen minutes, we may remember, these verses were 'composed.' But we need not dwell any more on the miraculous spontaneity of their 'composition' but to look at what they mean and suggest. The spectacle of the world, of the world transitory, is not self-contained, it reveals a third dimension, a presence that permeates the world but is not of the world. There is a presence that presents itself in full in the part no less than in the whole, in the ripple no less than in the river or, for that matter, in the entire length and width of time and space. But this presence can only be a revelation, it cannot be discovered by human effort, it manifests itself and by itself. No technique can discover it, no discourse and no endeavour. This presence daily spends itself into the world and yet it remains full, not a trite of its fullness it ever loses. It remains full because its being consists in spending itself, it is nothing else than endless spending of itself. Sacrifice is it, sacrifice constant and eternal, without a let and a pause. It sacrifices itself to sustain the world, dies for each and every being, dies each and every moment for them. Sanctifying water it is, purifying and redemptive, this self-spending, this self-sacrifice. And man too has to live as that, as the sacrificial act, only that. There is no salvation beyond this sacrificial act. To be ever self-sacrificing is redemption, is liberation, is immortality and eternity. Man is given only one choice: To turn into dust while alive or else to be forced into dust. If on his own he turns into dust he will turn into God, if he does not do so, from dust will he move to dust, from the dust that is misery to the dust that is death.

To return, however, to our story. When the devotees had read these lines, Gurudeva said, 'This is enough for this place. At another place, the rest will flow out. You have taken the holy dip in the waters of the Word. The *Vairāgī* does not like that we stay here. Solitude alone is not enough. The Lord's will be done. Let us return to Thatta.'

Back at Thatta, his choice fell on the cremation ground; that was the place chosen to resound with the voice of the Word. The Word resounds when man dies, when the *human* person [in him] is dead and is burnt into the Word, not into ashes as it happens in the case of us mortals that do not burn themselves in the redemptive fires but cling to life. It was the first night of the lunar month of *Mārgaśīrṣa* of the year 1998 of the Hindu calendar, the middle of November 1941. The time: 1 A.M. The landscape was covered with a thick blanket of darkness; no voice could be heard, neither of man nor of an animal nor of a bird. Gurudeva asked Banārasīdās to bring some water from a pool in a deep and dark cave at some distance, which the Noble Devotee did, despite his fear and nervousness. He washed his face and hands and sat down on the ground to take down the voice of the Word in the glimmer of a lantern. He beseeched for the blessings of his preceptor, drank the nectar of his feet and readied himself to act as a fit recipient of the Word. The Master said, *'Premī,* write first the *Mahāmantra* and then write, *"Sat-guru-prasāda-amṛta,"* "The gift of immortality from the *Sad-guru*, the preceptor true." Yes, this is the gift of grace from the man who has become the Truth. Age after age it remains. Desire-free it makes of man. The Lord has willed that it fall to your lot to take it down. Take it down, understand it and fashion your life in accordance with it.'

The Word uttered the first couplet:

> Peace eternal is *Samatā*, no other has it to oppose it and no other to sustain it, this the very being of the Lord. Think of it as *That* alone, the predicate itself of itself.

After that couplet was commenced the section called *'Nāda-viveka,'* 'The Knowledge True of Nāda.' The Master said, 'When you have taken down nineteen verses, then say, *"dohā,"* "couplet".' The dictation started. 'It was' says the scribe, 'a bitterly cold night. At every pause, I would warm my hand on the chimney of the lantern. The flow commenced at 2 A.M. Mahārājjī remained sitting in one posture till 6 A.M. I found the time to change my posture barely two or three times. Sleep had fled as it were, only around 5 A.M. I thought of it. Like a fountain was it flowing out, the divine *bānī*. No human power could reveal the Self in this way. Blessed I felt myself then and was grateful that

Fate had chosen me for this spectacle that passes every understanding. Boundless was his grace, of my divine guru, the refuge of the lowly, who had given me the privilege of sitting at his holy feet.'

The *vāṇī* commenced with the description of Being, the beginningless beginning of the world, the Person that dwells in full as well in the individual as in the world entire. The light of the world is he, of the subtle and the gross – that mine of bliss, of creatures unhappy the creator. Ever the full is he, ever the extinct, that end of every misery, that ever full and ever extinct. Ever unborn is that ever born, without the *other*, without a second. Manifest is he in the world as the *Nāda*, the sound resounding ever the same. That is the form of the Being to be worshipped alike by humans, by demons and by gods. Not the Being that is no Being, but ever the same *Nāda*. The *Nāda* is the origin, the *Nāda* is the end, the *Nāda* is the name true; in every state, in every age it sounds alike, this seed of the world entire. In every being it reverberates, in creature each and every, this Word of the Person Extinct, this Word that Person Himself, the Person that is not. The Lord Himself is this His manifestation, this eternal manifestation of That which lasts and does not last. In varied names they worship the *Nāda*, this full on every side, this bliss supreme, this indivisible, of every stain pure, whether of the visible world or of the invisible, this ever unborn Person without either a base or a support. A mere note of it will set at rest the myriad concepts and desires, and contemplation of it the recurrence eternal of births and deaths. The knower is the *Nāda*, liberation is the *Nāda*, passive is it, this motion, this essence very of the Vedas and of the *smṛtis*, of what has been revealed to man and what he has thought in response to the call of that revelation. The man who worships the *Nāda*, the Person Full will he find It to be, that Way to his release and his liberation

The language of paradox is used here both for the Person, the Being, and its manifestation, the *Nāda*. Sometimes they are spoken of as one, other times as distinct, as a ripple is both one with water and is also not one with it. Three hundred pages are devoted to the ontology of the *Nāda*, its attainment and the fruit of that attainment. The reader has to go through these pages to bathe in the waters of the *vāṇī* to get a feel of it. We have perforce to speak about that unspeakable in terms plain but impoverished. When does the *Nāda*, the resounding sound, resound in man? When man, we may note, steps back from the senses, from the mind and the intellect and breath. When breath comes to merge into consciousness, then both the consciousness of breath and breath itself turn into bare consciousness-of-*the-Nāda*. This comes to be possible, as we have said earlier, only when one meditates on the Name vouchsafed to one by the Truth-become preceptor. First, the *Nāda*, we are told, resounds at the region of the navel, then it resounds at the root of the nose, between the two eyebrows. Contemplation of the *Nāda*, real contemplation, commences there. Man has to focus his attention only there, there alone. He is not to think about what gets revealed above the eyebrows, for that will bring him down to the level of the mind. What happens above is the function of the upward breath, of the *kuṇḍalinī* or of the Vedic Fire. The *yogin* at this stage of his journey has to, the *vāṇī* would repeat the point unwearied, let happen whatever happens; he no longer remains the pilgrim, no longer the contemplator, no longer the striver, no longer the inquirer, no longer the disciple. To be a part of the happening has to be his life, not to be its regulator or its director.

This passive contemplation will turn him, in the long run, into passivity itself. Actions will of course take place before him but he will not be their doer, for, stand apart will he from them. For, no *to* will remain for him, no *from*, neither the actual nor the ideal, neither the endeavour nor the goal. If he tries to look at, to *actively* contemplate, the *Nāda* as it manifests itself above the eyebrows, it will disappear from his sight, will desert him. The pure sound will turn into articulate words, passivity into thoughts and thoughts will become oriented towards the senses and the senses towards their objects. The bliss will turn into misery, misery great and insupportable,

For the man who remains content with being the passive and innocent witness or hearer of the *Nāda*, the face of the entire world will change. Instead of objects of perception, visual perception, he will find pure light, light without a form. The eye will find its being in that light, the ear in wordless sound, the sense of smell will find the smell sweet, the sense of taste the essence of taste, and the sense of touch existence instead of existents. And light too will find its being, so will sound, so will taste, so will smell and so will touch. Words too will find their home, so will thoughts, so will concepts; they will all turn into Being. All the five senses will sing in unison the song of harmony, for they will not run into divergent courses, one sense trying to dominate the others. Acquisition will give place to giving, self-freezing to flowing out, closing in to opening out. As the senses will flow into each other to turn into Being, so will the things of the world; they too will be interfused to turn into Being. The mind will no longer be dragged by the senses to this object or to that, nor will the intellect have any concept, for concepts too will melt into each other, those creators of fissures and distinctions. And breath too will have come to a standstill and so will acts and the propensity to act. When this happens, when, that is to say, the mind and the intellect cease to operate and breath too almost ceases to move, then the *Nāda* and the hearer of the *Nāda* will merge into each other to turn into the Word, the Word that is at once the name and the named, and the word and its referent, and the knower, the knowledge and the known, and birth, life and death.

The *Nāda* resounds when, as we have noted, one becomes the witness of the senses-mind-intellect-breath. It is in reference to the ear that the Being[?] of beings is called *Nāda*. For all sounds, in the absence of concepts, turn into a continuum of sound, words getting fused one into the other. With reference to the eye it is called the light without a form, for no perceptible objects can survive the death of concepts, only the light pure remains, only that. With reference to the sense of smell it is called sweet or holy smell; with reference to desire it is bliss, with reference to thoughts it is Being. And with reference to breath, it is rest absolute, the end of its motion, call it death if you like or immortality, or *śūnyatā*, nothingness, if you will. I shall dwell on the last form at the proper time when I shall try to analyse these experiences in existential and conceptual terms. Here the narration alone is the thing. The witness does not, however, die easily; from the witness of the sense-mind-intellect-breath, it changes into the witness of the *Nāda*, of the light, of the sweet smell, of existence, of nothingness or emptiness or of rest and repose. It is only when the witness and the light merge into each other that they turn into Being. And so do the *Nāda* and the hearer thereof when they become one; and so do the sweet smell, existence, nothingness and repose and the experience-r thereof. They turn into Being that is no Being, into the Word that is no Word. This happens, this merger, only when one becomes so passive as to cease to be. We will find occasions to turn to the existential and conceptual implications of this account. Here I confine myself mostly to summarising the content of the *vāṇī*. We may, however, remember that none can reach that state unless and until death has become a presence for him, *the* presence for him. In this matter, the voice of the Word leaves no one in doubt.

The first night the *bānī (vāṇī)* flowed out uninterrupted up to 6 A.M. when the Master opened his eyes and said, 'The sun has arisen, the guardian of the world. Now take care of your bath and other ablutions. And then read out what has come out.' The Bhagat wanted to have some sleep but that was not to be. He went to the pool of water, poured a bowl of it on the body to send a shivering through each and every pore of it, shaking off every trace of sleep. A little more of the pouring, and his bath was complete. He came back to the Master and started reciting the *vāṇī*. Recitation over, Gurudeva asked the Bhagat about the content of what he had written and recited.

'Mahārājjī,' said he, 'Of the *Nāda*, of the Word, is this *bānī* the celebration, the *Nāda* which makes visible all that we see. This is it that gods seek, and sages and *ṛṣis*. In every being this light shines. But a veil of delusion conceals the supreme bliss, barring creatures of the world from glimpsing it and seeking it. A net of folly and *Māyā* entangles all.'

'Premī,' said the Master, 'First, one has to think about that which though invisible makes every thing visible and sets in motion the wheel of the world; one has to have a conceptual understanding of that invisible. Then comes the turn of turning into it, for which one must strive hard to the utmost extent. To get rid of the bondage that *Māyā* has forged is not an easy affair. But easy too is it. For those who gave themselves up to the Lord, made Him their sole refuge and shelter could reach the other shore without much ado. One becomes aware of the glory of Being only when one comes across a person blessed and suffused with Being. Only he can inspire you to get oriented towards it and strive truly for it and, eventually, attain to it. Strive for it with faith and patience. It is not the way of those who will be in a hurry, patience, patience alone will help, not hurry.'

The Master made the cremation ground itself his abode. In the late afternoon alone would he go to the town for a few hours to give a brief discourse. The rest of the day he would spend in *samādhi* at the cremation ground itself and the Bhagat in sleep. During the daytime alone could the latter sleep, not during the night when he had to act the scribe. The third day, when he woke up at around 3 P.M., he found a funeral procession approaching the cremation ground. After setting aflame the dead body and the ceremonial bath, everyone came to the Presence. One among them, a devotee of the Master, recited these words from the 'Sama-darśana-yoga:'

> Sing the name true of the Ordainer, sing in unison, ye that would die into Him, sing in unison His Name true, for know you not when the body this will turn into ashes.
>
> With charms allures you the beautiful world, but false is its beauty, a tragic illusion, for none was there who was charmed by it and thereafter repented not.
>
> \+ + + + .
>
> Proud are you of youth, proud are you of wealth, but in a moment will fade away youth, and in a moment will flee away wealth, for as is dust so is wealth.
> Where is the glory of those of old, where is their splendour great? Deserted now are their palace-gates, no pipers there to pipe of joy, only crows to caw of decay.
>
> \+ + + +
>
> The world will not accompany you, your family will not accompany you, neither will your wealth nor will your glory. In humiliation will you go away, overwhelmed by time.
> Know the truth, know what it is and give up the deeds that bring you to ruin. This moment will not you find, this moment opportune. Wake you up from your delusions deep!
> Tear apart the veil of false delusions, take your shelter in the truth! Death will not remain to kill you then. Of Maṅgat is this the word, pay every heed to it.[4]

After the recitation, the Master said, '*Premīs*, this verily is the place of rest of all those who have come to be born. Of the rich is this the rest, of the poor is this the rest, of the high and of the lowly. This is the final end of all, of kings no less than of beggars, of the wise no less than of the foolish. In desire burn all, in the fire of desires, every moment they burn in it, every hour. The misery a being inherits ever follows him; in misery is he born, in misery does he live, in misery does he die. Strives hard he to get rid of misery, but striving adds to its weight, makes it heavier than before. To be born and to die is the disease he suffers from, the most deadly disease is it. None can be free from it without the vision of the truth absolute. He will think in vain and strive without a goal if he lives and dies bereft of that vision. Human birth will become fruitful only if one finds one's home the true in this very life. Only that finding will cure this malady, only that. The deeds that a being did in the past inevitably bear their fruit; his birth itself is the result of those deeds. Their bitter and sweet fruit he will have to taste, there can be no escape from it. But he will not meekly accept the results of those deeds; rather he will strive for other things, provoking thereby new births and new tragedies. As long as you do not follow the path that the Truth-become have shown, unrest is sure to follow you. Lord give you all the power to see the truth! This moment's dispassion that you feel now will end by the time you reach your home. This *faqīr* stays here for your service. Do attend the *sat-saṅga*, save some time for it!'

One among the audience said, 'We don't care to come here even during the daytime, not speak of the nights. It was necessity, sheer necessity that brought us here and gave us an opportunity to have a glimpse of the holy presence here.'

'Think not of coming here,' said Gurudeva, 'They will bring you here some day without taking your consent. This is the place that reveals the truth about you. Why shun it in fear? You people worship your bodies. If you cherish love for the Lord, you will go out of your way to come here. But for your sake, *This* is staying at the town. In the late afternoon, a *satsaṅga* is held there. Spare some time for that too...'

That night when Gurudeva and Banārasīdās arrived at the cremation ground, it was already an hour past midnight. The pyre was still burning; little flames arose here and there. The rest of the landscape was shrouded in dense darkness. Severely cold was the night, making Banārasī's hands numb. He sat near the embers of the pyre to warm them a little so that he could take down the *bānī* that was going to be revealed. The Master called him to the four-pillared structure built there, structure open on all the four sides. The Bhagat covered himself with a blanket to protect himself from the cold and biting winds. The Master went into *samādhi* and the flow of the *bānī* commenced immediately, the *bānī* which was to bear the title, '*Nāda-upāsanā,*' literally, 'Sitting near the *Nāda,*' that is to say, 'Contemplation of the *Nāda.*' The utterance went on without a pause and without an interruption making impossible for the scribe to warm his hands on the chimney of the lantern. All the time he kept on writing, alert was he to the hilt, having had a very little intake that night. There was no heaviness, no drowsiness or a shadow of sleepiness. The *bānī* the Bhagat noted down in the early hours of that day related to the yoga and the hard discipline it involved. In the morning after his bath he referred to the hurdles he faced while meditating the Name.

Devotee: When I meditate, I find my attention stray away both from the Name and the motion of breath. The mind starts weaving its own fantasies. I don't know when this weaving will cease.

Master: How can your attentiveness, how is it possible for it to get concentrated on breath and the Name without a long and arduous struggle. Birth after birth the intellect has been intent on fulfilling desire after desire. It never thinks of freeing itself, never tries to extricate itself, from the clutches of desire. The secret of yogic meditation is vouchsafed to a man when he has earned the ability to do it through many a life of noble deeds. Then alone is it portioned out to him. Unless he gives his entire attention to meditation, how can the intellect find breath as the anchor of its being? Concentrate your vision on the tip of your nose and meditate the Name as the breath moves in and moves out. Let your lips be closed, your spinal chord erect and your seat properly laid. Let not your neck bow down, that sign sure of drowsiness. Ever withdraw your gaze from the things around and concentrate it on the tip of the nose and let your mind be concentrated exclusively on the Name and the motion of breath.

Devotee: Mahārājjī, you too on occasions bow down a great deal and come back to the natural posture after a long time

Master: Of something altogether different, *Premī*, is that the sign. It indicates the disembodied state, that bowing down. When the intellect completely forgets that there is such a thing as the body, when, that is to say, it discards the body and becomes one with the cosmos, it gets lost in Bliss the transcendent. Beyond the sphere of *prakṛti* stays it then, beyond Nature the primordial, the first made and prior. Then is it that the trunk bows down, as you say, to touch one's lap as it were. Long effort is required to attain to this state....

As long as one is conscious of the Name and of the motion of breath and is trying to mingle one with the other, there is no sense in letting the trunk bend, even a little. Not until the

Word resounds in man can there be forgetting of the body. The process of this forgetting starts with the manifestation of the *Nāda*. While meditating, one's attention should be exclusively focused on the Name and breath. Those who eat much cannot do this meditation, nor can those who eat very little. Neither can those who sleep much nor can those who sleep little. Only one that eats with restraint, deals with restraint and associates with restraint can succeed in it and find, sooner or later, the bliss that is *samatā*, sameness....

And let this be a principle with every one who wants to succeed in meditation: Never to do it in public. Let him do it unobserved and unnoticed. Years and years may pass by but no one should know what he does. There is no room here for self-publicity.

Devotee: Only your grace, Lord, will put an end to our mental instability. We on our own can never hope for success.

Master: Say or not say, 'Allāh, Allāh' but be unto Sūraj true!

Devotee: What does it mean, *Mahārājjī?*

Master: There was a seer of a high order in the region of Pathavar, called Chohan Bhagatan. Sūraj was his name. Even now, his descendants are called, 'The line of *bhagatas*, of devotees.' A Muslim devotee used to bring him milk and stayed with him to serve him. One day he said to his mentor, 'Revered Master, show unto me too the way that leads to Allāh, to the One God.' To him said Sūraj:

'Shahānī is thy name, thy caste of those that deal in milk. Found have you Sūraj, the Master true. Say or not say, 'Allāh, Allāh' but be unto Sūraj true!'

The implication is that remembering the Lord is not indispensable but steadfast service of the guru is. That is the prayer true, that is the worship true! That alone is enough to bring you salvation.

A true seeker of the truth should surrender his mind to his guru, and also his speech and all that he does and would do. Shahānī was his name, and tending cows his profession. Found had he the true preceptor. The spiritual instruction he received had only one point to make that his guru should be his sole refuge. The members of his community opposed him and his ways but he stuck to his resolve up to the last breath. Steadfastness is *the* trait of the genuine seekers. One should take a leaf out of the book of their life.

Devotee: Mahārājjī, you have attained to the highest spiritual state, yet you speak words that only a seeker of the truth should utter. Words of utter humility like these should come out of his lips, not from the Lord's. But you say:

'A beggar I come to Thy gate, Thou that art the Giver for the givers. Those that came to knock at Thy door received in return devotion full. I too have come for that, Supreme Lord! Let unto the end with me be You. That is my prayer to Thee, my Lord, my humble petition! Grace abounding art Thou, let that fall on me, Thou Gracious. Let me be devoted to thy feet, O You the Lord Merciful!'

'A beggar at Thy door I come. Give unto me devotion, devotion alone for Thee. Let this be Thy grace that Maṅgat die into Thee!'

Master: *Premī, It* has received and given what was to be received and what was to be given. That process is now over. Words like these are the cry of those like you. Whosoever treads the true path is our own self. The wayfarers on that path will find their goings and comings come to an end by heeding to what is spoken unto you. These words will give birth to love for the Lord in the minds of those that meditate on them. *As for the man that has attained to the state Supreme, it behoves him to be ever humble, ever self-effacing.*

Devotee: Mahārajjī, sleep too is a great curse. One cannot get rid of it try as much as one may.

Master: Man eats and drinks to suffer, sleeps and enjoys his pleasures to suffer. Birth is suffering and growth is suffering, and so are youth and age and death. All is suffering. All these changes one thinks as one's own. This confusion makes one now happy, now unhappy. Not until one enters into [the state of] knowledge will the wheel cease to move on, unchecked and unhindered. It is imperative one think in these terms: what is this body, whence it arises, what are the changes that take place in it and how do they take place, who is it that speaks in it, and what is *that*, knowing which one will be free from all these changes and modifications? Is there something knowing which one finds nothing more to know, which knowing puts an end to all knowing? Not until one meditates on these questions can one tread the way true, the way that will, one day, lead one beyond the reach of these modifications.

The same day at the *sat-saṅga* at the town, Chanan Shah requested the Master to initiate him too into the path of yoga, to which request the Master asked him, 'Aren't you satisfied with what you already do?'

Devotee: Satisfied? Once a year we pay a visit to our family preceptor's seat, bow down before it and make an offering of Rupees one hundred and one if we wish to have a glimpse of the Holy Book. What kind of tradition is this? You cannot cast even a look at the book without this fine, set aside the question of reading it! You too, Lord, are composing a book. Please do not set up traditions of this kind.

Master: This revelation will remain open to all. No offerings will be made to the book. Directions will be issued in this regard. As you see it recited here at the *sat-saṅga*, so will it continue to be recited in the future too. For you, meditation on the *Mahāmantra* is enough. Do it daily, morning and evening. You cannot, at this age, sit for meditation for long. Do it with a support for help.

An hour past midnight, both the Master and his noble disciple left for the cremation ground. 'This place,' said the Master, 'seems to have been waiting long [for hearing the voice of the Word]. How quiet is it, how secluded! Are afraid?'

'It's the Lord's fearlessness that makes me fearless. Otherwise, I could never summon up the courage to come here alone and at this time.'

'Don't speak of fear here! Only the impurity of the mind causes fear. You are in the presence of Him, the Lord. Let His blessed joy and rapture overflow!'

The Master commenced the *Niśkāma-karma-sādhanā*. Half of it was dictated by quarter to six. In the morning, Banārasīdās asked the meaning of *niṣkāma-karma*, action without desire. To this question of his was given the reply:

> There is an action that binds; there is also an action that unbinds. Not for a moment can any living being extricate himself from action. An action done with desire for its fruit is *sakāma-karma*, the cause of his further births and deaths, of his comings and goings. Birth after birth he reaps the fruit of actions in various modes of embodied existence to sense pleasure and pain, attachments and aversions. Restless he remains because of this sense. When his good actions ripen, they bring him into contact with a truth-established seer who unfolds before him what *niṣkāma-karma*, action without desire, is. From that moment of understanding starts his pilgrimage to the truth ultimate. Instead of orienting himself towards self-serving he orients himself towards truth-serving. In other words, whatever action falls to his lot, whatever presents itself to be done, he does it as if ordained by the Lord. In obedience to His will he does it, not for the sake of satisfaction of his own desire. That is the way to wash your determinating faculty of all stains and make it aware of That which ever remains itself. The true desire-free state comes to be when the *Nāda*, the Word that is the Supreme Lord, manifests Itself within man. Then whatever he does he does without desire, to act with desire becomes just impossible for him. That is the moment that turns him into desirelessness itself. All wrong understanding changes into right understanding; the *buddhi*-with-forms changes into the *buddhi*-without-forms. [No image remains to comprehend and no concept to conceive, no awareness of them]. When you can neither perceive nor conceive, what can remain there to desire? When man sees himself in all, then doing or not doing no longer remains his concern. He finds them, doing and not doing, as ordained by the Lord. Now say what prompts you to do all this service!

Devotee: Not for the things of the world has this servant come to the Lord's refuge. That peace he seeks that Rāma and Kṛṣṇa, Kabīr and Nānak , the Buddha and other seers found and lived in, that peace he seeks. That alone is his desire, nothing else.

Master: Great is this thought of yours, *Premī!* But it must change into the goal, the exclusive goal, of your life. Not until you change this thought into your goal immediate and ultimate will your mind move in that direction. Great effort is required to set the mind in that direction. Blessed with grace you already are, with the grace of the guru. Now your own effort is required to lead you further. Service and other noble acts and dispositions are merely auxiliaries to the main factor that can lead you to your goal, the factor of yogic meditation. Let you be steadfast in the belief that the Lord alone is the doer of the deeds you do. Stick to this disposition with every resolve. You are to live this disposition to die ultimately into it. That is the beginning and that is the end - this surrender of your acts to the will of the Lord. Long time and effort are required to understand this thought. To remain absorbed in this thought is much better than talk about it.

That evening Gurudeva asked the members of the congregation at the town if they could understand the *bānī,* to which question one among the audience said that despite the lexical simplicity, the ideas expressed were difficult to follow. One could not, he added, fathom the depth without the Master's grace. 'Willing seekers,' the latter said, 'will not be left unaided. *This* comes here to wake up the people here, not for the business that flourishes here. Ever in search of the truth-oriented souls does *This* wander. But the people here seem all immersed in worldly affairs, deaf to the voice of the Truth. His *Māyā* has no end, encompasses it all in its folds! A land of waste is the land where people have no ear for the Truth and no concern for the deprived and unhappy.'

'A time was,' said Chanan Shah, 'when this place was a kind of a paradigm of service and *sat-saṅga*. So many *aśramas*, monasteries, are here, which once hummed with chants and discourses. But all are neglected now, are in ruins. We do not know what sin the people of this place committed that they have been deserted by the enlightened seers.'

Thatta, now a small centre of textile business and of loot, murder and plunder was once a centre of spirituality and meditative life. Forty miles away from the town was a giant cave that had space enough for thousands of people to sit in meditation. The entire area was once the abode of *ṛṣis*.[5] At that very place consecrated in ages past by the presence of transcendental souls was gushing out, once again, speech the redemptive. That night too it flowed out. Recalling those days, the Bhagat says in his memoirs, 'The four hours, from 1.45 A.M. to 5.45 A.M., fled away in a moment as it were, scarcely registering their presence. There was no drowsiness, no tiredness. Like a current of water did it flow out, the *bānī*, flow out all new and fresh; the words of one strophe were never repeated in another. Nothing was said that required revision or correction. All corrections owed their origin to my mistakes while taking it down, not to the speech or the speaker.'

It was that day, the seventh day of the Mārgaśīrṣa, November 21-22, when Banārasī asked the Master why the *vāṇī* was replete with words of Hindi and Sanskrit when the Master had all his education, whatever he had, in Urdu. His reply has already been quoted.[6]

In the early hours of that morning commenced the *Śūnya-karma-sādhanā*, 'the way that leads to where no action obtains.' The winter was advancing, every night was turning colder. The previous day, Banārasī had collected some firewood, which he lighted as soon as he reached the cremation ground. Its soothing warmth made him feel cozy and drowsy. 'For a week more put up with this cold,' said the Master.

Accordingly, he threw away the entire stock of firewood and devoted himself entirely to writing, which went on up to 6 A.M. When the Master came back to his human self, he said, '*Yoga* and *bhoga*, meditation and comfort, cannot go together. The choice is clear and unambiguous.'

After a brief bath he asked the Bhagat to say in brief what he had taken down that morning.

Devotee: The *bānī* reveals the first state in which *buddhi*, the conceptual and determinating faculty, becomes completely inward oriented. That is the state of no-action, the state where action comes to cease. No thoughts arise then, neither their negations; one comes to be one's real self. All that man does, he, unknown to him, does it to attain to this state. After attaining this state, the way should become smooth and easy!

Master: Smooth and easy! No, not at all! Identification with the body does not die down easily. One among tens of millions reaches this state. Name and fame are the temptations that can bring about his ruin. So he takes every care to stick to his path and endeavour. The deeper the establishment in this state, the greater will be his distance from the ways of the world. Many become mute after attaining this state, shaking off all worldly ties and stains. Only a

> few among them guide the beings of the world to the truth and make them attain to their purpose. But how can you know what *This* has attained to? Only a Buddha could or a Kṛṣṇa!

Next day, when Banārasīdās returned from the town after taking his meal, he found a Muslim devotee narrating the life story of Rabia, a woman saint of Egypt. A long story of suffering, torture and humiliations was it. An orphan, Rabia was helpless and starved, a bare piece of bread was beyond her reach. Her youth was spent in slavery, her master cruel and a debauch. Shattered alike in mind and body, she waited only for death; in that alone she thought she could find her deliverance. And awaited it she day in and day out. At last a day came when the bitter cup of her suffering overflowed its brim; Rabia found it impossible to bear any more the torture and the passion of her brutal master and ran away from his harem to put an end to her life. In the process of her flight opened out the gates within her and she found, to her wonder and surprise, a light burning bright within her. The narrator narrated this story of hers in details and with so much fervour that tears flowed out of the Master's eyes. As long as his narration went on, the tears too continued to flow down the Master's cheeks. The narration over, the Master said, 'Those who remember the One Lord meet the same end, be they of the East or of the West. Helpless he becomes, he who worships the Lord! He cannot but find every event as ordained by Him.'

The man bowed before the Master the Islamic way and left. 'Do you notice, *Premī,*' said the Master, 'the fervent faith of the man and the way he narrated the story? Rabia had attained to the same state of *śūnya*, of no-being, attaining which there remains nothing more to attain. To live as the Lord wills is the greatest worship. You too are writing about the same state where the blessed of the Lord dwell. One who has attained to that state simply cannot say: I am Brahman, I am God. Of *samatā,*[7] of sameness, is that state.'

That night saw, when another dead body was aflame, the descent of *'Nāda-dhyāna,'* 'Contemplation of the Nāda.' The silence of the night had turned into the silence of death as it were. In that desertion resounded the sound of the Silence itself:

> When the nāda-without-a-friction[8] is contemplated, one is absorbed by naught, one naught by the second and the second by the third.
> As the mind gets immersed within, a still peace comes to suffuse the body, peace that none can measure, none can fathom.
> In the lotus at the navel wave the waters of immortality, those very waters flow up in the nerve benign, in the the *suṣumnā,* from there to flow up to the sky, to the head, for the rare guru-oriented soul to bathe and exult in.
> There in the sky it resounds and reverberates, absorbing the attention of the heroic one rare, of one who knows where the three nerves meet, the *iṅgalā*, the *piṅgalā* and the *suṣumnā*.
> There he abides, in the silence within the head, having realised there the Word stainless and pure to turn into a soothing every pore of his body and to set at rest its burning and its torture. Quiet becomes he, tranquil and at peace. For finds he there the long sought for home.
> All illusions end there, all darkness is dispelled, with fourteen digits shines the moon full there.
> Blessed becomes he with vision and blessed his mind. All chains will break, all shackles crack when turns compassionate his guru true.
> The Person unndecaying finds he within, the Person that dwells transcendent in all, the Person the light eternal and blessedness supreme, finds he that Person to attend all passive to Him, to that Lord of the world, the worshipped of the worshippers.
> That is the moment to realise the glory of the Name, to realise it in mind, to realise it in the body. Blessed turns a man when the Name turns into the Word and discloses Its mystery unto him.

Fatigue and cold now no longer bothered the Bhagat; totally absorbed was he in writing now, with no thought of the hour or of sleep. 'Wonderful indeed,' he says, 'was that time, only the Master's grace made it possible for me to arrest that flow into the written word. I do not find any ability in me to accomplish that feat. In the beginning, I felt a lot of trouble, but now time was of no account. In a moment as it were arrived the dawn and the bright morning. No sleepiness was there nor heaviness.'

Daily was he given the dictation and daily its uninterrupted effusion surprised him. One day he expressed his feelings in these words, 'Every strophe comes anew every time. This surprises me in the extreme. The language is simple but the content is a hidden mystery.'

'*Premī*,' said Gurudeva, 'all this is the play of my Lord, His alone. What can this shell do and accomplish? Whosoever remembers Him will find all the mystery turn into a revelation. Within man rolls that immortal bliss, not without. Yet without too is it as well as within. But one can find it only by turning within. The determinating faculty, the intellect, alone can have *anu-bhava* of it, can turn into it, become it – not the body. In all the three phases of time, the present, the past and the future, shines self-same that light. The body decays ever, it decayed in the past, decays it in the present and will decay in the future too; never does it come to be itself. Despite this change, every living being thinks of it in terms of be-ing, forgetful of the bliss within. How much has he to struggle and risk for the sake of the pleasures it can give! But in spite of all the risk and trouble, it turns into ashes in the long run as has this body that burns before you. Yesterday it was alive and active but today it is what you see before you, a food for these flames. There is no moment, no fraction of it, when any being comes to be at peace with himself; all the time he suffers or is happy, as his past acts would determine. This is his being, to be happy and to be unhappy. This keeps him, this delusion, away from the immortal bliss that he truly is. Try to understand what you write. Only then will you succeed in interiorising this thought .. ..'

The next night too heard the peal of the Word. The dawn came without a notice and then the sunrise; the *vāṇī* was read out and the mistakes of the scribe rectified. It was the tenth day of the outflow. 'For six more days, said the Master,' will it continue. Then will come the time for you to rest.'

'It matters not now,' said the faithful devotee, 'whether it is six days or thirty. No longer am I distracted by fatigue or by drowsiness. Such has been the Lord's grace.'

Master: This is how the mind gives up its natural propensities. Outward oriented is it by nature. For little and trivial things it roams restless in the world. That is the net it weaves life after life to entangle itself in. It is only when grace smiles upon it that it turns to the way to the truth.

Devotee: There are moments when it is all pure and unblemished, given in full to service and meditation. And there are moments when these do not interest it. It seeks then the usual pleasures and comforts.

Master: Premī, the wheel of *guṇas*, of the three modes of being, moves on unabated in man. When the mode of *sattva*, of the transcendental thrust, dominates in man, he, as a matter of course, would seek the company of the truth-becomes, will serve them and the people of the world, will give himself up to meditation, to the coalescence of name, mind and breath. When the *rajas*, the mode of activity, dominates, he strives for sense pleasures and for self-glory and show, and when the mode of *tamas* dominates he would steal and play fraud and deceits. To go beyond these three modes of *sattva*, *rajas* and *tamas* is the purpose of sustained meditation. That leads to the state *nirguṇa*, the state free of these three modes. When one attains to that state, these modes, which are nothing but deviations from one's true being, shall melt away into that truth. Not a trace of them will remain. When the faculty that determines phenomena [that enframes what *is* in names and forms], when this faculty is purified a little in the true sense of the term, it no longer finds any interest in the objects it would enjoy in its tainted state. This disinterest leads it to the way of the truth. A time comes when it finds itself turn into that truth, discarding all names and forms. *You* may *stumble on the way, not once but on many occasions but that should not deter you from your way the true.* With discrimination true should you try to resume your pilgrimage.

On the eighteenth of *Mārgaśīrṣa*, the third [?] day of December, the effusion came to its end. The last section was '*Nirvāṇasiddhi*,' 'Attainment of Nirvāṇa,' the state where speech becomes silent and the mind becomes bereft of thoughts. They call it *śūnya*, *samādhi*, the Word, the One without a second. But not until one ceases to be conscious of the Word, not until consciousness itself becomes the Word, becomes the *śūnya*, becomes Brahman the Alone can one attain to that state. Where will then be Brahman, and where will be the Word, the *śūnya* or *samādhi*, that coming to rest of the mind? Words are they all, words of man, on him depend these all, on his concepts. Ineffable is that state, where distinctions melt away, each and every, where the Word is not different from words and words from the Word, *śūnya* from being and being from *śūnya*, the Absolute from the relative and the relative from the Absolute, Brahman from *Māyā* and *Māyā* from Brahman. *Samatā* alone is that state, only *samatā*, only sameness. Not even sameness.

In the ashes flowed that fount of immortality. For sixteen days it flowed in the solitude of that shrine of death. In the darkness shone that light, from the fear came forth the hope. That is the way to our home, the way called death. One has to burn into light, one has to die into life. Death is our home, our destination. We come to be when we cease to be. The *bānī* sounded this note of conclusion:

> Of the unknown is this the speech, this writ of the Person ever invisible. The Word shall resound in man, its secret all revealed, if with care he gives his ear to this Its speech, gives it in love.
> The Word dwells where the senses do not reach, indivisible is It, that life of life within and without. Perceive It thus and worship It thus if cross unto the other shore you will.
> The Lord of all is the Word, the worshipped of all is It, the holy Word unheard. Sing the song of the Word, of Person the Truth, sing you all that would hear the Word.
> Your wishes will find their fulfillment, fulfillment they seek in vain, if you in mind flow one with the song; your mind will be washed of stains and your body will shine like gold if you know in truth this word of the Word.
>
> No duality will remain nor will remain the thought that deludes. All shall be light within, bright and pure, and bliss eternal when each and every being turns into *Nāda*, of Itself own the hearer.

With the conclusion of the flow of the *vāṇī*, the Bhagat bowed low before his holy Master, who, all compassion, stroked his back with affection and said, 'Great is your fortune, *Premī*, chosen were you for this service. The Lord bless you with the vision of the Truth!'

He drank the nectar of his Master's feet and, with fervent emotion, bowed before the cremation ground, once an object of fear but now holy and consecrated, fit to be worshipped and adored. Once the abode of seers and sages, as evidenced by the ruins of *āśramas* and monasteries, that fearful landscape seemed alive to the man whose ears had heard the voice of the Word. To his prayer it seemed to respond, or, rather she seemed to respond, for alive had become that place for him. Benedictions divine it seemed to shower upon his bowed head, freeing him from every fear. Is the Vedic vision of *pṛthivī* irrevocably lost and gone? Can that lost paradise be regained? For the simple servant of the Lord, the answer was unnecessary because the question was unnecessary. He was not, then, in the state of mind that asks questions and seeks answers. You commune with the living earth, you do not ask her, 'Why art thou, and how art thou?'

Another week passed in reading out the entire *vaṇī* revealed there and correcting the scribe's mistakes. During this *tapas* too Gurudeva had lived only on tea, one glassful in the morning and another in the evening. Even fruit and vegetables had been bidden goodbye. The climate of the place was rather harsh for his frail body; the dry cold of the nights spent in the open and his bath in the heavy water of the pond there could not but play havoc with it. His body had developed several fissures, oozing a white watery substance the moment he but scratched it a little. Wounds were visible at many spots, blood seeping out of them. He would not submit to medical treatment, despite all the persuasion of the devotees. Sometimes a little guess, a hint, a passing remembrance can do things that conscious human efforts cannot. The Bhagat had once observed the Master take raw radish. So he decided to make him have some daily. The simple radish worked and healed the wounds, though after a considerable time. Where the devotees were worried about his health, the Master was all indifferent; absorbed he remained in the depths within, depths unknown. It seemed now that his human self was resting in repose and calm. His own words too confirmed this impression. *'Premī,'* said he, 'This heart is now at rest. To those that stray and wander in search of being in the never to be world, this speech of the Lord, this grace abounding, will bring comfort and repose. The seeker of the truth that reads it and listens to it and follows in earnest the path it shows him will find the invisible within him become visible. He will find the inbeing of life, the true in-being, that seeker true. Not until this Inner Light shines in him, man cannot but wander, lost and blind. In striving lies the achievement, in struggle is the reward. So read it with care, think over it and bring this testament to the notice of others too. This way will you find the reward of your strivings and so will the others.'

Notes

1 Generalizations of this kind share a good deal of exaggeration. There are people who give a less flattering view of their friendship.

2 Because of his bad health. *Vide,* Ch. 13.

3 The *Samatāprakāśa,* pp. 1083-84.

4 The *Samatāprakāśa,* pp. 112-14.

5 The place seems to have been, originally, the abode of Buddhist monks.

6 *Vide* Ch. 5.

7 For the truly blessed man distinctions between Brahman and Māyā and between God and Creation no longer remain relevant. Of sameness alone is he the seer.

8 or, less probably, the *nāda* without an end

10

The Five Principles

Up till now our story has been concerned with the man and the Word, the man who died to be the Word and the Word that consented to disperse Itself into words. We cannot, however, say that like the man the Word too died into words, for the distinction that we draw between the Word and words is our distinction, not in or, if we may say so, for the Word. There is, however, one rider. We found the man we call Gurudeva feel, as he said, his heart at rest after the final articulation of the Word at Thatta. Does this not show that the man too was part of the articulation, part as its receiver and its tool as it were? Can the Word peal out on its own unless there is one to articulate the peal, the mortal communicator of the immortal Word? After his stay at Thatta, the outflow of the *vāṇī* became intermittent, irregular and occasional to become eventually mute and silent. It is not that the revelation itself came to an end, it continued to show itself forth in the awesome silence of the enigma that his face was, his entire body was, the one absolutely non-human, the other a mass of glow as it were. The peal of silence was perhaps more loud than the peal of words but only, but only if and when you were lost in the enigma before you, in the person that was no person, emphatically no-person. But here the onus of opening out lay with the beholder, not with the Word. You had to spend a lifetime, more than a lifetime to fathom what was revealed in that face and, more importantly, what lay concealed behind it. But of this later.

There was also what may be called the recognisable man in him, the man that breathed, talked, acted and related, the man that Gurudeva described as 'a mere shell,' shell that his devotees took as their Guide and Master but which he himself rejected as of no account. For, the Guide and Master, he said, was the Word, not the shell. Our story, however, can now, now when the Word has almost ceased to articulate itself, be of the man only, of the 'shell,' not of the Word that is not the Word, the Word that expresses itself now in words, now in the deep mystery of the [no-]expression of his face and bearing. What did that man do and what impression did his talk, actions and thoughts leave on those that saw him, heard him and paid attention to his thoughts? Could they hear a ring of the Word in his conversations and of the Ineffable in what he said? Were his words like our words, words that sought to relate, vainly, to their referent, or did they reverberate with the referent, with the Real that ever abides beyond the reach of our noisy speech, as if that unapproachable lay immanent in them? And how did the arrogant respond to him, and the humiliated, the self-complacent happy and the insecure unhappy, those sure of their being and status and those totally unsure of it, even unaware of it? We have to watch the man now and see how in the midst of his human limitations and errors, one could see or feel the Presence that remained untouched by those limitations and those errors.

When man resurrects in the *sat-puruṣa*, one that has become the Person True, he resurrects as a being related and situated, related to others and situated in a social context and its *other*, the world. The Alone gives place to a being that is a being along with others, others known or unknown. So, the man becomes active but active in a different way from the way of common people. In what way Gurudeva became active can be glimpsed from what he wrote, in a letter, to one of his devotees:

> *This* seeks in you a propensity for the good, a fervent desire to do good unto others and to serve your country. *This* seeks others' pain in you, others' anguish and others' sorrows. *This* wishes that you followed the path laid down by the wise persons of old. *This* desires that the light of *samatā* shine bright in you, *samatā* that has no *other* to confront or negate. *This* desires that you devote yourself to your preceptor and give yourself up to the Lord. Will you, devotee fit and true as you are, slake *Its* thirst?

There is an irreconcilable contradiction in man. As a being in the world he lives as a being along with others, he cannot do without others when dealing with the *Other* that Nature is. But there is also the Narcissus in him, a rotten interior that recognises nothing except itself. Desire is its being, desire that would fulfil itself at any cost, even at the cost of the life of the communality that man is. These two realms, that of blind desire and that of communal action, do not get easily, truly, related to each other, despite the efforts of civlisations. Desire triumphs, in the long run, over man the social being to make of him a slave to serve its purpose. This blind fury was named *Id*, It, by Freud to emphasise its independence from man. It rules over him completely and absolutely, even his conscience, his superego, is rooted in it, even the norms of civilisations are only its other face. Out of this infernal being, Gurudeva would fashion a being that is truly related to others, lives with them and as them, a being that breaks loose his narcissistic confines. Notice the different note struck in this letter from those that civilisations chime day in and day out. He does not ask the devotee to become a constituent of a collective effort, theoretical or practical; his expectation can in no way be linked with the expectations of civilisations from their members. Civilisations seek to relate human beings, one with another, in terms of collective work but not in terms of what may be called collective enjoyment. When it comes to enjoying the fruit of their collective effort, civilisations let human beings remain self-serving; they find nothing wrong in working communalities turn into enjoying individualities. Here, on the contrary, the individual is asked to live as others, suffer with others and enjoy with others. He should be expansive enough to become the others, must have that capability, the capability to be a no-being in order to be every being. He is to live as an individual, only as an individual, but an individual that can live and perceive and know as other individuals do. One must have what may be called existential empathy, the capability to become each and every being. Civilisations would undo the individuals by directing their blind destructiveness against themselves, by turning their sadism into masochism. Here you are to remain an individual, but not *this* individual but every individual.

The way to the state of *samatā* lies, the letter says, through breaking your individualistic confines, through empathising with others' pain and misfortunes; others are to be your concern, your end, not you. This does not of course mean that you, in the vein of a Kant, treat humanity as an end. For, humanity is the slave of desire, whether in your person or anybody else, whether rational or irrational. When you try to idealise rational humanity this way, you cannot escape the devastating sneer of a Freud, that seer infallible almost of our inferno.[1]

But how to escape from the coils of desires that choke you with their grip? Through, says the letter in effect, two things: sincere and earnest devotion to the guru, that expression of the Word, articulate or silent, and through surrendering your will to the will of the Lord. If your mind is in the grip of thoughts, then pay heed to the thoughts that the Word reveals, if your mind is calm, then let it rest on the face of the no-person that the guru is. Action that results from conscious will is, despite its appearance to the contrary, centred in narcissism, in the pleasure principle, in the *Id*, in the blind instinct or , if you like, in the structure of your nervous system and the brain. Every effort is blind, every discourse is ignorance, be it naive or sophisticated, the product of faith or science, for they are all rooted in the blind desire, even reason is under its grip.

However: you cannot have whole civilisations fashioned this way; you may dream about them but you cannot bring them into being. Utopias they have been and utopias will they remain. Findings of psychoanalysis or of modern psychiatry are to an impressive extent true but about man the communality. In him lives desire of every kind: civilised, primitive, savage and animal. The wolf of the wild steppes seems to have possessed the inner being of every being-with-others. Not until has he been made to endure much, and endure without hope will he pay heed to the call of the Beyond as enshrined in the voice of the Word. The Word appeals to the transcendental urge in man. And only the man that can pay heed to that call of the Word can escape from his self-enclosed being, can live with others and *as* others. And by living with others and as others, each one of them, he will no more live as we do. For, to be each and every person means to be no person. It is to become Brahman the *Absolutus*, the Unrelated, the Alone, not merely the all-in-each, but also the negation of the all-in-each.

So the Master moved from place to place in order to fashion **some individuals** in the mould described in the letter. We have to look at the cultural conditions of the Punjab of those days in order to know the human stuff that the Master wished to mould in that mould. The Punjab, that Land of the Five Rivers, the five tributaries of the mighty Indus, was at one time the cradle of the early Vedic civilisation, a civilisation that looked upon every being, living or non-living, not merely earthly but also cosmic and divine.

And corresponding to these three dimensions of his/its being, that civilisation also envisaged *trayī-vidyā*, threefold knowledge: knowledge of *pṛthivī*, earth, called *ṛgvidyā*; knowledge of *dyu*, heaven, called *sāmavidyā* and knowledge of *antarikṣa*, interspace, called *yajurvidyā*. That *trayīvidyā*, that threefold knowledge, manifested itself along with Creation and every being, we are assured, is blessed with it but the temptations of the world do not let him know it, let him become aware of it – not easily. A victim of desire, he finds it difficult to realise that he is a part of the act of sacrifice that Creation is for that vision. It was natural that men of the world should reduce that sacrificial vision into mere ritualistic formulas and practice.

Before the rise of the Vedic Civilsation there was another Civilisation that flourished in the Punjab and other far flung areas, called the Indus Valley Civilisation with its town planning and idol worship. That Civilisation also had a deep spiritual aspect in the form of Śaivism, which the *bānī*, as we saw, has highlighted on many an occasion for us. But as the Cosmotheandric vision of the Vedic culture became, in spite of the Upaniṣads, distorted in the hands of the greedy, so did Śaivism too got, in spite of seers and saints of Kashmir and of other places, reduced to mere idol worship in the hands of worldlings. In what a decadent way these various strands of Indian religious culture survived in the Land of the Five Rivers may be gathered from the following incidents.

In February 1942, Gurudeva happened to visit Daurangala, a village or rather a small town, in the district of Gurudaspur and spent the night at the temple there. The Bhagat and another devotee accompanied him; the latter had some relations there. At the said devotee's invitation, some persons did visit Gurudeva but finding a frail body clothed in white, they left him without a word. Early in the morning, quite a few people came to the temple, rang the temple's bell, saying, 'Hail! Hail to the Great God

Śiva!' and came to sit at the Verandah outside the room where the Master stayed. A good many among those visitors thronged there to partake of the tobacco pipe and to indulge in gossip, in jokes or in discussing their day to day matters at home or of business. The morning, of course, was the same that made their ancestors sing the *sāman* with the sacred *gāyatrī* preceding the song. No mystery these visitors saw in the birth of dawn out of the darkness, in the night brightening into the morn, no relationship with it, no necessity of participation in it. 'What hypocrisy,' remarked Gurudeva, 'flourishes in these temples, what trivialities and decadence!' He asked Banārasī to call them in but none cared to respond. Only one among them, one Amarnath, entered the room and sat down after prostrating himself before the Master. Gurudeva asked him, '*Premī*, the temples are surely places for *sat-saṅga*, for knowing the truth from falsehood, they are not smoking centres! Are they?'

'Mahārājji,' said the man, '*sādhus* and saints come here; the holy fire keeps on burning for them. The people of the town too get a puff or two with them. But pardon my asking, who are you and from where do you come?'

'A physician is *This* to cure you of the malady that inflicts you, for sick are you all. Show the *faqīr-s* a solitary place where you could be attended to and cured!'

In the green fields outside the village, there was a room that was found suitable for *tapas*. Nearby was a well of drinking water. The devotee that had accompanied Gurudeva was sent back and Banārasīdās was asked to make his own arrangement for his daily meals. In the afternoon was held a *sat-saṅga* that some people did attend but could make no head or tail of it. A woman, dignified in look and gentle and restrained in speech, said, 'Mahārājjī, people here can't understand what you say. They do not know what contact with the truth is, they have had no experience of it. Lofty are the Lord's words and profound are their meaning. It is our good fortune that brought you here.'

She invited the Master for a meal but the Master declined the invitation, saying, '*Devī,* gentle lady, let your relatives come here. Then will the decision be made. Eating is a thing of the past; hence no question is there to accept the invitation.'

The Bhagat explained to her that the Master lived only on a bowl of tea, that alone was his sustenance. Surprised and baffled she bowed and left for home. 'What a place,' said the Master, 'and what people! But in the midst of crows, there are some swans too. Let's see what the Lord wills.'

In the evening, the Bhagat went to the market place and prepared tea for the Master at a sweet seller's shop and appeased his hunger with milk and some pieces of rusk. There was no inn or a restaurant at that place, where one could get a meal. On his way back two among the audience at the *sat-saṅga* met him and said , 'Why did you come here to prepare the tea? You could have asked us for this little service.' 'It is not our way to ask for anything,' replied Banārasīdās, 'if someone desires to serve the Master, he has to make a request to him, beseech him for that purpose. I am here only to obey him and his command. But when we have come here, to your village, take we must something, we have to. Existential conditions can't be ignored and set aside.'

In the morning after his bath, the Master sat basking (?) in the winter sun, when an elderly man approached him; smart and agile he looked, despite his age. '*Namaste,* "My respect and greeting!'[2] Standing, he said these words, a mere formality, without caring even to bow his head in gesture. 'Are you, Mahārājjī a *dvaitavādī* [*dvaitavādin*] or an *advaitavādī* [*advaitavādin*], an exponent of the doctrine of dualism or of a-dualism?'

'*Premī,*' came the answer, 'Sit you down first.' When the stranger sat down, the Master said, '*This* sees a-duality in duality and duality in a-duality. The *buddhi*, the faculty of knowing, or the intellect, will turn into the vision of *samatā* only when it sees the two states as one. By what name are you called?'

'I am Pundit Guruprasad Dogra, retired sub-inspector of police. Last evening, my sister, Sarasvati Devi, told me that a seer of a high order has come to our village. So I came here straight from my morning walk. My prayer is that from today onwards both the morning and the evening meals will be served from [my] home. Be gracious enough to agree to my request. And if there is any other thing needed, kindly let me know.'

'Do grace this place with your presence. That alone is the need here, nothing else.'

On deaf ears fell these words. 'Be kind enough to ask your devotee to bring here milk and tea.'

His persistence forced the Master to give in. 'Go, *Premī,*' said he to the Bhagat, 'let the giving and receiving that remains be settled.[3] When we have paused at his door, something will have to be done.'

'All belongs to you, Lord, nothing is mine.' Saying this, he caught hold of Banārasī's hand and virtually dragged him towards his home.

The Master's *tapas* could not but affect the people. Not long after the people of that town started taking interest in what he said. Many became his lifetime devotees, and sought to fashion their life in accordance with the word of their guide and mentor, their 'all,' as they would describe him.

There were towns and villages that presented a much worse picture. In the year 1943, Gurudeva went to Golara, a town that fell in the district of Rawalpindi. Uninvited he had gone there. Bhagat Banārasīdās had a distant relation there, named Palshah, so he took the Master to the house of this relative whom he had never met before. The people there showed no interest in the Master, were rather indifferent to his presence. But the spirit enshrined in the Upaniṣadic saying, '*atithidevo bhava*,' 'be unto an uninvited guest what a devotee is to his god,' had not yet disappeared from the unconscious psyche of the people, despite all the cultural poverty that a long history of invasions had wrought upon the Land of the Five Rivers. So, notwithstanding the fact that this was the first meeting between the Bhagat and Palshah, the rules of formal hospitality were not ignored. Palshah did not hesitate to take the two to his house. But that was a mere formality and Banārasīdās felt uneasy about it. Gurudeva reassured him about the positive result of their visit. We know that Gurudeva spent his nights in the open but that day he chose to stay in the host's house. Palshah was a compulsive drinker. His misfortune was that his dear bottle was placed in a cupboard in the very room the Master had occupied. All the night the latter remained sitting, lost in *samādhi* and all the night Palshah kept waiting for the Master to go to sleep to give him the occasion to end his torment. Neither of the two went to sleep that night, one remained in ecstasy, the other in torture.

In the morning, the Master asked Palshah to show him a place away from the village. At a distance of about four or five hundred metres he found a place suitable for *tapas*. A room built near a well with a forest nearby for his nightly vigils was not an unattractive place. The man made all the arrangements for his stay there, made them carefully and meticulously, and while returning asked the Bhagat, 'Is it indeed true that the Master does not sleep at all, that his nights are spent solely in meditation? And does he live only on a bowl of tea?'

'Years and years have passed away,' said Banārasī, 'since he got a wink of sleep. And it's true that a little tea alone sustains his life.' This was too much for Palshah, nothing less than a miracle for one whose life was little else than eating and drinking. So he lost no time in talking to friends about the Master's *tapas* and his self-denial. People flocked in numbers to have a vision of the unbelievable miracle of Nature that they discovered he was. The people of Golara were undoubtedly gifted with the Upaniṣadic spirit of hospitality, hospitality to the *atithiḥ,* one who comes unannounced and without a date, a total stranger; they were polite in their speech and demeanour but the majority were given to meat eating and drinking. Palshah was a local celebrity for his hedonistic ways and so was his uncle, Kashinath, 'The Guardian Spirit of Kāśī, of the holy city of Benaras.' When Gurudeva came to know about their ways, he summoned the entire adult population of the village to his presence and called upon them to give him a solemn undertaking that they would give up both drinking and meat eating, adding a warning to the effect that if they did not do his bidding, he would leave the village, rejecting their hospitality. That was indeed too much a penalty for retaining their habits, so all of them swore in the name of their God that they would not touch these things in the future. The entire village or town was in turmoil to see the unbelievable transformation.

Noticing the decay of spiritual culture among the people, the Master laid down the five principles of **Samātavāda**, its cardinal principles, and explained them in details.[4] The five principles were: 1) Simplicity, 2) Service unto others, 3) Truthfulness, 4) *Sat-saṅga*, 'association with truth', and, 5) *Sat-simaran,* 'remembrance of the truth', that is to say, the yogic meditation, the confluence of the name, mind and breath. We have had a long and leisurely look at the yogic meditation and also a somewhat brief reflection on the others.[5] For the Master's own version of these principles and the author's comments thereon, the reader should consult *The Radiant Sameness* Chapter 10. For fear of repetition I would rather refrain from commenting on the implicit critiques of modernity that these five principles present before us.

I would, however, emphasise a point here even at the risk of repetition: Of these five principles, let me reiterate, the first that of simplicity, is primarily related to what is called the inert world. It is what the ancients in India called the *bhūta-yajña*, sacrifice to the elements. It also implies sacrifice *to* the animal kingdom, a sacrifice that makes a man realise and live his mortality. Simplicity thus also means what the ancients called *pitṛ-yajña*, sacrifice to fathers, one's dead ancestors. It has social implications too, for simplicity discourages consumer culture and gives rise to empathetic disposition. The second principle, that of service, is truly a social principle in the sense that it can be practised only in society, though to live at the service of others does not mean to be a being along with others. By living at the service of others you, paradoxically enough, isolate yourself from others, you make yourself vulnerable to the exploitable narcissism of others. Service leads its practitioner, that sacrificer, to the status of the *act* of sacrifice. As for truthfulness, it simply makes man the truthful live at the mercy of others, rendering him defenceless in the extreme. Such a man cannot retain his identity, identity as a being *along* with others. And a being in isolation, in absolute isolation, cannot retain his communicative speech, with the result that all concepts that inform that speech become weak and, eventually, inoperative. Many are there who make the claim that communicative language is the informing principle of a human being, that he is born in language and cannot escape from this his existential status. All talk, they add, about going beyond language is a mere pastime of certain mystics and has no validity or truth about it. Truthfulness, however, is a way to transcend this, our condition, this our condition of ignorance, for no language can ever lead us to the real: an inevitable gap falls between the real and what we think about it in terms of our linguistic concepts. Interested reader should consult the *Radiant Sameness* for elucidation of these admittedly very terse remarks. The fourth principle, that of *sat-saṅga,* de-situates man from his existential contexts and transforms him into a being identified with the transcendental principle, the principle that negates every identifiable state of being. This principle has the same implication as had the ancient principle of *ṛṣi-yajña,* sacrifice to the seers. The fifth principle, of course, is the same as *brahma-yajña,* sacrifice to Brahman, sacrifice that transforms man into a moment that encompasses within itself birth, life and death, the moment that we mortals call immortality, eternity, *śūnya* and infinity, blasphemies with which we pollute that what *is.*

Perhaps I should also add here that sat-saṅga does not merely mean contemplation of the *vāṇī,* the speech that is its own speaker or the contemplation of a seer's person that is no-person, the seer lost in *samādhi.* There is also another kind of *satsaṅga* in which the guru or the seer speaks neither as the no-person nor as the Word but as a man. Hearing his words those who have experience of a long series of hurts, rebuffs and humiliations will find their despair turn into hope and their pain into a balm. Even those whose faith in life and its promises is intact may not, will not, go unrewarded. We may, in this connection, listen to what the Master said in 1943, at a mosque at Sarayasala in the North-West Frontier Province of British India. Unfortunately, only a summary of the discourse has been preserved; we miss the images, metaphors and ring of his words. But despite that deficiency what impact his words had on the supposed fanatics may be gauged from the following:

> Embodied in clay souls come and go, have been coming and going ever since He that created Himself willed that there be a world and the order of the world. As long as bodies are there,

there are worlds too, of each being a world of his own. A creature of misery is every being, amazed and confused – every being, be he a human or a beast. Those who could cure this malady of misery too have been coming into the world, in every part of it, in the West no less than in the East. And continue to come will they. Creatures that followed in their footsteps, thousands of them, found deliverance everlasting and bliss immortal, their minds coming to rest forever. But the souls that came to deliver the Command of the Lord, the Command out of the ordinary, had to undergo many a hardship and affliction. But their Truth Perfect made the malevolent meek and the hostile self-submissive. No sacred writ will ever permit you to harm any creature for the sake of your own desire. For teach they, without exception, service unto them, to each and every being, man or beast. The Self-created One, the Lord Supreme, is not the property of any being, for, with His light, of Being the Supreme, is illumed all that is. And the man that denies that Being Supreme is a *kāfir*, an infidel.

A faithful seeker will comprehend the light that the Lord is if he sees no *other*, finds no second. He alone is a true follower of his guide and prophet who perceives the presence of the Lord in every being – in the birds of the air, in the beasts of the pastures and the forest no less than in man. A man of this mettle will have nothing but love and affection for every being. And he lives as the Lord wills him to live, for his desire is nothing else than the Lord's will. In his eyes, all belongs to the Lord, to Him alone: his belongings and his possessions, his mind and his body. When all is His, and His alone, where is the room for self-glory? That alone is infidelity, this sense of mine. Do you have anything of your own that you could offer to the Lord? Consider it well. For the sake of satisfying your desire, you get cruel where you are to be compassionate, you kill creatures of the Lord and call them sanctified and eat them. The creature killed by the Lord forbidden and the creature killed by man sanctified, this sanctified and the other not! What a wisdom, what a vision! A fabrication is this all, fabrication woven by your own desire and craving. And reap you shall the rewards, the wages, of your sins. If you would glory the Lord, then glory the death of desire and selfhood. For, that alone will propitiate the Lord. Those who ever live as the Lord ordains them to live will wake up from

> their benightedness. And those who live entrenched in their selfhood will never find their mind come to have the rest it seeks. With faith let Him bless you, with patience and with humility!

This was the discourse he gave to the fierce Pathans that are supposed to be fanatics. How is it that they listened to his reprimands meekly and intently? An example of another discourse given to Hindus and Sikhs should also be paid heed to. Again, we have to be content with a gist of it. We have the precise date of this discourse: January 17, 1951. The place: Tarantaran, the seat of a famous Sikh shrine.

> From the moment he is born up to the moment he dies, each being lives as a creature of worry and activity. No moment can he find that is not a moment of occupation and assiduousness. His days are active and so are his nights. The wheel of action moves on to engage without a respite every embodied being till the very end of his pilgrimage. Consider for a moment the condition of being human. Every man is immersed in the instrument of activity, this body. Not for a moment will he pause to think what this body is, this instrument of action is. Speaking, he will not consider who the speaker is, seeing he will not pause to think who the seer is, nor will he think who the hearer is and who the thinker. This is how his life is spent away, in thoughtless activity, without an inkling of where he came from and where he is going. Activity is innate in him. To eat and to drink comes to him as an inheritance, and so do other activities like seeing and hearing, but not the power to distinguish between the good action and the evil action. All ignorant of this is he born
>
> Blessed is this human birth, for in this birth a being can attain to the Supreme Being that ever is Itself, that Immortal Soul Supreme. But man lives as given up to the body, given up to it so blindly as to lose the sight of what truly is his and not his. Greed prompts him to evil and so does infatuation. Every place has something to please him and distress him, and so has every time and every body. At his birth itself he inherits ups and downs, those results of some actions he did in the past, actions that have begun to bear their fruit. His birth itself is a result of a part of the countless deeds he did in the past, an inevitable result. The inevitable will happen, is bound to happen, despite the self-forgetful busy body

that his greed and attachments have made of him. The Lord has vouchsafed to man the power of thinking to discriminate the truth from the untruth, the good from the evil, and not for acquisitions of the pleasures of the world, which his past deeds alone will ordain for him. Understanding not the inevitability of his portion of pleasure and pain, man wastes away his power of thinking on these his [so-called] goals and ends. That is his ignorance, the densest one. Half of his life is spent in sleep, the other half in fret and anxiety. Before long visit him age and its helplessness and days and nights of worries and insecurity. From woe to woe he goes, no rest remains for him, no freedom from vexatious worries. The memory of the happiness that is no more distresses him, the future holds no promise for him, for death confronts him there. Whatever he earned his children waste away without a thought and consideration of his sweat and struggle. Himself he lived a miser, spent little on himself or on others, nothing on piety or in the service of the unhappy and distressed. The prodigality and extravagance of his children upset him a great deal, but in vain are his protests and reprimands. In infatuation for them, he earned and hoarded, spent not a trite of his acquisitions in good deeds. His entire life was spent in expanding his family and bringing it up, thinking not for a moment that what he thought were his riches were his penury. The wealth he accumulated through lies and frauds will be of no avail to him, for everything will be left back here itself, nothing will accompany him. A man inflicted with stupidity can never understand that the true wealth consists in good deeds, in these alone. They will determine his lot in lives to come. But if he sows the bitter, the bitter shall he reap.

There is a belief popular in India, especially among the Hindus, that one's descendents will take care of one's redemption. When they, in this life, make an old man live at the outer fringes of their house, turn a deaf ear to his call, or, if they respond, they do so heaping insults on him, call him senile and a glutton, how will they, under what compulsion, bother about what fate he meets after his death? For whose comfort he dedicated his entire life, they find his subsistence a burden and a strain. Unstable is this world, unstable are all relationships here, all anchors. When he dies his family takes care to observe every custom, will make his funeral procession a grand affair, a thing of show to win the applause of the people. In his death, the same man that was a burden for them becomes an object of celebration, a means to win respectability. This is what they call relationship, this empty show. What good he did in life – that alone will be his anchor: his meditation, his *tapa,* the service he rendered to others, the generosity of his soul, his care and concern for those in distress. These alone will accompany him, neither his family nor his riches.

Aware of the fact that their life is a short-lived affair, some people spend it in doing some good to others. In that alone they find their own good, in doing good to others. Such people alone are awake, for they think right and do the right. The world, however, teems with people who, all unaware of their goal, live with no thought of the direction of their life and its purpose. They live as their desires prompt them to live. There are others who think right but act wrong – under the compulsion of their greed and blind infatuation. He alone is free who thinks right and acts right, takes more care for the right action than for the right thought. He alone is wise. So long as a man does not come to be convinced of the reality of the Eternal Being, he cannot take steps in the direction of his true wellbeing. May He that is Gracious to the lowly bless all beings with the thinking stain-free! May He shower this blessing upon creatures so that they may know what is right and what is wrong! The days spent in pleasure were the days spent in vain. Of time they became the food. As for the future, it is all uncertain. So remember the Lord and make your life a success. That is the highest gift of human birth, remembrance of the Lord.

After this *upa-deśa,* this pointing out, one in the audience said, 'When will our attachments to the things of the world end? If our mind were immersed in one thing, we could, possibly, withdraw it from that thing and direct it towards meditation. But endless are the thoughts, desires and inclinations that arise in the mind, countless are they as are the waves of the sea. Distractions persist, with all our efforts. I live in comfort but my ways are not straight; fraud and deceit are there to tempt and overpower me. The entire day is spent in the court, where all sorts of people come with all sorts of inclinations. Hard is it to comprehend His sport, His play!'

'Endless is the mind's fashioning,' said the Master, 'no limit is there to its reach. A duality is this mind, and that is what gives rise to delusions, this its nature to perceive the *other*. This propensity towards the *other*, this desire, inflicts each and every being. Mind is the abode of distinctions like "mine," "yours" and "his". In the mind arise thoughts of giving and taking, weal and woe, virtue and charity and so on without an end. Its restlessness is the world, that alone. The bondage of ignorance is fashioned by the mind. That is why when it tries to study the world, the latter shows new faces of itself, faces which one can neither count nor comprehend. When you control the mind, when, that is to say, you orient it towards the meditation of the Name and breath, meditation done with devotion, faith and self-surrender, it comes to be one-pointed and restful and does not move outwards. Not without meditation can its restlessness cease nor can its feverish broodings. The entire world is nothing else than the mind. So long as his mind thinks in terms of me and mine, man, and, for that matter, every being, is in bondage.

'To break it, this bondage, man must give himself up to devotion to the Lord. When he comes to know the Silence within, and, pure in mind, self-surrenders to It, to the Silence that has become the all, that will be the moment when his orientation towards the world will come to an end. Who can measure this show astounding of the world, who can determine what it is? There is only one way: self-submission to Him that is ever gracious unto the lowly and the poor. That alone can redeem and save one, this spirit of self-submission. Think of your own freedom and liberation. Countless are the number of beings and countless are their tensions. Who can resolve those tensions, who can reconcile them?'

'So try to dispel your own restlessness and your own delusions. The world at large is miserable because it thinks of the visible as real. Can you dispel this ignorance of theirs? Try, if you can! Few will always be there who will know that the Lord alone is real and not the world. Coming to rest of the mind, its cessation absolute, is bliss the true. Attaining this state of mind-lessness, one becomes free of the stain of dualities. When your sense of identification with the body ceases through *tapa* [*tapas*] and meditation, then alone will you know the state of true repose, the state of *samatā*. And that will be the moment when your mind will come to rest.'

> When in all he finds the one, and in each being the self-same Lord, his breath shall be He and He his being, in that End of fear shall he end and cease.
> Break shall his ties of *karma*, of this dweller in the abode on high. The Lord shall he meet there, in the crown of the head, with eternal bliss his fare.
> No *me* will remain there and no *mine*, within him will open the eye divine to perceive the one in all. Melt away will his fears all and so will his delusions, each one of them.

Notes

1 Freud came in for a good deal of unsympathetic criticism by some feminists and those wedded to the scientific principle of verification. But the criticism turned out to be rather hasty. For, inspite of Feud's naiveté as a philosopher and his inadequacy as a scientist, his insights and findings, when we have applied some correctives to them, remain relevant and true. One may put them in a different way but one cannot escape from their compelling force.

2 Literally, 'I bow to you.'

3 The odd sounding phrase, 'giving and taking', has reference to past lives. It is the transactions done there that have to be settled in this life. A seer lives only to exhaust his *prārabdha*, actions that

are in the process of unfolding their results as and in the present life. No longer is he a doer but only a witness that is no witness of the results of those acts. He is a witness that is no witness because distant is he from the passive witness too, all innocence he roams about in the world. His wisdom, his astonishing and incredible nobility and his lapses happen on their own. Unconscious he lives and unconscious he dies, though, apparently, all conscious he seems, all wise and sage.

4 The article in question was later included in the collection of his writings or dictations, *Samatāvilāsa*. See *The Radiant Sameness*, pp. 95-128.

5 See Chapter 7, pp. 10-14.

11

The Call of the Forest

Of the five principles enunciated in Chapter 10, only yogic meditation, the confluence of name, breath and mind has the potentiality to make death a presence. That is not, of course, an easy affair. For, even when a man *becomes* breath, and, further, having become breath becomes the witness thereof, there still persists in him consciousness of the emptiness within, consciousness that refuses to die down. For, the joy of contemplation is so serene and so innocent that a man who has once tasted it would not like that it should ever leave him. He would repose in that placid and balmy state, the wounds that fate inflicted upon him all healed as it were. His exalted joy would make him, as would the wretched vanities of life an ordinary man, oblivious of the end portioned out to us mortals.. His long and hard endeavour, it would seem, proves, in most cases, of little use to undo the primal ignorance, the ignorance that makes a man think, 'He *is*.' Therefore, one that has achieved this state is asked to have recourse to solitary *tapas*. We already know how the Master spent his nights in the open, did *tapas* in dangerous forests or at cremation grounds, not in the comfort and security of a home.

Even when he had attained to the *sahaja-samādhi,* he would spend at least a few months every year in the solitude of forests. There was no need for this seer of *samatā,* in whose eyes the forest was civilisation and civilisation was the forest, life was death and death life, to resort to this kind of *tapas*. It was meant, as he would say, as an inspiration for his disciples and for the good of the people at large. We have already seen how during his *tapas,* revelations would descend in profusion for the good of mankind. But there were spells of solitary *tapas* where practically no revelation descended. The silent *tapas* was a sure indication that every genuine seeker of truth has to pass the test of insecurity. Without this act of *presencing* death, one could not possibly attain to the highest goal. The ancient way of life is relevant even today. The centre of civilisation, its creative centre, lies in the forest, not in villages, towns and cities.

So, let us cast a brief look at his stay in extremely unsafe forests, where his days and nights were spent more in silence and less in the articulation of the *vāṇī* to have, if we can, a glimpse of its significance. Two examples should serve our purpose.

In May 1942, he entered the Sarūpā forest in Kashmir. About six miles towards the direction of Kohala from Chinari, the turbulent Jhelum passed through a deep gorge over which hung a bridge for pedestrians and ponies. Two miles ahead across the bridge lay the town Sharian and about half a mile from Sharian started a thirteen-mile long footpath through the dense forests of what the locals called *ceerha,* a species of the pine family, resembling the deodar but lacking in the latter's tall majesty. Their needle like leaves invigorated the spirit with their strong pungent smell and soothed it into a tranquil quiet with their soft breezy sound. Other kinds of fauna too one found on the way to dispel for a moment one's fatigue and fears, trees of various shapes and hues, some with thick large leaves, others with tiny and soft ones. The path culminated at a small clearing beyond which lay the mighty Sarūpā. Hills after hills of the green, here light, there bright and there dark, presented themselves to the eye up to the farthest limit of one's vision. It seemed as if at the horizon the green met with the blue, the green of varied shades and the blue the same everywhere, from the horizons to the zenith. There was only one point in the landscape that reminded one that the breath-taking sight that opened up before one was of this earth and not of heaven – the majestic Farkhan mountain peak. The mountain seemed to break itself loose gradually from the green of the earth, its lower reaches overspread with the oak more dark than green and its higher presenting a look of bareness, of rocks and earth then bereft of winter snows.

On the margin this side of that forest was a clearing, where a hut-like structure had been built through the effort of a disciple, Faqir Chand. Two walls had been raised against a huge rock with the wood and grass serving the purpose of the roof. There was no water nearby. The Master went down a little from the improvised hermitage to a thick cluster of trees and shrubs and asked his disciples to dig the earth at the spot he indicated. With a little digging, a spring of water, clear and clean, flowed out from below. Bitingly cold was the water, a little, brief dip would make the hands and fingers numb, though the clearing was not more than eight thousand feet high. Beyond it was the fearful density of the jungle. Many kinds of trees covered range after range of hills, one kind covering this range entire, the other kind the other range, trees of varied hues and sizes, some among them so huge, tall and thick that not a drop of rain could pierce through their thickness. Safe havens were they for the beasts when rain and lightning lashed that wilderness. Virtually impassable was that forest, its thickness impenetrable, a haunt of leopards and bears that roamed about freely during the day and the night, their roars and cries frequently shaking its stillness. Curious tales were told by the locals about the forest that they had never dared to enter. They talked of the trees there that would drag a beast or a man that approached them; they had, they asserted, that gravitational force in them, and would not let it or him go until they had sucked all the blood and consumed all the flesh. When a mere skeleton remained of the man or the beast, they would throw it away. All truthful, they said, were these accounts, for many had seen those skeletons under their malignant shades! Truthful or not, they did indicate the dread that the forest held for those locals.

Like at other places, here too the Master's nights were spent not at that apology of a hermitage but on a rock two miles inside the forest, where he would lose himself in *samādhi*. Severely cold were the summer nights of that solitude, so cold indeed that the disciples could not sleep without a fire to warm them up. But the Master had only his rough blanket to protect him from the cold and the frost and no defence against the beasts that teemed the forest and prowled freely and unchecked. Add to these, the danger of cloudbursts, a frequent happening there. Such was the place the Master chose for solitary meditation. A solitude indeed!

In that forest descended the *vāṇī* entitled *prārthanā*, prayer. What kind of prayer was it? Let us contemplate a little the first couplet of the first strophe:

> In the beginning was That Unstained, in the beginning of the world and in the beginning of its ages. Ever itself is That, that Word, the Presence suffused with every power. To that my obeisance, to that my obeisance.

An infelicitous though almost a literal translation! The cause of the world, the cause of every phase of it ever remains unstained; creation and the changing in that creation do not affect it. It remains itself in the beginning of the world, during its endurance and at its end. It is the Word that is Its own referent, Presence It is, full Presence, Presence that creatures ever seek but find It never. Transcending the world, It is immanent in the world, the cause of the world It is, the primordial cause and yet stays It alike with causes and effects that the world is, stays among these as their being, as their presence. I cry for It, the world is a cry for It, every word is a cry for It, for the presence that ever is. In the insecurity of the forest that cry turns much more fervent than in the humdrum of civilised life where we are made to sleep over that urge of us, the deepest urge of us.

In the summer of 1945 too the Master stayed in that forest and at the same place for two and a half months. Faqir Chand, the Moon of the Poor, a man of a happy temperament and soothing generosity had done everything possible to make the stay of the disciples comfortable. Quite a few among them visited that place, covering the hard path through a difficult terrain, men prosperous and used to comforts. There was one Amolak Ram who had resigned his job and, like Banārasīdās and Divān Singh, had dedicated his life to the service of the Master. With devotion great he had built an *āśrama* at Gangothian and stayed there permanently. There was another, Paramarthi, the owner-editor of a religious journal, well versed in scriptures; there was the highbrow and capable physician, Dr Bhagat Ram, all but westernised during his student days in England, with a flourishing practice at Lahore, his patients coming from every part of the Punjab. And, of course, the Bhagat, now busy with collecting the stray prose writings of the Master into a book form. Some others too came there, forsaking their comforts and taking the risk of walking through unsafe jungles. But stayed they all in the hermitage, spending their days in meditation and in the holy company of the Master, their minds oriented inwards, the silence of the forest penetrating into their noisy minds

One day at around 11 A.M., Parmarthi sat concentrated, reciting with devotion the *bānī,* the devotees, sitting in a semi circle, repeating it. The Master sat silent under a tree, absorbed in himself [?]. Presently, there appeared a huge white grey snake to move towards the Master, touching a foot of Parmarthi on the way. Noticing its presence, one among the listeners cried aloud, 'Snake!' There ensued a confusion, the devotees jumping away for their life. The snake moved on undisturbed until it touched the left foot of the Master and, then, turned back to disappear into the forest. The cries and shrieks of the devotees woke up the Master who sat unmoved, saying, 'Let the recitation continue. Creatures such as these are found every where, in towns no less than in the jungles. The Lord is the protector, here as well as there.' From the Master's look it appeared, say those who were present there, as if a devotee had paid a visit to him, not a deadly snake. So happy he looked, so cheerful. Evidently, the forest and its creatures remained the *others* for the devotees, despite their stay in its interior. With cool detachment, I am making an analysis of the states of mind of the *premīs* of the Lord. What would have I done if I had been present there? Surely, more nervous than them would I have been, more frightened!

There was, however, a soul that had truly heard the call of the forest; not one among the disciples of the Master was he, but one who no one would notice, no one would care for. A seeming nonentity he was. A few days after the visit of the creature of the jungle, he came from the outskirts of civilisation. An old man was he, a Muslim cowman, with a bowl of milk on his head. Placing it before the Master, he saluted him and sat down, humility itself.

Gurudeva: From where come you, Elderly One?

Visitor: Last night, Holy One, I saw in a dream that a *faqīr* had come to these environs. 'The heart prompted that I pay my homage and offer my prayer to the holy presence.

In the morning I made enquiries and came to know that Chaudhary Faqir Chand's preceptor, a great man of God, has taken his sojourn in this jungle. So, I started at 4 A.M. and have reached here now.'

A distance of twelve miles the old man had covered on foot.

Master: How many sons you have?

Visitor: God has blessed me with two.

Master: On the way fall thick jungles. Didn't you feel frightened?

Visitor: If man holds God in awe, there is no creature that will not fear him, will not fear his shadow. But when his actions turn evil and hostile, other creatures too turn hostile. Otherwise the beasts of the forest never transgress their nature, never violate the Law, only man will transgress the forbidding line, not they. Look at these lines of the banakhorī, of wild walnut trees, how homogenous are these, how do they expand with an even uniformity! On the other side are the lines of the leafy tilapatrā,[1] on the third are those of the deodars. You do not find one kind intruding into the place of the other kind. Even these trees, lifeless though we call them, have this sense of propriety; they do not tolerate violation of the dividing line. Only man cannot retain his natural self and becomes good and evil as his willfulness would determine, though the noblest among creatures do they call him.

Master: A noble *faqīr* are you, Noble Elder. The forests are you dwellings and God your anchor and refuge. Remember Him you ever. Every creature reaps what he sows, good or evil. Good acts fashion good nature, evil actions evil nature. May God bless every being with noble understanding and noble resolve and noble acts!

Visitor: Blessed Master, pray to God that He grant faith and patience unto me.

Master: Doubt not, friend! Ever gracious is God to each and every being.

Having said these words, the Master asked Faqir Chand to extend him a liberal hospitality. To be non-intrusive was his principle and his life. The forest responded to this his disposition by stealing into his dream. What peace was in him that could bring together the two, the dream and what we call the real, objective world? Who was that man, what was he that could see our reality as a dream and our dream as reality? We had better paused before we become judgmental about his formulations.

The *premīs* too could not but feel tied to that wilderness. That quiet and still beauty unconsciously sank into their mental landscape, became a part of it; they had, later on, only to recall it to find it a vivid presence. Banãrasīdãs has this to say about the bonds that had come to be forged between the forest and its stray dwellers:

> In a happy association were spent our days, the Master spoke and the disciples listened, all attention. One day all the premīs left, only three or four of us remained to stay back. The time passed away quickly and July 15, the date fixed for the departure, drew near. No longer the forest seemed, as it had during our stay, a place teeming with life and activity; its loneliness began to register its heavy presence. Everything seemed to be slipping away from the hands. Another visit seemed out of the question. Things so beautiful to the eye seemed to lose their colour and beauty; they had, it appeared, no joy to give, no cheer to stimulate. Mahārājjī too said during a *sat-saṅga*, 'On fate depends another visit. The wheel of *karmas* moves relentlessly on to weave all kinds of patterns. Strange is the Lord's *Māyā*. But His will be done!' On the day of departure around 10 A.M. we bade goodbye to the jungle. A feeling of nostalgia came to seize the mind, sad and moving. Repeatedly I looked back to cast a last lingering look at that happy place of our sojourn. Noticing this act of mine, Mahārājjī said, 'Let coming be not an occasion for happiness, and going not a cause for pain./ A seer of *samatā* will you be when alike they become, the coming and the going.

> Tie not yourself with any thing of the world. Impressions will leave behind these ties to force you to come back to this place, in what shape one cannot say. Give no thought to the visible, for therein lies the seed of your future births and future deaths. Let loss and finding be one for you!'

We enter now another forest, called 'the Jungle Failān' by the local population, a forest in the vicinity of Chinari. On May 4, 1944 the Master entered that forest. From Chinari to Ūpī, another small town, the Master and the disciples went on tongas, two seated carriages each drawn by a horse, but from there on they had to follow a path meant for ponies. On the way they had to wade their way through a stream to its other bank from where started two and half mile stretch of a steep ascent. The path was covered with needle like leaves of the pine, making it slippery and rendering the ascent a toilsome and difficult task. Often the leaves would enter into their shoes making their walk uncomfortable and hurtful. Having covered that distance, they reached the rest house of the forest department, a four room wooden structure with a kitchen at a short distance. Nearby flowed a spring with its icy cold water. In the very thick of the forest the department had built that structure. At some distance were a few hamlets of Muslim shepherds; on another hill was a hamlet of the Sikhs. The rest house was situated at a height of only [we are speaking about India, not Europe or North America!] six thousand feet but severely cold was that place even in the hot summer months. At some distance started the forest of what they called the *tung* trees, inordinately tall and widespread, doing the function of pens and shelters for the shepherds: for not a drop of rain could reach the ground, so thick and luxuriant were their leaves.

Extremely dense was that forest, impassable and inhospitable, to enter into its interior was to virtually lose oneself in a labyrinth. No one could summon up the courage to venture beyond the end of the path the forest department had laid. Beautiful is not the word for that place, despite the majesty of the trees and of the snow-clad peak Pīr-kanṭhī and despite the beauty of the hamlets, with steps of fields below and above them and of the green that stretched up to their very doors. Grand and sublime are the words to describe that place. For, anyone who sat in the midst of the tall trees could not see anything of the world around, except the tall peak. Only a little of the sky was visible from there, otherwise all around was the silence or the music of the trees that would often seem to rise up to the sky as it were. One could not raise a prayer from there; there was no openness, no beyond to address a prayer to. One had only to wait for the light to fall from the sky, wait for its blue to enter one's being. Here human effort seemed to be purposeless, only grace seemed to reign there, grace supreme. A recipient alone could one be there, not an invoker or a contemplator.

On May 21, the Master wrote in his own hand *Samatā-bodha*, wherein was expounded the doctrine that *vāsanā*, desire, is it that fashions the visible world and all that exists there and functions. Man is not an independent being that desires, rather he is merely a function of desire [and vice versa]. Obviously, this startling doctrine demands a careful look and consideration. First, to translate some lines from the text:

> The entire world is nothing else than the visible form of *vāsanā* with its three modes of *sattva*, *rajas* and *tamas*. *Vāsanā* is the cause of creation and dissolution. The visible net of *prakṛti* is the expression of *vāsanā* itself. This truth comes to be revealed when one becomes what one truly is. Therefore, one should strive to attain to one's self, the Supreme Being that is ever Itself and is the light of consciousness, its revelation. One should strive to attain to this Supreme Being because no desire obtains in It, in that expanse of infinite peace. ..
>
> The three modes determine the way a being acts in the world. The change in the modes intensifies the darkness of *vāsanā*. Once

> entangled in *vāsanā*, every being finds himself a prisoner of the pleasures of the body, and, having got entangled in them, he wanders in the visible world as one ontologically or existentially tied to it, to the world fashioned by *vāsanā*...
>
> A prisoner of the three modes, every being sets up states of affairs of different kinds, affairs strange and past his understanding. And busies himself he to bring about the fulfillment of his desire in and through these phenomena that he has set up. But how can his wandering in the perishable phenomena of *Māyā* bring about that fulfillment? Despair alone falls to his lot when he gives up his body. (5.1.13 – 15)
>
> *Vāsanā*, to summarise some of the ideas of the **Samatā-bodha**, *vāsanā* which is the cause of the phenomenal world, is itself caused by the sense of one's being as a doing being. The sense that one is a doer gives rise to the desire, *vāsanā*, for the fruit of actions, which fruit is nothing 'but a modification of the five gross elements' (5.1.10). There is no way to determine the why of this sense of doership; indeterminable is this, this uncaused cause of desire; the very being of *Māyā* is this false appearance (10). As long as this false sense persists, there can be no end to *vāsanā*. And where *vāsanā* is, there will too be the body-world.

'Vāsanā' is derived from the root *vas*, to dwell; it means that which stays unconsciously in the mind – the impressions and dispositions derived from one's past, from one's past lives. *Vāsanā*, the creator of the present world is itself conditioned by the past world. In other words, *vāsanā* is desire but desire not free but conditioned; at once the creator and the creature of the world is it. This conditioned desire for things is the product of 'I am the doer'-sense. The doer is the meeting point between the past and the future; rather he is the present moment. But a doing moment is never a stable moment, never a *present* moment; its being is a being that has been and is to be. The 'has been' is no longer there and 'to be' is yet to be here. So the doer is dead and yet to be, he is an absence that would be a presence. As the present moment is not really and truly present, so the doer too is not really and truly a being. *Vāsanā* too is, as already mentioned, an indeterminable appearance; it too is informed by the has-been that is no longer there and the will-be that is yet to be. It is the experiential face of the sense of doership, having the same ambiguity, the same indeterminate being[?]. As the cause cannot be determined so cannot be the effect.

The phenomena of the world that the conditioned desire sets up too share in the same indeterminate nature. Desire seeks to invest them with an appearance of being, but they never share in being. Every single phenomenon that seems a presence to desire is constituted by a concept, by a universal. And a concept or a universal is equally constituted by every single object encompassed by the universal concerned. The implication is: without the universal there can be no particular, and without the particular there can be no universal. And universals too are interconstitutive, as images and percepts are interconstitutive; there are no percepts or objects which are not constituted-negated by other percepts or objects and there are no universals which are not constituted-negated by other universals. The world is a totality of facts that are not facts, a totality of states of affairs that are no states of affairs. The world is anchored to the facts that are not and the facts are facts in a world that is not. And it, the world, is a totality that is no totality, for it too is indeterminate, its being constituted by the facts and states of affairs whose reality is itself in question. So nothing ever comes to be, neither the world, nor the facts, neither the objects nor the concepts. 'Vāsanā' describes the world as no abstract term can. It connotes not only the undecidable nature of phenomena but also highlights the tragedy inherent in that undecidability. Desire, that negation of every concept and every phenomenon, is the being of every being, living or inert.

How does desire set up the world and phenomena before us, the world and phenomena that seem so solidly real to us? Conditioned desire is always a desire-of, desire object-tied. There can be no desire without objects and there can be no objects without their *place*, the world. So desire can function only in the context of a world. Common sense would have no difficulty in accepting this proposition. It will, however, feel every difficulty in accepting the obverse side of this proposition, namely, that there can be no world without desire. The 'objective' world, however, has a past that is always 'yet to be,' for, until the present comes to condition the past, comes to differentiate it from itself, the past cannot be the past. The past has to wait for the present to come into being. But the present is the moment between the past and the future, the moment to be constituted by these two, its constitutive yet-to-be *others*. So the present, too, is yet to be as are the future and the past. So we live in a world that, like desire, is a self-negating presence. It is the *other* of desire, that self-negation par excellence. Desire and the world are the two faces of the same phenomenon, the subjective face so-called and the objective face so-called. 'So called' because you cannot draw a clear line of demarcation between what are called the subjective and the objective. They are as indeterminable, the subjective and the objective, as are the past, the present and the future. You cannot say here begins the objective and here ends the subjective. But we do mark, existentially speaking, the boundaries between the subjective and the objective, between the spatial objective and the temporal subjective. The medium through which we draw this distinction is the body, the space suffused with time and the time suffused with spatiality. It is through this ambiguity that we draw the line of demarcation between the two realms of the subjective and the objective. But the objective realm, the so-called realm of space as against the so-called realm of time, is not the unambiguous space that it is normally taken to be. For, it is the present moment of time, this space. The present moment that eluded us as the moment of time makes its 'reality' felt – mark the word 'felt' – as spatiality.

In other words, at the moment of perception, at *this* moment of perception, I cannot distinguish between the world and my perception of it. The world as an objective reality, as the present moment of time, has to borrow that reality from time the past and future. So it is the elusive past and the elusive future that invest it with reality and objectivity, this present moment of my perception, moment that is as elusive and problematic as are the past and the future.

There is another aspect to this matter to consider. There is no phenomenon in the world that ever comes to be itself, ever comes to be a substance. It exists not as and in itself but in relation to the entire complex of phenomena called the world. That constitutive *other* of a phenomenon, the world, never lets it remain itself: the latter ever and always would intrude into it to disrupt its fragile being. However, this fragile being, this little phenomenon that never comes to be itself, is the condition of the being of the world, its existential context and ground. Without its coming into being the world too cannot come into being. The tension between the part that would be and the whole that would be (or, between the individual and the world, to put the matter in human context) is the very embodiment of desire that dwells (*vasati*) within us.

If desire and the world rise simultaneously, how can we say, as the *Samatā-vilāsa* clearly does, that desire gives rise to the world? How can we invest desire with this ontological priority? Desire is always desire *for* something, the moment it arises that something has also to be there with its ground, the world. The rise of desire cannot occur without the *other* that it seeks. The assertion that desire *and* the world rise simultaneously is an assertion, though implicit, of their independence. There are, however, no independents like desire *and* the world; there is only desire–world. Two faces of the same coin are these, desire and the world. You cannot divide the two. And yet desire is the first term in this duality, not the second. The world cannot be there without desire, for it is desire that invests the world with reality, makes it look the solid *other*. As a desiring being you experience the world, there is no such thing as the world in itself independent of the desiring being. When desire dies down, there will remain no sense of the past and the present and the future, nor will remain distinctions of *here* and *there.* Time will turn into space and space into time. Each thing in space will be infinity and eternity as will be each moment of time infinity and eternity. This statement is, however, an understatement or rather a misleading understatement. For, with the death of desire and doership, the world, along with every thing in it, will show itself as something entirely different, which no blasphemies like 'eternity and infinity' can ever pollute.

Nevertheless, the statement that desire creates the world is a more sound proposition than the unintelligible that the world *and* desire rise simultaneously.

There is another aspect of the argument that one should consider with attention, viz., that there are no such distinctions as the body *and* the world; there is only the body–world complex. Where the body is, there will also be its constitutive *other*, the world. The body is a complex of sensations and also an instrument of action. The senses are the seats of *vāsanā*, and the motor organs that of activity and actions. These organs, the sense organs and the motor organs, have for their constitutive *other* the world. The senses are directed towards the world and the motor organs are projected towards it. The body is the seat, therefore, of *vāsanā* and *kartāpan*, of desire and doership. *Kartāpan* finds the world as the world-to-be; it finds it a presence-to-be-forged, whereas *vāsanā* finds it as if it were already a presence. *Kartāpan* (*kartṛtva)* finds uncertainty and unintelligibility everywhere, but is not ready to accept that uncertainty and unintelligibility: it will strive to bring about presences where no presences are or could ever be. *Kartṛtva* is called a delusion precisely because of its refusal to accept the truth of things, their uncertainty and *anivarcanīyatā*, their un-sayability.[2] Desire is one step removed from doership because it is not, unlike the latter, aware of the truth of uncertainty about things, much less is in a position to accept that truth of uncertainty. When desire dies down, *kartṛtva* too will die down because *kartṛtvā* is prompted by the passion to convert itself into *vāsanā*: the struggle to bring about a certain state of affairs means to *presence* that state of affairs, which means to make it an object of desire. *Katṛtva* and *vāsanā* cannot, strictly speaking, be separated from each other, *vāsanā* is inherent in *kartṛtva*; the latter inevitably transforms itself into the former.

Of the three modes of *prakṛti* and of the subjective and the objective spheres of the world, we have had occasions to speak. Desire prompted by *tamas* makes one cling to the present state of being, the desire informed by *rajas* makes one change oneself and the world, desire informed by *sattva* is desire for pure transcendence. The desire informed by *tamas* is tragic desire because in the changing world you cannot remain coincided with yourself. This kind of desire makes one a neurotic, a creature of a killing anxiety and insecurity. The desire informed by *rajas* is frustrating because no state of affairs can turn into a presence that this passion would make it to be. The desire informed by *sattva* is, as we said above, is desire for pure transcendence; it does not seek to cling to what is and is not interested in substituting one state of affairs with another state of affairs. Disillusioned with both, with the given *is* and with what is to be brought about, it turns into pure moving forth, pausing at no state of being. It can become redemptive, this aspect of desire, if it resists the temptation of becoming conscious of itself, of becoming a witness of transcendence and the joy and bliss of being that witness. For if the witness remains, it can, it may and will, sooner or later, become a prisoner of the *rajas* and the *tamas*. So the witness has to die into pure transcendence, and with its death pure transcendence too will die, for no consciousness will remain of it. With the death of consciousness will come about the final death of *vāsanā*. We are not to forget that to be the witness of transcendence also means to *vas*, to live or dwell. That too is *vāsanā* and must, for this reason, die for the redemption of man – the witness that is the final facet of *vāsanā*.

I have discussed the entire thought in impersonal term; I have spoken about *kartṛtva* and *vāsanā* as if they were agents. But the text, we find, speaks in a more personal strain. 'A prisoner of the three modes,' it says, 'every living being sets up states of affairs of different kinds, states of affairs strange and past his understanding.' The implication is that though it is *jīva*, the living being, that creates states of affairs, yet he creates them in a way that they look ontologically prior to him, beyond his ken and understanding. In other words, the creator finds himself a creature, not a creator. Why has this being, this creator–creature been introduced in this way in the text? Without consciousness, the answer would be, no *kartṛtva* is possible and no *vāsanā*. To the witness consciousness, the world would appear indeterminable, the world of which nothing could be predicated. But once this consciousness gets involved in that world, world the indeterminable, it will become prisoner of the *to* and the *fro*, *this* and *that*, *here* and *there* and of conceptual differences with their *other*, the world of objects. So it is this consciousness, the prisoner of the sight before it, that creates the world to find itself a prisoner in it, a world that it can neither comprehend nor control, despite its pathetic successes, termed the triumphs of civilisations.[3]

This was the message that descended on those spots enclosed from all sides by the tall trees that seemed 'to connect'[4] one with the sky. The message of desirelessness was it, for, here you could not strive for anything, for any goal; you could only let things happen, and let yourself be lost in the happening. There could be no *karanī*, doing, for you, no *kathanī*, saying; there could only be *honī* and *rahanī* for you, only happening and only be-ing for your.[5]

Notes

1 The tree with sesame-shaped leaves.

2 For the ontology of name-named relationship see Chapters 7 and 8.

3 For a detailed analysis of this point, see Chapters 7 and 8.

4 Wordsworth's phrase in Tintern Abbey.

5 For a more detailed analysis of the doctrine *vāsanā*, the reader should consult *Anubhava* Five of the *Radiant Sameness* (pp. 279-329) and also the Notes appended thereto.

12

Among the Seekers and the Sought

1. The outskirts of Daurangala in the district of Gurudaspur in the Punjab, December 1943: One day the Master sat basking in the winter sun outside a room near a well, the place of his sojourn there. Presently came there an ochre-robed monk – old, sad and serious. Gurudeva asked Banãrasīdãs to make a seat for the visitor. Taking his seat, the stranger said, 'What kind of glory is of the bliss in which remain absorbed the Great Ones? Could one perceive that state with the eyes? To what extent can speech articulate it?'

The answer came in the form of *vāṇī*:

Ineffable is that in-being, beyond the reach of speech,
yet its glory I'll sing for thee;
for, in my ears does speak a Man,
the Man from where one cannot say.

To know that Being is to be that Being,
so rare is the singer of Being, singer without being.
Of Wonder shall he speak and of Wonder hear,

of That which ever abides as That,
taking no stain from the passing world.
Within the body dwells that Being,
stays therein as being without being.
When you live as the body, the mind will rove,
and the body will it kill, the impatient mind.
When the body melts into the Word,
and lost too is the mind in It,
of unfoldment will the moment then arrive,
of *that* the vision which ever is *that*.

When the aged man heard these words, he prostrated himself before the young Master. 'A sharer I must be,' said he, 'in the blessed portion meted out to the world to see the Lord face to face. And without an effort, without a struggle! Where can one find blessed presences like the Lord! Only grace abounding can vouchsafe their sight. Blessed is this moment, blessed this place and blessed are the people these. Be gracious unto me, Blessed Lord!'

Master: Noble One, what can one say, what could one possibly say, about That, attaining which one becomes That Itself. Speech cannot find it and the ear cannot hear it. Beyond the reach of the senses Is It called. Before whom can one speak of that Bliss? Who will give his ear to that 'speech'? A time was when seers would speak of That with one another, whole congregations of them. Now, saints come together to share the pipe. Rare is the sight of a person like you, given to devotion to the Word of the guru. In the company of genuine seers alone can be found the bliss that one seeks, every creature seeks. Bereft of their company, one finds it hard to break one's ties and choose the path that leads to the truth. The body will perish sooner or later, death is inscribed into its being. But creatures would find bliss, the real bliss, in this very body, in this very death. Only a soul blessed will seek the company of seers. But these are the days of bankruptcy. When saints observe no rules, what can one expect from men of the world? Only their *tapa(s)*, their bright, holy self-burning can make the people think of abiding in the truth. May the Lord bless every being with wisdom true!

For some time the old man sat mute and contemplative. Then he reverently bowed before the Master and left. Gurudeva saw him off a few steps away from his seat but asked the Bhagat to accompany him up to his place. On the way, the old man said, 'Bhagatjī, is it true that Mahārājjī lives merely on a bowl of tea?'

When answered in the affirmative, he said, 'This too is a mere form, for a man like him can live on bare air. Fortune smiled benign on you when it ordained that you live at his feet. Otherwise, where would seers of this order let people approach them?'

On his return, the Master said, 'Somewhere, sometime you do come across persons of promise. A seeker true is he.'

2. Golara, District Rawalpindi (now in Pakistan), March 1944: A temple near a ravine wherein lived a recluse. All the day he would remain within the walls of the temple, only at night would he come out a little and that too rarely. People said that he had been silent for twelve years. His intake was about two liters of milk and an equal measure of curd a week. Every Sunday two of his devotees would bring the milk and the curd around eight in the morning, serve the mixture to him and return. For the rest of the six days of the week he would neither eat nor communicate.

Very few people at Golara knew about his presence at the temple. One day, a little after sunrise, Gurudeva asked the Bhagat to accompany him to the said temple. On reaching it, the Bhagat opened the door in obedience to the desire of the Master, laid a seat for him; he himself sat on the bare floor in a corner. The sage was reading some book. A tall figure wrapped up in the white, soft complexion, every vein peeping out, the face all aglow and arresting:

this, in brief is the description of the man from Bhagatjī's pen. The Master folded his hands, accompanied by a slight bow, the traditional way of greeting an equal; the Bhagat prostrated himself before him. The courtesy of 'How do you do, or how are you?' through gestures of the hand, not through speech. A piece of paper lay there and also a pencil. Gurudeva took hold of the two and scribbled these lines:

> Which is the land and which is the place
> from where you deign to come,
> Why should you wear this decaying form
> that mortal men roam in?

Pat was written the answer:

> I come from no land, I come from no place,
> neither mine nor yours,'
> I abide in the Being that ever is the same;
> the Same is my wear, the Same is my worship,
> with thy grace benign.

And:

> Which was the way that led you to it,
> to this blessed state supreme,
> And who was the guru that uncovered for you
> the secret hidden and true?

Answer:

> The outgoing breath and the incoming breath
> brought forth this immortal fruit,
> The Word was the guru
> that led *this* up to the blessed state supreme.[1]

Having written these lines, the sage smiled. Then added he another line, '*Cidghana*, consciousness enmassed, alone abides beyond the Being that is *samatā*. Now nothing remains to do, no duty to perform. Time passes in silence and in quiet. No more is the joy of coming and no more the regret of going.'

Gurudeva stood up and bade goodbye to the sage, his

hands folded. The sage too came out and bowed a little with hands folded and went in and bolted the door. On the way, Gurudeva said to the Bhagat, 'What did you see, Premī?'

'Only seers,' said the Bhagat, 'can understand seers. The world is not empty of the Truth-becomes. But if the Lord too had retired all silent into a corner, who would have shown the Path to us lost souls? Grace abounding indeed are you, my Lord and Master!'

'A seer of a high stature is this soul. Refrain from propagating this incident. Let him live absorbed in Bliss.'

3. **Abohar**, Punjab, January 1947: The year was the tragic year when the Hindu–Muslim divide had turned into an intense hatred, resulting in wide spread riots and killings and, eventually, in August, the partition of the British India into Independent India and Pakistan. By January itself the atmosphere had become tense and violent causing countless deaths. In remote towns and villages, they talked only of the riots and of the impending danger. At Abohar, a small business town, too people could think and talk only of the uncertainty and insecurity, even those that came into the presence of the Master. None could summon up the patience to talk about the ultimate goal and reality. One afternoon at about two, something happened out of the usual and ordinary. Gurudeva sat mute in *samādhi*. A man, clothed in shabby clothes, almost rags, came there and sat in the presence of the Master. Ordinary he looked in every sense of the term, less than ordinary, penury itself seemed that stranger.

Gurudeva opened his eyes and said, 'Where live you, *Premī?*'

'Here, Revered Master,' said he, placing his hand on his chest.

The moment he uttered these words, his body trembled

and he closed his eyes. Gurudeva went on looking at him, all smiles. When, after some time, he opened his eyes, he said, 'Your grace is upon me, your grace in abundance. Some bricks I lay for a living. Nothing else is required.'[2]

Bowing in humility, he left the place.

'A pearl in rags!' said Gurudeva, 'Intoxicated they live, such beings. Did you have the occasion to meet him earlier, *Premī?*'

'He goes,' said Bhagatjī, 'to the well for water before the break of the dawn. One day as I too went there to fetch water, I found him standing there. When I bent down to pick up the rope, he stepped back in confusion, thinking I was going to touch his feet. "A servant," he said, "am I of you, Holy Guru!" Since that moment, I have carried a high opinion about him. There near the still waters below, he lays bricks. Unbaked they sell. Very rarely he talks. This is the general report about him.'

'What use is,' said Gurudeva, 'talking? *Faqīrs* behave as their *svabhāva* prompts them to behave, their nature fashioned by their modes of life in their previous births. My Lord showers His blessings wherever He wills. Riches don't count for Him nor does penury. Penury of this kind is a blessing indeed, for takes it one to this state. The earth is not empty of noble beings. But rare are those that show others the path. Mute turns one when one attains to this state. Those that strive will, ultimately, reach the blessed state. Ever look out for such souls, *Premī*!'

4. Srinagar, Kashmir, June 1950: A devotee, Pundit Radhakrishna, brought to the presence of the Master a man who looked in hypnosis as it were. The Pundit bowed before the Master, but the man-in-hypnosis kept standing. Immediately, the Master removed the blanket under him and spread it on the floor and requested the stranger to take his seat, expressing his annoyance at the Bhagat for his lapse in showing respect to the newcomer.

'Mahārājjī,' said the Pundit, 'a great one is he, one attained to his Self. On the way I met him and brought him here.'

Many a time the Bhagat entreated him to take something, but the other did not reply. He went on gazing blankless at him. Then he said something that would be offensive to every civilisation. He equated food with faeces and asked the latter to prepare some for him. He went on repeating this sentence, 'Eat shall I the faeces, prepare some for me.' The Pundit said something to him in Kashmiri language, to which he said, 'The faeces should be good. Let him prepare two loaves of bread with sauce of onions and black pepper.'

The Bhagat made two loaves of bread and also prepared the sauce. The stranger took those loaves in his hand, threw away four pieces in the four directions, and then bowed down before the loaves calling them with same offensive name. He took four or five mouthfuls, placing the remnants at the foot of a tree nearby. Then, using the same word, he made a request for water.

All the time Gurudeva looked on what was happening before him. 'This state,' said he, 'can do no good to others. *Avadhūtas* they call such beings, ones that have shaken off their entire worldly being. Unaware they live of the body, to bless is not for them nor is to curse.'

'People,' said the Pundit, 'pester him a lot, Muslims no less than Hindus. Once he utters a sound, it continues to be uttered on its own. Some try to construct these sounds into words and interpret them in their own ways.'

'The land of Kashmir,' said the Master, 'is a land of seers and sages. Here the great Kaśyapa did his *tapas*. In those days three-fourth of this land was immersed in water. A time was when every man here was a *ṛṣi* or a sage.'

Hearing these words, the Pundit narrated the story of Lāladevī, a woman saint of Kashmir. Her sayings in the Kashmiri language, he said, are read with great devotion even now. One of her saying reads, 'I gave no birth, neither was I born. No ginger I took. Before the sixth came I and after the seventh.'

Hearing this puzzle, the Master said, 'As only a seer can know what the Bhagavadgītā says, so only a seer can know what this saying means. A seer of a very high order indeed was she. But people can understand a seer only when he says something.'

'If the Lord too had chosen to remain silent,' said the Pundit, 'who would have waken us up from our slumbers?'

No reply was given to this question.

Notes

1 I may mention that the verses in the original were written in totally impersonal vein, all bereft of *I* and *yo*u.

2 Again, there was no use of the *I* in his answer. The genius of Hindi and other languages or dialects related to it are well suited for impersonal vein.

13

The Suffering Man

Into the Word died the man his disciples called Mahārājjī and the Word died into the Ineffable, the Ineffable turned into the Word and the Word into words. The Word spoke to redeem man and, through his redemption, redeemed Itself. The Word spoke through silence and through speech, but what became of the man neither the Word considered nor the Ineffable. There was no way the man should not have got scalded in the fire that burnt unabated in the mountains and the forests, in the wildernesses and the cremation grounds. The effect of that self-burning became visible even at the Nikhettar Parbat. On the day of departure from that Starry Mountain, the Master asked the Noble Devotee to take him to the spring from where he brought water. At the spring itself, he said, he would have his bath. A distance of about a mile down he had to cover. But even this walking proved tiring for him, for, reaching the spring he sat down under a tree to recover himself. After a little rest, he started his bath but two or three bowls of water were enough to make him say, 'The water is very cold. Was it from here you carried the water up?' The Bhagat saw that the Master's body had turned almost blue. 'It appears as if the body was not there, appears something almost different!'.[1] Saying these words, he stood in the sun to warm himself up a little. The steep ascent was obviously too much for him, a few steps and he felt exhausted. 'The way down.' he said,' was not tiring, but now there is breathlessness.' He sat down, spent and worn out. The Bhagat helped him to walk up with the support of his shoulder but the Master said, 'Slowly, Premī, a little slowly!'

'Mahārājjī, milk should take the place of tea. What good could boiled water do? We stand in awe of the Master and dare not speak, but . ..'

He could not complete his sentence. In a soft, low voice said the Master, 'There is no pretence or show. Such is the Lord's command. It cannot but be obeyed.'

We know when he left the mountain he urged Faqir Khan, the milkman, to ask for a boon for his and his family's prosperity. I may also mention that when he was about to leave the Failan Forest, the shepherds and milkmen came to his presence to make him a request, 'Holy Master, be gracious unto us, Allah's devotees. Our cattle and herds are ill and yield no milk. Their feet decay and ooze out blood and puss, their mouths discharge saliva. Please pray for their cure and health.'

They were all Muslims, those simple folk. The Master kept mute for some time, and then asked his disciples to pour some water on a huge stone nearby, reciting the *Mahāmantra*. After the *premīs* had done his bidding, he asked the shepherds to pour some milk on the stone and pray to God, to Him that cures.'

That was his response to others' distress. But how helpless he felt when overwhelmed with weakness and exhaustion! When the seer spoke, he spoke as the one transcendent, but here was the man, man the sufferer who lived in obedience to the command of his God, with no power of choice, no ability to think what was right for him or not right for him. In ignorance he lived, in weakness. Where had gone the seer, the one whom obeyed the elements, who could shower blessings on all that moves or does not move? For, said he on one occasion, 'The tree is redeemed under which a seer does his *tapas*, and so is redeemed the stone he sits on.' And yet that self-same seer is weak and helpless and feels the pain of exhaustion more intensely than 'a man of strong character' would do! This paradox of self-trancendence and self-surrender should never be lost sight of. A seer, says the *vāṇī*, gives up the care for the looks of the body and the beauty of the mind. Distanced he lives from these. When he comes to live as these, then the doer is [for him] the Self or the Word, not he. He will endure and live all weaknesses, all humiliations and all trials but would not think of borrowing the power of his inner being to undo them. He will not borrow even the power of endurance from it. In meekness he will live, and in helplessness. Only those who have seen a seer true can understand the truth of this paradox, and its beauty. The man in the seer lives as his past deeds have fashioned him. Some, like the Master, live as men of *tapas* and also as meek sufferers; others may not do *tapas* but endure calmly and without ado what destiny chooses to inflict upon them by way of their share of human suffering. Hasty judgements would be foolish.

After his terrific *tapas* at the Failan, his left ear developed an acute pain, which, in a short time, turned shooting and piercing. Whatever domestic treatment was available was administered but to no effect. It persisted unabated for months making it difficult for him to give a proper discourse at the annual *yajña* at Gangothian. All the day he stayed indoors, his face wrapped up in a piece of cloth. But when at night the murmurs of the Trail beckoned him to its banks, he went there to spend the night in *samādhi*. Then remained neither the pain nor the weakness. It had drained all the strength out of the body, that strange pain. When, despite very many traditional efforts, there appeared no sign of improvement, the devotees took the Master to Rawalpindi for a proper medical treatment. Up to the railway station at Mankyala, he had to be carried on a *pālakī*,[2] so weak had he become. Specialists examined him, prescribed their treatment but to no effect. Seeing his condition, the devotees forced him to rest on a bed. A month passed by this way.

One day, the Master asked his host to bring him a book of his late father's, a physician in the indigenous school of medicine. He selected a formula that to a modern physician would appear simply bizarre. The medicine prepared according to this formula consisted of equal measures of the liquid extracted out of the donkey's dung, sesame oil and onion juice. But when this strange mixture, heated a little on fire, was poured into the ear, he felt some relief. 'The shooting pain,' said he, 'seems to have decreased. Perhaps, this oil may do some good.' His ear was running pus and the doctors had prescribed some oral drugs to dry it up. The Master ridiculed them. He could not understand, as he said, why they administered oral drugs when the pain was in the ear! Was he unwilling even to shed off the prejudices against modern medicine widely prevalent among the village folk in those days? Even ignorance would he not shed, not to speak of ordinary weakness and frailty! As the Word he lived, beyond even the Word. What had he to do with the shell called the human person? How did it matter whether that shell was ignorant or well informed, rational or irrational, open minded or prejudiced? If there is nothing in the world without the Word, the Word lives alike in the wise and the foolish, the timid and the heroic, the arrogant and the meek. As the Word does not disown all these Its manifestations, so doesn't a seer his human self and its frailties. Alike he looks on the strength of the Spirit within and the weakness of the flesh.

A few days of that treatment [?] and the pain disappeared but not the debility it had wrought into the body. Never could he regain his strength, whatever little he had. On the insistence of the devotees, he took, for a few days, two slices of bread and a small measure of black gram gravy, but only for a few days. Eating was really too much for him and he came back to his normal daily intake of tea. In 1945, after his *tapas* at the Sarūpa Forest, the pain appeared again, and continued to trouble him off and on. Commonsense would, no doubt, attribute the condition of his health to his insufficient intake and the severity of his *tapas*, and so would, perhaps, medical science. One could cite evidence, too, for this conclusion. Once, in deference to the wishes of a devotee, he took an orange a day. On the fourth day, he found the pain subsiding a little. But again he came back to tea with, as we shall find, disastrous results.

In the summer months of 1949, the Master was staying at Jakhu in the upper reaches of Simla (now spelt 'Shimla'), at one time the summer capital of the British India, now the capital of the small Indian State of Himachal Pradesh, the Land of the Mountains. Jakhu is exposed to the cold winds that blow from the snowy mountains in the West and to the winds from other directions too. Near its top he stayed, spending his nights under a tree. With the onset of rains his *tapas* in the open proved too much for his worn out body. One Sunday evening after the *sat-saṅga* he complained of an ache in the left side of his belly and asked the Bhagat to prepare a cup of black tea for him. Barely half an hour after he had taken the cup, he vomited, the discomfort having increased. Some lemon and black pepper brought some relief, but the pain persisted. The following morning after his return from the *tapas* in the open, he again complained of the pain. He felt, he said, a disorder in his stomach.

In the midst of this trouble, he wrote in his own hand the *Jīvana-saphalatā-bodha*, 'On Life the Successful'.[3] Success means, the essay says, withdrawal from sense pleasures and putting an end to the cause and source of those pleasures, the body-ego. As long as the sense of identification with the body persists, one remains a prisoner of sense pleasures, the prelude sure and inevitable to one's undoing. The man who can see the tragedy that inheres in sense pleasures alone is wise, and the man who can distance himself from the body, finds it as other than him, alone is successful, for he alone will truly come to be himself. The other, the one who seeks his self in the body and bliss in sense pleasures lives to no purpose. Unfulfilled was he born and frustrated will he go, his life a tale of meaningless events. So let man withdraw himself from the body and find the self within, the true self that is the self of each and every being, moving and non-moving.

That was the message for those who live immersed in the world but how did he live, he who had already distanced himself from the body and had become all? As a man humble and common did he live, did not assert and show that beyond the body he 'lived,' beyond even the Word. As men of the world lived, so did he. Like them did he suffer and like them did he endure the portion meted out to him. The body-ego had died into the self and the self into the world. No distinction had remained between the sublime Word and the pathetic man.

Yet despite the complaint, he would not subject himself to treatment. He gave clear and explicit instructions to the Bhagat not to make a mention of his complaint to any one. Only black tea and lemon-water continued to be the means of cure for that obstinate trouble. When things went from bad to worse, the Bhagat, ignoring his command, informed the devotees about the Master's state of health. Dr Bhagat Ram came from Dellhi to examine him. He excluded tea from his diet and prescribed, in addition to a drug, olive oil and a boiled apple a day. The treatment benefited him but only for a few days. After a fortnight, he felt the same disorder within and went back to tea, giving up the drug and the apple and olive oil. Modern physicians were absurdly fastidious, he said. The system could not, however, absorb the tea and, after two hours, threw it out causing great distress to the Master. It was late night when the Bhagat heard the Master vomiting. He rushed out of his room to find him very ill, his face pale, his body shivering, with drops of perspiration on his face and forehead. He brought the Master back to the latter's room and made him lie on his blanket, rubbing his feet, legs and hands. After about five minutes the shivering declined but the face continued to remain pale and colourless. The Master regretted the trouble the Bhagat had undergone and asked him to take rest in his room.

However, the trouble did not mean that the body would be spared the severity of *tapas* during the night in the open. Only after sunrise did he return, with clear signs of the ravages that the cold of the night had wrought upon his body. He could not have his daily morning bath that day. 'It is no use for *faqīrs*,' said he, 'to retain a sick body. Why not throw it down the ravine in the early hours?'

'The Lord of the entire world are you, my Master! And of this body too. Create it can you and destroy it too. Your will is all. What good destruction of this body will do? Pray, do not bring us ignorant to test! Why this trouble?'

'*Faqīrs*, too, *Premī*, are under obligation to reap the wages of the deeds done in their past lives, they too have to clear their debts. Upset *It* is not by these happenings, *It* only watches what the Self within you speaks. Many will have to pass through a test, for each one of you will have to endure much with *It*. There is a time to be happy and, also, a time to be unhappy. That is how the world moves.'

Next morning, when he came back from his *tapas*, he said, 'Another bowl disappeared into the ravine below. That the things of the *faqīrs* should disappear this way is not something to be taken as of no account. Their loss is a sign of a coming physical ailment. This second loss is a warning that the malady will not disappear easily.'

A bowl had disappeared earlier too, slipping from the hand of one of his disciples, Mukundlal.[4] One day, Mukundlal stumbled and fell down, the said bowl sliding down the ravine. He searched for it long but in vain. The Master was furious. 'Careless are you all! This loss of the bowl is not an ordinary event; a signal sure is it of an impending illness for *It*. Came you here to serve your Master! Service indeed! If you did some service, you did it for your own benefit. Be careful lest grace should change into something else!'

Why this burst of anger and harsh words? Speculate shall we not on these matters, this sport strange of the Word. We shall let the events speak for themselves. So, to come back to our story! September was drawing to its close but the complaint remained unabated. Dr Bhagat Ram advised that the Master should come down to Delhi where he could be treated properly under his care. Accordingly, he went down to Delhi and stayed in a hut in an orchard. His devotees were deeply distressed to notice his condition, an assemblage of bones almost he looked with a thin coat of flesh over it, his face frighteningly weak and pale. 'To serve the *saṅgat*,' said he, 'came *This* to the world but odd is the condition of this body. Without a notice come bouts of pain. The morning was without a discomfort but now heaviness is there. A vomit may bring some relief. Of little use may be the *faqīrs* now. So alone should *This* be left. Unhappy indeed is the company of the unhappy.' But despite his trouble, he continued to give *upadeśa* three times a week.

However, his trouble refused to mellow down, gave no promise of its end in spite of all the care that Dr Bhagat Ram took to bring the Master back to health. Twice did he visit the Master every day but whatever treatment he prescribed would become ineffective in two or three days.

Rather it would add to the discomfort. No effort on his part proved successful, with all his undoubted abilities and his high degrees from a prestigious British school of medicine. Many a time, says the Bhagat, the Master would complain of his malady as men of the world do. This kind of behaviour, he says, made him and others very distressed. But the very next moment, the *premī* adds, the veil of *Māyā* was removed and the man that spoke before one was no longer the man that complained but the man that spoke from the region of the beyond. Who was he? The man that suffered or the Word that spoke, or one who had transcended the Word too into. ..? Of what did his face 'speak,' his pale and sick face, when he would come back from his *tapas* in the morning?

From the medical point of view, the Master's illness did not seem incurable. Dr Bhagat Ram could not see how his treatment should not prove effective. But of no use were his services as a disciple and his abilities as a physician. His Master's health, he could see, deteriorated almost every day. Winter had arrived and the nights had become bitingly cold. Exposure to the cold during the nights could not but have its effect. The Master developed pneumonia. Proper and expert treatment was given but the nights continued to be spent in the open. No one could interfere in this matter, neither the disciples nor the disciple-physician. None had the courage to do so. Even mild and indirect protests were set aside as of no account.

Needless to say, the pneumonia wrought havoc on the body but no word of complaint or discomfort escaped from his lips. With a stony stoic spirit, he endured the disease. After the pneumonia had been cured all that he said was, 'This shock too had to come. In abundance showed it its power.' Some improvement in his condition ensued, giving some hope to his disciples. For two weeks no signs of his other malady were visible. He appeared to be, so the devotees thought, on the way to recovery. One afternoon, however, he had a sudden attack of the same discomfort resulting in a vomiting, his face turning pale and his forehead wet with drops of perspiration. The attack was much stronger than the earlier ones, the shivers, the perspiration and the pale colour of the face showing its unmistakable intensity. The Bhagat followed him and wiped out the drops of perspiration from his forehead. In a feeble voice spoke Gurudeva, 'Only tea is *Its* intake. Then, why this trouble? Bring some black tea for *This*.'

Tea, the cause of the malady, was sought for the alleviation of the discomfort. Dr Bhagat Ram was present when this attack of the disorder occurred. It seemed advisable to him to have another medical opinion and he suggested the name of a colleague. That day, the devotees remained in the hut up to late in the night, their worries and misgivings not letting them go back home. Only the Master sat indifferent in *samādhi*, the pale of his weak and haggard face and body and the shadows of death that lurked there could not conceal their soft and mellow splendour, of the face and the body. Up to eleven in the night he remained immersed in that unearthly oblivion. That night too much before the break of dawn, that frail body had to sit in the open, exposed to the chill and the cold winds blowing from the north.

On the request of Dr Bhagat Ram, the said physician, well known for his expertise and high degrees, came to examine the Master an hour before noon. With utmost care he examined the condition of the patient. After examining him and getting all the information of the history of his trouble and the way of his life, he said, 'I have been treating patients that lived on cereals and other things but not one that lived only on a bowl of tea. It is difficult to prescribe any medicine for a patient of this nature. He has starved himself into this state, his nerves have become weak; his entire system is malfunctioning. Increase of intake of milk and vegetables are the clear imperatives.'

On the very first day the treatment showed adverse results. Gurudeva refused to accept the second dose and asked his devotees to leave everything to the will of God. Human ingenuity, he said, was of no use. So he came back to his old routine, tea becoming his sole diet. The day he would spend in the room, with the door closed. The devotees came, prostrated themselves at the threshold and returned without seeing the Master. Speaking, they knew, was too much of a strain on him. But the call of the night and of the open sky was still irresistible, there was no let to his nocturnal 'awakening into light' in the open. Forgetful of his body and its trouble, he would sit immersed in *samādhi* and would come back with the same calm or no-calm writ large on his face. But that could not reassure his disciples, this his enigmatic transcendence. It was his human presence that they sought and longed for. And that was in clear danger now.

Disappointed with modern system of medicine, they took refuge in the indigenous system and the Greek system that the Muslims had brought with them during the medieval ages. They also consulted a *yogin* who traced the cause of his trouble to tea and advised that he should take milk, butter and cereals and almond oil. Listening carefully to his advice and his exhortation, the Master said, '*This* gave up cereals and other things not out of self-will. No interest was left for these things. That appeared to be the Lord's command. Convenience of the devotees too was a consideration. It is tea that has wrought this havoc; each and every nerve seems to have become addicted to it. But it is difficult to find a substitute for it. Let us see if some alternative could be found.'

The *yogī* wanted the Master to switch on to fat but Dr Bhagat Ram was against this advice. So the devotees could not act upon the *yogin's* prescription. The indigenous and the Greek systems of medicine too proved of no use. As for the Master, he remained indifferent as if his life was not his but of his devotees' concern. Dr. Bhagat Ram made another attempt but, as before, failed in his effort. He advised a change of climate. Many places were considered but none in the vicinity of Delhi was found suitable. At long last, it was decided that he should be taken to Tajewala, where he had done *tapas* in 1948. The decision was taken in accordance with the wish of the Master who said, 'Leave everything to the will of the Lord. The *premīs* too had to endure much. If the Lord wills that *This* should serve His people, He would show the way out. If this does not happen, then this useless body would be thrown into the waters of the Jumna[5] there.'

February 27, 1950 was the day of departure for Tajewala. The train reached Saharanpur at 3 A.M., hours before the dawn. Despite the early hour, the bus for Chakarota was standing outside the railway station. Gurudeva sat in the bus along with four or five devotees who had been permitted to accompany him. The way through Jagadhari was more convenient but he selected the inconvenient way lest he should cause trouble to the devotees that had come to settle at Jagadhari after the partition of the country. Now his resort was going to be the bank of the blue watered Yamunā and the solitary hills, away from the ways of men and their methods and strategies.

When the bus started, the dawn was about to break. Not long after the sun rose with its cheerful rays falling on the green fields and hamlets on the way. Gurudeva sat silent, immersed in *samādhi*, his pale and almost lifeless face stood in stark contrast to the awesome transcendence that shone forth through that manifestation of death. The bus was passing through the countryside and stopped frequently to take in the voluble and noisy passengers or let them alight it. This commotion and tumult did not disturb the placid oblivion of the Master nor did it cause excitement or irritation among the frozenly depressed devotees. When the bus arrived at the outskirts of a hamlet called Mirzapur, five miles this side of Tajewala, the conductor asked them to alight. No means of transport was available to take them further. The entire distance had to be covered on foot, an undertaking beyond the power of a person in the Master's condition. But he had insisted on going through that route, giving up the straight one via Jagadhari. So after a brief breakfast, the journey started. For about eight months, the Master had practically lived on air. That he had managed to live and breathe for that long was nothing short of a miracle. But that skeleton that resembled a human body was walking that morning ahead of all the devotees, so fast was his gait and so nimble. Only one devotee could keep pace with his gait, the strong willed Amolak Ram. On arriving at Tajewala, the group spent the night on the bank of the river in a tent.

A whole literary tradition of romance has clustered around the Yamunā: of the anguish and ecstasy of love and the song of the melodious bird *koel*, the cool easterly winds and the long looked for dark rain-laden clouds. That day too the same Yamunā flowed before those five persons but her glory was going to be celebrated in an altogether different way. The sister of Yama, the god of death, is she said to be, the entire world dissolving in her dark bluish waters. For that boon had Gurudeva come to her, for that death which puts an end to every further death.

Next day, arrangements were made for stay at Hathinikund Bungalow, a little over a mile above Tajewala, much favoured by tourists. But we are speaking of the days when civilisation had yet to ravage the place and its rich wild life. Yet, despite this rude intrusion, the beauty of the place takes away one's breath and its sublimity simply overwhelms. The bungalow is built on a plain spot; beds of grass and flowers and lines of trees with walks in-between give you the tranquility to look above, around and below.[6] About sixty feet below flows the softly murmuring river, almost calm and quiet having left, a little distance above, the hills and mountains. The blue lucidity of its waters is much more arresting here than in the plains down. On this side are the hills of Haryana, on the other side are the vast plains of the state of Uttarakhand, with an old fort of the days of the Mughals towards the left. On the left are the hills of Himachal Pradesh and, at a distance, the vast ranges of the snowy mountains, a virtual meeting of them from many a direction. On a clear day, after rains, these distant mountains seem to transgress into the plains. At a short distance, I said, is Hathini-kund from Tajewala, a few turns of the road and you find yourself at it, but it appears, on a rain washed day, as if you had entered into the very interiors of the Himalayas. To enter this vale, on such a day, is to enter into the domain of the timeless. One hears, almost palpably, the words of the Sanskrit poet Kālidāsa, 'If thou hast undertaken these austerities to attain to the world of gods, vain is thy effort. For thy father's land, this Himalaya, is itself that world'.[7] In the midst of this vale, the nearness of heaven and earth is the gift of one's sight and vision, not of one's belief or faith. To think of their difference would be an aberration, a perverse distortion of a palpable truth.[8]

On March 1, the Master entered a servant quarter attached to the bungalow. The bungalow was vacant but he preferred the servants' rooms. Those days the environs of Hathini-kund presented a sight of almost a wilderness; the haunts were they of tigers, leopards and wild boars; frequently one could see their pug marks on the sands on the banks of the river. The British had built this bungalow for the purpose of *śikār*, for hunting these animals. To this wild had the Master come, snapping off all relationships with the human world, even through letters. With him were the four devotees, the peaks of snow with the blue sky above them and the flowing waters below. 'If the Lord wills this body to remain for some time,' said he, 'ways will He show for that purpose.' What a rebuff to civilisation and its faith in human praxis! In these days when Nature is no longer considered enchanted, when God is supposed to have died, when the source of all meaning is man and his discourses, his theories and praxis, this disposition would appear not only quixotic but weird, archaic and incongruous. But before we hasten to deify man and his discourses, we should wait for what comes out of this surrender to the elements of Nature bare of every trace of the human in them.

On March 4, he wrote *Sāra-nirṇaya-jīvana*. *Sāra* means essence; *jīvana* means life and *nirṇaya* (*nis*, into, or negation; *naya* from *nī*, to lead) = to be led into a conclusion, or where leading reaches its culmination, its cessation. Are we led into a conclusion or does the word suggest that where leading ceases there alone is truth, that coming to an end of instruction is the dawning of truth? Is *nirṇaya* the instruction that eventually negates itself to let the truth replace it? Let us have a look at some of the passages to find out what is the truth of life whose essence lies in negating itself.

> One should think of the body and the world as informed by transience, think of them this way with conviction.
>
> To lead life in deeds pure and stainless is the paramount duty. One should bear no malice towards anyone or nurture ill will. For all will change, nothing will stay as itself. Therefore, that life is the best life, which is guided by love.
>
> Think of the world as a storm fierce and deep. Nothing is there except dust, confusion and unrest. Freedom from this storm and its dust and confusion is possible only when one finds the support of one's being in the Lord. This conviction led many a gifted person to their salvation.
>
> The glory of human birth lies in being good unto others, to the best of one's capacity. In this perishable world, this noble approach alone can bring man peace, the real and genuine peace he is in search of.
>
> Let man strive for the peace of his mind and his senses, the bliss that ensues when all desires have come to rest. That is the quality

> search and research, this striving for the coming to rest of all desires.
>
> To know with conviction that the world one experiences is the world perishable is to move upwards. And also to purge the mind of all desire, to, that is to say, establish it in the That which is ever Itself, with no concept to predicate of It and no context to place It – to establish the mind in It with no thought of any thing else. He alone will rise above himself who thinks and acts this way.
>
> This is the final truth of life and about life. Gifted people should pay heed to it and live in accordance with it. This is the way they can redeem themselves.[9]

The change of climate, to turn to our narrative, proved of no use. Nor could the yogic exercises suggested by a *yogin* who somehow stumbled into the Master's presence. The exercises rather injured his spinal chord. Yogic exercises, he said, were for the well fed, unnatural were they, fit only for those who were interested in physical well being. Daily walks too proved futile. The body somehow was bearing the burden, the too heavy burden of life; it was beyond its power to bear the additional burden of nocturnal *tapas*. But to spend a night under a roof was not its portion. His life seemed a flicker on the point of extinction; a life-in-death was it, this life posthumous. Finding no improvement in his condition, he said, one day, to his devotees, 'Find out where the waters are deep. It's time this body should be offered to them.'

The remark evoked anguished protests from the devotees. The thought was too painful to entertain.

One day, he asked Bhagat Banãrasīdās, 'What did you find in the company of the *faqīrs*?'

'As proximity to a river makes one cool so does the Master's presence. No worldly idea rises up in the mind or any selfish thought.'

To other devotees: 'If this composite of the five elements, this body, comes to disintegrate today, people will ask you what prompted you to remain devoted to your preceptor. What answer will you give them?'

They spoke of his *tapas* and his incredible renunciation but confessed their inability to fathom the depths in him that tied them to him as if to a tether. They asked him to explain what was there in him that kept them glued to him as if he were their sole anchor.

To them said he, 'Make some use of your own thinking powers, *Premīs!* If someone asks you about the nature of the Lord, then read out the *Mahāmantra* to him. If you are questioned about the nature of a true *guru*, then read out the *Gurupada-siddhānta*[10] to the one questioning you. As human persons, *gurus* and incarnates have different bodies, different personalities and different outward forms and life situations. Some may be born as princes and behave like them; some may be born poor and abide their time in poverty and deprivation. All these matters depend on their *prārabdha*, actions responsible for their present birth. But with all these differences in terms of personality, behaviour and life situations, there are certain inner traits that are common to the great ones. You will find them all free from desire, meek, risen above the affairs of the world, stable and full of compassion and care for others. When Rāma conquered Lanka he did not keep the kingdom for himself, he gave it to to Vibhīṣaṇa, the brother of Rāvaṇa, the slain king. A garland of flowers was the only gift he accepted for himself. The same way, Kṛṣṇa never made himself a king, though many a king he anointed and dethroned. He, along with his wife Rukminī, meekly pulled the chariot of Durvāsā, his preceptor, through the streets of Dvārakā, submitting, without a question, himself and his wife to the latter's cruel whip. And when this humiliating ordeal was over, he had only this much to say to his preceptor, 'Lord, be gracious enough to command me another act of service!'

His days were spent in the service of his people and his nights in the solitude of the jungles. In his interior self, every desire had been extinguished. Only fools present that *yogī* as a *bhogī*, an epicurean. He lived as a prince, but he could also dance on the hood of a monstrous snake, playing his flute. In every state of being he remained absorbed in his true self. He had every pleasure at his command but no pleasure ever came to be *his* pleasure, ever distant he remained from them. Of the feet of Sudāmā, the poor friend of his student days, he drank the wash, gave to the Pāṇḍavas everything of the kingdom he had helped them win, keeping nothing for himself. He tried to bring the wrongdoers to sense, first through affection, then through persuasion and, when these and every other measure failed, through the sword. So much did he do, so much change, so much transform but all through the rise and the fall of things and affairs, he kept himself aloof.

'Anyone, *Premīs*, who is gifted with traits like these, is called a guru, a guide and an incarnate. Only such souls, gifted with these traits, can dispel the darkness from the world. Whenever people sewer from the right course, someone appears God willing on the scene to show them the right and straight path. His life and presence make them adopt the right way and live in harmony with and love for each other. To live as the Lord ordains one to live and to stick to purity in the midst of adverse situations gives rise to the disposition of disinterestedness. To believe in the Lord as the light eternal and to perceive, every moment, the body as passing and ephemeral will give rise to the disposition of humility. To meditate with sustained intent on the true self within, to find oneself anchored to it makes one rise and stay above the turmoil of the human self and its world. Steadfast will make one this transcendental state. He alone can stay above the world, he that finds the body and the world as false appearances and lives absorbed in the Lord to the extent of becoming one with Him, finding in Him his being and his delight. One can do good to others only when doing everything one finds one's deeds as ordained by the Lord and not willed by oneself.

'When the *buddhi* finds itself suffused with these traits, its ignorance falls off and it attains to the state of *samatā*, that bliss eternal. *Sat-saṅga*, sustained meditation and the spirit of service free man from sins to make him all-victorious. Let not your talk harp upon your faith, lest it destroy the latter. Until a man of learning does not strive hard to turn his precepts into living truths, vain will be his learning and vain his discourse. When the learned turn mere talkers, they bring only turmoil and unrest for themselves and for others. The *faqīrs* have brought into the open every secret, have given their life and blood so that you may change for the better. These are the days of *māyāvāda*, of belief and faith in the visible and the measurable. Things external alone have become the truth for the people. When people seek their life and being in these things, in them alone, misery falls to their lot. To deliver people of this sort from these their taints, the *faqīrs* have to take upon themselves a share of their misery. To undo their sins, of such people, the *faqīrs* have to do penance, especially to undo the sins of those that live in their proximity. Whatever articulate the depths within them mingles into the air to bring about a transformation of the people. On those that are awake and open, their words will not fail to have their impact.

'The word "*samatā*" has appeared again. And for reasons special has it appeared. Not that it was absent in the ancient scriptures. It was there but in an oblique, hidden way. Now it appears focused, its glory manifest and its meaning explained. It is the command of the Lord that this word should appear in this way and in this light. Peace will come about when *samatā* becomes the base and the goal of all endeavours. At this time *This* is there to protect you. No compulsions of desire can make you helpless. But ruin will await you if, after *Its* departure, you let thoughts of pride, honour and wealth sway you. In *Its* absence do not give yourselves up to wealth and woman. Undo you surely will they. These are the temptations that make you wander in the world, birth after birth. The Lord has blessed you with this human birth, destroy it not through pleasures. Let you not be blind to the dangers that lurk in them. Let your life be spent in meditation so that you may come to rest in your self. Now the last hour arrives. Fashion this way your life after the death of this body.'

Time passed away unnoticed in conversation. The shadows lengthened and the time of sunset drew near. The Master stood up to go down to the bed of the river. A few words escaped from his lips all spontaneously: 'Of man is woman the wife, of woman man is the son. Having given thought to this, the *avadhūta* gave up all, shaking away all his ties and sins.'

Below flowed the Yamunā in two currents; the current this side was shallow, beyond it lay a bed of sand and, beyond the sand, flowed the main, deep current.[11] Beams of wood lay on this side of the shallow course. Gurudeva sat on one of them, the devotees on others. 'Since the morning,' said he, 'the same discomfort has been felt. Only the Jumna (Yamunā) can cure this disease. How deep are the waters there?'

'Let the Lord,' said a devotee, 'take almond oil for a week. It may improve things.'

For quite a while he dwelt on the curative efficacy of almond oil. Another devotee, Amolak Ram, opposed this suggestion, referring to the medical advice. The devotee, Pandit Girdharilal Rishi, did not like this blind faith in Dr Bhagat Ram. 'There at the Headworks[12] too,' said he, 'there is a doctor. Why not consult him?'

'Do,' said the Master, 'whatever you deem fit. *This* has no desire to torture the body. *This* tries to protect it as much as is possible. Come, let's see how deep are the waters there.'

They crossed the shallow current. The blue of the waters had taken in the gloom of the evening. The sun had left the plains and the hills and had come to linger on the far off snowy peaks. Stones lay in numbers across the minor current. Sat they on these stones, beyond which swiftly flowed the main course. Seeing it, the Master said, 'Tomorrow is the holy day of the new moon. Tie this body with these stones and throw it into these swift flowing waters. It will be a good thing if mother Jumna (Yamunā) accepts this gift of the body.'

A lingering look he cast around with a soft smile on his face. 'On this Jumna Kṛṣṇa spent his childhood. Here the air is pure and clean are the waters. A sanctity is there in all the atmosphere. *This* likes this place very much. Most appropriate is it for death. Holy will this place become for you, the place for pilgrimage.'

They looked at him, at his demeanour and bearing. An assemblage of bones looked he, a skeleton, his face pale and wrinkled, his eyes thrust inwards. Yet there was an extraordinary depth in his eyes, a captivating lucidity, emanating a love for all that is from the living to the inert, a love without a trace of self-reference. How out of tune with that outflow, that love, were the words he had just uttered! An awe came to seize those that heard him in the soft dusky sound of the waters. Not a word could they utter in response to his request. Silent they sat, looking down. The dusk deepened and darker became the waters. Mute they sat, all the devotees, in that descending darkness, concealing their tears. Biharilal Rishi alone somehow summoned up the courage to break that painful silence. 'Mahārājjī, if this body, as the Lord says, belongs to the *saṅgat*, then it is for his devotees to decide about its fate. Allow us to deliberate about our options tonight. We do not want to lose our guide and refuge.'

'O.K, *Premī*, take your decision tonight.' There was a smile on his face.

They returned to the rooms, the Master to his, the devotees to the one adjoining it. To Bhagat Banārasīdās said the Master, 'They want *This* to take almond oil. Do you think it will do some good?'

'May I,' said the other, 'bring some?'

The Master laughed a soft laugh. '*This* too,' he said almost in a whisper, 'knows the way out. *This* only watches the *premī*s and their ways and acts.'

The words reassured the Bhagat. He felt that the Master was only testing the mettle of the devotees. For that purpose alone did he suffer and, in a sense, appear to suffer. Every cure was there at his beck and call. Were things as simple as the Bhagat thought? Was he testing his disciples or taking upon himself their own share of suffering, their own *prārabdha*? Or, was it that the last and final fire had been ignited for him to burn into what they call or miscall salvation or life eternal?

Outside the room it was all darkness, the chirping of the birds had ceased, only the soft sound of the waters of the Yamunā could be heard. In the dim light of a lantern began the *sat-saṅga*. The Bhagat started the recitation of the *vāṇī*, the Master went into the yogic oblivion, his eyes closed, his trunk bent forward a little. The expression of seriousness gave place to that of transcendence. Eventually, that too disappeared. The eyes of the devotees closed, their attention, all serene, focused on the rhythmic flow of the recitation. A deep passivity came to occupy them, replacing their thoughts, even the thoughts caused by the words of the *vāṇī*. At the end of the recitation, they became quiet and serene, forgetting almost their anxieties and fears. The Master slowly returned to his human self. Drinking in this calm, a devotee saw a snake moving towards the Master. In a moment fled their serenity and their passivity. One of them caught hold of it but his trembling hand could not sustain the grip. Another devotee caught it firmly and went out to throw it away at a distance. In the tumult and agitation, Gurudeva sat calm and aloof, the traces of transcendence still visible on his face.

They sat silent facing him, the devotees. 'Today again,' said he, 'the unrest is there. The change of climate has been of no use. Nor has the intake of the vitamins. Only the Prompter can change the things, if He chooses to prompt someone.'

He lay down and covered his face and head, the Bhagat rubbing his feet. Full of doubts and fears, the devotees went to their room and deliberated long how to dissuade the Master from his resolve. His presence was the presence of peace for them. Even in his illness he could soothe their thoughts into a calm they could not comprehend or express. How could they think of losing that presence? In about half an hour, the Bhagat heard the Master's vomiting outside his room. He rushed out and helped him wash his hands and face and brought him to his seat. A cold wind was blowing but the Master was perspiring, his face expressionless. The Bhagat's nerves almost failed him but he did not call in the other devotees. 'Since the noon there has been a feeling of nausea. The Lord does not seem to will *Its* recovery. So where is the point in using human ingenuity? Go and take some rest!'

The morning did not fail to see the Master in the open, lost, as ever, in the yogic oblivion. A beautiful morning was that, the sun rising behind the snowy peaks to spread his rays first upwards and then on the hills and the plains. In the midst of that unearthly beauty returned the almost lifeless figure of the Master. He asked the devotees to have their breakfast. When they returned to him, he inquired of them about their decision. They told him in one voice that they would consult the doctor at the barrage.

'How can he,' said the Master, 'succeed where highly qualified doctors have failed?'

The devotees stuck to their resolve and went to request the doctor to examine him.

That very afternoon arrived from Gurudaspur a very simple, plain and almost illiterate devotee, Babu Ram. The Master asked Banārasī and two other devotees if they had informed the new comer about his illness. The Bhagat had not disobeyed the Master's command but the other two had. Babu Ram prostrated himself before the Master and said in a voice trembling with emotion, 'My Lord and Master, how could I remain at home knowing about your condition? Hard it is to bear this sight!'

'Graciously,' says he, 'the Lord granted me to stay with him. I came to know from the lips of the *premīs* that the Master was of the mind to give himself up to the waters of Ma Jumna. That day too he expressed the same wish. The *premīs* could not agree to this proposal. "Pitch," he said, "a tent here, then. *This* will enter the final *samādhi* in the tent itself. In the morning take hold of this body." In despair I heard these words. "The learned." said I, "say one should not put an end to one's life. Sin they term such an attempt." The Master administered a stiff reprimand to me. Weeping, I went out of the room and went down to the bed of the river, walking up and down along its margin. 'Ma Jumna, forbear to accept my Master's body. Have no such intention! Otherwise, not one but very many bodies you will have to accep!'

That evening was an evening of despair and lost hope. No *sat-saṅga* was held, no *vāṇī* was recited, no meditative passivity permeated the souls of the devotees. The doctor at the Barrage had promised to visit the patient after two days. The morning came, beautiful but blank and cheerless. No one could think of eating that day. But the wolf in the belly had to be propitiated. So a course meal was offered to that ravenous beast. In the evening the Master sat at a platform of the bungalow from where the breathless beauty of the valley was visible with its full glory. Sitting there, he repeated his desire to throw away the body into the Yamunā's turbulent waters 'in the early hours of the morrow.' The spot he had chosen for that painful offering lay towards the right direction of that platform, the waters running there swift and deep. The resolve of the Master seemed firm and determined, causing great distress to his devotees. Helpless would be they without him, the prop and support of their being. Their tears were the only response to his words.

Seeing what transpired in their minds, he said, 'Where meeting is, there separation too is. One comes alone and goes alone. Not forever can one live with others. You have done your best. The Lord, it appears, wills that this body should find its final rest.'

They requested for his compassion, for his grace. But silent he left the platform and went back to the quarters to sit under the mango tree. Despair seemed to have seized the devotees. One among them, Shesh Raj, wept bitterly and decided to drown himself in the river. A fit of madness seemed to have seized him. With great difficulty was he restrained. The evening saw the Master's condition deteriorate still further. He asked them to hold the *sat-saṅga* in the adjoining room. No meal was prepared that evening, for none had the appetite. Their efforts of months had proved futile and useless. They prayed, prayed long but a mere anguished cry of despair was their prayer, not of fervent hope and faith. The Master summoned them late in the night to know their mind. His voice had changed into whispers; his life seemed a flicker, his body a wreck. That he had managed to live for so many months was itself something beyond the pale of credibility. Who could summon up the courage to see him drown? They kept mum, except Biharilal Rishi. 'We do not,' he said, 'have the nerves to imagine that scene, much less to see it with these old eyes. Besides, there will arise many complications. There will be investigations and postmortem reports.'

'*This* will leave behind a note. You will have no problems then.'

'We are not thinking of our problems. We do not want that this holy body should be subjected to police and medical investigations. Allow us to wait for another day or two.'

'Let a few heavy stones be bound with the body. It will sink to the bottom and the fish will make a good feast of it. There will be no investigations and no postmortem.'

'We wish to take the advice of the doctor at the Barrage. We also wish to see if almond oil produces any results. If nothing works, we shall act as the Lord commands us to do.'

Rishi was almost obsessed with almond oil and would lose patience if someone questioned his faith in its efficacy, though the medical advice was explicitly against its use.

Another day ended and another night came to brighten into another morning to find Gurudeva lost in *samādhi* in the open as before. Babu Ram saw him come back, his feet covered with dust. All the daylong he swept the entire path, removed the pebbles and sprinkled water on it. Next day, when Gurudeva returned from his *tapas* he found the devotee sprinkling water on the path. The devotee fell at his feet and wept with inconsolable anguish. The Master stroked his back and asked him to get up. Babu Ram saw a moisture of love in the Master's eyes. Would the waves of the Yamunā, could they ever engulf that embodiment of love? That was the question the *premī* put to the Yamunā and his God.

The devotees decided not to sit near the Master for long. His talk about death through water was becoming unbearable for them. Men of the world cannot understand the suffering of those who have attained to their goal. Otherwise, why should the entire *saṅgat* have kept away from him? His command that he should be left undisturbed they faithfully followed but not the other ones, the inconvenient ones. The very souls for whom he was 'burning' feared to approach him, those unhappy souls. Those who were given the opportunity to burn with him, to share in his *tapas,* they too had started fearing him. Inheritors of sin that we are, we cannot see, are blind to, our own redemptive moments!

All of them, these men of wisdom, busied themselves in some work or other to escape from their pain. Some got busy with collecting fuel from the jungle around, some brought water from the river and some got busy with cooking food. Dumb they became even to each other. Among these busy bodies the Master laid himself on the cemented base of the mango tree, his face covered with a sheet of cloth. In a short while, he uncovered his face and asked the Bhagat busy with cooking to feel his pulse. A devotee felt his pulse and found it very faint and irregular. He was an indigenous physician and could not mistake what the pulse indicated. 'Finish with your meals as quickly as you can,' said the Master and went down to the river. All the devotees left their work and, helpless and almost paralyzed with misgivings, saw him disappear. Only two of them went after him, trembling and sweating with fear. From under a tree about three metres above the sands they observed him move slowly towards the river's bed. About two metres this side of the edge of the waters he walked up and down, covering about a hundred metres each way.

The high noon sun of that hour lent a flashing splendour to the sands and the waters, the floating white bars of rainless clouds of spring eclipsing it in-between. The snow on the distant peaks and the green of the hills nearby glowed with an unearthly beauty; and in light and shadow glimmered the waters of the river. A nervous watch the two kept of each and every step the Master took and its distance from the minor current. When he turned back to move near them, they felt as if the entire agony of mortality had come to be concentrated in that one face, so deep was it and so intense. A time was when the fire of an oven had soothed his feet. Would the cool waters of the Yamunā 'scald' them today? Was that place aglow with that unearthly grandeur, the two asked themselves, the place 'suitable' for his death? For about 40 minutes he walked, the distance between him and the waters remaining the same. The *premīs* could not summon up the courage to go near him and speak to him. But they kept on praying to the Yamunā, for instinct with life and concern seemed she to them. Asked her they to spare their Master or accept them too in her waves. In a short while, Rishi too joined them in their watch. After about five minutes he went near the Master to accompany him. For quite some time he walked mute with him, uttering not a word. Then he managed somehow to break the silence and started some conversation. The two watchers felt their life return to them. Hoping that the Yamunā had heard their prayers, they too joined the Master.

For over an hour he had walked. With hesitation, Rishi requested him to return. The Master took the way up, walking with a slow gait to find the Bhagat and other devotees waiting for him, their faces ashen and colourless. The Bhagat spread out a seat for him.

'Your doctor is yet to arrive!'

'Tomorrow morning will he come,' said a devotee.

'Who knows what the morrow has in store for you?'

Then he turned to Amolak Ram, 'Babu,[13] take a photograph of *This* in these last moments.'

With tears flowing down his cheeks, Amolak Ram brought his camera. The Master called the Bhagat. The latter approached him and stood nearby. 'Rogue, you are standing here! Bow down here. Keep ever in memory this moment!'

Amolak Ram took three or four snaps but none turned out to be well shot. The Master stroked the Bhagat's back with affection. He took Amolak Ram behind the room and asked him to look after Banãrasīdās in his absence. Mistakes, he said, Banārasī committed in plenty. Let him not, he added, be led astray from his path

Up till now the Master himself had been Banārasī's guide and guardian. Many a time, prompted by his relations or his own feelings, he had asked for the Master's permission to go back to the world. On one such occasion he had left the Master without permission and had made plans to start some business. That time too the Master had sent Amolak Ram to bring him back. When, after a good deal of persuasion, he agreed to go back to the Master's presence, the latter told him, 'You do not know what kind of relation is there between you and *This*.' With eyes wet with tears, the Master touched his feet and said, 'Let you be *Its* guru and *This* your disciple! Say, what you want. The *faqīrs* will do everything for your happiness. Whatever thing you wish will be procured for you!'

Deeply moved by these words, the Bhagat came back to his normal self and requested the Master to let him stay at his service. That day too when the last hour of life seemed to be near, the Master's affection for the Bhagat had not decreased. Amolak Ram promised to take every possible care of Banārasī after the Master's departure. Returning to the other devotees, he said, 'Two days more are given to you. After the doctor's visit, you will know about the Lord's will.'

In the evening after the *sat-saṅga*, the Master looked at Rishi and said, 'If this doctor prescribes almond oil, then you may seek permission of Dr Bhagat Ram.'

There was no need, said Rishi, to have anybody's opinion. The Master's own permission was needed. He had come there, he added, to take the Master to Pathankot, his home town. Rishi had complete faith in the Master; he was convinced that the Master would not desert them, doctor or no doctor.

'Your stubbornness may bring about wonders, Rishi. *This* too observes what goes on in the minds of the *premīs*. No one is insistent in his request like you. Pray to the Lord that this doctor's treatment may be successful.'

Next morning, when he returned from his *tapas*, the same old glow shone on his face, the same mystery and the same depth. That light soothed the tortured hearts of his devotees, supplanting all thoughts of his death. After tea, he said, 'What a sunrise! The day succeeds the night, the night replaces the day. Centuries pass away this way. The sun shines far above all that happens in the world, all that comes and goes. Nothing can touch him. *Prārabdha* decides who is to come and who is to depart, who is to meet and who is to separate. Even if you know what is in store for you, you cannot change what is decreed by your *prārabdha*. So, see what the next three or four days unfold before you.'

At about 11 A.M. the doctor arrived and examined him carefully and asked the Master to take almond oil. No other medicine was needed, he said. He too requested him to give up tea. The Bhagat had some almond oil with him. Mixing it in tea, the doctor administered it to the Master. He was convinced that it was tea that had wrought that havoc. 'Be gracious enough to give me three days for this treatment. With the Holy Guru's grace,[14] it will bring about the desired result.'

The simple almond oil did what expert medical treatment had failed to do. At about three in the afternoon, the Master said, '*Premī*, your oil has done a miracle. No discomfort has reappeared. Rishi, your constant persistence with almond oil may bring about what seemed impossible. The Lord is there to make your service fruitful. If another three or four days pass by without trouble, *This* may regain the lost health.'

Things improved slowly and gradually. The doctor received the Master's blessings, the devotees got back their lost hope. 'Perhaps, *This* is destined to do some more service to the *premīs*. True disciples ever remain true to themselves. But few people are there that remain faithful to their own truth. Devotion to the guru is hard to attain, much harder than devotion to God. To stick to *dharma*, to the right and straight path, is like treading the sharp edge of a sword. Now, take your food and spend the evening in meditation. *This* is and will remain ill.'

During the days of recovery, the Master dictated the following instructions for his disciples:

1. After *Its* departure, no one should think that anything belongs to him. Look at every living being as a member of *Samatā-saṅgat*. There should be no discrimination between a Hindu, a Muslim, a Sikh or a Christian or between those initiated or not initiated. The *bānī* has manifested itself for every being and so have the sayings.

2. To frame elaborate rules for the management of the property and land of the *saṅgat* is a great obstacle in the way of spiritual uplift. The *āśramas* have been, or will be, established so that the *premīs* may gather to think and meditate and live in harmony and to deliberate how they can uplift themselves. Those who have retired from their service or business should stay in them for *tapa*. Self-interests of clever disciples often bring a bad name to their preceptors.

3. These days the people at large are not interested in meditation of the ultimate real, they don't feel the need of attaining to the self that is the self and being of all. Whatever was to be propounded about the philosophy of *samatā* has already been fully propounded. Nothing needs to be added to it. That is the Lord's command. What is needed today is not the doctrinaire exposition but *bhikṣūs*, men of renunciation that embody in their life the precepts of *Samatāvāda*. Given to righteousness and not to themselves, their life and time solely dedicated to the good of others, let them bring to the notice of the people what *samatā* stands for

and how it can be attained to, through what means and ways. Their exemplary life alone can do any good to others; only persons of this mettle can make people adopt the right ways. Let the five principles of *Samatāvāda* be the guiding principles of their life. Let them be an example unto others in this regard. That alone will make it possible for others to regulate their life in accordance with these principles.

4. Glory will be his alone who gives up all that he has in the service of others: his life, his possessions, his thoughts. Who, awake or asleep, wishes well of all, be they high or be they low. And who, with no thought of mine and yours occurring to him, empathises with the agony of others, making their pain his own.

5. Let not anyone find faults with others, when he has faults enough in himself to find. You are not the guardian of the world to pass judgements. Not through judgements can you change anyone but through what you do and what you are. How you live and what you give alone will affect others, not your faultfinding.

6. When you propound the truth of *samatā*. before people, you are not to pass adverse judgements on others. No *premī* should act in a way that may stain the good name of *samatā*. He should be very careful in this matter.

7. The *bhikṣus*[15] should make every endeavour to free people from wrong acts. They should see to it that they themselves do not become victims of wrong customs. Instead of fabricated myths and stories, they should make people acquainted with the *samatā* literature. Fashion is to be given up and so are cinema, smoking, meat and liquor. The *bhikṣus* should make every effort to make people give up these things and lead a life of simplicity, simplicity in food and dress. This way of life will save them [the people] from many an expense. That saving they should be urged to spend in service of the deprived and needy.\

8. The *saṅgat* should give thought to how it can best serve the people. Its members should spend their savings in service of the deserving, on education and towards making people

> eligible for employment. That is the way to serve the Lord and their guru.

'The Jumna has declined,' he said one day, 'to accept this body. Offer some gift of grace to her.'

The truth-becomes flow out to the lifeless as much as to those that live and breathe. They look alike on the sentient and the insentient, on man and on beast. We see the rivers as bereft of life, we who are careful not to anthropomorphise Nature, we who would let no enchantment bedim our rational and pragmatic approach to things. We explain the flow of waters in terms of cause and effect; we perceive no purpose in that flow, no striving to reach the goal of creation. But seers see in that flow the same thirst that they see in man. Once he said, 'A wave of a river dashes towards its bank in search of the same peace that prompts a man of the world to his pleasures and a *yogī* to his renunciation.' With that gift of grace, appeased was the thirst of the restless waves.

At last came to an end that divine sport and that love for the pain, for our mortal pain, which we all would escape from. That body suffered and burnt and with its burning burnt out the sins of the living and the inert. The *tapas* went on for the world which noticed it not, not even those who called themselves his faithful disciples. Who has ever seen the Sustainer and the agony He endures to sustain the world? He suffers as one with all, as one with suffering. In his immanence lies his transcendence, the suffering suffer but not suffering.

The day (March 6) melted into the dusk. The birds chirped loud in the trees and slowly went into sleep, quiet and silent. The night enfolded in its folds the forests and the hills. The stars appeared in the sky, bright and splendid. They sang the song of the Word, those *premīs* of their Lord. But today the Word could not bring about the peace and the passivity that It had brought about on the days of anguish and distress. For nine months had they suffered, those devoted souls. On the morrow they would take back the shepherd to his flock – safe and sound. Heard had been their prayers, not in vain had been their tears; their faith had been vindicated. Where had this hope and faith any room for the passivity that the *vāṇī* would generate in them, who among them had space enough in him to let the peace that passeth understanding replace his happy thoughts? Only the Master sat aloof from hope and joy, immersed in *samādhi*. The same old stillness his weak and frail body wore, the stillness that neither our joy could encompass nor could our pain. The Beyond was there, in that frail flesh, the Beyond that erased even the Beyond.

Darkness deepened outside, the stars shone in clusters numberless. There is something of the immeasurable about night, something awesome, something like infinity itself. That kind of night was it that descended upon the river, the hills and the mountains. But deaf to the call that the night made, the call to keep awake and receive her blessings, the creatures slept deep, oblivious of their loss. The birds hailed the coming of the morn with their songs, the cows with their lowings, men with their cheerful prayers and energy. But none could find the night as the day, the darkness as the light, suffering as redemption. For the sake of the creatures the Master suffered but the creatures knew not the meaning of his suffering and their own suffering, they knew not the dignity of pain and the redemptive face of death. Happy were they that morning and so were the Master's *premīs*. Did these latter love him as they thought they did? Yes, they did in our human sense of the word. For suffer they did with him during all those months but could not find the ecstasy in the pain, the light in the darkness, the day in the night. And until they found the *samatvam* between the day and the night, between the ecstasy and the pain, between light and darkness, how could they say, how could they claim that they were the *premīs* of their Lord and Master? But have I attained to the state of *samatvam* to pass this kind of judgement? I should remember, with every humility should I remember, the words: JUDGE NOT LEST YOU BE JUDGED.

Before leaving, the Master gave an *upa-deśa* to the people at Tajewala and resumed his old ways.

Did a change occur after that *tapas*, the *tapas* that men of the world called illness?

Notes

1 Or 'distant.'

2 A device by which four men carry a person on their shoulders.

3 *Samatāvilāsa*, (2007) pp. 445-51; *The Radiant Sameness*, pp. 431-34.

4 Once a reckless profligate, drunkard and prosperous gambler. Far and near he went for gambling and made quite a fortune for himself. The shock of his life came when the Master refused to accept his hospitality; not even a cup of tea would he take from him. A *faqīr*, he said, could not accept hospitality from a man whose soul had been soiled by tainted lucre. Pass through trying and dangerous circumstances he had to before his tea could be accepted. His trials were to be severe and long. Of these we shall speak at the proper time. See Ch.14.

5 Yamunā, a tributary of the Gaṅgā or the Ganges.

6 This is how the landscape looked at the time of writing. The bungalow is now in ruins almost and the garden a waste. Now a barrage has been built here changing the topography of the landscape. There remains nothing to attract the tourists. Everything looks here drab and bleak. Earlier the British had built the barrage at Tajewala. The passage of time had made it frail and weak. So, it was shifted to Hathinikund.

7 *Kumārasambahva*, The Birth of the Hero.

8 I have left the description as it was at the time of writing. Today, the landscape will fail to evoke such emotions.

9 See the *Samatāvilāsa*, pp. 451-54; *The Radiant Way*, pp. 431-34.

10 A chapter in the *Samatā-vilāsa* (pp. 237-51) on the nature and qualities of a genuine guru; also *The Radiant Sameness* pp. 227-37.

11 That was the topography of the river before the construction of the barrage at Hathinikund.

12 The dam or barrage at Tajewala.

13 Gentleman; the term used for Government clerks in those days.

14 Guru Nanak. The doctor was a Sikh gentleman.

15 Mendicants.

14

The Social and the Alone

I

Before the advent of the Muslims, Hinduism and Buddhism, the two dominant religions of India, were vibrant enough to absorb into their folds the hoards of invaders that poured into her plains from the deserts and steppes of Central Asia. When Muslims came to finally settle in India, Buddhism had virtually disappeared from her soil and Hinduism had entered a phase of decadent self-oblivion from which it is yet to awake fully. A large number of low caste Hindus called the *śūdras* converted into Islam, quite a few among them through the power of the sword and very many[1] because they found their own faith too oppressive and humiliating. Their new faith did not give them what they hoped for, for honour and opportunities were denied to the poor as much in the new fold as they were in the old. But no longer were [the lowest among them] considered the unclean untouchables. If someone among them rose in the economic ladder, he was sure to find a relatively respectable place in the new order unlike in the old. At least the hope of rising up was there, if not the promise. Birth no longer determined the mode of their life, their achievement could. So the hatred of the poor converts for the high caste Hindus was perfectly understandable, augmented by the untouchable status they still retained in the latter's eyes. The Muslims in general too were, if not exactly untouchables, but 'unclean and impure' in the eyes of the Hindus, and so were 'their' water and food, which a 'clean' Hindu could not think of drinking or eating. For centuries this kind of relationship [?] continued, augmenting their hatred for each other to a degree that made it almost impossible for them to live in the same areas and locations. Only the rich and powerful among the two communities would not submit to ghettoization, their pride would not accept it nor would their education.

Years before the partition of the country, Gurudeva would impress upon the Hindus that they give up their hatred for the Muslims. He held them responsible for the communal mess that India found herself in. It was their fault that they could not withstand the invaders, and it was their fault that a large part of their membership had deserted their faith. Thus on May 9, 1945, the last day of his stay at Golara, he said during a discourse, the last one, 'Such opportunities do not frequently come one's way. This might be the last visit of the *faqīrs*. This is the time to live in concordance and in harmony. Good will and good feeling for each other alone are one's support in adverse situations. Utter not a word of offence to anyone. In the long run, only God is one's succor and support.' Similarly, on January 13, 1946 he spoke in the same vein at Daurangala, 'Perhaps, another visit here may not come to pass. Be favourably disposed towards every creature, dispel all thoughts of fanaticism from your mind. Enmity will bring no good to the land; selfishness ruined the Hindus in the past and may ruin them in future. Times much worse may be in store for them. Regard for others is the need of the hour. But some *premīs* are there that seem to prefer conflict and division to harmony and concord, taking these ruinous traits as the signs of their patriotic dispositions. They should understand that this kind of patriotism brings in only discords and conflicts. Wellbeing, whether secular or spiritual, comes to be possible only when people orient their thoughts to the truth. Fraud has never done any good to any one. Plans based on mean thoughts result only in disaster.'

How much the two communities were divided from each other may well be gathered from what happened at the last *yajña* at Gangothian in October 1946. Gurudeva gave a discourse on the states of bondage and liberation. He spoke at length on the ontology of suffering and the ways of deliverance from it. After the discourse a rich feast was given to all the audience with the usual extravagant abandon. Most villagers swallowed things with embarrassing greed, and, as it was their wont, packed a large quantity of them to take it home. After this virtual loot, they looted the shoes of the *premīs*, of those who were taught to love every creature in the spirit they loved their Master! The earth was rough, thorny and overlaid with sharp, piercing pebbles. The devotees had to go back barefoot. The looters too did not fare better. For, hardly anyone among them could find a full pair. It may be noted that the majority of those that enjoyed the feast and looted the shoes were the poor among the Muslims, the descendents of the converts. This was the effect of the years of *sat-saṅga* and *yajña* on them! That Gandhi could not persuade the majority of the Muslim leaders to give up their demand for a separate State for Muslims should hardly come as a surprise, given the estrangement of the two communities from each other. When the British decided to vacate India, things really went out of their hands, those of the authorities and of the leaders, Hindu as well as Muslim. The Master found himself in the very thick of the turmoil and disorder, loot and murder.

It was the second day of March 2, 1947 in a predominantly Muslim lower middle class locality of Lahore. Moments after the afternoon *sat-saṅga* held at the house of his host there came some people, shaken and trembling and out of breath. 'Riots,' said they, 'have started! Master Tara Singh[2] tore apart the League's[3] flag!' The devotees, those who had come to attend the *sat-saṅga,* left the place in a hurry with the Master's permission. The owner of the house squarely bolted the doors after the devotees' departure. With the coming of the evening, thuds and shouts by running crowds could be heard and so were gun shots. A tenant arrived at about eight to report that killing and stabbing were in full swing in the localities that fell on his way. His account, augmented with lurid details, mostly actual but some the products of his fear-oppressed mind, unnerved in the extreme his already shaken listeners. A Sikh gentleman took hold of his gun and went up to the roof of the house to shoot any one who meant mischief. His heart, as he confessed, was beating fiercely. Gurudeva said only this much, 'Don't be nervous. The authorities must be taking some steps to bring the things under control.'

All the night they remained awake to keep a careful watch on the situation. Gurudeva remained immersed in his yogic oblivion. Much before the break of dawn he left the house, asking the Bhagat to accompany him. On the way back the two, the Master and his disciple, saw the beast in man let loose, let loose with all its ferocity and thirst for blood. With batons, axes and swords in their hands, hordes of Muslims [for that was a Muslim-dominated area] roamed about in the streets howling and shouting. 'Allah is great, Allah is great!' was the slogan they raised with animal fury. When they reached near the said house, they saw his hosts, Parmarthi and his wife, nervously beckoning the Bhagat to hurry on. Both were in the grip of a wild fear, for the mob was about to enter their area. But the Master, reports the Bhagat, walked on with his head bowed a little, walked on as if in a trance, he following his preceptor trembling and in fear of a stab in the back. Hardly had they entered the house, when the mob arrived at the open space before it. A fierce exchange of fire ensued, the Muslims and the Hindus firing at each other from their respective localities. The police somehow persuaded the mob to disperse but the shots continued to be fired throughout the day and, also, the day following. The third day saw the firing soften down a little but it was only on the fourth day that the authorities could bring it to an end, but not, as the carnage that followed soon showed, to the final end.

Amritsar and Multan too had been engulfed by communal frenzy and so had the countryside around Rawalpindi. The train service had been badly affected. Next day, March 8, 1947, Dr Bhagat Ram managed to come to the presence of the Master. He was requested to make arrangement for the Master's departure the next day, which he somehow managed to do. Reaching the railway station, they found it overflowing with crowds but with a death like silence prevailing outside and inside it. With great difficulty they could find some place near the door of a first class compartment. On the way they came to know that the rule of law had completely broken down in the city of Rawalpindi too. At the Jhelam railway station, a *premī* chanced into them and forced them to alight. Gurudeva asked him, many times, to let them go but he did not agree. 'The report is that the entire city of Rawalpindi has been,' he said, 'encircled by the Muslim mobs from the countryside. The railway station is overcrowded; one cannot find room enough even to stand there. I just heard on the radio that gunshots were being freely exchanged. Many buildings have been set ablaze.'

The conditions in Jhelam too were not different. The Bhagat suggested that instead of going into the town they should move on to Jammu. [And right proved his suggestion, for soon, too soon, the town was to see unprecedented carnage.] However, their deliberations ceased, when they saw a train entering the platform – the Sindh Express, running thirteen hours behind the schedule. They bought the tickets and somehow managed to enter a compartment. In the nearby compartment they could hear, almost without interruption, shouts of 'Allah is great, Allah is great!' 'Long live Mr Jinnah,[4] Mr Jinnah!' Hindus, Muslims and Sikhs in their compartment sat silent in fear, their heads almost buried in their laps. After much confusion and uncertainty, the train left the platform. On the way, the passengers said that the train had been attacked at Rawalpindi, Sehala and Mandra, and a large number of Sikhs had been butchered. At practically every station on the way, the same chaotic conditions prevailed, the same fear and overcrowding. At Wazirabad junction, where they were to change for Jammu, they alighted, almost a day late.

The train for Jammu was to leave the next day at 1.30 P.M. The waiting room literally overflowed with people. In a corner, the Bhagat found some room to make a seat for the Master. Nervous and insecure, the people were talking, some trying to drive away their fear through jokes and laughter. Death, they said, was inevitable, so why die in anticipation of it? Some were showering abuses on political leaders, others on the British rulers. Sometimes Gurudeva would go into *samādhi*, sometimes he would listen to what the people said and smile. At the break of dawn, he left the waiting room and went out of the station. As long as he remained absent, the Bhagat was all anxiety, his heart beating at a high pitch. On the return of the Master, he prepared tea for the latter and took his breakfast. At 1.30 P.M. they left for Jammu.

India was going to be independent and partitioned into Independent India and Pakistan, attended with a terrible bloodbath resulting in, according to an (perhaps exaggerated) estimate, about a million deaths[5] and an exchange of population of about nine to ten million people.

The massacre started on March 2, 1947 and did not stop until Gandhi was martyred on January 30, 1948. The Hindus and the Sikhs fell victims to the fury of the Muslim fanatics in what is now called Pakistan, the Muslims in the Indian Punjab and in Delhi and some other parts of Northern India to Hindu frenzy. Bengal and Bihar too fell victims to maniacs thirsty for blood. The beast in man was let loose. The land of peace was transformed in one day into the land of savage murders, plunders and rapes. The rule of the mob in its worst form replaced the rule of any law.

Jammu, being a part of the native State of Jammu and Kashmir, was as yet unaffected by the riots. When the Master reached Jammu he was received with a surprised welcome. Many influential people of the city and the court came to visit him. The Master gave his usual discourses three times a week. As for the Land of the Five Rivers, it was engulfed in the flames of an unprecedented communal unrest. Amolak Ram came from Gangothian to break the news how Gangothian had been saved by Captain Mohammad Yusuf and Mohammad Ibrahim, the priest of a mosque nearby. Other Muslims too protected the Hindus from the fury of the mobs. But the rest of the area was a scene of massacre, loot and rape. Amolak Ram too had barely escaped death on the way where murderous mobs prowled freely in search of 'the infidels.' He could undertake that impossible journey all alone on the strength of his faith in his Mahārājjī. Hearing his account, the Master said, 'The way of *dharma*, the way of righteousness, is meant for trying times like these but even the paradigms of patience lose their balance in such times. Only faith in the Lord can give man patience in such hard times, and his [past] noble deeds protection. One sees these days nothing but unrest everywhere; hatred and brutality have come to sway the mind of almost every one. Only care and regard for each other can extinguish this all-consuming fire. But it will be some time before people come to realize this truth. ..'

The Master wanted to spend some time in solitude. Thakur Zaffar Singh, a devotee of the Master, made arrangements for his stay at Anant Nag. On April 10, the Master left Jammu. Zaffar Singh had rung up Raghunath Mattu, a minister in the court, about the arrival of the Master. There at the bus stand, a man was waiting for him. But the Master preferred to stay at Matan with a disciple. In the evening came the minister accompanied by a rich landlord, Pandit Radhakrishna, and other officers of the government. With deep respect and reverence they requested the Master to accept their hospitality. The Master declined the invitation but Pandit Radhakrishna persisted with his request, his hands folded in touching humility. In the meantime, they saw a whole caravan of cars behind the house. All welcomed the caravan with bowed heads and folded hands. On questioning, the minister said to the Master, 'His Highness is returning from the river after angling. '

'The world,' said the Master, 'is in flames and he is busy with his pastimes. He has no thought of the impending troubles.'

Pandit Radhakrishna was a rich landlord of an unmanageably vast estate encompassing many villages and orchards, many among the latter remaining neglected for lack of proper management. But despite his riches, of which he could hardly keep a count, and his great power and influence, he was a man of incredible humility and gentle demeanor, virtually a paradigm of hospitality. He had built a vast dining hall for formal occasions with all the modern paraphernalia and all that goes with the table. His private meals, however, were served in the traditional Kashmiri Brahmincal manner. He and his family would sit on mattresses spread on the mud floor, sanctified with the sprinkling of holy waters and the chanting of the sacred *mantras*. Special dresses had to be worn at that time, dresses untouched by the impurities of the outside world. When he sat at his meals, a large number of guests, friends and strangers were inevitably present. If a stranger came at the time of his meals for business or a favour, he was not allowed to express the purpose of his visit before he had partaken of the hospitality of the rich man. So his meals inevitably turned into banquets, for there was hardly a day when people did not throng at his place for some purpose or the other.[6] Gurudeva understood the mettle of the man and had no choice but to accept his invitation. Accordingly, tents were pitched at a beautiful spot at Karkutnag. For two days, the Pundit personally supervised the entire arrangements. On May 1, the Master started his *tapas* there.

The inevitable bears and leopards were there also to give him their protection and company. As the unrest in the country increased, so did increase the intensity of the Master's *tapas*. The Maharaja's passion for angling did not spare the sanctity of even that solitude. Gurudeva asked the Kashmiri Pundits accompanying the ruler in his pleasures to bring him to his senses. But either they could not summon up the courage to tell him the truth or he disregarded their advice.

Pundit Radhakrishna was worried about the shape of the things to come and the uncertainty that surrounded the big estates like his. India was going to be free, and Mohammad Abdullah,[7] a close friend of the future Prime Minister, Jawaharlal Nehru, wanted radical changes in the laws. Egalitarian ones were undoubtedly in the offing. 'Changes will apply to all. Often do they take place. The Lord is the sustainer of each and every one.' This was the reply he got from the Master.

Many devotees flocked there from far and wide to spend some time with their Revered Master, away from the petty concerns and worries of their lives. For two and a half months the Master stayed in the solitude of Karkutnag. Some sayings were composed there, which we will attend to after we have seen him at Srinagar, the summer capital of Kashmir, where he arrived on July 19, 1947. For, we must have a look at the tragedy of those days and also the depth of the patience and faith of some of his disciples during those cruel times.

There at Srinagar came one day a devotee of his, Divan Devi Chand, once his host at a village called Chhajian. Extremely dejected he looked and woe-stricken, broken and dispirited. The Master was surprised at his sudden appearance. How happened he to be there, he asked. The man could not summon up the energy to speak. His tears alone were his response. With effort could he manage to speak out his pain and anguish. 'With difficulty great,' said he, 'have I managed to come here. My entire family and relations have perished in flames. *Premī* Shiv Nandan has been slain. When the riots broke out, all the women and children went into a house for safety. Only men stayed back at their respective homes. One night, some men went up to the roof of the house where women and children had taken shelter, dug it open and poured petrol into the rooms and set the house on fire. Then came the turn of the houses where the men had stayed back. All the children and women were burnt alive, not a soul escaped the conflagration. Men saw the fate of their women and children, and broken in heart and soul ran from their burning homes to the hills to escape from the shrieking mob. We stood helpless before this spectacle of burning and running for life. The entire town was in flames. In the morning we found the burnt up bodies. Not a single soul was alive. The fugitives too had not escaped, they fell victims to the spears that followed them in hot pursuit. Some of us went to Haripur and wired to the authorities about the state of things. Accompanied by an army contingent, we went back to find the dead bodies, their shapes intact. The severe cold had protected them from decomposition. Under the protection of the army personnel, we cremated the corpses. Thereafter, we went to Haridwar to immerse the ashes in the Ganga. From there have I come to the holy presence.'

Their hair stood on end, of those that heard the narration that almost choked the current of their breath. Gurudeva alone retained his impersonal calm. 'Destiny,' he said after a long pause, 'is all powerful. How happy they lived there! May God bless you with patience and faith, *Premī!* Creatures are bound to separate from each other, sooner or later.'

'In the holy presence I have at last found some solace. I will not remember these things hereafter. Be gracious to me, Lord! Let this distraught mind come to be stable a little!'

Another devotee – we have had occasion to say something about him during the Master's stay at Simla – too had come to Srinagar from Jhang in West Punjab. Only a year before had he taken refuge in the Master. A profligate he had been, a professional gambler and a drunkard, going to distant towns and cities to try his luck at the dice. The first discourse he attended laid emphasis on honesty in one's professional life and on purity of one's food. No one, the Master said, could tread the internal way unless he was careful in his dealings with others and about what he ate and drank. The person who ate meat had a natural propensity for evil, fraud and cunning. The wealth earned through fraudulent ways would only bring about one's ruin in the long run. After hearing these words, Mukund Lal, for that was the name of the devotee, requested the Master to permit him to serve him tea the next morning. The Master turned down his request, sternly reminding him of his ways. 'You first become,' said he, 'like the *faqīrs* or make them the likes of you. Think carefully before you repeat your reques!'

'I was,' he says, 'surprised. I could not make out how the Master came to know about my life. I could not forget the way he had spurned me.' For the whole night, he kept awake, weighing his ways and the worthlessness of his possessions when he was little better than an outcast in the eyes of the Master. Next day, he went again to the Master. Some discussion was going on about pitching tents for the Master's stay at the outskirts of the town. Mukund Lal wanted to bear the expense, but his request to that purpose too was turned down. In the evening the Master spoke about the meaninglessness of worldly life and the misery that sense pleasures give rise to. Having heard these words, Mukund Lal said, 'I have given up meat and wine. My friends will bear witness to my resolve. Be kind enough to give me a place at your feet!' The request evoked no response. Another day, the Master spoke against smoking. Mukund Lal took out a packet of cigarettes from his pocket and threw it away. His resolve was firm, his determination strong, his faith exceeding the faith of the faithful. In December, he was accepted into the fold of the disciples.

When Punjab was plunged in riots, Mukund Lal could not know the whereabouts of the Master. At last in the month of July he came to know that the Master was staying at Srinagar. When the Land of the Five Fivers had become a land of murder and loot, when every morrow was uncertain and even every hour, Mukund Lal left for Srinagar, leaving his family to the care of his Master. Every day during his stay there, he heard accounts of barbarism, of beastly cruelty and greed, accounts that often made him worried about the fate of his family, with whom he had lost every contact. He wanted the Master to give him permission to go back, but the Master seemed to be indifferent. He would not think of making a request on his own. The Master would often talk about the calamity that had visited other disciples but was strangely silent about the condition of his forsaken family. Fifteen days passed away, fifteen days of anxiety and worry. The country was about to become free. Already the exodus had started, of the Hindus from the would-be Pakistan and of the Muslims from the would-be Bharat, Free India. Mukund Lal did not know what had become of his family, what fate they had met. One day, he lost patience and made a request to the Master to let him go back. 'Where is the hurry, *Premī?*,' said the Master, 'Have faith in the Lord!'

He obeyed the Master's command and stayed on, without a question. Another fifteen days passed away this way. At long last arrived the long awaited date, the fifteenth of August, the day alike of glory and of tragedy. The country became free but not without the trauma of a partition. The province of the Punjab too was divided into the Indian Punjab and the Pakistani Punjab. The unprecedented exchange of population started accompanied by deaths in hundreds of thousand. Every day, Mukund Lal heard of incidents of incredible bestiality but did not have the courage to violate the Master's command and to go back, not to his family – for he knew not where they were – but to seek their whereabouts, if indeed they had survived the terrible holocaust. One day, the Master himself said, 'Do you have any care for your family or not? Why don't you go to know what had become of them?'

He accepted the reprimand without a question, as if he had stayed on out of his own will! He left Srinagar in search of his family. To enter Pakistan was not an easy matter, with all the means of communications in total disarray. Every railway station presented a sight of corpses left unburied or uncremated. With great difficulty he managed to reach Amritsar, the last city on the Indian side of the border. Every day trains of refugees from Pakistan arrived at the railway station, many of them bringing in only dead bodies. When Hindus were fleeing away from Pakistan, he was going back to it! One day he stumbled into his father at Amritsar who told him that his house had been burnt down and his property looted and that his family had left for Layalpur. What had become of them, his father did not know. Somehow, he managed to reach Layalpur to find his own but robbed of practically everything they had possessed barring the gold ornaments of his wife. He brought them to India, with a very uncertain future staring him in the face.

I will divert a little from the account of the Master's stay at Srinagar to continue with the trials and tribulations that Mukund Lal had to pass through in order to graduate as a host for the Master. His business partner, Savan Mal, too had migrated to India, penniless. Mukund Lal parted with half of his wife's ornaments; the partner in business turned into a partner in calamity too. Reestablishment of business was difficult, all his ventures going awry. His trials became all the more distressing when the Master asked him to contribute towards the funds needed for the printing of the *Samtāvilāsa* and the *Samatā-vijñāna-yoga.* The Master never asked anyone, not even his disciples, to contribute money whatever the purpose might be. That was a principle with him. But Mukund Lal had to pass a test, a hard and severe test. For too long had he pestered the Master for an opportunity to serve him. His prayers were heard but with a deadly irony. He had no money left to offer the Master. He folded his hands and said, 'Mahārājjī, this servant has been rendered penniless. Only some ornaments are left. Let the Master give me permission to sell them.'

With indifference, said the Master, 'Yes, sell about half of them!'

Soon after this cold command, he received a severe reprimand for a trivial matter. He was cut to the quick and said that he would sell the ornaments and fulfill his promise but he would never visit the Master again. But where else could he go? He sold away the ornaments and became almost a pauper. All the money that he had made through evil ways was gone. With the pride relating to the me and mine gone, he went back to his only resort to receive his blessings. From that day on prosperity visited him again, never to forsake him.

A day came, the long awaited day, when he truly graduated to serve milk to the Master. That day was December 10, 1951 when the Master graciously agreed to stay at Hodal, the place of his new home. Hard had been his test, severe his trials. This should not be taken to mean that he was taught only the hard and stern way. Love too broke his pride. The occasion was the *yajña* at Jagadhari, the first one after the partition of the country. Tents had been pitched for the stay of the devotees. Dr Bhagat Ram chose for himself a relatively comfortable tent and stayed alone in it, while the rest of the *premīs* had to share their tents, each with some others. Considering the age of the doctor, this should not have been objected to but Mukund Lal was seized with righteous indignation and found faults with the doctor for his 'preference for that kind of exclusive comfort.' Against the very spirit of *samatā* he had acted, Mukund Lal argued with persistent and loud emphasis. His protests evoked a spirited discussion and the matter reached the ears of the Master, who summoned Mukund Lal and others of the same persuasion to his presence. Mukund Lal repeated his arguments with the same dogged confidence. In the home of the seers there could not be, he argued, any difference between the high and the low. He too had a right to stay in that tent, as had the doctor. 'Truth' was on his side, so his enthusiasm was great, his confidence unflagging. The Master listened to him in silence until he stopped speaking. Then came the soft words from his lips, '*Premī*, to whom you are devoted heart and soul, where does he spend his nights? Under a roof?'

The words sent a shock in the strong frame of the devotee. Tears flowed out of his eyes. Silent he sat, his head bowed with shame and embarrassment. After some time Gurudeva asked him to go back to the *premīs*. One can easily imagine what Dr Bhagat Ram thought when he heard about this incident.

But to come back to our story. 'When people forget the right way, when they fail to draw a line between the right and the wrong, the Lord's wrath descends upon their heads. These days, there seems to be no distinction between humans and beasts. Goodwill and good feelings have deserted men's hearts, only hatred rules them. Those that recite the names of Rām and Karishan [Rāma and Kṛṣṇa] have forgotten their message. They no longer seek the self in the body, the unconditioned in the conditioned; their anchor is no longer the Spirit but stones [images]. Murderers have they turned into, those who are expected and supposed to search the imperishable self in the perishable. But hatred will only complicate the matters. There is still time to discard it and live in harmony with each other. Patience and faith alone can make your minds stay quiet in these unquiet times. Self-centred people can do no good to the country. Only those who have no axe to grind, those who live in poverty devoted to the Lord can serve and have been serving the country, not the self-centred worldlings.'

Words of warning that few could understand and appreciate in those monstrous times!

II

When the country was partitioned, the native princely states were given the option by the departing British to remain independent or join either of the two states, India and Pakistan. The Maharaja of Jammu and Kashmir craved to be an independent ruler, a status too big for him. Pakistan would not countenance it, nor was it (as the later events showed) acceptable to India or, for that matter, to the people of Kashmir. Rumours were afloat that the Pathan tribes were making preparations to invade the Muslim dominated Kashmir to force its merger into Pakistan. Rattled and upset by these reports, the *premīs* of Chinari came to the Master's presence to take him to Chinari, presumably thinking that the divine presence of the Master would 'save them from the invading beasts.' Strange were those people, those inhabitants of the beautiful landscape of Chinari. Seen had they the Master's *tapas,* heard had they his teachings about how man is to live and strive to free himself from his existential bondage, but with little or no effect. There were some among them who had not been able to restrain even their food habits, not to speak of their dispositions. When the possibility of the invasion loomed large, they requested the Master to hold a *yajña* at their village in the hope that it might save them from the impending disaster. 'What have you people,' said he, 'learnt from the life of the *faqīrs*? *This* would not like other people to partake of your food earned through evil ways. It will do evil to those who partake of it.'

They promised, once again, that they would not deviate from the Path and that they would observe purity in their private and business dealings. Insecure they were and uncertain, the threatened loss of their homes and business spelled ruin for them. They wanted to escape from that disaster through religious strategies, for little else was what they deemed to be religious life: a mere set of observances to ensure their safety and interests. After the *yajña,* the Master said, 'You cannot but live as the times dictate you to live. The old joys will be the things of the past. As long as the rule of the Maharaja obtains, stick to this place. If there is a disruption, then think of some way out. Either the Maharaja does not know the truth or he has some support somewhere. Carelessness on his part will end up in futile regrets. To be over-clever often means self-deception. Destiny is indeed powerful, very powerful; before it strikes, it impairs one's judgement. Heedfulness is the need of the hour.'

At the time of the departure from Chinari he once again asked them to wait until the last hour, the hour of the invasion.

When the hordes of the Pathans entered the State, Chinari was a place of chaos and confusion. The people were at a loss to know how to save themselves from certain death and disgrace. The Maharaja was utterly unprepared for the contingency, his government was in disarray, his own life and that of his family in danger, of the man who could think of nothing else than his pleasures. How could his decadent rule provide any help or succor to his subjects in the hour of their misfortune! No count could possibly be kept of those that perished in that invasion, how much of property was destroyed, how much of their possessions plundered, how many women were dishonoured. Rumours were afloat with inevitable exaggeration of a truly appalling tragedy. The fear of the people of Chinari was, therefore, perfectly natural and real. At that moment of black despair, fifty *tongas* laden with fruit arrived from Srinagar on their way to Rawalpindi. When the *tonga* drivers heard of the invasion, they unloaded the boxes of fruit to go back to Srinagar. On the request of the people of Chinari, they took them to Srinagar, asking them to alight near the airport.

Srinagar was in the grip of panic, its fall seeming inevitable and imminent, the Maharaja and his ministers having fled from it to the safety of Jammu, the winter capital of the State. Helpless and baffled, the prodigal and careless ruler was forced to make a request to the Government of India to send its troops to save Srinagar from the impending disaster. When the refugees from Chinari alighted from the tongas, the airport was being cleared for the landing of the Indian troops. The air thick with fear and rumours, people were rushing to their homes. The unhappy refugees did not know what to do and where to go. In that hour of despairing distress, a plane arrived from Delhi with troops on board. The people of Chinari boarded that very plane and reached Delhi in about two or three hours. Homeless had they become, deprived of their possessions but safe in person. Their old joys were really now the things of the past. A hard life, a generation long hard life waited for them to regain their comfortable living.

We have had an occasion to mention the happy and hospitable disposition of one devotee, Faqir Chand, the same Faqir Chand that had converted a tiny part of the terrible forest, Sarūpā, into a place of comfort for the devotees. He was with the Master at Karkutnag and Srinagar. One day, he was asked to shift his family away from the unsafe Sharian, his village. Faqir Chand wanted to attend a wedding at Domail before going to his village, but the Master explicitly forbade him to do so and asked him to go straight to his home. On reaching Sharian, he thought of first depositing his money with a relation at Domail before shifting his family to a safe place. He did manage to deposit his money with the relation but that very night Domail was attacked by the Pathans. The relation was slain but Faqir Chand managed to escape but not for long. While crossing the bridge over the Jhelam at Domail, he fell into the hands of 'the hosts of God', who took no time to butcher 'the infidel' and throw the dead body into the river.

There were *premīs* of the Master who had literally concealed their achievements within the garb of ordinariness. One such devotee was our familiar, Thakur Divān Singh, the Man Friday of Banārasīdās, whose devotion to the Master was second to none, but whose resolve to remain an anonymity had no parallel. It was he who attended upon the Master whenever the Bhagat had to go somewhere else. He too perished in the riots that accompanied the partition of the country. Nothing much is therefore known about his inner state after his initiation into the path of yoga but a few incidents do indicate the man that was emerging out of the hard *tapas* he had undertaken. One devotee reports how he saw the Thakur at a *yajña* licking the remains off a pile of leaf-plates. The said devotee, a lad of eleven, was deeply surprised to see this scene, for he knew the status that the Thakur, despite his humility, enjoyed among the devotees. Years later, he remembered it vividly, each details of it. For high devotion he saw in this act, degrading though it may seem to the orthodox and the modern alike.

Shortly afterwards, his impression about the depth of the Thakur's devotion was, for him, confirmed. A painful growth appeared in his armpit, to treat which he was admitted into the Civil Hospital at Rawalpindi. The Thakur happened to be in the town but left it without paying a visit to the patient, an act that displeased the Master. In a few days, he returned to Rawalpindi and attended upon the patient every day, without a meal or a drink of water. Often his eyes remained closed. When the young patient requested him to take rest, he would immediately open his eyes and start reading some book. Sometimes, after much persuasion, he would take lunch with the patient, mixing some water in the food if he found it rather too salty. When questioned, he would say, 'This body has to perish one day. Why care for taste, then?' For about two months he served the young patient with every care and attention.

There was a reason behind this unique devotion of the Thakur. Once he went to see the Master at Gagothian but found that the latter had gone to another village. The Thakur and his companion sent him a message about their arrival and awaited his return. When the Master received the message, he left for the village at 2 A.M. to walk on foot for full six hours. It was the duty of the devotees to go to the presence of their Gurudeva, their divine teacher, rather than call him back to Gangothian. His long journey on foot embarrassed them very much, especially the Thakur, who, on that day, became a different man, as much different as we can dare to expect from our frail human nature. He became a life long servant of the Master. To wait in silence for his preceptor's command became the one principle of his life. That he too had to perish in the riots should have served as a warning to other disciples against their calculating faith and ethics. But not many could understand the meaning of self-surrender. Men of the world would often weigh the worth of their piety in terms of what it can bring them in return.

The Master left Srinagar for Jammu in October 1947, barely a few days before fear and panic seized the city, factual reports replacing rumours. The riots had spread to the Hindu dominated Jammu province of the State too, where hordes of Muslims could be seen moving towards the borders of Pakistan, driven away from their homes and hearths. Village after village were on fire between Udhampur and Jammu. This is how the Hindu faith was being protected through arson, loot and murder of the 'cruel and inhuman' Muslims. The Maharaja's overweening ambition had brought his State close to a complete ruin. At long last, he realised his mistake and acceded to India. When the Master heard about the accession, he said, 'Now there should be no cause for anxiety. For too long did he delay the decision.'

After signing the deed of accession, the Maharaja was an embodiment of distress and frustration. His actions had alienated the Government of India, his accession to India being more of a compulsion than a choice. Srinagar had been saved but his ambition had been thwarted. He now lived in Jammu, deprived of his rule, his pride and self-esteem deeply wounded. Some courtiers came to the Master to make a request to him that he console the Maharaja. The call, the Master said, had come too late. Earlier too the courtiers had tried for a meeting between the Master and the ruler but he was too involved in his pleasures and his self-glory to listen to any suggestion. Now the Maharani had beseeched the Master for a meeting with the Maharaja. After some hesitation, he agreed but on the condition that no gifts would be offered to him, that the Maharaja and the Maharani would sit on the floor with a white sheet of cloth spread over it. Further, there should be no decoration in the room and he should not be pressed to eat anything.

When he was about to leave for the palace, the Bhagat brought a freshly washed dress for him to wear but the Master said that the condition of his clothes could not console the Maharaja. Rags alone, he added, became the *faqīrs*, not clean dresses But the Bhagat insisted that he change it; he did not want, he added, that people should find faults with his devotion. With a smile, the Master acceded to the Bhagat's request. When the Master came back from the palace, he carried rather an unfavourable opinion about the ruler. The Maharaja wanted, he said, to leave the State. He was advised not to do so until things settled down. If he had let the State merge with India earlier, he, said the Master, would have done it with dignity. But surrounded as he was with flatterers, he did not understand the things. It was good, he added, that Sheikh Abdullah[8] was with the Congress,[9] otherwise Srinagar too would have fallen.[10]

III

With the struggle for Independence coming to a successful, though, to a painful extent, tragic conclusion, the great problem before the leaders of the movement for Independence was to decide what kind of government and society should evolve in modern India. India is a country of diversity; people of different faiths live here, though the majority of them are Hindus. The Hindu society is, however, not a homogenous group; it is divided into varied castes and sub-castes. How to bring about harmony among these castes, especially between the upper castes and the lowest of castes, which the traditional society spurned and despised, was an immediate and critical problem facing the leaders of the Freedom Movement. The enmity between the Hindus and the Muslims, augmented by the partition of the country, too was a problem, especially in the northern parts where the pain of the partition was especially felt. But more acute than these social problems was the problem of poverty that was crushing the people. More than four million people had migrated from Pakistan to India. To rehabilitate them was a task that seemed beyond the capacity of the new government to handle. Moreover, India was to start a new life and the responsibility of shaping its future fell, as noted earlier, on those that had led the Freedom Movement. To meet the daunting challenge, they and the elite of the society decided, after long deliberation, to opt for a democratic set up for the country, more or less similar to the Westminster model, with some powers given to the varied states that constituted the country. Given the people's deep faith in religion, the proposed democratic state could not be secular in the Western sense of the term and be indifferent to religion. At the same time, in view of the varied faiths that flourished in the country, it could not prefer one religion to another. The State had to be equidistant from but well disposed towards every faith, had to be secular only in this sense of the term.

But the most momentous task before the elite of those days was modernisation of their land where medieval ways still prevailed, with the resultant ills of poverty and superstitions. It is not that they did not, generally speaking, admire the strands of high moral idealism and spirituality in their tradition, but it was to modern Western Civilisation and its rational and scientific temper that they looked to in order to redeem their country from the mess it was in. But before we try to assess the soundness or otherwise of their approach towards modern disposition and traditional way of life, we should, I think, pay adequate heed to 'The Voice of the Truth' that articulated itself in the solitude of a jungle about the matter in question. That will help us to assess the legitimacy or otherwise of contemporary man's faith in modern disposition and post-independent India's commitment to it. While he was doing *tapas* at Karkutnag, the Master 'as one with the truth,' wrote down a few sayings that have a bearing on social and cultural issues. The most important among them read as follows:

> Life unfolds two states of *buddhi*, the knowing faculty, the state of *samatā* and that of *mamatā*, the states, that is, of sameness and that of mine-ness. When human beings get immersed in the body, when they find their being enshrined in and encompassed by the body, by that alone, the net of *mamatā* spreads out wide and extensive. When, on the contrary, they lean towards the *ātman*, towards self the real, then the light of *samatā* shines bright and radiant. *Mamatā* alone is ignorance. For, when the knowing faculty becomes dull as a result of its immersion in the body, it does deeds black and wicked to reap for itself the fruit of suffering. To delude beings this wise moves the wheel of *prakṛti*, of Nature subjective and objective.
>
> When the sense of identification with the body gets deep and intense, there ensues an intensification of desire, intensification that converts creatures into destroyers of one another. This ravenous disposition brings about disruptions, upsetting and devastating. Those who are born humans should ever keep in mind these two dispositions, that of orientation towards the body and that of self-submission to their real self. In order to strive for one's salvation one should know clearly what these two dispositions imply.
>
> The knowing faculty is by nature prone to orient itself towards identification with the body, which, in turn, gives rise to the desire for the pleasures of the senses. The desire for the pleasures of the sense prompts it to do all kinds of self-destructive deeds. When such deeds become habitual, they bring about nothing but adversity to their doer and for those around him. This life of darkness ever proves disastrous for every being. A man who has the awareness of the tragic implications of the sense of identification with the body would ever seek to orient himself towards his self the true and surrender his personality to that self. He would reap for his reward the attainment to the state of *samatā*, of peace all pervasive the dispenser.
>
> From faults and stains of the mind spring all actions that embodied beings do, acts right no less than acts wrong;

compelled are they to do these actions under their compulsive force, of those faults and stains. When they live self-submitted to the truth of their being, embodied beings strive hard to attain to the state of redemption. The path they choose for that end is marked by renunciation and nonattachment, and by a sense of affinity with others and love and regard and service for them. Of truthfulness is their path and of virtuous disposition and serene contentment. These unearthly traits of theirs constitute the way to universal peace and bless man with freedom from all bondage, freedom that is self-sovereignty, self-sovereignty in the form of *samatā*.

When, on the contrary, beings take the body as their being and truth, and live and act entrenched in this faith, to darkness blinding do they lead themselves. Pleasures of the body alone become their good and their end, so deeply immersed in them do they become. To lying they resort and to theft, and to fraud and jealousy, and hatred and inordinate greed, and to excessive attachments and sensuality, and anger and pride. They resort to these only for one end: to get those pleasures. Acts and disposition of this sort become the guiding force of their life to bring about discords and tensions destructive and without an end. Of fear and death are they the harbingers, these demonic traits, no less for the perpetrators of these acts than for their victims. It is imperative, therefore, to orient one's life towards the truth. Therein lie the essence and worth of human life.

To suffering move all beings and to death, move they inexorably towards them under the overriding force of *prakṛti*, of this wonder they call Nature. In opposition to this unhappy natural way of life, there is the way that liberates man from every striving, the curse that falls to the lot of every being that has come to live. Of self-surrender to *sat*, to truth, is that way. Understanding well what a predicament his life in its truth is, let man shed the physical and mental taints and evil that go with embodiment and self-submit to the *sat*, to Being, and dedicate his life to the good and service of others. That is the way to self-sovereignty, self-sovereignty true and supreme that only the state of *samatā* is. Only one right man is given, only one right does he inherit: the right to redeem himself through truth, renunciation and service the disinterested. Claim to this right alone can bring

> about peace, peace the absolute, and self-sovereignty ever secure and firm. To the lot of the unsurpassable hero will fall the victory absolute, the victory called *samatā*, to him who lives distanced from the very sense of me and mine – from that ignorance and bondage – and who, when he acts, acts without any personal interest to serve. For, ever self-submitted to the truth he lives, that man of genuine heroic disposition. He alone is great, he alone is all-wise; he alone knows what the supreme sovereignty is, he alone and no one else.[11]

True sovereignty does not mean mere political sovereignty. True sovereignty lies in freeing oneself from 'I am the body'-sense and attaining to one's own true being, abiding in it and becoming one with it.

The country had attained political independence but chose to tread the path that modern rationality and scientific temper had laid down, the path that ultimately culminated in consumer culture. The Enlightenment had purged man of his faith in the goodness of Nature, it had found the earth cold and unresponsive to what man would desire and cry for. So, he distanced himself from earth, and sought to change what was thought to be his home into a territory and possession, into an object of study and manipulation within the context of a workable and revisable conceptual framework. Earth showed forth no meaning on its own, man had to seek meaning in it, for there could be no revelation of truth, only a search, an active search for it. In other words, man could not abide in truth as one with it; he could only perceive it as an object of his understanding. Truth thus came to be virtually identified with discourse; it was in the latter that it obtained. This *hubris* could not possibly endure for long, for knowledge of things found itself surrounded by ignorance, it found itself, eventually, constituted by ignorance. For, there was no thing, no object of knowledge that did not exceed the bounds of that knowledge, did not transcend the limits of its very framework and its ontological assumptions, assumptions indispensable for the very being of that knowledge.

However, instead of accepting its defeat, modernity went ahead with its pursuit of knowledge, revising the latter's frameworks as far as practical, as far as the revision was consistent with its passion for knowledge. However, it soon found out that the *other* could not possibly be eliminated, the *other* of knowledge and the *other* of discourse. No doubt, man received from Nature what he gave her but Nature could not be equated with mind or with discourse, it was more than mind, more than discourse. Even a small familiar thing, a seemingly insignificant thing, spurned with disdain man and his powers to know. He had no concept, *a priori* or *a posteriori*, that could encompass the little thing before him. Nor had he a framework open enough to accommodate that thing in full, for infinite were the depths of that thing and infinite were its dimensions.

But there was such a thing as progress in knowledge, our understanding of things deepening with the passage of time. If man did not, could not, understand fully the thing in question, if his knowledge could not exhaust its depths and its widths, even of the smallest thing he perceived, he could, at least, improve his knowledge of it, could know more of it than he had known earlier. So the search went on and the research and 'enrichment of understanding.' Relentlessly he indulged in that passion for knowledge and, through it, sought to grasp and manipulate Nature and, despite the obvious limitations of his little knowledge and power, he came to regard himself the supreme sovereign, the dispenser of meaning and the source of all power. Man thus came to replace God; he killed the latter to anoint himself the ruler and master.

That master turned out to be Man the thinker, not man the living soul, Man the concept, not Man that exceeded the concept. And the world that Man the concept grasped or sought to grasp was not the world in excess of the concept but the world as circumscribed by the concept, informed by it and constituted by it. And so were the objects within this his world. The mystery of things he refused to acknowledge, and so did he the mystery within him. He found no disclosures in an appearance that exceeded the limits of the concept, no possibilities in the inadequacy of the concept. The depths that the melting of the concept revealed, depths within and without, appeared too eerie for his thought and practice. He was frightened by that mystery, the mystery that seemed to swallow up his own identity, the identity of the man in him. So he dismissed it as unreal and shadowy. Nature, that object of discursive knowledge, thus fashioned a new being out of man, man the category. Man the living being can live only as long as he lives oriented towards the beyond, the absolute beyond, call him God the Unknowable if you like. When he becomes Nature oriented, as did modern man, he dies to give place to the monster called the *cogito*, the conceptualiser.

Man frozen into a category in this way could only be a being in relationship, banished from his in-being, that dispenser of his life. This is how modernity visualised him. This view of him ultimately degraded him into a producing machine and a consuming animal that lived with others as a producer and enjoyed himself as an individual. His individuality came to be equated with what and how he came to consume. Otherwise, he was merely a tool, a part of the system of production. That was the distinction, almost the only effective one, which could be drawn between man the sociality and man the individuality. They spoke of his duties as the former and his rights as the latter. So exploitation widened its sphere from Nature to man. As a sociality he was exploited and also as an individuality, the former through rules and regulations, the latter through flattering temptations. All other distinctions outside the context of this distinction between sociality the producer and individuality the consumer gradually came to be eroded, came, for most people, almost to collapse. Distinctions between good and evil, between you and me, between the *arche* and the *telos*, eventually even the distinction between the external and the internal, reality and discourse almost lost their content and relevance. In this unprecedented cultural confusion man was obliged to perform one duty meticulously: to establish his credentials as a producer. Otherwise, he could not claim the right of being an individual, individual the consumer. The proponents of this philosophy called it pragmatism and poured scorn on every view that questioned the soundness of their beliefs. Their success was great and so was their arrogance and self-complacence. What troubled others as ambiguities and uncertainties, they found perfectly intelligible. For confirmed consumerists there is no legitimate question that is not an answer in the making. Pensiveness they ridicule, clarity and certainty they want and cherish. The consumer is very certain about his pleasures; they are his answer to any intellectual or existential puzzle or ambiguity.

Dedication to pleasure is, as Gurudeva said, natural to man, inherit does he it at his very birth. But our passion for knowledge of the so-called external world, world the material, has intensified it to self-destructive proportions. Thus he says:

> Investigation of matter, howsoever deep, cannot bring about the satisfaction that man seeks, unless and until investigation of the Spirit, the dispenser of life, is undertaken, of the principle of life that is *samatā* itself.
>
> No nation or country can go on prospering and flowering, not for long, if it has chosen to increase desires and wants. It has to supplement its investigation of Nature with investigation of the desire-free Spirit and Life within. Increase of wants often proves disastrous. Let there be no mistake about it.[12]

Independent India opted for 'investigation of Nature' rather than 'investigation of the desire-free Spirit and Life within.' The new rulers paid lip service to her spiritual tradition, but, as time went on, the lip service became rare, even embarrassing. But investigation of matter, too, requires a good deal of self-discipline and a serious commitment, which those that were interested in political power did not know how to generate. The result was that desires and expectations arose as never before without the accompanying theory and practice, so essential for scientific knowledge and technological power. Any serious talk of spiritual needs was simply out of the question. Despite the poverty of theoretical rigour and commitment to work culture, economic progress became the talk of the times as if that was the sole end of life. In view of the serious economic problems facing the country, the concern of the political leaders about economic progress seemed legitimate to many. Finding himself in this situation, a devotee wrote to the Master seeking his views about the matter in question. The reply he received was as follows:

> Your second question relates to economic reform. Every embodied being is engaged in economic activity – it is ingrained in his nature. There is no need to pay particular attention to what is inevitable and innate in man. To what extent economic progress is desirable for man's well being is the question that should engage your attention, not economic activity as such, which, at any rate, is bound to happen. The other thing that should be of concern to you is the way man should live when economic prosperity has been attained, so that he retains enough of sense not to degrade his life into one of sensuality and pleasures. But today men of intelligence do not think on these lines, they find no occasion and no need to do so. People in common have made economic prosperity and the resultant consumerism[13] their sole and exclusive purpose. The time is not very far off when this prosperity will reveal its ruinous face. This is the way of *Prakṛti* and her law. Economic prosperity can be a good thing only when it is accompanied with spirituality, not in and by itself. Only so much of economic prosperity is desirable as does not stand in the way of life dedicated to the investigation of the Spirit within, does not undo one's belief in that Purity. That alone is true economic progress, the progress that does not dim one's awareness of the Spirit within and without; that progress alone is in accord with *samatā*.

Only that much of economic progress is desirable as does not make man forget that he is a visitor to this world, not an inmate of it and that he has come to die and not to live – forever. If he forgets this truth, he will be so occupied with getting and spending that he will have no insight left with him, insight into the Spirit within him. His knowledge will change into cunning and cleverness, ending up in his and others' misery. This is as true of nations as it is true of individuals. Regarding this matter, the following words deserve careful consideration:

> [. ..] one may gather as many means of self-protection as one can, means internal and external; one may enjoy all kinds of pleasures and have at one's command all means of security; one may bring under one's rule every being or undo all one's enemies to live in a splendour unchallenged and unrivalled, but with all the power and accomplishments, one cannot escape the inevitable end. This arrogant way ultimately ends up in misery, remorse and repentance. ..
>
> Over-protection of the body leads to its decay, sooner than later. The same is true of societies too. If societies fashion and set up every defence for self-protection, do it out of unbridled greed and arrogance and do not pay heed to the Existence that informs each being and each phenomenon, they will only bring ruin upon themselves, again sooner than later. All efforts for physical wellbeing and for social and national progress should be in accord with the life dedicated to the investigation of the Truth. That alone can be beneficial, that wellbeing and progress, and not the one that is accomplished at the cost of man's openness to the Truth [of his and the world's being]. **Though this latter progress too cannot last forever, for that is the law of the *Māyā* of the Lord. Only the Self is the ever-abiding Being, that alone.**[14]
>
> ..

Modern world swears in the name of progress. Science and technology have given it unprecedented power and means of enjoyment, with a prospect for more of them, practically without an end. The result is the birth of consumer culture and, as we noted, blurring of distinctions, distinctions indispensable for life. This culture received a rather severe censure from the Master:

> To find matter alone as the sole reality, to live oriented towards it and dedicated to it is to get entrenched in the pleasures of the sense. And this disposition spells absolute disaster for mankind. When common people get blindly addicted to these pleasures of the sense, when their life becomes a mere orientation towards consumption, their desires increase manifold to bring about everywhere disorder and unrest. For people so dedicated and oriented can think of only undoing their rivals. And that becomes suicidal, this tendency to undo others. This truly is the end result of [this kind of] decadence.[15]
>
> One should clearly know what dedication to consumer culture brings about, and also what naturalism can result in and what denial of the Truth. With this insight into the nature of wrong investigation, one should strive to find out what makes the inert instinct with life, what the life principle is. That alone can ensure peace, within as well as without. If one worships matter and consumption, if one has fashioned one's life as dedicated to matter and consumption, desire will burn man each and every moment, making him a creature of gnawing unrest and disquiet. And chattering about peace in the world while one's own mind is burdened with unrest and disquiet is nothing but an act of self-deception and hypocrisy. For, a man who knows no peace within cannot know how to bring about peace without. The first duty of man, therefore, is that he free himself from the disquiet and unrest within and attain to the peace fearless. Only then can his life and words do any good to others.[16]
>
> Dedication to matter can in no way bring down wants; on the contrary, it constantly increases them. It turns human beings hostile to each other, resulting in afflictions, distresses and despair. One must give up this life of distress and frustration, give up the thought of it and dedicate oneself to the life force within, life force that is the Truth itself. One should, therefore, strive hard to bring down one's wants, as much as one can. Therein alone lies the way to redemption, to purity absolute. .. It is indeed imperative that a check should be put to materialistic inclinations, to self-hood and to consumer culture. This can be accomplished only if one leads a life of purity and dedication to

> the Truth. These [materialistic and consumeristic[17]] tendencies have, in these times, magnified into a dangerous deluge, which, if not checked, will acquire devastating proportions, plunging these times of show and pomp into one of despair and darkness. For, this is how consumer culture often culminates. All gifted persons should investigate their life[-principle], investigate as it should be investigated, so that they may know what is pure renunciation, what it is to be disposed well towards others, what is fearlessness, what is peace eternal, know these and attain to these. For that constitutes the real goal of life, the attainment of these dispositions and attitudes, attainment that makes one realise the being and dispenser of life.[18]

With the memories of the Second World War having gone faint and the fears that lurked in the phase of the cold war having subsided, modern world has become dangerously self-complacent, notwithstanding the threat posed by terrorism. We are fast entering the domain of decadence. Religion is superstition for us, literature a strenuous pastime, art a mere means of decoration, philosophy a barren exercise. History is no longer of importance for us, for we see no purpose, no *telos,* to which it can point out. Science interests us more for technological requirements than for conceptual encompassing the *other* that Nature is. Our heroes are sportsmen and actors, not men of bravery and courage; our lawgivers are personalities of the media, not prophets and seers. Our analysts are journalists, not thinkers, our creators of beauty are no longer artists but fashion designers. Our thinkers we have banished to the academies to get sterile and barren in the absence of a contact and communication with people in real life-situations. Our poets are not there to sharpen our perceptions but to be ignored as of little or no use. Scientists are important but more for reasons of economics and power than for reasons of what modernity used to call knowledge. Add to this decadence, the arrogance of Enlightenment, of faith in reason and of contempt for 'obscurantism.' Folly has really led us into an endless maze. One could not imagine bankruptcy imagining itself as plenty with greater abandon and flamboyancy.

More than six decades ago, the Master gave a warning that Modern Civilisation can ignore only at its peril:

> Whatever actions a living being does, he does it in accordance with the *vāsanā* of the three modes of being [the *sāttvika*, the *rājasika* and the *tāmāsika*]. The being of every being is constituted by these *guṇas*, these modes. One endowed with *sāttvikī vāsanā* is inclined towards noble deeds, noble in the extreme. Truthful will be he and given to service of others, forgiving will be he and anchored to the Lord and gifted with uprightness and contentment, simplicity and disposition of kindness. Live will he to be a comfort to others, this embodiment of these traits. Only a man of *sāttvika* disposition of this kind can attain to the state of no-*vāsanā*, the state of the infinite bliss that *samatā* is.
>
> A being that lives bound by *rajoguṇī vāsanā* lives to procure desirables of every kind. He would subdue the entire world to serve this his end. But these very desirables, these pleasures that he seeks for self-gratification show forth their other facet, that of pain, when the time for death arrives and he departs from the world with frustration, frustration in the extreme, as his lot. A man constituted by *rajoguṇī* nature lives only for the pleasures of the senses, given in the extreme to sensuality, anger, greed and pride. Not for a moment can he find a respite from self-concern, the passion that darkens one's being and soul. For him there is only one purpose, only one: to seek the pleasures of the senses. Dark and darkening is this *rajoguṇī vāsanā*, not for a moment will it let man breathe free and fearless.
>
> A being given to *tamoguṇī vāsanā* lives in disquiet in the extreme to do deeds wicked in the extreme. Sense-gratification and consumption become the sole aim of his life, his sole joy and delight. No sense of proportion has he, no sense of limits and bounds, this being given to this mode of desire. Of deviations becomes he a victim, of perversities and depravities. Fraud, deception, shamelessness, theft, murder and beliefs dark and blind constitute his life and its purpose. A torment great will be his end and his lives to come a punishment.

> The wheel of the world moves as dictated by these *guṇas*, these modes three. When the *sattva* dominates, then the way true determines the lives of beings. In peace they live then, striving to free themselves from the sway of sense desires. To be peaceful in mind becomes the sole aim and purpose of their life.
>
> When *rajas* dominates, then beings live for acquisitions, for attached do they live then to pleasures of every kind. Under the force of this passion, wonders after wonders they discover and invent for self-gratification. Physical wellbeing and sense pleasures constitute the sole purpose of their life, its entire meaning. Their days are spent to fulfil that purpose and so are their nights. Marvelous means do they forge for material progress, means that make them forget that there is such a being as God to rule over the world, so obsessed do they become with them. Physical wellbeing becomes *the* thing for beings of this mode, their obsession with physical enjoyments making them oblivious of mental peace, lose all sense of it. A time comes when even material progress becomes impossible for them, not to speak of spiritual progress, so great becomes their obsession for physical pleasures. With vengeance then arises the *tamoguṇī vāsanā*, that stained harbinger of disaster great and misery great. This is how the *Māyā* of the Lord plays its strange sport.
>
> When *tamoguṇī vāsanā* comes to sway the life of beings, then self-centred do they become, these victims of this mode of desire, so self-centred and selfish indeed as to snatch away through whatever means what belongs to others. If they have to resort to murder for that end, they will let no hesitation, no scruple to stand in their way. In no way can they live in harmony and peace; to deceive they live and to undo one another. Such is the depth of their depraved and dark desire that they live only to cheat and deceive, not a word of truth and transparency ever slipping from their lips. ... Evil comes to inflict the world then and decadence and distresses and afflictions. That is the fate ordained for beings inflicted with the *vāsanā* of the *tāmasika* mode.[19]

Societies at large cannot be expected to generate on their own the spirit of self-restraint with regards to both knowledge and desire. They require a *saṅgat* to serve as an inspiration to move in that direction, move *to an extent,* despite their natural propensities. A true saṅgat is composed of genuine mortals, of those that do not sleep over their mortal lot but live ever aware of it. Only authentic mortals of this kind can be true beings-with-others; only they can help bring about a just society. For, it is the sense of our common mortal lot and our ultimate frailty and failure that makes us share in the pain of others and realise the redemptive possibilities of failures and non-success, even the possibilities of what we call abnormalities. We perceive, if we have been thus subdued into sobriety and into expansive sympathies, perceive with utmost clarity, that those that succeed in life are not necessarily the best of beings, that the unsuccessful may have much to give us and the abnormal to instruct us, instruct us into sanity. And that our tragedies are not always what we take them to be, damning. It is this kind of insight that can see through all the masks that inhere in all our social relationships; it is this kind of insight that can ever hope to turn *a little* our cruel come-together-s into a society sane and truth oriented. But this insight does not come to us easily. The better among us have to keep it alive in some part of society through their exemplary life, their conduct and their words.

Thus only men of this deep insight and expansive sympathies and empathies can save societies from disaster. **But they can do so only when they keep themselves away from power and influence, away from wealth and possessions.** Their simplicity, their innocence, their care and regard for others, their truthfulness and meditative mode of life alone can help save societies from arrogance of knowledge and power and from consumerist[20] mode of life. Philosopher kings cannot fashion human beings in this mould nor can assemblies and parliaments of politicians; only seers can do so, seers who live anonymous and poor. Only they can wake up humanity to the deeper dimensions of life, make it self-critical and contemplative. Solitude is the saviour of society, aloneness of relationships, forest of civilisation, innocence of knowledge, contemplation of action, no-being of being. The *other* that sustains true intersubjectivity is not Nature but the *other* that a transcendental soul is. It is the soul that is the seer of the truth that can turn human beings into a *saṅgat*, into an assembly of true subjects, into an assembly that shares in the same endeavour, follows the same path to reach the same destination. Individuals as we find them in societies not sanctified by the presence of such seers, pursue different goals and purposes because they have no true goals and purposes, they have only desires to satisfy, whims to pursue and vanities to appease. Their goals and aims are bound to be in conflict with each other. But the man who has given himself to the transcendental thrust, to the sense of *ought*, has only one aim: to turn death into a presence, into a *living* presence, for that is what death is when it becomes a presence. And death as presence does not admit of differences and conflicts, it puts an end to all differences and conflicts. And that is the end that is chalked out for every mortal, the goal of *presencing* death. And only the presence of a sage, the man that has died into death, that life the true, that can make man pursue that goal, the goal of each and every being. That aloneness, that seer of the alone, alone can fashion a *saṅgat* because it is he who inspires human beings to follow the same path to reach the same end. **Or can deep and intense suffering**. For, those whose fate has been to suffer much in life can also pursue the same goal of *presencing* death provided they have the patience to endure their suffering and the non-attachment to contemplate it, contemplate their agony, their pain, their sorrows, even the pain of their bodily limbs. The seer that is dead unto himself is our guide and the patient and contemplative sufferer our co-pilgrim. The successful, the powerful and the rich have a place in divisive societies, not in *saṅgat*, that assembly of mortals that find in death their hope and their salvation.

Needless to say, only a few among mankind can participate in a true *saṅgat* but these few will be a reminder to the society at large that there are other goals to pursue, other victories to win and other ways to follow than the ones it pursues and follows. If they remain steadfast and true to themselves and do not try to win the attention of others, they will serve as an antidote to the disease of interobjectivity that the so-called societies reduce every man into. Societies are bound to ignore, to insult and humiliate genuine *saṅgat*-s. If the latter meekly submit to such humiliations and insults and remain steadfast to what the seers of the truth have revealed as their aim and goal, they will, sooner or later, purge society at large of the malady of ambition and self-interest, ***though only to an extent***. 'Only to an extent' because so long as man does not die into death to make the latter alive, he cannot purify himself of these stains. And that is possible only for a seer of the truth. For even in a *saṅgat* relationship does not give place to aloneness. **Man the alone, man the true mortal, alone can presence death, not a member of a *saṅgat*. The latter can only be a being *towards* death, not being *in* death. No society can be ideal, no *saṅgat* can be. For all relationships are contaminated with self-love. A genuine seeker of the truth has to bid goodbye even to the *saṅgat*. As alone can he attain to the Alone.**

Notes

1 The lowest among them considered untouchables.

2 Leader of the Sikhs.

3 The Muslim League that demanded the partition of the country as a precondition of her freedom. Mohammad Ali Jinnah, the future Governor General of Pakistan, was its unquestioned leader.

4 The leader of the Muslim League.

5 The estimate is hardly better than a guess. Some would put the number to be less than a million – three to four hundred thousand. No one is in a position to speak about the matter with any certainty.

6 Those guests took their meals at the place marked for them.

7 A leader of the people of Kashmir, the future Prime Minister and, later, Chief Minister of the State [after an amendment of the State's Constitution].

8 The Prime Minister, and later, Chief Minister of the State after its accession to India.

9 The Indian National Congress, the party that led the freedom movement and, after Independence, ruled over India for about four decades. Now (I am writing in May 2002) the main opposition party in the Indian Parliament. Today (2014), it has lost the elections to operaten as one of the opposition parties.

10 The Master asked the ruler to face the new situation as a true *kṣatriya*, a true warrior prince. He reminded him of his *dharma*, duty, as a warrior prince, to be alike in defeat and victory. His rule, he said, was meant for service and not for pleasures. Let not his distress soil the dignity of his station. The Master spoke to this effect in the author's presence. December 10, 1951. To his regret, the author cannot recall his actual words.

11 The *Samatāvilāsa*, pp. 410–11, sayings from 7–12. See also *The Radiant Sameness*, pp. 397-99.

12 *Ibid.*, pp. 408–09; *The Radiant Sameness*, p. 396.

13 *Vide* note 35 below.

14 *Ibid.*, pp., 415-16; *The Radiant Samenesss*, pp. 401-2; Sayings 4-5.

15 *Ibid.*, pp. 493 –94 (7); also *The Radiant Sameness* p. 463 (7).

16 *Ibid.*, pp. 495-96 (9); *The Radiant Sameness* p. 464 (9).

17 I use 'consumerism' not in the sense that some economists use it but in the sense of dedication to consumption.

18 *Ibid.*, pp. 499–500 (15) *The Radiant Sameness* pp. 466-67 (15).

19 *Ibid.*, pp. 294–97 (Sayings 16–21). The concepts of *vāsanā* and the three *guṇas*, the three modes of being, those of *sattva*, *rajas* and ta*m*as, of, that is to say, transcendence, of activity and of self-coincided- ness – of *ekstasis*, *stasis* and of the tension between the two have already received our attention. *Vide* Chapter 11. See also *The Radiant Sameness*, pp. 285-87(16-21).

20 Vide 17 above.

15

Yajña – 1953

October 16, 1953: Noon is melting into afternoon. The time is around 3.30 P.M. Four miles away from the Yamunanagar Railway Station, a *tong*a is moving on the road that links Yamunanagar with Chhichharauli. The moment it arrives at the spot where the road to Jagadhari branches off, three rooms, located at some distance from each other, become visible beyond the trees and the fields. The road to Chhichhrauli is a one-lane road, barely sufficient for one vehicle to pass. On either side of the road are fields, spotted here and there with trees, mostly of the neem and the mango variety, occasionally of the peepal too. On the right side, the fields stretch into a long distance up to the great wall of the Himalayas, which at this moment, wears a dim and faint look against the clear blue skyline shining bright and radiant. There is virtually no traffic on the road, with the exception of an occasional cyclist who often combines his driving with a song. Otherwise, you can hear no sound except that of the movement of the wheels and that of the hoofs of the horse. There are occasions when the silence gets so deep as to be audible to the ears. When the tonga approaches a tree, some stray chirping of a bird may also be heard, deepening one's awareness of the silence that the entire landscape breathes.

The fields have been ploughed for the winter crops. So no greenery is visible on their vast stretches. You can, however, see the thick clusters of the sugarcane here and there, breaking the monopoly and the monotony of the plains shorn of the green. A tranquillity broods over the smooth vast earth that extends unendingly as it were to fade into a distance, into the dim outlines of the mountains and the forests that lie at their foot. The trees mostly are silent, no leaf flutters in this stillness, no birds sing their chorus. A mild, serene warmth pervades the air and an unobtrusive pale of the sun. A mile away, in the front, starts a dense forest stretching up to miles and miles into the hills. Tigers, leopards and boars dwell in it in plenty. Sometimes their roars and screams have been, we are told, heard here in the early hours of the morning.

The rooms we have been talking about constitute an *āśrama*, a hermitage. You espy its gate as soon as you reach the spot where the Dadupur road braches off. Brightly white washed is this gate today. Entering the gate, one sees on the right a well, on the left a small field on which still stands a crop of plants, ripe enough to be harvested. At about a hundred yards away there is another gate, a small one, an entrance, one soon finds out, to the kitchen of the *āśrama*. Outside the *āśrama* proper are the well ploughed fields, the property of the *āśrama*, with a number of tents pitched therein for the stay of the *premīs*. Beyond the tents, there is a *pandal*, a relatively vast tent for *sat-saṇga*.

The moment the newcomers enter the kitchen gate, they meet Bhagatjī, with quite a few *premīs* clustering around him. The strong and sturdy Laddha Ram is busy, even at this late hour, with his usual job of cleansing the utensils.

As soon as they see the newcomers, their faces get bright with pleasure, eagerly they run to gather the latter in an embrace, take hold of their luggage and guide them to their respective tents. No newcomer is allowed to carry his own luggage. Every local *saṅgat* has its allotted tent/s.

The outer boundary of the āśrama is fenced with wires of iron, the inner boundary with a low wall about two feet high. The silence that broods over the fields and the road broods here with a greater, palpable depth. It appears as if this silence has enveloped not only the vicinity of the *āśrama* but also the distant mountains and the sky. The afternoon sun has lent a soft glow to the earth and the sky, a glow that does not please the eye but appeases it. There is a gate to enter the inner part of the āśrama, no one ever thinks of jumping the low brick boundary. Young plants of fruit cover that inner part; they will in due course grow into huge trees. On the other side, touching the boundary stands the hut of the Master. A virtual crowd of people has gathered there, but silent and tight lipped. Every one has to take off his shoes before entering the hut. A *premī* stands there to help wash the hands of those that would enter it.

The hut consists of a room, ordinary looking and old fashioned and a small verandah. The windows are grilled with iron bars, the roof has light beams of wood for support; there are two almirahs and two doors, painted dull grey.[1] On the opposite side of the door to the right sits Gurudeva, fully awake at this time, giving a smile, perceptible and vivid, to every newcomer. The latter place baskets of fruit in front of him and prostrate themselves all reverence and emotion before they sit in the midst of the devotees. Gurudeva asks each one of them about their well being. A clean carpet covers the floor on which everyone sits. The Master's seat consists, as always, of a blanket and a piece of rough white cloth spread over it.

Three years and seven months have passed by since he left Hathinikund and the Yamunā. The face is still pale, with an occasional gleam of the crimson. The eyes seem bright with love. The no-person that normally peeps out of that forbidding face has strangely been suffused with an expression of love, a love recognisably human. The beyond seems to have become proximate, the transcendence the immanence. Yet it is not absent, for it keeps on intruding into the human person that he is today, marginalising him, if not supplanting him. The body has seen only fifty years but wrinkles have already appeared as if decades had been added to the fifty. Yet the same softness it has and the same glow. Each limb is replete with it and also with the soft fragrance that body exuded.

What could be the cause of this parental look, this care and concern? How is it that this rock-like person that is literally no-person is compelled to love mortals that are fragile and weak, cunning and self-concerned? Fifteen years have passed by since he started wandering over the length and breadth of northwest India. From town to town he moved, from village to village to give his message of communal harmony, yet what effect could it have on the people around him? Before his very eyes, humans turned, as we have seen, into ravenous beasts and killed each other without mercy, without a second thought. That tragedy took him again into the deeps of forests, made him suffer for the sake of humanity, do a penance on its behalf, take its sins upon himself and suffer for those sins. As a result of that self-burning came forth the voice of the Word for the good of the newly independent country. But the new rulers forgot the tradition of simplicity and got busy, despite their conscious intentions, with fashioning a society devoted more to consumer culture than to work culture. They could not perceive, or perceived only dimly that the modernity they were trying to emulate had already passed its creative and energetic phase. Looking back, we can see how cunning, fraud, deception and easy money gradually became the way of life of many among the powerful in India, proving true the prophetic fears of the Master. Where the country, in the Master's view, was leading itself in the direction of a stillborn progress, the *saṅgat* too hardly fared better. He found this small sub-society of barely a few hundred too weak in its resolve and faith to resist the onslaught of that remarkably premature decadence.

However: with all his disillusionment, the Master could still exude love and affection, more than ever before. Now when I am writing, the memory of that demeanor arises before me with a vividness that arrests all my attention. I can only contemplate it in silence, cannot talk about it. It has taken me some time to remember that I am to proceed with my writing.

At 4 P.M. started the afternoon *sat-saṅga* with the recitation of the *vāṇī,* the Master entering into *samādhi*. The participants listened to the recitation, all attention with eyes closed. I felt my thoughts turn soft and calm, the motion of breath gentle, the mind a mere succession of the words and their slow, arresting rhythm. No feelings remained and no thoughts, only the flow of the words interspersed with short silent pauses. The recitation over, Gurudeva opened his eyes and commenced his discourse at a pitch extremely low and barely audible, the audience exclusively attentive and concentrated. Slowly the pitch rose to the level of that of the ordinary conversation to turn into eloquence, persuasive and evocative, yet retaining, strangely, the force of intellectual vigour. You could not, despite the eloquence and the evocation, spot any emotion in that voice, so impersonal it seemed, so, one might say, prophetic. Of the tragedy of life did he speak, of the existential and ontological dimensions of that tragedy, touching deep the souls of the listeners, their feelings or their calm welling up in tears they scarcely noticed. As for me, it stirred up no emotions in my mind, that impersonal voice of that no-person, a stillness deep and mute having come to suffuse my mind and body setting at rest my anguish and unrest. For twenty minutes the Master spoke, transforming the person in me into the no-person that could contemplate his tortures and dry despair without distress and without turmoil, as if they happened not to him but to someone else.

There came a sound, noisy and rattling, of a bus moving in the direction of Yamunanagar. That a rattling sound of an old, worn out country bus could be so soothing was an experience I could never anticipate and imagine. The rattle deepened the prevailing quiet and sent a gentle thrill in the body. The thrill and the shiver continued, sustained and augmented by the *vairāgya vāṇī,* the Word of Dispassion that invariably followed the Master's discourse. My hair stood on end, a cool sensation pervaded the body, absorbing every thought of mine. The cool of the body led to the flow of tears, soothing, emotionless and tranquil. Desire, said the *vāṇī,* burns the body as a fire would 'burn' a cooking vessel placed on it. Without a let it burns, without a pause and a hindrance. From death to death would move the man that sought life in this death. Like unto a leather bellow would he breathe, without being and life, the breathing setting aflame his desire as would the bellow the dying coals.

The recitation continued at a slow, lingering pace. At the end of every line there was a pause during which I heard a soft, low hum in the ears, like the soft sound one hears in a narrow vale or a gorge where no water flows, killing almost every thought. I recall that state as almost hypnotic or semi-conscious. I was conscious of the body but the thoughts or the mind seemed to be ebbing away, as if the body had replaced them. Could I identify the body as I do when I am fully conscious? Did it have any solidity then as to be termed 'a this?' What was it then? Was it the body, could it be called the body, that shell, that emptiness? A tranquillity was it then, a peace, a soothing something less than a sensation.

The recitation over, the prayer was sung and the gift of grace distributed. The time was about quarter to six; the sun had grown faint, a light shadow, so to say, enveloping it. The fields, bare of vegetation, shone as gold, the mountains showed their outlines with vividness, whole ranges of them stretching from the west to the east. The Master left the assembly tent; the silence changed into a chatter, the devotees leaving it to have a stroll on the Dadupur road, on which humans stepped but rarely. Today crowds of them walked over its almost virgin smoothness, breaking the silence of the place with their voices. But how mild were those voices, how smooth, as if the peace and the silence of the earth and the sky had mingled with them! They came to gather there year after year, very many among them but never was seen that harmony, that communication that was communion. One thought with others, talked through others, almost lived in others.

The light melted into twilight, traces of light on the distant snowy peaks keeping it at bay but only for a few minutes. The *premīs* returned to the *āśrama*, now plunged in darkness but for the faint glimmer of a few lanterns, especially at the compound of the kitchen, where many among the devotees were busy making preparations for the evening meal. Others had gathered in and around the hut of the Master, some sitting near the shoes, listening intently and eagerly to his words. A bell rang to announce the time of the meal. Row after row of them sat on the mats, the servers serving them with a devotion that had to be seen to be believed. None felt tired, none irritated; there was peace in the noise, tranquillity in that tumult. Many of the servers would vouch for the truth of the statement that while they, to all appearances, were feverishly busy, their mind, breath and name moved in unison, their bodies were light, their minds a passivity. All this when they had worked continuously for hours!

After the meal, the devotees went to various tents to be introduced to the new devotees, their faith making them life long friends at the exchange of the first greeting itself.

At ten all went to bed. I woke up at 3 A.M. to find the name, breath and mind melting into each other without an effort, without a struggle. The breath was moving slowly and gently, the ideas faint and dim, like little ripples on deep and placid waters, rising only to melt and disappear. The dawn came without a notice and brightened into morning without a waiting. Coming out of the tent I saw a different mien of the landscape, transformed into something resembling the ethereal, almost the celestial. From behind the mountain peaks rose to the skies the rays of the invisible sun, a cluster of them moving down from a little depression between the ranges. The sun itself was hidden behind the mountains but it had already dyed the sky crimson and red. Flocks of birds flew in the sky, rows after rows of them. At the well moved the persian wheel drawn by a pair of sturdy oxen, the *premīs* having their bath in the soothingly warm water from the underground. Soon after, the sun rose up from behind the mountains to light up the earth along with the sky and to set aglow the āśrama.

From his almost night long *tapas* came back the Master with the same old gait, swift and steady, the devotees making him obeisance, many among them almost laying themselves on the bare ground. But on went he towards his seat, casting no look on anyone and giving out no smile. A stillness froze on his face, an awesome stillness that would not melt into a human expression. Life and death seemed to have coalesced there, death alive and life dead. A concealed revelation was that face or revealed concealment, the emblem of the mystery, the very mystery of life and death. In the presence of that disruptive revelation or lack of it, the ethereal beauty of the dawn and morning seemed prosaic and dull, for who could have noticed it when death had turned into life and life into death?

After a brief bath, the Master went to his hut where had gathered a virtual crowd of men, women and children. All of them prostrated themselves before him as soon as he took his seat but where was the man to acknowledge that silent greeting and expectant devotion? For, the moment he was at his seat, his eyes closed and he was lost in samādhi. The organisers wanted to discuss important matters regarding the future constitution of the *saṅgat* but his yogic oblivion would not give them the opportunity. The Master had instructed Amolak Ram, the primary organiser, not to turn the property and the land of the āśrama into a thing of profit and loss and to refrain from saving money, and also to distance himself from every managerial function after the constitution had been approved by the *saṅgat*. After a long deliberation, the premīs had prepared a draft to place it that day before the general body of the saṅgat for its consideration and approval. But it could not be given the final shape before the Master had examined it. So they eagerly waited for the 'return' of his human self. The self-forgetfulness, however, abated slowly as usual. But even when he had regained what is called 'normal consciousness' he did not evince much interest in the matter in question. A disposition of disinterest, of aloofness had come to stay with him. To be disinterested was ingrained in his nature right from his boyhood but now it had become pronounced and conspicuous. Most of the time, when he was 'awake,' his eyes often remained fixed on the ground, his trunk bent forward a little. This disposition could not, in any sense, be equated with sadness. It spoke more of a distance, of transcendence than of disappointment. His own thoughts and views no longer seemed to be of concern to him, no longer seemed to be his. Some devotees did talk of his disillusionment with his disciples with their obstinate worldliness; they often quoted his stray remarks that he wished to throw the entire *vāṇī* into a river rather than leave it in the hands of the slaves of desire that most of them were. But these remarks, it was quite evident, were remarks of the suffering man, not of the no-man and the no-Word that he was. One could see that transcendence as immanent in his silent looks and his gestures.

A democratic set up of the organisation was proposed and approved that afternoon by the general body, the Master refraining from participating in the deliberation and the brief discussion. It appeared he seemed to disown his own past: the revelation and the teaching, the saṅgat and its aims and goals. That day in the afternoon he explained the meaning of *dharma*, of the way to the truth. In the concluding part of his discourse, he said:

> Meetings and contacts of this kind occur rarely in life. He who stands today will fall one day. The opportunity vouchsafed to you now may not fall your way again. Think of the end approaching you, approaching you ever. Who knows if what you perceive and hear now you will perceive and hear again? This body is bound to change in the end, it cannot stay for ever. With great fortune can one hear the voice of the Truth. Ever think of how you can redeem this life. The burden is yours, and yours is the responsibility, nothing will happen on its own. Do not think mere sight of a seer will save you; you have to reorient your life in accordance with some principles.

Earlier too, in the summer of that year, he had given the same kind of warning:

> Premī, life is uncertainty itself, those who live today may be dead tomorrow. .. Set aflame have you this redemptive fire; flicker will it for long to attract many a person, many a person that would willingly burn into redemption. .. You and others have inherited whatever belonged to *This*. So lose yourself in what you have taken down. ..

> 'Know you well, Banārasī, the condition of this body. The time of separation is now not far off. Whatever has been dictated, under the command of the Lord, unto you, take it as your Guide and Master. In solitude you will remember this time, in grief will you do so, in sorrow deep and tearful. So save yourself before this body of yours comes to fall. Otherwise the cruel wheel of birth and death will continue ... Distant will become your goal and long your pilgrimage.

Call it a chance or an act of grace, the *vāṇī* that was recited that afternoon at the *sat-saṅga* was a call to awakening in the same vein:

> Hard is it to come across a guru but harder still is to become a disciple true, for of himself has he to make the offering. Gracious turns first he, the one to be instructed.
> First becomes he the dispenser and the giver, then does become the guru the hidden treasures to open out, seeing the gracious giving up.
> The home true shows the guru, but toilsome and hard is the path he shows; die must man to tread it, keeping ever the Word before him.
> In the Word has he to die, in the word of the guru, to find its meaning and its essence, to find the cure for the unrest that life after life has pursued him, and death after death.

The following day was to be held the *yajña*. A little after nightfall, cooking started, a nightlong process of it, for a large quantity of food was to be prepared. For water there was only one hand pump, its little trickle was expected to cook food for over a thousand guests, perhaps more than that number. For hours a single person would pump out the water, then would another take his place. In the kitchen the formidable Laddha Ram and his associates were preparing the dough, like machines were they working, allowing themselves no pause and rest. In the meantime, Laddha Ram started the narration of his meeting with the Master, which his companions listened to with a rapt attention:

> The Master was then[2] staying in Delhi in an orchard in the outskirts of the city. One day, Laddha Ram, reading a hand written notice on the boundary wall of the said orchard and following the instructions given therein reached a hut.[3] A strong, wrestling physique turned steely by a regular, vigorous exercise over the years! The *pathan* dress, a salwar,[4] a shirt and a turban with almost a foot of the first end of its starched cloth left loose to stand erect on the head like a snake, showed the stuff he was and was made of. Add to this the large and staring black-dyed

eyes. Could one require more to intimidate the impostor that this sage too, in his belief confirmed over the years, undoubtedly was? It had been an interesting pastime for Laddha Ram to expose the hypocrisy of fraudulent saints. The temptation was too strong to ignore. But hardly had he taken his seat in the hut when he received a severe blow to his pride and self-esteem, 'What makes you intrude so rudely here? Sit there behind the last row!'

The hard, tough man was not ready for this kind of welcome. He received a jolt, but managed to say, 'When others can sit here, why can't I?'

'Get back!'

The voice was firm and stern and intimidating. The man obeyed, without knowing why.

Next day, he brought some sugar with him. Sugar was in short supply in those days of scarcity after the partition of the country. It was rationed along with wheat and other cereals. Laddha Ram ran a ration shop and thought that some sugar would easily tempt 'the saint.' So, he came to the presence of the Master, but before he could make his obeisance he received another reprimand, 'You again here?'

'Mahārājjī, what makes you spurn me this way? I come here to do service to the Lord. All the daylong milk and tea boil in the kitchen here. I have brought some sugar for that purpose.'

'The *faqīrs* do not accept gifts from the likes of you.'

'What's wrong with me?'

'Remember your deeds and your ways. In sin you earn and sin you bring here.'

The man was overawed into silence. For quite some time, he uttered not a word, but continued to sit there, thinking. And then, 'I hear the Master has written a book. Please give me a copy of it. I want to read it.'

'What will you do with the book, what good will it do to you? Go away, don't waste the time of the *faqīrs*!'

Here his narration paused and so did his hands. A smile, broad and expansive, came to soften his hard face. 'This *mahātmā*, this great soul,' I said to myself, 'is indeed a difficult game to catch!' On the way back, I thought of various strategies to lay the snare for him. I was determined to expose in full this imposter of a faqīr, as I thought him to be. The following day I put two notes, each of a hundred rupee value, in my pocket, fully confident of success in calling his bluff. But the moment he showed but a little inclination to accept the money, I would put it where it belonged, in my pocket.'

With great 'humility' he prostrated himself before the Master, placed the two notes in front of him and beseeched him to do him the favour of accepting that trifling. Repeatedly he made the request but to no purpose. When he persisted with his requests, he was sternly asked to leave the place and that too immediately. In silence he went out and sat on the platform outside, confused and puzzled. For quite some time he sat there, when a devotee of the Master complained that the man with the *turrā*[5] on his turban was still there.

'Drive him out. Who knows who is he and what is he? A shady man he seems!'

The man who could knock down half a dozen men when roused up could not be expected to bear this kind of insults. But the narrator became serious, very serious in recounting what happened afterwards. 'The moment I heard these words, my heart sank, my body shivered and was in sweat. With a difficulty I caught hold of my bicycle and went back home, giddy and restless, my heart beating strong and loud. It seemed as if I was going to die on the way itself. That night I was to play the part of Hanumāna[6] at the Rāmalīlā, the stage show of Rāma's history, which I found impossible to make it, to the great embarrassment of the organisers. I lay on bed, restless and troubled causing great anxiety to my wife, who asked me not to meddle with the affairs of seers, whose one word of anger could bring ruin upon us all. And to do such pranks at a place where they had no relations, no one they could call theirs! I asked her to keep silent. The whole night passed in distress and panic with not a wink of sleep. I thought my end was near. At the break of dawn, I prayed in repentance, "My Lord and Master, be merciful to me!

I will never repeat this act of blasphemy again. Forgive me for my sin this time!" For long I prayed and fell asleep. In the morning, I felt well but could not summon up the courage to go to the Master. For full one year, I did not pass that way, did not have the courage to do so. The very sight of its direction made me tremble and panicked.'

Deeply reflective and pensive he became while narrating this incident. So did his audience, who, unwittingly, had stopped preparing the dough; too absorbed were they in the story. Outside they sang songs in praise of the Lord, women making loaves of bread, men preparing the fragrant *halavā*. Two of his listeners went out to deposit the dough near the 'ovens', huge plates of iron placed on fire, requesting Laddha Ram not to resume his story until they came back. At their return, he resumed it. 'When the time of the annual yajña here arrived, Lakshmi Chand asked me to accompany him. But the very memory of the Master was a terror for me; there could be no question of seeing him face to face. I expressed my inability to do his bidding, telling him in brief what had happened to me. "If you go," he said, "with a clean mind, nothing will happen to you." I felt reassured a little and came here with him, though gnawed by anxiety and fear all the way. There was, however, one consolation: I was not going to the Master with any bad intention. All knowing he was, he would not spurn this repentant.'

On reaching the āśrama he bowed low on the very threshold of the Master's hut. 'You have come here too!' said the latter the moment he saw him. But now there was a broad smile on his face, not the forbidding frown that the *premī* feared so much. 'A beggar,' said the repentant man, 'I come here, seeking the Lord's grace.' The Master's mien reassured him a little. 'Go, do some service for the saṅgat,' he was told.

In the orchard in the interior of the āśrama, earth was being bored for installing a tube-well. Laddha Ram made a promise to himself: Not until the Master himself came to stop him he would continue with the work at boring. With a rough digging-tool in his hand, he went on digging hour after hour until blood oozed out of his fingers and palms. But on he went with his work, caring for neither the time nor the pain in his hands and a whole bath of sweat. Time and again he would paste earth on his wounds to stop the flow of blood but would not stop his work, despite the repeated requests from the premīs to rest and refresh himself. At last he felt a darkness enveloping everything before him, the landscape whirling in a circle as it were. But as long as the Master's heart did not melt for him, where was the use of rest and health? When everything was becoming dim and faint, he was shaken out of his near faint by a voice saying, 'Premī, it is the Lord's command that you stop work and take something at the kitchen.'

'Is this the command of the Master himself?'

'Yes, this is his command,' said Amolak Ram, for he was the messenger.

His heart melted into tears, of that seemingly cold and hard man. Too soon, he felt, had grace been showered upon him. Concluding his narration, he said, 'One day, the Master said, "You came here not out of your own will. You were just dragged to this place."'

Deeply moved were all those that had listened to his account. In silence they continued to make the dough and carry it out. Many a gunny bag of flour had been turned into dough. Heaps of loaves of bread had been piled up; layers after layers of halavā had been laid on vast circular plates. The entire night was spent in hectic activity, accompanied with the recitation of the holy Word. Before the dawn peeped in the east, the entire food was ready.

Back from his *tapas* at the break of day, the Master went straight to the kitchen immediately after his bath to cast a long, lingering look at the food. He sprinkled a few drops of water on it and blessed the premīs that had worked so tirelessly to prepare it and went to his seat. The same old inscrutable no-look was writ large on his face and the same familiar sheen radiated out of his skin, the same depths swallowing him as they had done before. That day, a long sat-saṅga was to be held after a light breakfast. The Bhagat brought a bowl of milk, now his diet after his long illness. He took it with almost a sense of aversion. The expression on his face clearly indicated that taking milk was a task for him, an unpleasant task. After this his breakfast, his lunch and dinner all in one, conversation started about the sat-saṅga and the persons that were to speak therein. Along with some others, Dev Raj Gupta too was asked to express his views at the *sat-saṅga.* The latter said, 'Gone through the ordeal have I! I cannot repeat the act of blasphemy.'

'Today, it is *This* that asks you to speak. Do express your views!'

Seeing the expression of a paternal love on the Master's face, the *premī* gave his consent. Only a year before, this very *premī* had virtually invited himself to speak in the assembly. Gurudeva had asked some other disciples to speak but had ignored Dev Raj Gupta. A young man was this devotee at that time, confident with a rich gift of self-esteem. Since childhood had he been a speaker on the stage, had a command over eloquence. With conviction he spoke and with emotion, with ideas clear or neat enough to produce an immediate effect, that asset of orators. Add to this his newly acquired degree in philosophy, which lent a ring of authenticity and learning to his speech. It was but natural that this observed of the observers should get impatient with the preference given to the persons who, in his eyes, had neither understanding nor the gift of speech. 'Mahārājjī, I too may be given some time to speak,' escaped from his nervous lips.

'Let the premī too be given ten minutes,' said the Master to the organisers with a ring of indifference in his voice.

'What can I say in ten minutes?'

'Let him be given twenty minutes, then.'

Twenty minutes could serve for only a prelude to the song, a preface to the text. But he hesitated to ask for more time, despite his dissatisfaction. Many had heard him converse with the Master, had been impressed by his remarks and insights and by the free praise the Master had showered upon those remarks and insights. They waited with expectation for his turn, thinking that his speech would be a delight and a thrill. Things, however, turned out to be contrary to all expectations. As soon as he rose to speak, he found his mind stray and wander, his thoughts dispersed into a confusion, every effort on his part failing to bring his mind into a focus. His tongue became dry, his throat blocked. He sipped some water to make another trial but every effort proved vain. At last, he sat down, saying, 'I do not know what is happening to me. I am compelled to be silent. This kind of thing has never happened before.'

Frustrated he felt and mortified, but the Master did not refer to that incident, though he discussed other matters with him, with every affection, even with enthusiasm, to the extent enthusiasm could be associated with him. So when that day, the Master asked him to speak at the satsaṅga, the devotee remembered that incident, how he had stood up inflated and sat down deflated. That day, too, he appeared before the audience but not to impress them with his abilities but to do the bidding of his Lord and Master. He did not care to prepare his speech, letting his breath and vocal cords utter what they would. When, however, he opened his lips, he felt a flood of thoughts come to seize him to pour themselves out without any effort on his part, sometimes even without his consciousness of them. Thought-less he spoke casting a hypnotic spell on the audience, who, on two or three occasions, raised a slogan or two by way of applause, a practice strictly prohibited. The twenty-five minutes allotted to him passed away in no time as it were. He concluded his speech but the audience insisted that he continue with it. The speaker, however, refused to overstep the limit of the time. The Master who sat nearby asked him to continue, giving his warm approval to practically everything he said.

After finishing his speech, the devotee sat down in a corner, in all humility, the members smiling their warm and eloquent approval. The silent praise made him feel small and abashed, for he knew where flowed the source of inspiration, who was the speaker and who was the recipient. He who was the master of every wisdom and every speech had ever spoken in the ordinary language of rustics. There was no consideration for grammatical niceties and lexical finesse in his discourses, no enthusiasm and no eloquence. What he said evoked reflection, more accurately speaking, pensiveness, for no idea could stand the test of retrospective scrutiny. He compelled his listeners to think, to think in existential terms, and to live his precepts and to outlive them. Where man has to weigh what has been meted out to him and what awaits him, there is no room for applause, even for a thought of it. Dev Raj could see that where everybody was busy praising his speech, none seemed concerned with its contents or concerned superficially, not existentially. Serous thoughts he had expressed about the kind of political and social set up that could keep alive in man the thought of his mortal destiny, did not let him sleep over it and get degraded into insensitiveness. But who was there to think about his thoughts in any serious way? Where the Master's words compelled thought and action and disowning of both thought and action, the devotee's words did not evoke even a serious intellectual response. So where was the use of that learning and that eloquence? Deeply introspective became he that day of praise and acclaim.

After the devotee's speech commenced the Master's discourse. A wooden bed with a white sheet of cloth spread over it served the purpose of the stage. Thereon had sat he, listening to what Dev Raj Gupta had said. He was not in samādhi that day before his discourse as was his wont. So when the discourse began, there was no softness in the tone, but clear and firm articulation. There ensued a complete silence among the audience, for everybody was attentive to the hilt, his/her eyes concentrated on the Master. Words flowed out in a steady even flow, with practically no rise and fall in intonation, his hands on his lap, his trunk erect, his body still, interspersed with an occasional motion, slight and barely perceptible. On two or three occasions the tempo increased, the intonation intensified, the voice modulated but the silence of the audience continued to remain deep as before. Their gaze remained steady and fixed on the person of the Master; some tears they shed but knew not when they flowed out and when they dried up. The gist of what he spoke could be summed up as follows:

> You have gathered here for instructions that could ennoble you and bring about your wellbeing. Thanks are due to you all for sparing the time for that purpose. Some thoughts are going to be offered to you. Give an attentive ear to them.
>
> This body is the world itself. Coiled in it beings wander in the world: men, birds and beasts. For joy real and authentic do they strive in varied ways but the joy they seek never falls to their lot, only death does. For that is the end fashioned out for them, not the end that they seek. He who does not understand this truth is not a human being. Beings wear this body of the five elements in search of a secure fulfillment but where in the world ever on the move can that be found? It is imperative that man understand this paradox, therein lies his wisdom – in the understanding of this paradox. For that is what makes of him a human. The pleasures he seeks to grab through evil ways are infirm and insecure and cannot give him the satisfaction he seeks. Like unto fire burns creature each and every, no effort on its part can extinguish that fire, no endeavour can ever appease it. So give up this desire for pleasures. Let service of others be the purpose of your life, with the Lord as your sole anchor and support. Otherwise, you will find yourselves as prisoners of the body, find yourselves merely the body and helpless prisoners of sense pleasures. They [the latter] will become your goal and purpose. To death will you go if you find not the Lord as your refuge.
>
> Let there be a limit, the truth-become say, to the appeasement of your desire and the satisfaction of your wants; let you not exceed

and transgress that limit. Take what happens to you or does not happen to you as ordained by the Lord, let your happiness and unhappiness be His concern, not yours. Let your concern for your happiness change into a concern for the happiness of others. Let your means be at the disposal of others. This disposition will lead you to a state beyond the range of frustration. To satisfaction will you attain, that long sought after goal.

There is no limit set to lying these days or to fraud. In sleep is humanity lost, in sleep of ignorance. Rest and unrest are the results of the choice you make about what you should do or should not do. Stick to the noble act, for the evil deed is there to take you to disaster. It destroys your life and injures your spirit. Neither thereby is served your self-interest nor your supreme interest. So let your own individual life be pure, let your effort be directed towards that end. Let your deeds be noble, your food pure, your dealings upright. This way will die the evil desire in you.

You have been vouchsafed this body so that you may tread the true way and attain to the end of your long pilgrimage. So let truth be your companion in it. There is no wisdom in giving up the striving while on the way.

Blessed are you all! Lead a noble life to wake up the culture of this your Land. Faqīrs can make only a request. The choice is yours and yours alone. Be you ever friendly towards others, be you ever their companions the true. That is the *tapa* chalked out for householders, for those who live as men with a family. To relate to others in and through the Truth alone will save them.

Let noble thoughts occupy your mental landscape. They will result in noble deeds. They will supplant thoughts of me and mine to orient you towards the Truth. Thereby shall the Path open up before you. Let the Lord bless you with insight so that you may attain to peace the true, and so may your society and your country and your family.

With the end of the sat-saṅga commenced the public feast that went on into late afternoon. The autumn afternoon soon transformed itself into *sandhyā*, into a meditatively calm confluence of the day and the night. The public dispersed but the devotees remained to gather, very many among them, in and around the Master's hut. Every local saṅgat was anxious that the Master visit them on his first move but the Master had no inclination to do so, no interest to resume his wanderings. Some thought that he was unhappy with the devotees and their ways. Therein they found the cause of this unwillingness. But said he, 'Unhappy is *This* with no one. But wandering *This* would rather avoid. How much time has been wasted this way! Now *This* would rather sit alone, does not wish to interact with people.'

A recantation of the very tone and tenor of his own discourse that day!

Devotee: May I, with the Lord's permission, say something!

Master: Yes, *Premī*, say what you will.

Devotee: A beggar was given half a loaf of bread. When the hungry man had taken it, he was asked to leave. The beggar said weeping, 'You ask me to leave now, when your half loaf has inflamed my hunger. Better would it have been if you had not fed me this little. I felt no pangs then as I do now. Cruel has been your bounty.

The Master did not respond to these words, a smile sad and indifferent was all that they could evoke.

The devotee was none else than Dev Raj Gupta. Dejected was he that day at his weakness. He had overeaten a little, overeaten even an unsavoury dish. If he could not resist the temptation for a wretched dish, how would he reach the end of his lonely pilgrimage? How could he reach it without the Master's support and blessing?

Gurudeva kept looking down on the floor, the smile had long left the face, giving way to an impersonal seriousness.

'Many a birth will have been spent when the goal is reached!'

'Yes, *Premī,* long is the way and distant the goal.'

'Can a guru shorten the length and the distance?'

'One has to earn one's salvation; it won't come as a gift.'

'Can the guru make the disciple see his self, can he do it by his grace?'

'A true guru can do everything. But where will the unripe disciple find the power to absorb and keep intact what has been given unto him?'

Having said this, the Master narrated an incident in the life of a *sūfi* saint, Bullah Shah or Bulleh Shah. A seeker true and earnest was he in his youth, this famous saint. Even though born in a family of the Saiyyads, the clan that claims descent from the family of the Prophet himself and is, for this reason, held in great respect and esteem, Bullah Shah became a disciple of Inayat Shah. A great seer was Inayat Shah, though a lowly grower of vegetables. When Bullah went to meet him for the first time, he found the latter working in the fields. Bowing before him, Bullah expressed the purpose of his visit. Seeing the man in distress, the Master assured him that the goal he sought was not distant, that to have the vision of God was as easy as replanting of the seedlings. From being placed in the mind–body complex one had only to place oneself as a witness thereof. So where was the difficulty? Why fret for that which one could win without much ado?

Bullalh was intoxicated, for found had he, he thought, what he had sought. He did not care to knock any more at the door of his Master. So proud he became and self-opinionated, ready to be a light and guide to all that came near him. Inayat Shah waited long for his wayward disciple but the latter did not care to turn up. The preceptor himself went to the disciple to wake him up from his dismal stupor. Bullah Shah was then sitting in the midst of his admirers, many among them Saiyyads. He did not think it becoming of him to bow down before a mere vegetable grower, and that too in the presence of his own people. He did not even care to rise up to greet him, but merely extended his hand towards his preceptor. The preceptor held his hand for a while but the moment he released it, Bullah found his vision gone, his ecstasy turn into misery, his borrowed wealth all snatched away. The deprived found himself deprived again, his crest fallen on the dust. Before he could utter a word, the preceptor had left.

Shame and disgrace would not allow him to pay a visit to his Master. In silence he prayed to the latter, prayed for long, during the day and during the night, beseeched him to forgive him and take him back into his fold but to no effect. Ultimately, he decided to burn down the pride of birth once and for all. He went to a dancing girl, though a Saiyyad, went to her openly and in the public eye to win the displeasure of his community, for there could be nothing more disgraceful for a Saiyyad than proximity to a dancing woman. But Bullah did the unthinkable; he prepared her smoke and served her as a servant would his master. Only one thing he asked of her for this public disgrace: she teach him how to dance like her. A complete outcast he wanted to be, a man out of the fold.

On certain occasions in that area dancing girls would dance before the public. Bullah, now an expert in that art, clad himself in her clothes, covered his face with a veil and, in Bullah's own words, 'danced before the people as a fallen woman would.' He could play the incognito before others but not before his guru, who immediately recognised who he was. 'Are you Bullah?' he said aloud.

'No, my Lord, I am not Bullah but a *bhūllā*, a forgetfu!'

He removed the veil, that confirmed outcast, and fell at the feet of his Master. Grace came to descend upon him once again. The way now ran smooth and straight.

Having narrated this story, Gurudeva said, '*Premī*, everyone has to fend for himself. The gift of a vision will not ensure you will have the power to absorb it.'

'Where grace vouchsafes the vision,' said the devotee, 'it can also bestow the power to absorb it.'

The Master gave no reply to this question.

'Can a perfect guru,' the devotee asked again, 'give him the power to absorb the vision?'

'Yes, he can, if he wills it so.

'Mahārājjī! why these ifs and buts? Why not a straight answer?'

The Master sat silent, his trunk, as usual, bent forward. Very serious he became. So none could speak in familiar terms, none had the courage to do so. There could not be any answer to questions of this kind. A long way a man has to go, a weary and hard way, to understand what the Master's words implied. He has to learn, first of all, that a man becomes himself when he ceases to desire that he become himself, finding this desire itself an obstacle between what he is and what he finds himself to be. He has also to learn that as long as the distinction between the guru and the disciple, the guide and the guided remains, there can be no vision of the self as the all. He has also to realise that there could be no revelation of the true, ontological self as long as the world is there and others are there, and, consequently, he himself is there. What a Master can bestow upon a disciple ambitious of self-knowledge can only be a semblance of it, at most an approximation to it, not the revelation of the self itself. All talk about the loss of the self, the attainment of the self, about bondage and liberation springs from selfhood; it is the pastime of the ambitious, not of those who have been chastened enough to see through such great ambitions. In other words, one who is actively involved in *sādhanā*, in contemplation and holy acts, cannot find the self. He alone finds the self who perceives every state of being as the state of salvation, every fall a redemption, every hell a heaven. But this one can find when all concepts have died down, and the *other* of concepts: the sense and mental content. The devotee in question was still thinking of ends and means, of the way and the goal and asking how to attain to the state of *samatvam*, the state in which all such distinctions lose their meaning. He did not know what he desired and asked for.

There remains, however, the question about the Master's answer that a true seer can gift away any state of being to a disciple, if he so wishes. But can he wish so? Where is the *other* for him to make him wish this way, for one who sees all as one, fall as redemption and redemption as fall, Māyā as Brahman and Brahman as Māyā? His role as a guide is only his play, a play that he has to play under the dictates of his *prārabdha*. The Master too played that role under the same compulsion, but not for long was he to do so, for we already find him distancing himself from it. Willingly had he let himself to be the dupe of the hope of saving individuals and enriching cultures – these vain illusions – had borne that burden as much as he could. At long last, he was going to throw it away, but throw it away with indifference, for where was the difference between this burden and the relief therefrom? A seer of *samatvam* may gift away a vision to someone but that will be a spontaneous act dictated by the inner, unconscious call of the disciple. Bestowing of grace will be of no account for him as will be withholding it.

A little discursive, a little doctrinaire diversion was necessary to undo the hope and illusion that many, too many, faithful often nurture and cherish in their naive minds. That evening, the Master's solemn silence palpably conveyed the frivolity of such hopes and illusions. So, none could speak in that vein again. After some time, when the mood of solemnity seemed to have sunk in the minds of the devotees, the Master himself broke that silence through narrating another story. When Kṛṣṇa, he said, became a celebrity, adored of many in his own land and abroad, his preceptor, Durvāsā was a man of worry. So one day he appeared at Dvārakā, the seat of power of the Yādavas, Kṛṣṇā's powerful clan. When Kṛṣṇa came to know of his sudden arrival, he, along with his wife Rukmiṇī, presented himself before his Master, all curious to know about the reason of his unannounced visit. 'How is it that the Master deprived me of the pleasure of welcoming him in person?'

'Much have I heard of the beauty of this city. That prompted me to have a look at it.'

Kṛṣṇa put his royal chariot at the disposal of the sage, which the sage could not accept as his carriage, saying, 'A renunciate like me, given to nonviolence, cannot accept this carriage. We cannot trouble the horses; this is against our way and vow. But you are our disciple. If you and your queen consent to draw the chariot, there will be no violation of our vow. A guru can accept the service of his disciple without inviting blame on himself.'

Kṛṣṇa promptly unharnessed the horses and requested the sage to ascend into the chariot, his queen and he pulling it and the sage whipping them without a mercy. Drops of blood appeared on their backs, lines and streaks of it but no let was given to the cruel whip. The citizens looked with horror at the couple and with awe at the great sage; incomprehensible was that sight for them, unbelievable and unthinkable. When the chariot had passed through all the lanes of the city, Kṛṣṇa stopped the chariot and Durvāsā alighted from it. With hands folded, the disciple asked the guru, 'I hope the Master felt no inconvenience. This servant will indeed be blessed if the Master thinks him fit to render him any other service.'

The master took his disciple in an affectionate embrace. Said he with emotion, 'Today your *sādhanā* is complete, your pilgrimage ended. Nothing more can I teach thee, nothing more have I to convey.'

After narrating this story, Gurudeva became silent. They talked of grace, but how many among them knew what it was. On Śrī Kṛṣṇa grace descended in the form of the bloody strokes of a whip. In what form did they want it? Who can know and experience that grace without knowing its preludes: the ordeals, the hardships and the misery. Self-realisation means self-extinction. None can desire it, none can cherish an ambition for it. Those who seek the grace of the guru for self-realisation do not seek self-realisation but self-glory. Vain is their request and false their talk.

Next morning, the devotees came into the presence of the Master, some alone, some in groups of two or three. They came there to get his permission to go back home but would not say it in words. It was left to the Master to ask them about their wish and grant them the permission. That morning too the Master gave his permission but not with affection and mild, soothing emotion but with a seriousness that could only be termed forbidding, almost scaring. With the permission granted, the devotees would go out of the hut without a word, without the usual feelings of sorrow. They seemed frightened and scared, everyone among them. Outside the hut they felt some relief, a release from a choking. He seemed so distant from them, so far away that they dared not think of relating to him or communicating with him. You do not establish relationship, a personal relationship, with a breath taking Himalyan peak. Memory of that unforgettable day is a memory of a forbidding dread. For knowing the inevitable no one wished to know that that was the last glimpse and the last meeting.

In a week the āśrama came to wear a look of desertion. Most of the devotees had left for their homes, only a few remained behind. The Master was not willing to wander any more but under the repeated requests from the local saṅgats he decided to make a tour of the Punjab. Before the date fixed for departure, November 1, the Bhagat went to meet his relations at a town nearby. He, however, did not turn up on the said date. Once more, the Master sent Amolak Ram to bring him back. On his return, the Master asked another devotee to speak to the Bhagat. After a long conversation with him, the said devotee told the Master that despite years of association with the latter, the Bhagat had not truly understood the Master, had not truly communed with him. He took his meditation rather casually. The Master should, he added, ask him to appropriately orientate his life.

'Where is the use of repeating the same thing? Many a time has he been asked to be regular in his meditations, but to little effect, it appears.'

The Master once again chalked out his daily programme, which the Bhagat could observe for only a few weeks. He could not, he said, observe that discipline.

'O.K., *Premī!* Soon will you be freed from every duty and every obligation!'

The last phase of the Master's life had started!

Notes

1 It would be vain to seek any resemblance between that hut and its crude distortion today. The Master's disciples changed the austere simplicity of that structure into a more 'presentable form', displaying an aesthetic sense peculiar in the extreme.

2 Laddha Ram did not mention the year. He met the Master after he had migrated from Pakistan to India. Probably 1949 was the year. This cannot, alas, be confirmed now. The devotee is no more with us.

3 The features of the landscape consisting of the orchard and the hut have been described in the Prologue.

4 The Pathan version of pyjamas loose in the middle and narrow at the ankles.

5 The first end of the turban left loose to stand erect on the head.

6 A character in the Indian epic, ***Rāmāyaṇa,*** portrayed as a paradigm of devotion and heroism. Rāma, the hero of the epic, an epitome of virtue and propriety, is portrayed in *Rāmacaritamānasa,* the Hindi version of the epic by Tulasidāsa, as an incarnation of Viṣṇu, of God the Immanent. The Sanskrit version by Vālmīki presents the hero, despite some hints to the contrary, as, basically, a human character.

Death and the Epilogue

Delhi, February 4, 1954. News arrived in the evening that the Master had attained to *mahāsamādhi* early in the morning at Amrtisar and that the body was being brought to the Jaghadhari āśrama. The train for Jagadhari left Delhi at 10.30 P.M. Throughout the night heavy rain fell as it had been falling since the day before. The clouds thundered and the lightning blazed. Around 3.45 A.M. the train reached the Jagadhari railway station. The rain had, by that time, turned into a drizzle, some stars were visible in the midst of the floating clouds. A little before the break of dawn, the devotees reached the āśrama. By that time the rain had stopped. A devotee stood at the gate, with a lantern in hand. In its glimmer, the group moved mute and silent towards the Master's hut. In the hut too a lantern burnt to dispel the darkness. The body lay where the Master used to sit, just opposite the door to the right. One eye was open a little, the lower lip a little under the grip of teeth. The turban had been removed; the body from the neck downward was covered with a sheet of white cloth.

They gazed on the still and inert body, gazed in silence and without an expression of emotion. In a little while the silence gave place to sighs, moans and tears. After some time when the tears had stopped a little, they asked the Bhagat, who sat near the feet with the eyes swollen, how it had happened. For, despite hints and suggestions to the contrary, none had really expected the end to be so near. A long spell of diarrhoea had, they were informed, made him very weak. His condition deteriorated soon after his arrival at Amritsar on January 31. On the third of February he found it difficult to walk. That day in the morning, he asked the Bhagat to prepare a herbal mixture for him. He did as he was told but the milk turned sour. The second preparation too did not fare better because the Bhagat, in sheer nervousness, poured salt into it instead of sugar. The third preparation the body refused to accept; the entire drink it threw out. The Bhagat's service, it seemed, had reached its end. 'No need,' said the Master, 'to prepare anything else.'

The whole day passed in discomfort increased by two or three motions. Between three and four in the afternoon, while the Master sat alone in his room and the devotees in the verandah, the latter heard, all at once, a cry loud and of pain and rushed into the room. They found the Master sitting at his seat, uttering softly, 'Oh, what's happened, what's happened?' Immediately, hues green, yellow, pale and others appeared on the face to disappear almost immediately, followed by shivering of the entire body. A devotee requested him to cover his body with a blanket. The Master stretched his hand towards it but it could not reach the blanket. Silent he looked at this sudden change in his body. The devotee covered him with the blanket and made him lie down on the mat. Another devotee ran to bring a doctor. The Master lay still, his eyes closed. In between his eyes opened on two or three occasions but not a word, a sigh or a moan escaped from his lips. The doctor came and examined him, tried to see if there was any sensation in his feet and hands. Only when the doctor wanted to give him an injection, he raised his hand a little, perhaps to indicate [?] his disapproval. The devotees explained to the doctor the condition of his constitution, his intake and way of life and the history of his reactions to medicines. The doctor did not think it proper to give him the injection. While leaving, he said that the Master was exceedingly weak. If they saw no improvement by the morning, they should, he added, get him admitted into a hospital.

After midnight the body stretched and contracted after short intervals. But no words escaped him, neither was manifest any sign of pain or relief. The eyes did open two or three times but only for a short while. The peace or more than peace that his face showed forth in samādhi came to rest on the face, the continual stretching and contracting of the body notwithstanding. Before the break of dawn the man in him had died finally into *mahāsamādhi*, the great samādhi.

The devotees that witnessed the passing away of the Master were naturally more sorrow-stricken than observant; otherwise they would have been able to recall in more vivid details the condition of his face and the transcendence immanent in it. The state of samādhi had always been a state of holy dread for most of us and much more, very much more, must have been the state of *mahāsamādhi* – that irrevocable and final death of every trace of the man in the Master, even of the dread holy and awesome. So we must be content with this little report they gave. With the morning arrived many devotees from various towns. After three days of continuous rains the sun rose bright and splendid revealing the sublimity of the Himalayas, the deep blue of the sky and the green of the earth with unbelievable vividness. A deep calm breathed the earth, the mountains and the sky, a cosmic calm, which many among us may perceive and feel but find it hard to interiorise. They were reciting the *vairāgya vāṇī,* the Word of Dispassion, but how out of place did it sound in that peace that the world *was* at that time! For that peace had nothing to do with human emotions, it seemed more than human, even more than cosmic. And how thin, dim and faint seemed the reality of things then, even the reality of the earth and the sky! And the sight of that death! So unreal it seemed that one had to remind oneself of it.

The body was given a wash and was laid outside the hut, the head tied in a turban, the face open, a sheet of white cloth covering it from the neck downwards. Some pale had come to cover the face but it could not conceal the traces of still peace that still lingered on it. Devotees came in numbers to have the last glimpse of their Master and bid him a tearful adieu, silent and solemn.

The peace seemed to deepen; an aura of the unreal seemed to envelop that white wrap and that face. The eyes perceived the face to be the face of a dead person but somehow the mind could not register the thought of death. A strange splendour, soothing and tranquil, seemed to emanate from the white cloth and the pale face. In the afternoon the body was laid on the pyre in the presence of a large number of men, women and children. How different the rising flames looked, how unfamiliar! To call them beautiful would be a gross understatement, a crude distortion. For difficult was it to recognise them as flames, the name 'flame' seemed so quixotic and out of place. One had to remind oneself that it was the scene of death and cremation, not of light and revelation. For years and decades, that glow remained a mystery for the writer, that sense of the unreal that was so exalting and so liberating. I do not think that life became him so much as did death. A liberation it was, a melting, sending to almost a naught our percepts and precepts. Never had I felt that peace before, the peace that spurned every concept of 'peace!'

After the cremation, the saṅgat was served a simple meal. When the meal was over, the sun was setting. The entire cosmos bathed in a unique, extraordinary crimson. The snow on the peaks flushed like saffron. An awesome view of ranges of mountains opened out that evening, stretching from northwest to southeast. Above them the sky too flushed crimson. The same elating sense of the unreal suffused them, the same peace that was in the flames of the pyre. A calm blank one experienced within at the sight of the sky and the peaks as one experienced in the presence of the flames. That evening left an indelible impression on the mind.

The fire burnt itself out by the morning. The ashes were collected and put in an urn. The devotees decided that they be immersed in the same current of the Yamunā to which the Master had once desired to offer his body. On the third day, a little before sunrise, started, through dense forests washed fresh with the rain, a twenty six mile long pilgrimage on foot by twelve persons. An extraordinary silence was in them, in those forests shining bright in the brilliant sun. When the sun was going down in the west, the pilgrims reached Hathinikund. The same unearthly beauty breathed there as it did when the Master had come there as a skeleton. Only the fresh rain had enriched it manifold. The sky, the snow on the mountains, the vale and the river seemed to resist every thought of the familiar vis-á-vis them. Strange they looked, familiarly strange. The mango tree, that familiar, loving and living tree no longer seemed to spread out that soothing, languorous shade as it had done earlier. Its very look, of that inviting shade, seemed to deepen the quiet emptiness within. How could death be so soothing and so elevating, sending to a naught the world and one's rotten self? How could this body, this seat of cruel passions and tumults, be so peaceful, so soothing, absorbing within itself all thoughts and even, to an extent, sense perception? A deaf peace it seemed to have turned into,

into an elevating blindness as it were. Where had gone its flesh and its bones and its solidity?

Below flowed the Yamunā; the devotees walked along the shallow current for some time where once had walked the Master all alone, but today they walked along it without the gnawing anxieties of that day. They crossed the shallow current to reach the spot where the Master had wanted to drown himself into *mahāsamādhi*. The main current flowed swollen with the rainwater, shining bright blue in the afternoon sun. At last, the Master's ashes mingled into the waters so beloved of him. The devotees looked, as long as they could, at the remnants of the ashes floating on the waters and on the waves that carried them away. The evening descended upon the mountains and the vale as it had done the day the Master had come to get an idea of the depths of the waters. That day the dusk of the evening had not been able to conceal the love that the Master had for his disciples, for all creation, from the inert to the living. Today what remained of his body had reached the desired destination. Could that parting break the ties of relationship between that transcendental immanence and them as it does in all human cases? That was the question that knocked at their hearts for an answer.

Epilogue

More than like a hero did he struggle, more impersonal was he than God, God of our imagination, yet he allowed himself to suffer as I would suffer and you would suffer. Enlightenment itself was he but he let himself remain ignorant, ignorant of the things we cherish for our security and power. The hero negated the man in him, the man the hero, the god both the man and the hero, and the latter the god himself. He could have entered into samādhi, and, as he said, from samādhi into death but he chose the ordinary way of dying, the way of pain and of suffering. Who was this man, this hero, this god that was neither man, nor hero nor god, this man of wisdom who would choose and love ignorance? 'Who?' alone seemed to be his name, for mystery alone was he, mystery that forces us to ask of it, 'Who art thou?' but which will admit of no answer.

I remember the beauty that his death was, remember its sublimity and its cosmic dimension. I can recall it clearly and vividly as if it were a presence and not a memory. Yet soon after I left the āśrama, I found my torture return, and the frozen and freezing pain that would cry for a tear that would not come. I was in the grip of a gnawing sense of insecurity augmented by hard and straitened circumstances, by poverty, insults and humiliations. I have to recount these circumstances and some of the incidents associated with them in order to show who led me through that inferno: the man I knew, the Word I heard or the guru that resided within me as my in-soul or under-soul. I was afraid, as I said in the beginning, of men and women, even of children, of trees and rocks and hills. The sky was a weight on my eyes and my perceptions a weight on my mind. I had never imagined that sight could be so painful to the eye and so smothering for what I called Me. The body was little else than a bundle of burning sensations, the head burnt and so did the temples and arms and feet. Joy, my companion almost from my birth, had deserted me and so had fled the beauty of the sky and the earth. My feelings turned into sensations, physical and stony, my living anguish into a dead, inert pain and my sorrow into a choking. It was not a question of regaining my lost paradise; it was a question of regaining the living hell. I wanted to feel, feel my pain, I wanted to breathe, breathe freely. But could not. I suffered without knowing why I suffered, I knew the want but did not know what I wanted, I wanted to weep but knew not for what I should weep.

For years this went on, without a break, without a respite except on occasions when some beauty would make me dream of her. But the elation was fleeting, the dream a passing shadow. For, who had the courage to entertain, much less cherish those feelings and those dreams? And who had the breath to articulate those emotions and sentiments that were more of visitations than the expressions of something native to me? And who had enough of an identity to think of her as an identity, a human identity? A dream was she, a fleeting shadow before whom the no-man that I was could never hope to voice my feelings before that phantom. Dreams can truly be devastating, our happy youthful dreams that make, they say, youth so beautiful! For what consolation can a woman give to a youth whose feelings have been frozen, whose body has turned into a succession of scalding sensations, who cannot feel that it is a thing and he a being with an identifiable character? And how could he possibly know a woman as a living, understanding soul when he himself has as many identities as he has sensations, one succeeding another without a connection except that of fear. For, that alone is his self, this sense of being disrupted as self.

Yet I went in for marriage without having recognised myself as a man with a soul. Marriage means relationships and the responsibilities they involve. A man without a soul cannot be a man in relationship. You yourself have to be a being of some sort before you become a being in relationship. So instead of giving me the security of a being with an identity or a fixed character, marriage merely augmented my self-negating anxieties and timidity. A constant fear of things getting worse or going out of hand darkened my days and disrupted my dreams. I may mention here that I became a college lecturer, a position that should, as in the West, make one secure and respectable. But lecturers were poorly paid in those days. It was really hard to manage things in an expensive place like Delhi, especially for one in my circumstances. Those were the days of abject cultural crudity. It was the policy of the State to give incentives to small entrepreneurs to establish their small industries. They produced shoddy goods and often sold their imports in the black market with the connivance of petty officials. Easy money lay in such transactions, not in production of quality goods. People of this class boasted of their new acquisitions, of their gadgets, of their property without a trace of embarrassment. A new class of mean bourgeoisie was emerging, rude, boastful and incredibly crude. Learning had always been respected in India, but it became an object of ridicule in the eyes of this smug and self-complacent class. They found learned people living in miserable rented apartments, in barely two rooms on the top floor of a house with practically no comforts, not even a fridge or a T.V. and with no cooling device to protect themselves from the heat of merciless summers. It was natural that those people should despise the 'so-called' learned people, even insult and humiliate them. Even their clothes they would comment on, with evident delight. And the Government, too, with its passion to bring in socialism, saw to it that the 'privileged' middle class, which meant employees of the Government and of semi-Government establishments like the universities, should be denied the basic comforts in order to 'save' the poor from their miseries. So they decided to erode through heavy taxes whatever little 'the idle university people' or 'the corrupt Government employees' received, taxes which those in business or industry seldom cared to pay.

It was inevitable that, given my circumstances and temperament, I should find it difficult to order my life properly. I worked hard but hard in a straight and simple way. For cunning was beyond me, even planning. I thought, out of my simple faith, that if I was honest and sincere, things would automatically go right for me, if I believed in my guru or God, he would look after my interests. But this was a belief only of my surface self, not a conviction of my stormy dark and deep, fear-stricken and fearsome inner being. I had no soul to anchor to, no bank balance to rely upon or the comforts that 'bribe grabbers' or the black marketers around me enjoyed in abundance. So I thought this was my *tapas*, this my penury and deprivation, and I must take it as such, take it as a gift of heaven. Self-denial became the principle of my life. Guests I welcomed, thinking them to be bestowers of prosperity. And they never failed to grace my apology of a house with their presence. I was hard upon myself and hard upon my wife and children.

The discipline turned almost into cruelty toward my family and me. My children lived in oppression, and, I came to know later, they hated me for what they thought was my cruelty. But they also acknowledged my honesty, my straightforwardness and my sincerity and the hard, dull and uninteresting drudgery that I undertook to supplement my meager income. Only my wife was all patience, despite my faults. She suffered from acute depression, and so did my children one after the other. Diseases visited us frequently, an empty purse became our companion and my children's poor performance in studies a recurring event year after year. Their humiliation at school and college was painful for them as it was for their parents. If we had anything in common, it was our depression and our despair.

Life became a horror for all of us. Alone we lived, spurned by almost all our relations who came to stay with us but would never invite my children to their homes. But I will not say that some among them were not helpful and sympathetic. But understanding they did not have, or did not care to have. I would not blame them, for none can understand a family under what the pre-modern world called 'a curse' and which the modern world calls a disease. It was inevitable that tensions should develop among us. For shared suffering is distressingly alienating. However, through this my journey through hell the presence of the Master was always there. I felt his presence, as I said in the Prologue, behind me towards the left. But a cruel presence it was, out to destroy me, and out of this destruction to reveal, as I hoped, the joy and the beauty that lay somewhere within those dark and dreadful layers. For I knew that there was a fount of joy within me, for deep had I drunk at it in my childhood and boyhood. But the joy never came, despite my efforts and my hopes.

For full fourteen years I lived the first spell of this misery, only, let me emphasise, the first spell. For, as I shall show presently, it pursued me relentlessly for a long time to come, for decades, to be exact. But first about the first phase. In my early youth I sought, as I said in the Prologue, to find relief from my pain, even a self-forgetting fulfillment, in the sense of taste; later I sought it in love and its self-restoring touch. Reality was, however, too stern to be set aside by these morbid and desperate excursions into those 'pleasures' of taste and touch. [For years, I could not remember them without a shiver in my spine]. I had to face the reality, howsoever ineffectively – reality that was misery itself. Slowly and with shocks I was made to perceive how misplaced was my faith in suffering and my hope from it. I underwent, as I said, drudgery of every kind to add a pittance to my income, drudgery that I found degrading in the extreme. There was no escape from working as a crude man among crude men. I loved to think and to understand but could not, owing to my restlessness and my circumstantial compulsions. My educational background too had been poor, I did not have a good schooling nor did I have a regular university education. A self-taught man I was with all the limitations and the lack of refinement that goes with this way of learning, and also the inability to communicate. For you communicate only when you have received communications. What you learn through your own private sweat and blood becomes so much a part of your sweat and blood that you cannot easily turn it into words; it lacks the mobility required for that purpose. And what your suffering 'reveals' to you, it does so in intimations too dim and faint for immediate understanding. You have to struggle long and wait for long before they articulate themselves in words, words halting and of hints. Dark revelations of this kind do not come out easily in conversation, unless and until you speak to a soul that too has the cords to respond to those inner notes that pain and torture have fashioned for you. It is only in hell that you come to acquire that kind of responsive soul. Hell alone fashions a soul of this kind, rather the soul itself for you, and not social relations, these latter can make of you only a function. And functions can tolerate functions and not a soul that is autonomous and independent.

And what kind of a soul had my hell fashioned for me? A soul without relationships, a soul that sought to be itself but could not be, a deprivation it was, a disinheritance from itself. A psychiatrist could, they say, be of some help to me but he/she would demand money. And possession of money implies successful working relationships, which I had failed to forge. The deprived and poor can only be spurned and ignored, they are not taken back into the fold. Society for such people can be little better than a jungle, a place of fear and of hurts that never heal. So I had to pray to the Presence that accompanied me ever and always, that cruel and hard Presence. Prayers could melt my frozen tears but they brought me no solace and no change in my circumstances. Circumstances could be, I slowly came to realise, changed, to a little extent, by rational endeavour, not by cries of despair. But you have to be a sociality in order to think and coordinate, a lonely being, a being that is loneliness itself, can never manage to think and act rationally. Prayer is his only resort, and prayer fails him inevitably. I prayed and prayed until I lost the strength to pray. My guru forsook me as much as did those around me. So I resorted to action, action clumsy and pathetically ineffective.

Yet his presence was there, a presence, as I said, all painful and all wrathful. It was hard, very hard for me to retain my old devotion to that presence. One could, perhaps, say that this condition of mine was the projection of my own masochistic dispositions. I am sure I never enjoyed it but I cannot say that I did not repose faith in suffering, which, on occasions, meant suffering for others too, for those over whom I had some power, my own family. How sordid are man's faith and his righteousness? Without a notice, without giving an inkling would they turn perverse and evil! Creatures of sin do we ever remain. Our beliefs and acts are not of much account before the infernal furies that rage fiercely within us.

But before this masochistic-sadistic disposition came to characterise me, I felt the pain of the loss of my faith in my Master. My moods became black and I wanted to die. I had striven for some inner, liberating experience but nothing was vouchsafed to me. Every morning became oppressive for me, for it meant another day of life and its burdens. One day I felt my despair overpowering me in the extreme. How deeply I wished to die that day! I remember the date. It was the sixteenth day of February 1967. All gloomy was that evening, gloomy in the extreme. I lay down on my bed unable to think, to pray or even to weep. But soon I fell asleep. I woke up at about four in the morning. An inner prompting made me sit in the yogic posture and regulate my breath. A moment and lo! I felt a movement in the region of the navel. My spinal chord became erect and stretched upwards. I felt my trunk getting taller and taller until something at the navel rose, something imperceptible that waved darkling as a serpent would wave. My trunk moved uncontrollably from left to right and from right to left. Was my *kuṇḍalinī* awake? I wondered. I remembered the day of my initiation and the movement that I had felt in the region of the navel. But remembering my worthlessness I could not believe that I deserved that, to me, act of grace. However, despite my misgivings I could not deny the reality of my experience and let the *kuṇḍalinī* move, looked at what was happening without a reaction. After some time it went into sleep again as it were. I had my bath and again sat for meditation and found the movement reappearing in a few minutes. Again the *kuṇḍalinī* rose and again she waved. Whenever, on subsequent days, I sat for meditation, the experience would repeat itself. I spoke about it to a senior *premī* and he confirmed the authenticity of my experience.

I thought that everything was now within my reach. All that I had to do was to endeavour for my goal. So I spent most of my time in meditation. In about a month's time – in the evening of March 22, to be precise – I found the *kuṇḍalinī* rise up from the navel to the mid-point between the eyebrows with a violence so fierce as to make my body shake and tremble with uncontrollable intensity. But despair had ingrained itself so deeply into my being that I looked on the entire event with an almost total unconcern. Prepared was I for death, if at all this meant death! But when that force struck against an obstruction at that point, I felt as if my head would burst open and, in fear, I gave up the meditation. It was a matter of deep regret for me, this love for life. So I again went in for meditation and found that it, the *kuṇḍalinī,* was present where I had left it. For it became active the moment I started the meditation. Soon I found that I had only to look within to find it there, active and alive. My meditation increased in duration and concentration, until a time came when I could feel the kuṇḍalinī's activity even when I was in my normal moods, sometimes even when I was talking or giving my lectures.

There was, however, no let to my pain and anguish, to my unrest and fears. They continued as before; only the freezing and frozen pain had become a living pain, the dumb agony had changed into a felt sorrow which I could probe into, could even try to articulate to myself, though without a significant success. Agonised introspection took the place of the dumb and inert smothering. Introspection, however, could not change my circumstances, could not give the mental leisure for careful thought. With the rise of the *kuṇḍalinī,* I reestablished my contact with the *saṅgat*, would resort to retreats during the summers in the company of three or four brethren, giving all my time to meditation. I recalled that on the day of initiation the Master had told us that when the Word reaches the mid-point between the eyebrows, music of different notes is heard, setting at rest the flow of thoughts. I waited for those divine, redemptive tunes in the midst of solitude. Occasionally I heard a humming tone in the head but that was not enough to set at rest the torment my mind was. Increasingly, I felt that I had to escape from the mind to find the rest I sought, for (I knew) as long as the mind was active, the unrest too would continue to gnaw me. But no effort of mine could soften down, not to speak of bringing to an end, that unrest and that pain. One day I found to my surprise, that the kuṇḍalinī had really overpovered my thought but only my thoughts but, not my wretched body. It was obstinately there to afflict me, though, to be sure, not as the too solid misery that it always had been but as a dark, empty shell! And as long as the shell was there, the thoughts would not, could not die irrevocably, and so could not the sense of insecurity. But the body would not melt away, try as I might, it persisted inevitably either as what I have called as the solid misery or as an empty shell. There was no escape from its truth and reality. Often, I would come back from the retreats an unhappy and distressed man to carry the burden of a distraught existence.

My contact with the *saṅgat,* as I said, was resumed but I could not find myself comfortable at the *sat-saṅgas*, for trite and banal they seemed, totally out of touch with the realities that lay on the lonely road. So I did not care to attend them, those anchors, I thought, of the self-righteous and self-complacent. Another thirteen years passed away, thirteen years of troubles without and a restless body and mind. The domestic problems were on the increase, absorbing my unproductive attention. My physique was not strong enough to bear the burden of responsibilities and the oppression of the mind and the cruel freezing unrest in the body. However, during an illness, when I was down with an acute back pain, I felt a cool soft wave rising up in the spinal chord, a slow, soothing wave. From the root of the spinal chord it rose to move towards the back of the neck until it spread in the head. For a long time it continued to cool down the head and the body, setting at some rest the unrest and the burning sensations which latter had lingered on, through at a lesser intensity than before the rise of the kuṇḍalinī. It was in the month of August of 1980 when this cooling process started. Later on – I forget the year – I found that cool wave entering into a cavity in the crown of the head. Like a tiny wave of water or vapours it poured itself there, with a little whispering sound. With that softened down further the fret in the veins and almost disappeared the burning sensations. But the mind continued to be restless and troubled and also continued our financial worries and the problem of depression that stalked us from, so to say, every side.

In order to escape from these burdens and reaffirm to myself my faith, I wrote a biography of the Master in Hindi. It gave me moments of self-forgetfulness, even of elation, for I wrote not what I thought but what I saw, so vivid was the presence of the Master before me. After I had completed the biography and published it, I found the presence of the Master desert me. I became a lonely traveller on a lonely road leading to a destination I knew not, perhaps to a destination that was no destination. So without a hope of grace I lived, without a faith. I had no guru to resort to, no God to pray to. My meditations had been of no avail, and so had been my painful patience, my honesty and sincerity. What I thought was my innocence was proving to be my imbecility and my principles mere empty boasts. In the meantime, I was made to realise the truth of the Master's saying that the guru was not 'the shell,' which I, with most of the faithful, had taken him to be. The faithful often take every word that their teacher speaks as infallible, every opinion he gives as absolutely right, every guess he makes about the future as a prophecy. The man in him that the guru discards as tainted and polluted the faithful often worship as their God. Their faith speaks not of faith in the unknown and unknowable but in what they can know and comprehend. When the man I worshipped did not prove to be God, when some of his opinions and views did not seem to tally with the facts or failed to be prophetic, I felt myself betrayed and let down. The faithful often find it difficult to live in conceptual uncertainty and existential insecurity, those preludes to genuine faith. So was the case with me. I felt forsaken and deserted, my 'faith' eroded and my devotion gone. No longer could I remember him with the old fervour. There were occasions, much too many I should say, when religious terminology would make me feel sick.

Though he ceased to be a presence to invoke my emotions, I remembered him many times a day but without the immediacy and vividness of a percept. Unlike in my youth, he appeared now rarely in my dreams. My existential bonds with him were getting loose and he was no longer the most proximate truth of my being. The kuṇḍalinī, however, went on functioning, unconcerned, it seemed, with the person that I was, with the faith or no-faith of that person. That person lived on as before, but, despite the kuṇḍalinī, without a transformation in his nature. The old stupidities continued and so did the fears and the uncertainties. There was, however, one change, a remarkable change I would call it. I found myself incapable of thinking, incapable of planning; my thinking faculty seemed to have been locked out.' So I lived at the mercy of my impulses, annoying many people. I had no fixed, predictable character. I could not say when I would be pleased with someone or burst out in anger before him. I am genuinely surprised at the tolerance of those who knew me, people who were not remarkable for their tolerance. They avoided me but it appeared they did not hate me, most of them. They talked to me, they told me, because despite my outbursts I had no ill will against any one. They thought me unbalanced, not evil or cruel. This behaviour of mine made me lonelier than before.

In the meantime my daughters grew up to be young girls. In India you have to give a handsome dowry if you want to marry off your daughters. The way to home lies through hard cash in this 'most spiritual country in the world.' So the question of their marriage became a matter of constant worry for me. Years passed away in anxiety, in sleepless nights and the sneers of relations who were anxious to tag on to me the label of 'the irresponsible' without wasting any time. Then happened what these people called 'a miracle.' There came a time when the daughters of the poor man came to be married to young men who considered dowry a shame and a disgrace. At long last, the unthinkable happened, no one understanding how young men of this disposition came to save me from sure and certain wasting away.

I felt relieved but only for a short time. Within a year – in December 1995 – I had a heart attack. Hardly had I been taken to the hospital when I fell unconscious. When I came back to myself I heard the doctor in attendance uttering the words, 'O my God! O my God!' There was a great discomfort in the region of my head and I found myself crying in agony. My eyes were closed. When the doctor was uttering those words, I could see vividly a bluish and beautiful flame rising from the midpoint between eyebrows towards the head. I found the kuṇḍalinī active, rather intensely active, unconcerned with my agony and my pain and my cries. I was frightened by the intensity of its movement and tried to stop it. Again the flame rose and the doctor moaned as before. Then the flame came down from the head to the mid-point between the eyebrows and disappeared where I could not know. 'Now, it is all right, it is all right!' I heard the doctor say. My agony disappeared and my cries and moans stopped and I opened my eyes. I found a young doctor and a number of nurses surrounding my bed. 'The call appears to have been made, Doctor! It is perhaps the time to depart,' said I. 'Why do you,' said the doctor, 'speak this way? Let me invite your people inside. You may speak to them.'

They came, my wife, my eldest daughter and my son in law, came one by one. The doctor, I came to know later, had advised them not to show me any sign of anxiety or weep before me. My condition, he said, was very precarious. Twice my heart, I came to know, had stopped functioning. All attempts on their part had failed to revive it. They were about to put me on a pace-maker but before they did it my heart revived the way I have described. My family said that there was a deep calm in my eyes when they saw me. I could understand them and believe them. They say people see lights and other phenomena when they are, clinically speaking, dead but I saw the light when I had revived and was fully conscious, though in intense pain. I could see and feel the beauty of the flame even in my torture. The doctors had virtually given up every hope before I came back to myself. For six days my condition remained critical. One of the doctors said that a delay of half an hour would have meant my death on the way. Well, I was saved and I came back home to gradually regain my health.

A change had been taking place in me for some years, since 1986, when I was down again with my old problem of the slipped disc. One morning during that illness I found two currents, one from the left temple and the other from the right temple, mingle with each other almost in the middle of the forehead, and entering a sort of a deep tunnel there. With that came to rest, for a time, my thought process. There had also been, before this happening, occasions when I saw the entire world within me and myself in the world. And there were also times when the entire dome of the sky with its stars and the moon would appear as if within the reach of my hand! Sometimes my gaze would get fixed on the dark clouds to stay there for long expelling all thoughts from my mind. These experiences became more stable and frequent after I had been relieved of the anxiety about my daughters' future. There were moments, quite a few of them, when I felt my thoughts melting into the calm and happy sensations of the body, into its warmth and cool. I was, on such occasions, little else than those sensations, those calm and happy sensations. There were times when the blue of the sky would enter into my being, its light and tranquillity displacing my thoughts and emotions. Even the crowded, dirty streets, with their chaotic traffic wore the look of a strange and tranquil beauty, as if the streets did not belong to our world but to another one, quiet and celestial. But long years of anxiety and suffering had shattered my confidence. I could not face even small, trivial problems; they seemed insurmountable to me. I did not know how to convince and handle people. Anxiety had become a part of my being. I could not do anything without the fear of doing it wrong. Even when I had done a piece of work, I often felt I had made a mess of it. I tried to convince myself that I should not entertain such feelings but should attend to the sublime beauty that the world was, that even the noisiest streets were. But that was not to be. I was extremely forgetful, unsystematic and nervous about practical matters and could not but feel impatient with myself. In writing alone I found some relief. When I wrote I forgot about these nagging fears. Spontaneously I wrote, knowing not what I would say in the next paragraph, sometimes in the next line. Soon I would forget what I had written. Reading my own writings sometimes appeared unfamiliar to me – almost. I would not say that I felt that someone else had written them, for I knew I had written them but with effort could I recall the actual moments of their writing.

I found some of the great minds of the world reading my thoughts with respect as if I was their equal. Their response I could not understand. For the day to day man in me was never a man that knew respect and honour. His nervousness, his distraught thoughts, his unsystematic conversations, his occasional outbursts could not make him an object of respect. There was a great gap between the man that suffered and the man that wrote, as there was a great difference between the man that wrote and the man that flowed out into the world to almost lose himself in it.

A time came when I found my writing useless and my visions futile, for they had not brought about any significant change in my wretched life. I remained the helpless person that I had been since my early youth, since the time I lost my visions. Occasionally I heard a humming sound in my head but I did not attach importance to it, for it did not have the tranquillity that I felt when I felt myself as one with the world. There also came a time when these visions too lost all meaning for me, for they were no antidote for my life long malady. I could, whenever I liked, produce a state in which I would find the world residing in my eyes, I could become the seer of my eyes without much trouble but how to soothe the torture of my mind I did not know. Time passed away, mostly in writing and in walking in rose gardens and in woods, without finding the meaning I sought. I no longer cared for meditation or for better thoughts, I lived almost a slave of my impulses, with the inevitable problems that this way of life led me to. However, people around me did not any longer take me lightly as they had done earlier because they knew I was a thinker of some mettle, though not one who had got his due.

Five years later, I was again in the grip of my heart problem, despite my meticulous care and doctors' assurance about the soundness of my heart. I was advised immediate bypass surgery. I saw little point in undergoing the operation, for to renew the same old routine of life – writing, typing and proof reading – and the foolish round of killing anxieties and cares no longer seemed worth the trouble. However, the blind instinct to live, live without a meaning, forced me to sign the declaration. When I was being carried to the operation threatre my only thought was why I was going in for the surgery, for the whole exercise seemed purposeless and meaningless, an invitation to troubles vain and futile. Even on the operation table when they gave me an injection, the same thought haunted me. I feared life much more than I feared death. When I regained consciousness, the discomfort and nausea overwhelmed my despair. Sick people make good friends, though temporary ones. I felt happy to talk to some people there. Everyone had his own story to tell, his own troubles and problems. My fears of a futile life were not, I soon found out, useless; they proved absolutely right. My fears increased and so did my misery. Whatever little confidence I had was eroded still more. I was dragging this base life somehow.

A further change occurred. More and more I found myself, though imperceptibly and slowly, stepping out of my mind. I could not change and keep under control that beast from the wild but I could distance myself from it. A passivity would I then become, calm and tranquil, looking at my thoughts as if they were not mine. In this disposition, I found their fury soften down; there were occasions when they could not disturb me and some occasions when they almost disappeared. Except for the emptiness within – emptiness I have already alluded to – I neither could find thoughts within me nor could I feel the solidity of the body, though its margins invariably registered their presence. The layer of the skin was all that was left of the body. How to get out of that confinement was the question, out of that seat of the hell that I was and would continue to be as long as I was destined to live. Often, very often, I felt a great force striking against an obstruction in the crown of my head. I wanted it – that obstruction, – to be pierced open so that I could escape from the miserable body. But that did not happen. I could now clearly understand the Master's indifference to mental accomplishments, why neither wisdom was a matter of concern for him nor was ignorance. For these belonged to the mind, wisdom and ignorance, and the mind was the hell one should never try to refine. For infernal would it remain and demonic, despite the surface refinement and culture. There were passive depths within that one should be, not these thoughts that are a rack and all sinful. And where was the difference between good and bad thoughts that one should choose the former and reject the latter? Opinions of the Master no longer concerned me, nor did the way he chose to die. There was, I felt, nothing unfortunate in dying in pain and nothing sublime in dying in calm. For, the real calm belonged not to the mind but to something other than the mind. And it was that something one should stick to, not to thoughts.

And if there was no difference between good and bad thoughts, was there any difference between knowledge and ignorance? For, when I lived as identified with cognitive and motor organs, the world appeared as something to be captured, to be ordered, to be forged and made, captured through concepts and ordered and changed through action. And when I contemplated the world in passivity, then all that existed and perceived was perceived in the mind. And when I lived in the stillness of the silent depths within me then the world and I would merge into each other to turn into a blank darkness, infinite and without a limit. However, there still survived consciousness of that dark abyss, deep and unknowable. And as long as consciousness remained, I would retain some vestiges of the ego too in me with every possibility of sliding back into the misery that I am, that my senses are and my mind is and is their *other* the world. That ego has to die but not through its efforts but through waiting and forbearing. For all efforts assume the ego and its blemishes.

I have already said that the faith that I cherished, the faith that is said to ensure one's well being, I lost pretty early. I soon came to realise that he who sowed not and reaped not could not hope to be fed. The hope that faith could change and purify my mind too was, before long, lost. Faith in my guru, as I had taken him to be, could not purify and transform my mind nor could good acts; it remained the infernal thing that it was. I dare not think there is anything in me that I do not find sinful. There is, I feel, something primordial, original, about human sin. We live as constituted by it. My life is a long story of embarrassments and of guilt too heavy to be laid aside. I do not think I can ever be morally comfortable with myself. My mind is a shame and a burden, too sinister it is to be linked to. I feel at peace with myself only when I occasionally step out of the mind, when it appears *there*, as something objective, having nothing to do with me. A dark peaceful tranquillity then I come to be, untouched by the sound and fury of thoughts and passions. There is no feeling that I can respect, no thought that I find meaningful, no act that I find redeeming. All is dark, all is vain, all is stained and polluted. A choking horror is this my mind, as dangerous as is the world without. I fear my mind as much as I fear society or a wild forest.

Faith as a thought, as an idea, as a principle is, I find, a useless thing. But faith I still have, not the faith as an idea or a principle, but faith as ***viśvāsa***. When I step out of my thoughts, I find myself turn into a mere succession of scarcely felt thoughts, thoughts collapsing into stillness. There was a time when I liked to remain the empty peace that this stillness made of me but it could not be sustained for long, that state of peaceful emptiness, the fury of thoughts disrupting it, sooner than later. For, as I said, the body was there, the body as the empty shell, so its safety and wellbeing could not be ignored for long. Thoughts had to be entertained, thoughts more of worry and anxiety than thoughts creative or meaningful. For, with the possible exception of an actually starving man, no one else is as anxious as the man expelled from that stillness. Realising the futility of this stillness and calm I no longer cared for it. I sought refuge in the *kuṇḍalinī,* that dark, sheer impersonal force that worked totally unconcerned with my well being or ill being, even with my life and death. But to contemplate the *kuṇḍalinī* meant to be the mind, the mind contemplative. And that meant remaining distant from her.

I have to, I can now see, own up my bodily being, the empty bodily being, almost bereft of thoughts and feelings. I cannot go beyond this state with my own efforts. I am not to look back on the sublimity of the interflow of the subjective and the objective, of the interfusion of my living thoughts here and of the inert rock there, of the coming together of the tiny space within me and the vastness of the sky without me. No longer am I to feel thrilled by the sight of the rivers flowing within me or of the mountains stepping into me and me into them. Ephemeral visions are these, devoid of truth, bereft of meaning. I know that the hard reality of the world too is the creation of my desire, but desire seems to dwell in me at a deeper level than any of these visions can dwell at. Desire is indeed *vāsanā*, that which has seized me as its dwelling. So I have to escape from the emptiness, from the nothing that has the capacity to become everything. Unless and until I do it, my tragedy will not come to an end. Death will be the reward of my being, of my existence. I shall have to die, die each and every moment. I have to die every moment I live; rather I have to live-die every moment. In contemplation, passive contemplation of our mortal lot, each moment of life turns into a moment of life-death. A blessed moment it turns into, into an immortality that is indistinguishable from death. But this moment of bliss in which life does not assert and death does not negate is, as I said, a moment in contemplation. When mind becomes self-conscious and the body regains its solidity then the old distinctions and conflicts and tragedies rise up again to lead us to our futile struggles and vain achievements. So, how to live, to live as body-mind duality and yet die as that duality is the problem that seems to admit of no solution for the contemplative disposition.

Perhaps what we seek most earnestly has already been vouchsafed to us; our most saving discoveries are already our inheritance, our realisations mere remembrances. Dimly conscious of this finding, this discovery of the truth behind my 'discoveries,' I realise the futility of my repeated talk about them – of my bliss and the loss of that bliss, of the blessed contemplative moments of coalescence of life and death and their turning, without a conscious hint, into the sordid 'realities' of our what we call life. Today when I am getting weary of spiritual practices and elevating visions and experiences, the memory of an event suddenly flashes before me with the vividness of a perception.

NOVEMBER 2014: Two miles away from the town of Dalhousie a streamlet once flowed with its milky waterfalls and its gurgling currents on stones and pebbles. Just a few feet on the left side of the road [leading to that spot] with ankle deep waters of the streamlet flowing over it stood a rock cut into a seat about five feet long and four feet wide, with a wall about four or five feet high at its back. Around and below it flowed the waters that must have worked long in the past to turn it into the smooth tender beauty that it was. That grey-white rocky throne always had a strong fascination for me, had – I should say – a great power over me. I felt a cool and calm sensation near my genitals whenever I passed by it, a sensation that would slowly spread across my entire trunk, leaving me little else than that cool and that calm. I could never understand why that inert stone should mean so much to me, so much indeed that even a recollection of it would make me breathe as myself. After a gap of as many as sixty three years[2] the memory of my first contact with the stone suddenly arose in my mind to reveal the cause of my inexplicable relationship with that stone. I was only four at that time. I remember my age because I had often heard my parents telling it to others. I looked at the smooth and flat sun-lit surface of the stone under my feet, was, it appears, arrested by that look of it. With calm I stood there when I felt as if the vast sky had entered my head at its crown, with its height immeasurable and breadth immeasurable. With a flash it came and with a flash it disappeared, the memory of the event lying deep in me beyond any recall. The reason for the sudden revival of the memory was the photograph of the stone with my grandson sitting on it.[3] I brought home a copy of it, the stone rousing all kinds of nostalgic memories. Daily I looked at the photograph without knowing or trying to know why I felt so intimate with it. It was just by chance, spontaneously and without a notice that the cause of that intimacy resurrected from the depths of my memory.

I have seen, as I have said, the horizons approach me and enter me, I have seen myself in the sky and the sky in me. The stars have often come almost as near me as is the ceiling of my room. The mountains have often come to stay within this body of mine as have the rivers and miles and miles of the earth. I have lost, on quite a few occasions, consciousness of myself and the world too, a loss that ended up in an ecstasy and beauty that mortals like me can hardly bear. I have also seen the sky lie heavy on my eyes, the mountains as frightful monsters, the trees the agents of death, and every human face a fright. The world was a paradise, it was also a hell. The mine was the alien, the intimate the stranger, the home the exile. A bliss was the sky and also a curse, a protective dome and an oppressive horror; near at hand were the horizons and also far, far away. Joy was there to turn into an ecstasy oblivious of itself and, in its desertion, to turn into a burning that would scald the nerves and the veins. In ecstasy and pain alike I forgot the intimations of the intimate stone, the throne where I had been anointed. The bliss betrayed me and so did my misery. I forgot the stone but the stone did not forget me, never did it forget to make me feel forgetfully the forgotten intimations. The bliss I tasted flowed at the fount of poison, for, my mind was a shame and my body a tragedy, those tasters of bliss. The sky that descended there, on that un-forgetful stone, sky the benign, gave me an intimation of the possibility of redemption from my curse, the mind-body-breath complex. It, that sky, did not let that complex relate to it or even perceive it. I belonged to it, not it to me. The sky in the head was my innermost being, more intimate was it to me than my body, my thoughts or my breath. All else was the *other*: what I called me or the world. That infinity was my being, my self, the being where I was not, where I could not be, where nothing could be, not even infinity, not even being itself . Could my fading into it, into that my innermost [no-]being be so deeply redemptive that to call it peaceful would be a total blasphemy? That alone could be my salvation, that bliss where bliss is not, where what I call my self is not, where the sky itself is not. I call it the sky, but what is it for itself? That sky to which opens up the tenth gate is my home and my being.

Within this visible world of grace and shame, I saw whom I have called my Gurudeva, my divine teacher. Was he my teacher, one who now was the visible face of the invisible, now the word of the sky, now a prophet and now a man fallible? Was he my guide who bore his pain now like a rock and now like a man, who was more than man and also a man, man the extraordinary and man the ordinary? In my journey through hell he guided me, that contradiction, that Master forbidding and oppressive. He made me strive and endure and left me in black despair in my failure. He beckoned me on as had done the beauty of the earth and the sky and like this latter turned into an oppression when I obeyed his call – he deserting me in the long run. He could not be my guide: that miracle, that enigma, that extraordinary recantation of itself. The sky that the man in him revealed and concealed was my guru. I remember his words that the shell that we saw was not the guru. He was that sky that opened out for a moment in the head, which the Word concealed, the prophet concealed, man the extraordinary concealed and man the ordinary concealed. That alone was my guru who had intimated his presence when I was only four but whom I could not recognise until the present moment.

The Word says that that sky opens out when the tenth gate opens up. The nine gates open up to sky the misery, the tenth to sky the bliss. I am not to, my vision on the stone implies, try to rise up to sky the bliss, I am not to seize it, master it as I would the other sky. For, that sky, sky the bliss, is the absolute *other*, wholly unknown and unknowable. It will descend upon me when it will, that grace abounding to own me up and in owning me up to kill me. For, that will be the moment of my final death, the last death, the death that will not visit me again, for I would no longer be there to die again. Till that moment, I have to endure my miseries, my misfortunes, the sorrows and shame that come I know not how and from where. Till that moment, I have also to bear the fury of thoughts that rise up in me from which depths I know not. From a depth dark and invisible they rise up to coil me up in their grip, to force me to do, to desire and to suffer things without a count. A captive I live of these dark forces, their slave and servant, not a moment of respite is mine in which I may breathe and live as myself. And this self of mine, this miserable self that I would sustain is not going to remain mine, try as I may. This tragic loneliness that I am cannot be undone by pleasures, by ambitions and by relationships, that most treacherous of illusions. Only the sky can save me from this misery, sky the Other absolute of me and the Self absolute of me. I cannot rise up to it but it can come down to me to save me by killing me. For, I am the sin, I am the ignorance, and I am the misery. I am the mess that the world is, I am the confusion, I am the chaos.

On this negative note, I am forced to conclude my musings. For, I do not know how what I call the sky in the crown of my head is related to the misery that I am and to that place of exile that the world is and to the loneliness that society is. The Word says that *he*, that sky, is the sufferer, he is the doer and he is the transcendental, mortal is he and the immortal, the temporal and the eternal. I have tried in this work to invoke the concept of *samatvam* to undo the distinction between the immanent and the transcendental, between the confusion of the senses and the mind and the peace of *samādhi*. But to know how they are one, the bondage and liberation, I have to wait for the descent of the grace upon me, of the silence and the nothing, of death that is immortality. My striving has come to an end and so have my thinking and my struggles against misery. I have to endure, only to endure my frustration, my ignorance and my misery and my sin. I have to endure my self, this fragile self that is so hard, so impossible to kill.

I will however end with a prayer for forgiveness:

I mistook you, my Master, for the radiant body, for that transcendental immanence, I mistook you for the miracle of self-denial that you seemed to be, I mistook you for the Patience that you were, I mistook you for the fearlessness that you were, the tapas *that you were. And, above all, I mistook you for the Word that descended on the mountains and the wildernesses of the forests. I committed these deadly sins all my life. Pray forgive me for these, these my undoings. I ever tried to circumscribe you, to make you the knowable for the man in me. I strove to rise up to you to force you to retreat further off from me. Now, that I know my sins, deign to descend upon me, my death redemptive! But perhaps, you want me that I cease to pray too. Let this sin too be undone, if this be also a sin!*

Notes

1 There were occasions when my inability to think made it difficult for me to prepare my lectures. Earlier, when my 'faith' was intact, I sometimes would not – deliberately - prepare my lectures. My guru that abided within me would, I believed, speak the right things through me, for omniscient was he. The reader can well imagine the embarrassments I had to undergo as the result of my 'firm faith.'

2 Today, in the year 2014 I am running my eightieth year. The experience I describe here occurred in 1939.

3 It was just by chance that my son in law had a snap of it. Its look must have fascinated him. Now, with the tree felling and other reasons the streamlet has become dry and the stone looks drab and dirty with no waters lending it the beauty it had.

Glossary and Index

[NOTE: For obvious reasons, only twice does Bhagatjī find a place in the Index. His name almost pervades the body of the text. *Brahman* and *ātman* too are not included in the index]